AMERICAN ENCOUNTERS/GLOBA
A series edited by
Gilbert M. Joseph and Emily S. Rosenberg

This series aims to stimulate critical perspectives and
fresh interpretive frameworks for scholarship on the history of the imposing global presence of the United
States. Its primary concerns include the deployment and
contestation of power, the construction and deconstruction of cultural and political borders, the fluid
meanings of intercultural encounters, and the complex
interplay between the global and the local. American Encounters seeks to strengthen dialogue and collaboration
between historians of U.S. international relations and
area studies specialists.

The series encourages scholarship based on multi-
archival historical research. At the same time, it supports
a recognition of the representational character of all stories about the past and promotes critical inquiry into
issues of subjectivity and narrative. In the process, American Encounters strives to understand the context in
which meanings related to nations, cultures, and political economy are continually produced, challenged, and
reshaped.

Reclaiming the Political in Latin American History

ESSAYS FROM THE NORTH   *Edited by Gilbert M. Joseph*

Duke University Press   *Durham and London* 2001

▼

© 2001 Duke University Press
All rights reserved
Printed in the United States of America on acid-free paper ∞
Typeset in Quadraat by Keystone Typesetting, Inc.
Library of Congress Cataloging-in-Publication Data
appear on the last printed page of this book.

Contents

▼

Acknowledgments

▼

This collection, a labor of love on the part of the editor and contributors, affords us a means of celebrating the distinguished career of our mentor and colleague Emilia Viotti da Costa. The volume originated in the *homenagem* to Emilia at Yale University over the course of several days in May 1998 on the occasion of her completion of twenty-five years of service to the university. My first debt, then, is to thank Yale's History Department, Council on Latin American and Iberian Studies, and Center for International and Area Studies for sponsoring the conference "Reclaiming 'the Political' in Latin American History," and the Kempf Memorial Fund at Yale and the Andrew W. Mellon Foundation for providing the lion's share of funding. Their support enabled us to host thirty of Emilia's former graduate students and closest colleagues, who gathered in New Haven not only to honor Emilia's agenda-setting scholarship and provocative teaching, but for stimulating and often rambunctious debate—with Emilia characteristically leading by example. Her contribution to this volume originally served as the keynote address for the Yale conference in her honor. In addition to the colleagues whose work appears in this volume, we are also extremely grateful to Marjorie Becker, Susan Besse, Nelson Boeira, José Celso de Castro Alves, John French, Seth Garfield, Steven Hahn, Kathleen Higgins, Reeve Huston, Michael Jiménez, Bryan McCann, David Montgomery, Muriel Nazzari, Julio Pinto, David Sanders, Stuart Schwartz, James Scott, Sol Serrano, and Peter Winn, whose formal and informal *intervenciones* in New Haven substantially improved the discussion in these pages.

Thanks also go to Nancy Phillips, then senior administrator of the Council on Latin American Studies, for her deft logistical management of an event that gathered together the members of Emilia's far-flung intellectual clan from across the length and breadth of the Americas. Nancy and I were ably assisted by a campus committee of Latin American history doctoral students (two of whom have subsequently graduated and taken up full-time academic positions elsewhere): Seth Garfield (now at the University of Texas, Austin), Bryan McCann (University of Arkansas), David Sanders, Amy Chazkel, José Celso de Castro Alves, Andrew Sackett, and Todd Hartch.

As we moved from the conference to the book, I was aided by Barbara Weinstein and Heidi Tinsman in selecting this volume's ensemble of essays. (Emilia set the parameters somewhat in requesting that the volume focus on the work of her North American students.) Editorial and clerical costs associated with the preparation of the book were covered by a grant to Yale's Latin American Council from the William and Flora Hewlett Foundation. The manuscript benefited immeasurably from close readings by Brooke Larson and Peter Winn; and the essays by Steve Stern, Heidi Tinsman, and me are much the better for the commentary provided by Catherine LeGrand—and the lively exchange with the audience that ensued—at the panel "Reclaiming 'the Political' in Latin American History" during the January 2000 meeting of the American Historical Association. Yale doctoral student J. T. Way provided valuable help in preparing the final manuscript. As always, I have been supported at every stage of my editorial work by my editor and dear friend at the Duke University Press, Valerie Millholland.

I

The Politics of Writing Latin American History

▼

Gilbert M. Joseph

Reclaiming "the Political" at the Turn of the Millennium

▼

These are unsettled times for historians of Latin America. As the region
enters a new millennium in the viselike grip of neoliberalism—a global
project which in the name of "flexible" economic choices, "democratization," and the "rights" of individual investors implements policies that
sow insecurity and promote the methodical destruction of collective structures, habits, and forms of sociability—there are few inspirational paradigms for connecting scholarship to action.[1] Indeed, many lament that the
state of historical scholarship, teaching, and "the profession" itself has
never been more disoriented, fragmented, and contentious (though it is
perhaps comforting to know that Alphonse de Lamartine engaged in similar lamentations regarding intellectual life in nineteenth-century France!).[2]
We have witnessed the explosion of once-comforting master narratives and
have heard celebratory proclamations about the end of ideology and history
itself. Recently we have also observed esteemed colleagues on the Left
protest "identity politics," "political correctness," and the "trivialization"
of the research enterprise, bitterly attacking new trends in cultural history and area studies, their voices now barely distinguishable from more-
traditional opponents on the Right.[3] Some of these colleagues have gone
on to establish a new "Historical Society" to further their pursuit of "objective reality" based upon verifiable hypotheses.[4] Unfortunately, however,
much of the "newer" social and cultural history *also* defangs or expunges
the political, fetishizing "experience," "mentality," or "identity," reveling
in the "unfixity" of meanings and dissolving the subject and ultimately
nullifying agency.[5] Alternatively, others of its practitioners have sentimen-
talized "resistance" and "agency," seeing it everywhere and thereby dilut-
ing political analysis to the point of irrelevance.[6]

It seems entirely appropriate at this critical juncture, then, to rethink, remake, or reclaim the political in our work—in the sense of elaborating richer, more sophisticated approaches to politics and broader arenas of power. After all, there has never been an abandonment of politics within the historical profession: this is true at the most prosaic level in terms of the continued study of conventional politics, war, and diplomacy among North American historians of both the United States and Latin America. Moreover, politics—and political power—has never been underemphasized in the Latin American context. Historian and political scientist Peter Smith has observed that whereas many North Americans might turn away from politics as an act of rejection based on the assumed "ineffectiveness," "irrelevance," or immorality of politics, Latin Americans have no such luxury. The stakes are too high; the conflicts too real. Politics and political action are crucial determinants of everyday existence. Politics entails more than style, image or nuance: "It can be, quite literally, a matter of life and death."[7]

It is no doubt for this reason that most Latin American scholars did not blithely follow the North American academy down the fashionable road toward social history (and away from political history) in the 1960s and '70s—or toward cultural studies and postmodernism in the 1980s and '90s. Fifteen years ago, Brazilian historian Emilia Viotti da Costa pointed out that the "new history" of "experience" and "mentalities" carried with it a serious risk. It gave us "a fragmented picture of . . . society and often made us lose sight of the interconnections among economic, social, political and ideological institutions and structures." Viotti da Costa wrote: "In modern societies, even more than in the past, politics is at the center of human life. This centrality of politics is a result of both the incorporation of increasing numbers of people into the market economy and the overwhelming presence of the state in the lives of people. As a consequence of these two processes, which are intimately related, political decisions have come to affect economic and social life in ways never seen before. The life of a peasant in some lost village in the backland, the labor conditions of a worker in a factory, a woman's status in a society, the opportunities denied or opened to a black person—all depend not only on their own struggle or on the cold logic of the market, but also on decisions taken by those in power. . . . It is impossible to understand the history of the powerless without understanding the powerful. History from the bottom up can be as meaningless as history from the top down."[8]

The present volume, composed of original essays by Viotti da Costa and several generations of her North American students, embraces the challenge of writing a social and cultural history of Latin America that is not divorced from power and the political. It is inspired by her belief that we as historians, our scholarship, and our teaching are powerfully shaped by (and involved in the shaping of) political contexts, structures, and forces. The challenge, therefore, is not to retreat back to a more conventional, bounded political history and claim a piece of it; it is, rather, to revisit the political—both as a theme of historical analysis and as a stance for historical practice—and to inquire, to what extent has the political undergone an important transformation as we enter the new millennium? We also need to ask, as Steve Stern does in his essay, "How do we specify the new demands placed by historical and intellectual experience upon the politics of writing and teaching Latin American history?"

In their attempts to contribute to that enterprise, the volume's authors explore some of the strategic realms in which the political might be studied, as well as the new theoretical and methodological tools that might be employed. In a pair of broad-ranging essays in the book's first section, "The Politics of Writing Latin American History," Viotti da Costa and Stern examine how the political has continually been remade in the North since the 1960s, and they present somewhat different views on what the future of "the political" should look like. Viotti da Costa's contribution, the reworking of an essay criticizing many of the postmodern and poststructuralist trends in recent historiography, is a revealing point of departure for the essays of her students, several of whom, such as Stern and Florencia Mallon, have been leaders in the selective application of recent "posts" and "turns" to Latin American history.

The essays in the second part of the volume—by Barbara Weinstein, Mary Ann Mahony, and Jeffrey Gould—address how pivotal dimensions of the Brazilian and Central American past are remembered. Sifting through the sedimentation of local and national historiographies, scrutinizing an array of primary documentation and oral testimony, and in Mahony's case, also exploring local archaeological remains, these authors wrestle with how historical narratives of slavery and emancipation, modernization and backwardness, ethno-racial and national identity—and collective memory itself—are politically mediated, contested, invented, and reinvented.

In part 3, the largest and most diverse section of the book, four younger scholars provide fine-grained studies of how politics (and an expanded notion of the political) informs and intersects with constructions of class, race and ethnicity, gender and sexuality, generation, disease, and the nation in nineteenth-century Jamaica and Guatemala and twentieth-century Chile. These case studies explore new theoretical concepts and methods, and reexamine a variety of conventional wisdoms. Diana Paton contributes an essay in subaltern history as she attempts, on the basis of elite documentation and the fragmentary, state-mediated testimonies of freed black slaves, to explain why former slave women refused to work in Jamaican plantation fields after 1837. Greg Grandin follows with an exploration of disease as an elite metaphor for indigenous society and national backwardness in nineteenth-century Guatemala, which he then relates to the trope of anti-communism in the twentieth century—a discourse which would be used to justify the massacring of 200,000 Mayans during the civil war of the late 1970s and '80s. Thomas Klubock revisits his earlier research on Chilean copper miners, but this time to examine the role of race and ethnicity, not gender, in connection with nationalist ideologies, class politics, and strategies of social control employed by North American corporate capital. Heidi Tinsman uses both gender and generation to analyze the differential effects of agrarian reform on married women and teen-age girls; in the process, she tells us a great deal about the role that notions of masculinity and sexuality played in Salvador Allende's attempted socialist transition in Chile. Each author demonstrates that the identities of historical actors are multiple, overlapping, and often contradictory—never static or dichotomous. Thus, race, ethnicity, or sexuality is not the same for men and women, and class, contrary to earlier formulations, does not eliminate ethno-racial, gendered, or generational identities, though it may speak through them with important consequences for collective political action.

In the book's concluding section, "Historians and the Making of History," Florencia Mallon examines the everyday political linkages between intellectuals and subaltern groups. She not only focuses on the historical role of local "organic intellectuals" in Chilean indigenous (Mapuche) society, but also explores the evolution of her own interactive and often problematic relationships with the subjects of these communities and with their struggles—past, present, and future. In this essay, we are provided with a bittersweet meditation on the promise and pitfalls of ethnographic and testimonial strategies as the historian attempts to "bear witness in hard [post-revolutionary] times."[9] In the tradition of her other recent writings, Mallon candidly ponders the need to elaborate different narrative strategies, analytical categories, and modes of argumentation in order to write a multidimensional history of subordinate groups in societies and contexts that no longer rivet the world's attention. Her ruminations on the complex relationships between historical research, historical memory, and current politics, both collective and personal, synthesize a number of the collection's crosscutting themes. The volume concludes with a final reflection by Daniel James, Viotti da Costa's longtime colleague, which locates the significance of these new readings of the political dimension of Latin America's past in a celebration of her most important work.

A few observations are in order about the goals and parameters of this volume. It seeks to pose timely responses to some of the larger questions currently preoccupying Latin Americanists and scholars in other fields and disciplines, namely: How does politics, broadly construed, articulate with other variables and categories of analysis? How is the political realm mediated through historical memory? And how does a political sensibility influence the writing and teaching we do, and the roles we play in the academy and society? In this sense, the book is meant to stimulate discussion and debate, rather than resolve current disputes. In discussing generational remakings of the political in his contribution, Stern suggests that major theoretical advances have come about through what he calls "reverberations": "imperfect intellectual conversations, echoes, and trackings across research projects and across specialized fields." These reverberations give rise to "unplanned convergences" and provide an antidote to the scholarly fragmentation so lamented of late. It was in the spirit of fostering such reverberations that Stern and Allen Isaacman launched the collaboration between Latin Americanists and Africanists that yielded the fruitful volume *Confronting Historical Paradigms* (1993); it was in the same spirit that my three most recent collaborations were born: *Everyday Forms of State Formation* (1994), which brought together Mexican revolution scholars and social theorists working on Europe and Asia; *Close Encounters of Empire* (1998), which prodded Latin Americanist historians and anthropologists north and south of the Rio Grande into dialogue with U.S. foreign relations historians to reassess the multistranded engagement of the United States with Latin America; and the recent issue of the *Hispanic American Historical Review* (1999), on Mexico's "new cultural history," which brought poststructural cultural historians into freestyle combat with their more positivistic antagonists.[10] It is our hope that this volume will trigger similarly useful "reverberations."

If there is a common denominator in the volume's essays, it is their prescription for a politics of history writing that is integrative. In their synoptic papers, Viotti da Costa and Stern advocate a dynamic approach to political analysis that engages multiple levels of the world system, embraces both the state and its subjects, and understands that political discourses, symbols, and identities are intimately related to social relations, economic processes, and power. Thus, Viotti da Costa calls for "a synthesis that will avoid all forms of reductionism . . . (whether economic, cultural, or linguistic), that will not lose sight of the articulation between the micro- and macrophysics of power, that will recognize that human subjectivity is at the same time constituted by and constitutive of social realities."[11] Arguing along roughly similar lines (though somewhat more partial to poststructuralist trends in the "new cultural history"), Stern defends what he sees as a "partial transition"—"more a matter of emphasis than absolute contrast"—from studies of Latin American "politics and society" to studies of "politics and culture." Whereas the former "placed a premium on the complex interplays of agency and structure within the unfolding political economy of regions," the latter "asks how people constructed their political imagination within the [power-laden process] of state formation." Though their emphases differ, both Viotti da Costa and Stern counsel against a celebration of subaltern agency and emancipation that minimizes questions of power, structure, and hegemony. The contributions that follow Viotti da Costa's and Stern's keynote essays represent attempts to harness materialist analysis with "the interrogations of consciousness, constructions of political language, meanings, and authority" by both power holders and subordinate groups that Stern sees as emblematic of the best work of the 1990s on politics as cultural formation.

Thus, these essays move us beyond fruitless current debates about whether we should privilege material or cultural analysis—structure or agency—in our work. Such debates have often had divisive consequences and risk setting back certain fields, particularly Latin American labor history, where some influential practitioners adamantly argue the need to study questions of production and the workplace to the virtual exclusion of other sites and dimensions of working-class life.[12] But as theorists such as Fernando Coronil, William Sewell, Ricardo Salvatore, and Bill Roseberry have persuasively shown, " 'political economy' and 'culture' are ambiguous theoretical categories that refer both to concrete social domains and to the abstract dimensions of any social domain. [An exclusive preoccupation with material analysis] entails a neglect not only of domains outside the economy, but also of the cultural dimension of economic processes themselves" (e.g., the meanings that male and female laborers put on the work they do and the goods they produce).[13] Similarly, an exclusive preoccupation with representation and discourse ignores the material underpinnings of cultural practices.[14] Explicitly in the case of Stern's, Viotti da Costa's, and Barbara Weinstein's essays, more implicitly in the volume's other essays, the contributors take a stand against segregating material and cultural/discursive analysis—a dichotomy that is itself culturally constructed and rife with political meaning and consequence.[15]

Although this volume represents a view of the Latin American political that comes preponderantly from the North, the contributors' training by one of Latin America's most distinguished and broad-gauged historians has powerfully affected their encounters with the region's past. Indeed, the manner in which so many of Viotti da Costa's students have set their stories in broader contexts of power and culture, and sought, like their mentor, to achieve "a synthesis that will result in both a new historiography and new political strategies," has forged them into a somewhat distinctive discursive community within the profession.[16] Consequently, this volume does not pretend to exhaust or represent all North American scholarship on the political in Latin American history—a point made emphatically by Stern in his survey of the field over the last several decades—to say nothing of Latin American approaches to politics. Nevertheless, the nature of the intellectual encounter it does embody is significant in its own right and points up incipient trends of hemispheric convergence in the study of Latin America's past.

Multiple ironies surround Emilia Viotti da Costa's mediating role in this North-South intellectual encounter. Harassed by Brazil's U.S.-supported military regime and ultimately forced to retire from the history department of the Universidade de São Paulo in 1969, Viotti da Costa came to the United States, eventually securing a position in the history department at Yale University in 1973. Over the next quarter century, she reestablished and redirected her academic career, training generations of North American students, a good number of whom became critics of the kinds of repressive regimes that brought her into contact with them.[17] Formerly at the center of a cohort of young historians and social scientists who were recasting the history of slavery, abolition, and race relations in Brazil—intellectuals influenced by French and European formulations of dialectical materialism leavened with new forms of cultural and textual analysis—Viotti da Costa was now forced to engage with a North American academy that did not prize her incisive critiques of the liberal historiographical tradition.[18] Ironically, as she herself testifies, it was in the United States, in dialogue with maverick Americanist colleagues such as Eugene Genovese, Elizabeth-Fox Genovese, C. Vann Woodward, David Montgomery, and Edmund Morgan, as well as with her own restless graduate students, that she "discovered" Latin America. As a younger Brazilian colleague of Viotti da Costa has observed: "This was a fortuitous surprise that permitted her to reflect on Brazilian and U.S. history and culture from a comparative perspective and to lend her analysis a new and enriching dimension."[19] Admired over the years in Brazil for her contributions to the specialized literatures on Brazilian slavery and abolition and the history of the Brazilian empire, it was only with the translation of her recent essays on Latin America's new labor and cultural history and her widely acclaimed 1994 book on slave rebellion in nineteenth-century Guyana, *Crowns of Glory, Tears of Blood*, that Brazilian historians took notice of the expansion of her interests.

In a 1998 essay in the *Latin American Research Review*, U.S. Brazilianist Thomas Skidmore acknowledged the intellectual results of Viotti da

Costa's encounter with her North American students. Skidmore featured the work of several of her students—a group he dubbed "The Integrators"—to illustrate wholesome trends of hemispheric convergence in Latin American historiography. It is these scholars' preoccupation with comparative history, their penchant for integrating global, national, and local levels of analysis, and with elaborating anthropologically informed studies of power and popular culture (particularly "the subtle ways in which nonelites have shaped the cultures and discourses of elite-dominated institutions"), that Skidmore believes characterizes their work and combats the fragmentation that has bedeviled humanistic and social science research on Latin America.[20]

Viotti da Costa's students and colleagues have certainly played a part in fomenting the proliferation of international cross-disciplinary research initiatives that have brought Latin American and North American scholars into ever closer contact in recent years. It is "this widening and deepening of the scholarly infrastructure," as Skidmore terms it, that has hastened "a convergence of professional standards and the creation of a genuinely inter-American scholarly community."[21] Stern, for example, has been an integral member of the Social Science Research Council's continuing international project "Memory and Military Repression in the Southern Cone," led by Argentine sociologist Elizabeth Jelin, whose goal is to train a new generation of Latin American and North American researchers around cutting-edge approaches to this critical cultural and political issue. Working with anthropologist Charles Hale and ten Central American historians and anthropologists, Jeffrey Gould has mounted a multiyear research initiative, funded by the National Endowment for the Humanities, to examine "Memories of Mestizaje and Cultural Politics Since the 1920s" in five Central American nations. Daniel James is currently in the final stages of a similarly ambitious NEH collaborative research effort, "The Berisso Obrero Project," codirected by Argentine labor historian Mirta Lobato, which to date has gathered the testimonies of 250 male and female meatpacking workers as part of a broader effort to write a gendered history of work in this small industrial city south of Buenos Aires.[22] Greg Grandin's research on Mayan constructions of the Guatemalan nation has contributed to and benefited from related research initiatives at the Centro de Investigaciones Regionales de Mesoamérica (CIRMA) and the Asociación para el Avance de las Ciencias Sociales en Guatemala (AVANCSO); as a result of this ongoing collaboration, Grandin was invited to participate as a consultant to the Guatemalan Truth Commission, whose historic report on the origins of twentieth-century violence and repression he helped to write.[23] Similarly, Thomas Klubock, Heidi Tinsman, and Florencia Mallon, as well as Barbara Weinstein and Mary Ann Mahony, have fashioned research strategies that are highly integrated with the agendas of local universities and institutes in Chile and Brazil, respectively. At present, Diana Paton is launching a multinational collaborative project whose goal is to produce a gendered history of slave emancipation in the Atlantic world.

Of course, the recent "hemispheric convergence" that Skidmore and others are touting has hardly brought an end to scholarly fragmentation. Indeed, inter-American collaboration proceeds on a variety of planes, and not without some voices raised in opposition. In addition to the convergence around a "new political/cultural history" of Latin America, reflected in this volume, one could also point to the vital North-South collaboration linking postmodernist literary critics and cultural studies scholars in the Latin American Subaltern Studies Group[24] and the Red Interamericana de Estudios Culturales; the incipient working group on Latin American law and society;[25] and the network that has galvanized neoclassical exponents of a "new Latin American economic history," some of whose members have been rather antagonistic to the other patterns of convergence.[26] No doubt a variety of factors has enhanced these diverse inter-American collaborations—to wit, the revolution in electronic forms of communication, the recent surge in academic exchange between Latin America and the United States (particularly the migration north of ever greater numbers of Latin Americans to pursue advanced degrees and hold visiting appointments), and the internationalization of U.S.-based fellowship competitions, foundation boards, and elite research centers, which has enhanced the participation of Latin American scholars. Yet for many Latin American leftist and nationalist intellectuals, these trends merely underscore the penetration and ascendancy of the (neoliberal) "New World Order" and provoke from them a tepid if not negative response.[27] Some Marxist scholars are as opposed to the "new political/cultural history"—which, by accentuating agency, language, and multiple axes of "difference," undercuts more traditional, monochromatic explanations centered on class and imperialistic oppression—as they are to neoclassical paradigms centered on the market and rational choice.[28]

The essays in this volume argue that historians can and should bear witness to the ways in which abstract historical processes and institutions (e.g., markets, states, wars, capitalism, imperialism, positivism, slavery, patriarchy, dictatorship, and "modern" medicine) are inscribed on the bodies and memories of real people.[29] They eschew modernist binaries and teleologies in their analyses, and try to show that class, gender, and ethno-racial hierarchies and forms of oppression, although connected, do not move in lockstep and often have distinct logics and trajectories. In the process, the volume's contributors seek to reframe and reclaim the political in Latin American history.

The very fact that the political needs to be "reclaimed" says much about the state of the field and intellectual life more broadly. The failure of revolutionary struggles in Latin America, the lack of a cohesive social movement in the United States, and the explosion, as Steve Stern puts it, of "paradigms of inspiration" that might connect ideas to purposeful action—all add up to what Florencia Mallon describes as intellectual "hard times." Of course, progressive intellectuals have always contended with difficult times. Referring to the totalitarian and fascist forms of "darkness" of a previous generation, Hannah Arendt wrote of "the disorder and the hunger . . . the outrage over injustice and despair 'when there was only wrong and no outrage.' " [30] Yet, "even in the darkest of times," Arendt went on, "we have the right to expect some illumination, and . . . such illumination may well come less from theories and concepts than from the uncertain, flickering, and often weak light that some men and women, in their lives and their works, will kindle under almost all circumstances and shed over the time span that was given them on earth. . . . Eyes so used to darkness as ours will hardly be able to tell whether their light was the light of a candle or that of a blazing sun." [31]

For many of her students and colleagues, Emilia Viotti da Costa has been that blazing sun. And although she herself does not believe that the political needs to be reclaimed—for her, real history is always political—it is a fitting theme for a book in Emilia's honor. She has constantly reminded her students of the obvious: that history changes; that cycles of despair and hope are inextricably bound up with that change; and that what is important about methods for understanding the past is not their cleverness or their effectiveness in debunking what came before, but their usefulness in helping us engage politically with the world. At the end of her contribution to this volume, Emilia surveys the new hegemonic strategies that accompany the internationalization and technification of the economy under neoliberalism. She draws our attention to

> the improvement of the conditions of living of sectors of the working class at the expense of others . . . and the consequent intensification of ethnic conflicts which makes it difficult to promote class solidarity; the expansion of the informal sectors (where workers have no power or rights); the extraordinary increase in the participation of women in the labor force (generating conflicts in the domestic sphere); the renewal of putting-out systems (isolating workers); the multiplication of temporary workers (which makes it increasingly difficult to organize them in traditional ways); the transformations of residential patterns,

with the disappearance of working-class neighborhoods (which traditionally had been centers of working-class activity); changes in forms of leisure (isolating the workers in front of TV sets); the growing impact of a media in the service of the state and of business corporations; and finally, the generalization of a consumer mentality that intensifies the tension between privation and desire and emphasizes the individual at the expense of the social.

"This extremely complex scenario, which varies from one society to another," Emilia contends, must inform political practice and theory, as well as the new histories we write, for "the mere reproduction of traditional interpretations cannot account for this new reality." She recognizes, moreover, that despite the formidable challenges it poses to subaltern groups and activist scholars alike, the present political and intellectual moment is also alive with new possibilities. No matter how cruel neoliberalism or corrupt democracy tend to be in Latin America these days, no matter how corrosive of old solidarities, the current period is also redolent with new forms of identity and new modes of political and intellectual engagement—many of which are discussed in the pages that follow. It remains to be seen, of course, how influential or lasting Skidmore's notion of "hemispheric convergence," fueled by scholarly diasporas and enhanced communication, will be, either in intellectual or political terms. But it has already thrown shafts of light across these "dark times," facilitating strategies of North-South (and South-North) collaboration among scholars, labor organizers, environmentalists, feminists, and Native American activists, to cite the more celebrated cases.

This emphasis on the need to integrate, to achieve a historiographical synthesis that "will avoid all forms of reductionism and reification," has animated Emilia Viotti da Costa's discussions with her students for the past quarter century and is centrally at issue here. "The work of the historian," Emilia maintains, "is always a dialogue between past and present," and the good historian transcends earlier understandings and modes of analysis by means of dialogue and argument, rather than simply by displacing them. "Ideas do not die," Emilia reminds her students, even as some intellectuals declare the end of ideology, and of history as well: "Ideas never die; 1848 will come again. And when it does, you better be able to recognize it."

Notes

I am grateful to Brooke Larson, Peter Winn, John French, and Steve Stern for their thoughtful comments on an earlier draft, and to Greg Grandin for sharing reflections about Emilia Viotti da Costa and Hannah Arendt that inspired parts of this essay.

1 See, for example, Pierre Bourdieu's provocative correlation of social and intellectual trends in "Neo-Liberalism, the Utopia (Becoming a Reality) of Unlimited Exploitation," in *Acts of Resistance: Against the New Myths of Our Time*, trans. Richard Nice (Cambridge: Polity Press, 1998), 94–105.

2 See the epigraph to Emilia Viotti da Costa's essay in this volume.

3 See, for example, James Surowiecki, "Genovese's March: The Radical Reconstructions of a Southern Historian," *Lingua Franca* (Dec.–Jan. 1997): 36–52.

4 In its second national conference in June 2000, the Historical Society took dead aim at "the New Cultural History."

5 See Linda Gordon's critique of (and exchange with Joan Scott) in *Signs* 15, 4 (1990): 852–59; for other trenchant observations on this danger, see Florencia E. Mallon, "The Promise and Dilemma of Subaltern Studies: Perspectives from Latin American History," *American Historical Review* 99, 5 (Dec. 1994): 1491–1515; John D. French and Daniel James, "Squaring the Circle: Women's Factory Labor, Gender Ideology, and Necessity," in French and James, eds., *The Gendered Worlds of Latin American Women Workers: From Household and Factory to the Union Hall and Ballot Box* (Durham: Duke University Press, 1999), esp. 7–8; Leon Fink, "The New Labor History and the Powers of Historical Pessimism: Consensus, Hegemony, and the Case of the Knights of Labor," in *In Search of the Working Class* (Urbana: University of Illinois Press, 1994), esp. 135–36; and Emilia Viotti da Costa's essay in this volume.

6 See, for example, Lila Abu-Lughod, "The Romance of Resistance: Tracing Transformations of Power through Bedouin Women," *American Ethnologist* 17, 1 (1990): 41–55; and Sherry B. Ortner, "Resistance and the Problem of Ethnographic Refusal," *Comparative Studies in Society and History* 37 (Jan. 1995): 173–93.

7 Peter H. Smith, "Political History in the 1980s: A View from Latin America," in Theodore K. Rabb and Robert I. Rotberg, eds., *The New History, the 1980s and Beyond: Studies in Interdisciplinary History* (Princeton: Princeton University Press, 1982), 3–27 (quotations from 4, 26).

8 Emilia Viotti da Costa, *The Brazilian Empire: Myths and Histories* (Chicago: University of Chicago Press, 1985), xvii (emphasis mine).

9 In this regard, Mallon's essay sheds important light on the mediated nature of oral histories and *testimonios*, the issue which lies at the heart of the controversial debate between David Stoll and defenders of Rigoberta Menchú Tum. See, for example, the special issue "If Truth Be Told: A Forum on Stoll and Menchú," *Latin American Perspectives* 26, 6 (Nov. 1999).

10 Frederick Cooper, Florencia E. Mallon, Steve J. Stern, Allen Isaacman, and William Roseberry, *Confronting Historical Paradigms: Peasants, Labor, and the Capitalist World System in Africa and Latin America* (Madison: University of Wisconsin Press, 1993); Gilbert Joseph and Daniel Nugent, eds., *Everyday Forms of State Formation: Revolution and the Negotiation of Rule in Modern Mexico* (Durham: Duke University Press, 1994); Joseph, Catherine C. LeGrand, and Ricardo D. Salvatore, eds., *Close Encounters of Empire: Writing the Cultural History of U.S.–Latin American Relations* (Durham: Duke University Press, 1998); Joseph and Susan Deans-Smith, eds., "Mexico's New Cultural History: *Una lucha libre?* Special issue of *Hispanic American Historical Review* 79, 2 (May 1999).

11 Her argument here builds on earlier iterations: see, for example, Emilia Viotti da Costa, "Experience versus Structures: New Tendencies in the History of Labor and the Working Class in Latin America—What Do We Gain, What Do We Lose?" *International Labor and Working-Class History* 36 (fall 1989): 3–24; and *Crowns of Glory, Tears of Blood: The Demerara Slave Rebellion of 1823* (New York: Oxford University Press, 1994), esp. xiii–xix.

12 See, for example, John Womack Jr., "Labor History and Work," paper presented at the symposium "Industrial Relations in Latin America: A New Framework?" Harvard University, 5 November 1999. Womack is certainly correct about the need to reverse the trend away from research on the work process; it is his disparagement of those labor historians that do "cultural history" *tout court* that seems cause for alarm.

13 The quote is from Fernando Coronil's foreword to Joseph et al., eds., *Close Encounters of Empire*, xi; also see William H. Sewell Jr., "Towards a Post-Materialist Rhetoric for Labor History," in Leonard R. Berlanstein, ed., *Rethinking Labor History: Essays on Discourse and Class Analysis* (Urbana: University of Illinois Press, 1993), 15–38; Sewell, *Work and Revolution: The Language of Labor from the Old Regime to 1848* (Cambridge: Cambridge University Press, 1997); Ricardo D. Salvatore, "The Normalization of Economic Life: Representations of the Economy in Golden-Age Buenos Aires, 1890–1913," *Hispanic American Historical Review*, 81, 1 (Feb. 2001): 1–44; French and James, "Squaring the Circle" and *The Gendered Worlds*; and the essays by Diana Paton, Thomas Klubock, and Heidi Tinsman in this volume.

14 See, for example, William Roseberry, "Social Fields and Cultural Encounters," in Joseph et al., eds., *Close Encounters of Empire*, 515–24.

15 Gilbert M. Joseph, "Close Encounters: Towards a New Cultural History of U.S.–Latin American Relations," in Joseph et al., eds., *Close Encounters of Empire*, 3–46, esp. 14; Anne McClintock, *Imperial Leather: Race, Gender, and Sexuality in the Colonial Contest* (New York: Routledge, 1995).

16 For Viotti da Costa's role as a mentor, see Thomas E. Skidmore, "Studying the History of Latin America: A Case of Hemispheric Convergence," *Latin American Research Review* 33, 1 (1998): 105–27, esp. 119–20, amplified by personal communications with the author. The quotation is from Viotti da Costa's essay in this volume.

17 See Stern's essay in this volume.

18 See Weinstein's essay in this volume.

19 Personal communication with Maria Ligia Coelho Prado, 17 November 1999.

20 Skidmore, "Studying the History of Latin America," 115–17, quotation on 117. Skidmore focuses on the recent work of Florencia Mallon, Gilbert Joseph, and Steve Stern. He also alludes to the contributions that Tulio Halperin Donghi of the University of California, Berkeley, and other exiled Latin American historians made to a "hemispheric convergence" in the way Latin American history is written.

21 Ibid., 121. It bears repeating that many other North American scholars have played an active role in such initiatives. In his contribution to this volume, Stern draws our attention, for example, to the catalyzing role the Social Science Research Council played in organizing major international collaborations to chart new directions in Andean and Mexican history and anthropology. These projects were spearheaded on the North American side by scholars such as Brooke Larson and Karen Spalding (Andes) and Friedrich Katz (Mexico).

22 For preliminary findings from this project, see the essays by James and Lobato in French and James, eds., *The Gendered Worlds of Latin American Women Workers*.

23 Comisión para el Esclarecimiento Histórico, *Guatemala: Memoria del silencio*, 12 vols. (Guatemala City: Oficina de Servicios para el Proyecto de las Naciones Unidas, 1999); for an on-line version of the report and an English-language summary, see http://hrdata.aaas.org/ceh.

24 On the creation of the Latin American Subaltern Studies Group, see Mallon, "The Promise and Dilemma of Subaltern Studies," 1504–6; for the group's "Founding Statement," see the special issue on "The Postmodern Debate in Latin America," *boundary* 2, 20 (fall 1993): 110–21.

25 For a recent sampling of the "new legal history," which discusses the emergence of this international community of scholars, see Ricardo D. Salvatore, Carlos A. Aguirre, and Gilbert M. Joseph, eds., *Crime and Punishment in Latin America: Law and Society Since Late Colonial Times* (Durham: Duke University Press, 2001).

26 Two recent collections of the new economic history scholarship are Stephen H. Haber, ed., *How Latin America Fell Behind: Essays on the Economic Histories of Brazil and Mexico* (Stanford: Stanford University Press, 1997) and John H. Coatsworth and Alan M. Taylor, eds., *Latin America and the World Economy Since 1800* (Cambridge: the David Rockefeller Center Series on Latin American Studies/Harvard University Press, 1998). Haber has been most aggressively opposed to the new cultural/political history and postmodernism, which he invariably lumps together in his attacks. See, for example, "The Worst of Both Worlds: The New Cultural History of Mexico," *Mexican Studies/Estudios mexicanos* 13, 2 (summer 1997): 363–83; "Anything Goes: Mexico's 'New' Cultural History," *Hispanic American Historical Review* 79, 2 (May 1999): 309–30; see also Susan Migden Socolow, "Putting the 'Cult' in Culture," in the same issue, 355–65. Socolow labels the new political/cultural history "the latest gringo intellectual contagion" and agrees with Haber that it has had little impact in Latin America itself. For responses to Haber, see the commentaries by Mallon and Claudio Lomnitz in the same issue of *HAHR*, and Stern's essay in this volume.

27 See, for example, Claudio Lomnitz, "Barbarians at the Gate? A Few Remarks on the Politics of the 'New' Cultural History of Mexico," *Hispanic American Historical Review* 79, 2 (May 1999): 367–83, esp. 382–83, for a suggestive discussion of why many traditional Mexican historians have not embraced "the new cultural history."

28 See, for example, Francisco J. Carpintero, "Un proyecto académico exitoso? La nueva historia cultural del campesinado mexicano," unpublished manuscript, 1999. Other Latin American scholars who are in principle sympathetic to a synthesis of political economic and materialist approaches have problems with the weighting that is often given to them, particularly in scenarios where a preoccupation with gender and ethnic inequality impedes the historian's ability to critique underlying regimes of class and imperial exploitation (personal communications with Maria Ligia Coelho Prado).

29 I draw here on the eloquent discussion in Florencia E. Mallon, "Time on the Wheel: Cycles of Revisionism and the 'New Cultural History,' " *Hispanic American Historical Review* 79, 2 (May 1999): 331–51, esp. 349.

30 Hannah Arendt, *Men in Dark Times* (New York: Harcourt, Brace, and Company, 1968), viii.

31 Ibid., ix–x.

Emilia Viotti da Costa

New Publics, New Politics, New Histories:
From Economic Reductionism to Cultural
Reductionism—in Search of Dialectics

▼

These times are times of chaos, opinions are a scramble; parties are a jumble; the language of new ideas has not been created; nothing is more difficult than to give a good definition of oneself in religion, in philosophy, in politics. . . . The world has jumbled its catalog.—Alphonse Marie Louis de Prat de Lamartine, 1790–1869[1]

"May '68 we remade the world. May '86 we remake the kitchen." This caption, which appeared in an advertisement published in the French newspaper Le Monde, paid for by a company that sells modern kitchens, suggests a change in people's attitudes from the 1960s to the 1980s: from a period of political militancy to the "yuppie" generation. It is true that one might question the radicalism of May 1968 and doubt that it did, in fact, set out to remake the world—although there is no doubt that was the intention of many of the thousands of young and not-so-young people that gathered in the streets of Paris and other cities of the Western world. We might also doubt that the new generation is fundamentally consumerist, individualistic, and conservative. The advertisement probably expresses the hopes of entrepreneurs, not the attitudes of the consumers. But the advertisement—which was later reproduced on the cover of an issue of the Radical History Review devoted to the study of the impact of new forms of consumerism on contemporary culture and politics—is a good metaphor to characterize the state of mind of many historians and militants when they confront the new trends both in the histories we live and the histories we write.[2]

One just has to look at some of the articles published in recent years about contemporary events to detect a tone of concern, if not pessimism and despair, reminiscent of the "mal du siècle" that affected Alphonse de

Lamartine's and Alfred de Musset's (1810–1852) generation, which saw the early hopes of the French Revolution momentarily collapse during the Restoration. Even more revealing are some of the book reviews and essays discussing new historiographical trends. Concerned with the new tendencies that have taken historical studies away from traditional paths, enlarging the frontiers of historical research to areas never explored before and raising doubts about traditional approaches, methods, and interpretations (tendencies that often go together with new political goals and strategies), some historians have reacted as if these tendencies represent a dangerous rupture with the past and a threat to the future.

The field is polarized. On one side are those who view the new tendencies with suspicion and reservation, and who, unwilling to establish a dialogue with the new, continue to write history as if they were still living in the 1960s. On the other side are those who uncritically pursue the work of demolition of traditional approaches, embracing new fashions just because they are new, without examining their limitations and implications. Both positions are misleading. The first, because it refuses to incorporate at the theoretical level the extraordinary transformations that have taken place in the past thirty years, stubbornly clinging to theoretical schemes that no longer account for the world around them. Not surprisingly, those who adopt this position have lost the capacity to recruit followers among new generations. The second is misleading because, in its quest for originality and its seduction by new fashions, it simply inverts the assumptions of the historiography of the 1960s instead of integrating them in a new and richer synthesis. Thus, in spite of all its claims to novelty, it runs the risk of re-creating a type of history even more traditional than the one it repudiates, and—what is worse—in its eagerness to look for new themes, the "new historiography" ignores aspects that are crucial for understanding society and history. Readers of this new history are often left unable to situate themselves in relation to past and present, hence incapable of constructing the future. At its best, this attitude converts history into a mere rhetorical exercise aimed at entertaining the reader. At its worst, it transforms it into an academic exercise that, in spite of its authors' intentions, serves purposes fundamentally conservative. In this polarized field it is extremely important that we stop to think about these contradictory tendencies, not with the purpose of returning to approaches and strategies that have been obviously superseded by history itself, or to uncritically celebrate the new approaches, but to open new paths for a much-needed synthesis.[3]

To understand the epistemological rupture that has occurred in the past thirty years, we have to place it within its historical context: the changes that have affected both society and the conditions of intellectual production. Signs of tensions can be traced back to the 1950s. The work of Jean-Paul Sartre (particularly his *Critique of Dialectical Reason*) and also of his adversary Merleau-Ponty (especially *Humanism and Terror* and *The Adventures of Dialectics*) already contained the perplexities and doubts that led to the theoretical impasse we confront today. In an essay published in the sixties, Merleau-Ponty remarked that the dialectic had its own history. He called attention to the tension between freedom and necessity in the interior of the dialectic and noticed that depending on social praxis, historians were led to emphasize either impersonal and "objective" historical forces or the role of the historical subject, and thus of subjectivity, will, and freedom.

In fact, when we examine the changes that have taken place in the historiography of the past thirty years, we notice a gradual shifting from necessity to freedom: from an emphasis on what were once defined as "objective" historical forces to an emphasis on the historical actor's subjectivity, creativity, and agency; from a preoccupation with material conditions of existence to a preoccupation with perceptions, symbols, meanings, and rituals; and from a preoccupation with what in the 1960s was characterized as infrastructure to what was then conceptualized as superstructure. What started as a healthy and necessary critique of mechanistic interpretations, economic determinism, structuralism (as in E. P. Thompson's critique of Althusser, for example),[4] and the artificial separation between infra- and superstructure (a separation skillfully criticized by Raymond Williams in *Marxism and Literature*)[5] ended, against the original intentions of the authors, in a complete inversion. Culture, politics, language, and meaning, instead of being constituted (determined) became constitutive (determinant). Consciousness was again seen as determining the social being rather than the reverse—as postulated by the historiography of the sixties (leaving aside, of course, the conservative historiography, which has always asserted the transcendental nature of consciousness).

The valid critique of essentialist notions of class and of mechanical relations between class and class consciousness (so well problematized in Gøran Therborn's *The Ideology of Power and the Power of Ideology*),[6] and the new paths it opened for an investigation of the process of construction and articulation of multiple and often contradictory identities (ethnic, religious, class, gender, nationality, and so on), often led to the total neglect of the concept of class as an interpretive category. What started as a recognition that historians construct their own objects, and a critique of the objectivism characteristic of a positivist reading of marxism (which wrongly assumed a total separation between subject and object, asserting the scientific nature of historical knowledge), has frequently led to a complete subjectivism, to the denial of the possibility of knowledge, and sometimes even to the questioning of the boundaries between history and fiction, "fact and fancy" (for example, Hayden White's emphasis on "the fictive nature of historical narrative").[7]

Both the traditional and the new approaches are eminently anti-dialectical. They not only establish an artificial separation (opposition) between objectivity and subjectivity (or freedom and necessity), forgetting that one is implied in the other, but they also ignore a basic dialectical principle: that men and women make history, but not under the conditions of their own choosing.

The result of the shift from one theoretical position to another was an inversion: we simply moved from one reductionism to another, from economic to cultural or linguistic reductionism. To one type of reification we have opposed another. Both are equally unsatisfactory. Neither approach does justice to the complexity of dialectics and the theory of human praxis, but thanks to such an inversion, it may be possible today to attempt a new synthesis.[8]

The demolition of traditional approaches has had several casualties. One was the notion of historical process. Dissatisfied, and with good reason, with a teleological history that saw each historical moment as a necessary stage in a linear process that automatically conducted to an end already known, a great number of historians went so far as to deny that history had any logic of its own. They also gave up any attempt at totalization. This led to the discrediting of all theoretical models, whether they originated in the theories of modernization, dependency, world system, or modes of production. Consequently, theoretical debates, which in the past often lacked empirical basis and risked becoming scholastic and sterile, have been postponed if not abandoned altogether. Empiricism became fashionable again, not as a necessary moment in the elaboration of any theory, but as an end in itself, as if history would somehow reveal itself to whoever leans over documents. From a nondialectical, deductive approach that demonstrated more than investigated, and that seemed to know what it would find even before it started looking for it, we have moved to an inductive approach that never reaches theoretical levels. Instead of emphasizing similarities, historians emphasize differences; instead of privileging regularities, they privilege the unpredictable, the accidental, the unexpected, the irrational, the spontaneous.

The "histoire tableau" and the "historie de la vie quotidienne," which had been famous in France in the 1950s but since buried, were resuscitated in a new and more refined rhetorical garb. So were theories of national character, which everyone believed had been put to rest with the defeat of

Nazism in 1945, but which now reappear under the guise of "culture" or "ethnicity." Simultaneously, memory often took the place of history. A growing number of historians seemed more interested in gathering people's testimonies and collecting their memoirs than in writing their history. So important has this trend become that in December 1997 the *American Historical Review* dedicated one of its "forum" sections to "History and Memory." In the introduction, the editor stresses that "collective memory has become a compelling form of historical analysis." Following on the steps of the French historian Pierre Nora, the adepts of what soon became an overwhelming genre have created magazines, promoted international gatherings, and not surprisingly recruited ever more followers. Although most historians continue to use oral testimonies to supplement archival material, some have come to rely exclusively on interviews; thus memory takes the place of history, and oral history displaces archival research. This genre has become especially successful among groups committed to making the voice of the voiceless heard in the public arena.[9] But often, as Steven Watts put it, "eager to dispense discursive 'participation' to all excluded cultural groups, linguistic leftists failed to challenge the underlying socio-economic, political, and cultural structures that have excluded those groups to begin with and have sustained the illusion of 'choice.' "[10]

Because the traditional historiography had neglected the subjectivity of historical agents (transforming it into an epiphenomenon, seeing people as "bearers" of historical forces rather than as historical agents), the new historiography chose to focus on human agency and to write history from the point of view of those who had been silenced or forgotten. The number of practitioners of oral history grew, as did the number of studies based exclusively on testimonies and interviews—as if these contained the whole history, or as if history were nothing but a confusion of subjectivities and voices, a sort of Tower of Babel. The extremists claimed that the only way out was for each one to tell his or her own version of history. Historians would be limited to registering the many versions, and perhaps adding their own. There was a danger in this approach, however, that some scholars were quick to point out. Witnesses' accounts are always partial; one cannot grasp historical processes by hearing one side. And even after hearing many and contradictory testimonies, historians have to submit them to historical criticism. Otherwise they will miss the history behind the words.

Under the influence of Foucault, historians' attention moved from the global structures of domination, the processes of capital accumulation, the state, and the relations between social classes—all of which had been at the center of traditional historiography—to the microphysics of power.

This led to an extraordinary expansion of the frontiers of history: criminality, prostitution, homosexuality, witchcraft, carnival, smells, processions, rituals, the theater of power, myths and legends, cartography and other forms of representations (all of which had interested historians only marginally in the past) absorbed the energies of the new generation of historians. But only rarely did they attempt to establish a connection between the macro- and the microphysics of power. In some rare and notable exceptions these two approaches came together.[11] More often they ran parallel to each other as alternative ways of looking at history. The result was that in spite of the extraordinary expansion of the field of history and our understanding of the multiplicity and variety of human experience, the macrophysics of power remained in the shadow. Although this method of analysis, derived from a simplistic reading of Foucault, *did* help identify the many places where power is exerted—and this was a positive contribution to our knowledge of the past—it refused to explain how and why power is constituted, reproduced, and transformed. Contrary to Foucault's original intention, the micro-histories remained often as colorful pieces of a broken kaleidoscope never coming together to produce a design, fragments of experience without meaning.

The political strategies that in the past were based on the critique of the state and of economic and social structures were not validated by the new historiography. Other strategies found justification in the new history, which celebrates spontaneity, negotiation, day-to-day resistance, the "weapons of the weak," and preaches the subversion of language. But these trends that may mean emancipation can easily lead to a dead end, since it is difficult to take a position before a history that is characterized as arbitrary, chaotic, and without meaning or direction.

None of the tendencies mentioned here has contributed as much to the inversion of dialectics as the emphasis on discourse, be it the discourse of the oppressed or of the oppressors, the discourse of the reformists or of the conservatives—a tendency that one author has defined as "vulgar linguicism." As Bryan Palmer stresses in *Descent into Discourse*,[12] many authors who have adopted this approach have imported a terminology that serves only to decorate their historical texts, which otherwise continue to follow very conventional methods. "Discourse," "language," "symbolic," "deconstruction"—all have become common expressions in historians' jargon, although often as part only of their vocabulary, not of their theory. The next step, however, was the reification of language. This tendency appears clearly in influential studies of the working class.[13] Gareth Stedman-Jones, for example, in *Languages of Class*,[14] after asserting that there is no social reality outside or before language, concludes that Chartism "spoke a language of class that was constructed and inscribed within a complex rhetoric of metaphorical association, causal inference and imaginary construction"—something that is always good to remember, but in itself is not enough to understand class experience (as Neville Kirk has pointed out in his fine review of the literature on Chartism).[15] Criticizing Stedman-Jones for not carrying his methodology to its ultimate consequences, Joan Scott, in "On Language, Gender, and Working-Class History,"[16] went on to propose a method that would show how "ideas such as class become through language, social realities." This is a complete inversion of the traditional methodology. In this case, language determines social relations rather than the reverse.[17] In this text Scott seems to give priority to the concept of class over class experience when she says that "concepts like class are required before individuals can identify themselves as members of such a group, before they can act collectively as such."[18]

Discourse analysis is, of course, fundamental to the historian's work. In fact, it would be fair to say that there is no historical research that does not start with an analysis of discourse. But to recognize this fact is not the same as to say that discourse analysis is sufficient for understanding history. And certainly it does not mean, as some people would like to believe, that the only things that exist are texts upon texts, or that the work of the historian, like that of the literary critic, is nothing but an infinite deconstruction.

Terry Eagleton, describing the events of 1968 and the emergence of post-structuralism, commented on the irony that, incapable of subverting state power, the generation of '68 subverted language. In a review of Furet's book about the French Revolution, Lynn Hunt noticed in 1981 that the history of the Great Revolution—which for a long time had been associated with violence, hunger, and class conflict—had been transformed into a "semiological event." Furet had invented a new metaphysic in which language creates human relations.[19]

The new historiography has also shown a growing concern with epistemological problems; that is to say, with the discourse of the historian. This tendency is not new. In "Structure, Sign and Play in the Discourse of the Human Sciences," Jacques Derrida observed that we need to interpret the interpretation more than to interpret the things themselves.[20] His appeal would find many followers who were more concerned with discussing the limits of historical consciousness than with history itself. The categories used by historians in their interpretations of the past were brought into question, leading to obsessive speculation about the validity of applying our own categories to other cultures, and to other times and places. Can we apply categories born out of European experience to the "Orient"? Can the colonizer speak for the colonized? Can we write the history of the oppressed, or should they speak for themselves? Can the subaltern speak?[21] Can the theories about the sexual division of labor that we use to study the central areas of capitalism be applied to the periphery?[22] Doubts mount and multiply. More and more, we talk about what historians can or cannot do instead of talking about history. Here too, what started as a healthy reflection upon the distortions that historians' biases impose on the writing of history, and a critique of Eurocentric or Western-centric points of view, can easily be turned into a perversely gleeful denial of the possibility of historical knowledge. We are far from the many certainties that characterized the sixties. This can be good, but it can also be bad, especially if we become too certain of our uncertainties.

That the historiography which came out of a positivist reading of the classics of the dialectic left much to be desired is something that has been acknowledged for a long time, though the beating of dead horses remains one of our favorite intramural sports. In fact, much of what appears today under the labels of "postmodern" or "poststructuralist" found its roots in the work of a French philosopher who had a great impact in the sixties but was later ostracized, probably because of his political connections. Anyone who takes the time to read the first two hundred pages of Sartre's *Critique of Dialectical Reason* (the section entitled "The Question of Method")[23] will find a keen critique of marxist historiography as it was written by Sartre's contemporaries. Sartre criticized intellectuals who believed that they were serving their party by simplifying the data, neglecting details, and conceptualizing the event before they had studied it. He accused them of having transformed what was supposed to be a method of research into a new metaphysic. Commenting on Daniel Guerin's *La lutte des classes sous la Première République*, Sartre said that "this method is a priori. The author does not construct its concepts from the experience he wants to decipher. He knows the truth even before he has started. His only goal is to fit the events, the people and their actions into pre-fabricated molds."[24] Sartre also criticized the reduction of the political to the social, and of ideology to class interests. He condemned historians for not being able to integrate into their histories the perspective of the historical agents, and for dehumanizing history. Sartre also challenged those who established a mechanistic relation between individuals and social classes, between social class and consciousness, and between imaginary and real praxis. He insisted on the importance of mediations and condemned the teleological nature of historical explanations. Sartre also criticized the essentialist, functionalist, and static approaches that ignored the meaning of contradictions and the importance of the historical process. His friend and companion, Simone de Beauvoir, raised the banner of the new feminism.[25] She was one of the first to show how power is implicated in the construction of the other.[26] Thus already in the fifties and sixties, one could detect the perplexities, the conflicts, and the trends that came to dominate the new historiography. But the new generation of historians did not follow Sartre.[27] Their work is closer to Foucault, Derrida, and the new French philosophers.[28] This led them to a confrontation and a rupture with the historiographical traditions of Sartre's era.

It is perhaps in the field of labor history that the conflict between the old and the new is more visible. While in the past historians focused on conflicts between capital and labor and on the macrophysics of power, and were concerned with economic structures and the role of the state and of trade union leaders and political parties in the formation of the working class, the new historiography turned to the study of rituals, language, family, leisure, and day-to-day resistance. While in the past historians asked what impact industrial change and the state had on the workers' movement, the new history inverted the question and asked what impact the workers' movement had on the economy and on state formation. While traditional historiography was concerned with "the working class," which was assumed to be the revolutionary class, the new historiography problematized and historicized notions of class and class consciousness, questioning the essentialist view of the working class characteristic of traditional historiography. The new historiography also raised doubts about the alleged "natural" solidarity of the working class and exposed the internal conflicts that issued from the many and sometimes competitive identities— national, religious, ethnic, sexual, and so on—undermining working-class solidarity. Simultaneously, the new historiography repudiated teleological approaches that in the past had assumed that history marched inevitably toward socialism and that each historical moment was a new stage in that direction. The focus of attention moved from the labor movement to the workers, from the factory to the household, from the working man to the working woman, from the individual worker to his family, and from work to leisure and culture.

The new historiography of labor reexamined the relations between leadership and the grass roots, between the trade unions and governments. It challenged those who had assumed an automatic connection between the forms of consciousness and types of activities workers were involved in, and it repudiated the concepts of hegemony and false consciousness often employed by traditional historiography. In this process of revision, historians also incorporated into their analysis the urban nonindustrial workers who had scarcely claimed attention in the past. As a consequence of all this

revisionism, there was a great expansion of the boundaries of the historiography of labor, which came to include social movements, women, and
workers in the service sector. This, too, has been a positive movement, but
if carried to its extreme, it can have negative consequences because it
makes people lose sight of fundamental historical forces that affect not
only the lives of workers, but also their own lives.

The new tendencies in the historiography of labor have triggered great
debates and some negative reactions, particularly because they are directly
tied to contemporary political questions. This becomes obvious, for example, in Michael Schneider's 1987 essay, "In Search of a 'New Historical
Subject': The End of Working-Class Culture, the Labor Movement, and
Proletariat,"[29] in which he shows the direct connection between the new
historiography and political trends in postwar Germany—trends which
have led some writers to assert that traditional forms of proletarian consciousness cannot emerge in the present time, and even to predict the end
of the proletariat and of the labor movement, and the emergence in its
place of social movements such as peace movements, ecological movements, feminist movements, and so on. Confronting this challenge, others
look with nostalgia to a past that they describe as a time when the working-
class culture was integrative and radical, and blame the strategies of social
democracy for its disappearance. Schneider argues that the successes of
social democracy and of the trade unions within the liberal democratic
system and the market economy in Germany did indeed improve the conditions of workers, leading to an erosion of class consciousness.[30] The nu-
merical decline of the working class and the difficulties of creating class
consciousness led to a redefinition of political strategies and, simultaneously, to the search for new historiographical paradigms oriented toward the study of the politics of "ordinary" people's daily lives. Analyzing
the consequences of these new political and historiographical practices,
Schneider remarks that the solidarity among small groups of workers, or
the inhabitants of a neighborhood, may indeed create alternative islands of
culture and social reform, but cannot replace a more inclusive political
program. In his opinion, the projects that aim at exploring the political
potential in the lives of ordinary people, and which emphasize only the
negative aspects of more inclusive class and political party organizations,
may lead to a dead end. After pointing at methodological flaws in this new
historiography, Schneider concludes that many of the local and regional
studies that are following the new trends offer nothing more than an
uncritical compilation of details whose relevance is never questioned. They
remain a cemetery of sources, a museum of curiosities. There is also the
danger, he says, that the historians who cultivate this type of history will be

themselves unable to assess critically their own situation and their own vulnerability.

What Schneider does not seem to visualize is that what today seems to him so derivative may be a necessary moment to correct distortions and insufficiencies of the past historiography, and that it might lead to the production of a new and richer synthesis, and a new and more effective political practice.[31] For that synthesis to happen, however, we need to pay attention to both sides, and subject both to a serious critique. The need for such a critique seems even more important on the periphery, where intellectual fashions, instead of being a result of a reflection upon internal conditions, are often imported from places where the reality is profoundly different. When I hear Michelle Perrot, the famous French feminist and labor historian, say that the postmodern society is "a society in which the possibilities of individual expressivity have actually multiplied," that the "impact of dominant political and cultural models on people has been exaggerated, that people still have their private lives, their critical faculties, which are more and more important because people are more and more educated," I pause and wonder whether this really applies to Latin America. But when she goes on to say that "after all, post-modern society is a society in which class has a different meaning and in which people have greater respect for each other," I ask myself, in which world has she lived?[32] It certainly is not the one I know. Racism, torture, massacres of political leaders, death squads, increasing numbers of robberies and assaults, domestic violence, problems of survival that affect the day-to-day life of men and women of the periphery from Mozambique to El Salvador and Guatemala, the six million abandoned children of Brazil, the problems of the inner cities in the United States—these sorts of things do not seem to have entered the universe of Michelle Perrot, or that of many other intellectuals of the developed nations. Seen from the periphery, the celebratory narcissism and the forms of militancy of this new avant-garde, which ignores what happens in their ex-colonies, and sometimes even what happens in their own backyard, seem suspicious and force me to raise questions about the validity of applying analytical categories born out of such a diverse experience to other parts of the world, and perhaps even to our own.

The new tendencies of American and European historiography were born out of concrete situations. Some are similar to those we find in the so-called Third World; others are not. They are, in part, related to the crisis of the Soviet system and of a certain reading of marxism during the postwar period, and the ensuing critique of forms of organizations and strategies followed by political parties associated with the Soviet Union. In the periphery, this process was accelerated by political repression triggered by the Cold War. The failure of *soi-disant* socialist regimes in Africa and events in China generated doubts and perplexities among the academic Left. During the past forty years, East-West polarization and intense propaganda on both sides made a critical assessment of contemporary and historical events difficult. It was within this context that the new generations looked for new forms of political action, and the historiography searched for new paths. But this is only one side of the story. The other is much more difficult to analyze and has to do with the growing internationalization of the economy; the industrialization of the peripheries; the process of de-industrialization in the center; the adoption of new technologies and the shrinking and changing nature of the proletariat in the central areas of the capitalist world (though not necessarily in the periphery); the expansion of the tertiary and of the informal economy; the presence of growing numbers of migratory workers (Arabs, Africans, Italians, and Portuguese working in France, England, or Germany, for example, or Mexicans, Haitians, Salvadorans, Guatemalans, Vietnamese, Koreans, Chinese, and others in the United States); the improvement of living conditions of sectors of the working class at the expense of others (whites versus blacks in the United States, nationals versus foreigners in England, France, or Germany) and the consequent intensification of ethnic conflicts which makes it difficult to promote class solidarity; the expansion of the informal sectors (where workers have no power or rights); the extraordinary increase in the participation of women in the labor force (generating conflicts in the domestic sphere); the renewal of putting-out systems (isolating workers); the multiplication of temporary workers (which makes it increasingly difficult to organize them in traditional ways); the transformations of residential patterns, with the disappearance of working-class neighborhoods (which traditionally had been centers of working-class activity); changes in forms of leisure (isolating the workers in front of TV sets); the growing impact of a media in the service of the state and of business corporations; and, finally, the generalization of a consumer mentality that intensifies the tension between privation and desire, and emphasizes the individual at the expense of the social—all this has led to a redefinition of practice and theory.[33] It is within this extremely complex scenario, which varies from one society to another, that the new history was born.

After all this, it should be obvious that the mere reproduction of traditional interpretations cannot account for this new reality. And since the work of the historian is always a dialogue between past and present, it is not surprising that traditional ways of looking at history seem inadequate and that the past is rewritten from new perspectives. In this sense, 1968 really was a watershed. But the opposition suggested by the advertisement with which I started—"May '68, we remade the world. May '86, we remake the kitchen," militancy versus consumerism—may be more apparent than real, and is certainly reversible. Recent events in Europe and the new and recurrent crisis in the capitalist world, particularly felt in the periphery, suggest perhaps that we are entering a new historical period. The moment favors a synthesis that will avoid all forms of reductionism and reification (whether economic, cultural, or linguistic), that will not lose sight of the articulation between the micro- and macrophysics of power, that will recognize that human subjectivity is at the same time constituted by and constitutive of social realities—a synthesis that will result in both a new historiography and new political strategies.[34]

Let us hope that, in the next century, historians will be able to pick up the pieces in this field littered with fragments and create a richer and less chaotic vision that may help them (and others) to free themselves from the straitjacket of narcissism, to reinvent new forms of solidarity, and to find new roads to a more open and truly democratic world, where all people of different genders, classes, ethnicities, religions, and nationalities will come together to participate equally in the wealth of the world.

Notes

A slightly different version of this essay was presented as the keynote speech at the seventh Labor Studies Conference, Atlanta, Georgia, October 1991.

1   Cited by Clifford Geertz, The Interpretation of Cultures (New York: Basic Books, 1973), 221.

2   Radical History Review 37 (1987): 29–93.

3   This is what Jean and John Comaroff are trying to do in anthropology. See, for example, Of Revelation and Revolution: Christianity and Consciousness in South Africa, 2 vols. (Chicago: University of Chicago Press, 1991, 1997).

4   E. P. Thompson, The Poverty of Theory and Other Essays (London, Merlin, 1978).

5   Raymond Williams, Marxism and Literature (Oxford, Oxford University Press, 1977.) See also Williams, Problems of Materialism and Culture (London, Verso, 1980) and Keywords: A Vocabulary of Culture and Society (London: Fontana, 1988).

6   Gøran Therborn, The Ideology of Power and the Power of Ideology (London: Verso, 1980).

7   Hayden White, "The Value of Narrativity in the Representation of Reality," Critical Inquiry (autumn 1980): 6–27; "The Structure of Historical Narrative," Clio 1 (1972): 5–20; and "The Historical Text as Literary Artifact," Clio 1 (1972): 41–62.

8   I have attempted this synthesis in Crowns of Glory, Tears of Blood: The Demerara Slave Rebellion of 1823 (New York: Oxford University Press, 1994).

9   Daniel James, in "Meatpackers, Peronists, and Collective Memory: A View from the South," notices that there is a new boom in the academy "centered on the production of texts about memory, commemoration, and forgetting." He points out that "there is some convergence between the thematics of the academy and the wider popular culture." American Historical Review (Dec. 1997): 1404. For the problems involved in working

with memory as historical source, see James, "Tales Told out of the Borderlands: Doña María's Story, Oral History, and Issues of Gender," 31–52, and John D. French, "Oral History, Identity Formation, and Working-Class Mobilization," in French and James, eds., *The Gendered Worlds of Latin American Women Workers: From Household and Factory to the Union Hall and Ballot Box* (Durham: Duke University Press, 1997), 297–313.

10 Steven Watts, "The Idiocy of American Studies: Poststructuralism, Language, and Politics in the Age of Self-Fulfillment," *American Quarterly* (Dec. 1991): 652. For a sweeping critique of postmodernism's influences on historical writing, see Ellen Meiksins Wood and John Bellamy Foster, eds., *In Defense of History: Marxism and the Postmodernist Agenda* (New York: Monthly Review Press, 1997).

11 See my comments about Peter Winn, *Weavers of Revolution: The Yarur Workers and Chile's Road to Socialism* (New York: Oxford University Press, 1986) in Viotti da Costa, "Structures versus Experience: What Do We Gain, What Do We Lose?" *International Labor and Working-Class History* 36 (fall 1989): 3–24.

12 Bryan Palmer, *Descent into Discourse: The Reification of Language and the Writing of Social History* (Philadelphia: Temple University Press, 1990).

13 See R. Gray, "The Deconstructing of the Working Class," *Social History* 11 (1986): 363–373, and J. Foster, "The Declassing of Language," *New Left Review* 150 (1985): 29–46.

14 Gareth Stedman-Jones, *Languages of Class: Studies in English Working-Class History, 1832–1982* (Cambridge: Cambridge University Press, 1983): 90–178.

15 Neville Kirk, "In Defence of Class: A Critique of Recent Revisionist Writing upon the Nineteenth-Century English Working Class," *International Review of Social History* 37 (1987): 2–47. See also P. A. Pickering, "Class without Words: Symbolic Communication in the Chartist Movement," *Past and Present* 112 (1986): 144–162, and J. Epstein, "Rethinking the Categories of Working-Class History," in *Labour/Le travail* 18 (1986): 195–208.

16 *ILWCH* 31 (spring 1987): 1–14.

17 See the critiques of Joan Scott in the same issue, *ILWCH* 31 (spring 1987).

18 See Scott's reply to her critics in *ILWCH* 32 (fall 1987): 39–45.

19 Lynn Hunt, Review of *Penser La Revolution Française* in *History and Theory* 20 (1981): 313–323, cited in Palmer, *Descent into Discourse*, 97.

20 Jacques Derrida, *Writing and Difference* (Chicago, University of Chicago Press, 1978), cited in Palmer, 33.

21 Gayatri Chakravorty Spivak, "Can the Subaltern Speak?" in Cary Nelson and Lawrence Grossberg, eds., *Marxism and the Interpretation of Culture* (Urbana: University of Illinois Press, 1988), 271–313.

22 See, for example, Lynne Phillips, "Rural Women in Latin America: Directions for Future Research," *Latin American Research Review* 25, 3 (1990): 89–108.

23 Jean-Paul Sartre, *Critique de la raison dialectique, precede de question de methode,* vol. I, *Theorie des ensembles practiques* (Paris: Gallimard, 1960).

24 This is a free translation.

25 Another author of the 1950s and 1960s whose work was very influential was Roland Barthes, particularly his *Mythologies* (Paris: Seuil, 1957).

26 In the *Second Sex* Simone de Beauvoir argued that it was "by constructing the woman as 'other' that men in Western culture have constituted themselves as subjects." See Frances E. Mascia-Lee, Patricia Sharpe, and Colleen Ballerino Cohen, *The Postmodernist Turn in Anthropology: Cautions from a Feminist Perspective, Signs* 15, 11 (1989): 7–33.

27 Commenting on the experience of her generation in the 1970s, Florencia Mallon wrote that "some carried [to the field] volume I of *Capital* under their arms, others, *Reading*

Capital. Larger numbers traveled in the company of E. P. Thompson, E. J. Hobsbawm or Antonio Gramsci." ("Dialogues among the Fragments: Retrospect and Prospect," in Frederick Cooper et al., *Confronting Historical Paradigms: Peasants, Labor, and the Capitalist World System in Africa and Latin America* [Madison: University of Wisconsin Press, 1993], 372). If we continue following her metaphor, we would say that the present generation has gone to the field carrying Foucault and Derrida.

28 Ironically, in spite of their differences, these authors tend to be antihumanist and anti-historical in their approach. See Kate Soper, *Humanism and Anti-Humanism: Problems of Modern European Thought* (London: Hutchinson, 1986).

29 *ILWCH* (fall 1987): 46–58.

30 Similar improvement is noticed in England in the two decades after World War II, as James Cronin has indicated. Cronin and Jonathan Schneer, eds., *Social Conflict and Political Crisis in Modern Britain* (London: Croom Helm, 1982).

31 Alf Ludtke tries to establish a bridge between new and old in "The Historiography of Every-Day Life: The Personal and the Political," in Raphael Samuel and Gareth Stedman-Jones, eds., *Culture, Ideology, and Politics* (London: Routledge and Kegan Paul, 1983), 38–54.

32 "New Subjects, New Social Commitments: An Interview with Michelle Perrot by Laura Frader and Victoria de Grazia." This interview was conducted by de Grazia in Paris, 20 September 1986. *Radical History Review* 37 (1987): 27–40.

33 *Radical History Review* 37 is devoted to the study of the impact of consumerism.

34 Walter Adamson, "Leftist Transformations: A Clash between the Feasible and the Desirable," *Radical History Review* 37 (1987): 94–100.

Steve J. Stern

Between Tragedy and Promise:
The Politics of Writing Latin American History
in the Late Twentieth Century

▼

Is our task to reclaim the political in Latin American history or to remake
it? Is the one inseparable from the other? In this essay I argue that the
political—both as a theme for historical analysis, and a sensibility that
informs historical research—has infused a great deal of innovative scholarship on Latin American history between the 1970s and 1990s, but that the
meaning of "the political" for historical writing on Latin America has
undergone an important transformation. In this context, "to reclaim the
political" implies not so much a rediscovery of an abandoned theme or
sensibility, as an effort to specify the new demands placed by historical and
intellectual experience upon the politics of writing Latin American history.

Some parameters will help specify the focus and limitations of the discussion. First, this essay focuses on scholarship. The "politics" of doing
Latin American history, however, takes many forms, some of them more
important than the writing of scholarship and rather untethered from a
conventional spectrum of Right, Center, and Left. Which is the more politically meaningful or engaged act in the life of a scholar-teacher of Latin
American history? Is it research and writing about themes directly related
to questions of power and social justice? Research about any theme in
which the dialogue of past and present is informed by political sensibilities? Is it teaching critical thinking? Is it teaching knowledge that inspires
a break with parochialism or complacency? Developing a democratic ped-
agogical style? Seeking out and mentoring socially disadvantaged students
with potential, in addition to the obviously well prepared and polished star
students? Or does the politics of doing Latin American history sometimes
become more important outside the standard academic arena of scholar-

ship and teaching? During the Central American wars of the 1980s, were scholar-teachers more meaningfully political when they spoke at solidarity rallies and teach-ins, or when they debated State Department representatives on public radio? Or more subtly, when they shared historical background information with church-related groups about to venture out on their own direct encounters with Latin Americans, or when they translated statements by refugees taken in by churches?[1] Finally, how does one assess the politics of international intellectual relationships—whether the politics of collaboration and "giving back" to Latin American colleagues and people who have given and taught us so much, or more uncomfortably, the politics of international academic inequality?

Simply to pose such questions reminds us that the "politics" of doing Latin American history is too multifaceted to reduce to its scholarly dimension. The values of academic life grant the scholarly pursuit of knowledge primacy of place. But this valuation, the raison d'etre that pulls us into networks of scholarly conversation, reading, and debate, can also lead us toward overblown appraisals of (or accusations about) the politics of scholarship. Placed in the context of the full range of the ways in which we are knowingly and unknowingly political, scholarship is usually a modest and indirect form of political engagement. Indeed, its most important political aspect may emerge not in the scholarly writing itself, but from synergies that develop between the process of scholarship and the processes of teaching, mentoring, community work, and international collaboration mentioned above.[2]

One limitation of this essay, therefore, derives from its focus on scholarship, one among several paths of political engagement in the life of scholar-teachers, and arguably not the most important. (Obviously, I am also leaving aside here the question of scholarship as a currency of power, reputation, and privilege within academia, a subject that merits discussion in its own right but which lies beyond the scope of this essay.) Moreover, the "political" that has informed serious scholarly writing of Latin American history is subtle rather than crudely mechanical. The problem under review here is not that of pseudo-scholarship—the marshaling and twisting of apparent research to suit a particular political line or agenda. The focus, rather, is on two more nuanced issues: 1) the political sensibilities, framed by generational historical experience and a wider social and intellectual environment, that influence the questions historians of Latin America have asked, and the conceptual approaches they have found useful; and 2) the visions of politics and power that subsequently emerged in scholarship on Latin American history.

Two additional limitations of this essay require mention. First, it concentrates on the meanings and remakings of the political in writings by U.S. scholars of Latin American history. There are valuable stories to tell, of course, about the meanings of the political in historical writing by Latin American scholars, situated in their own social and political contexts, between the 1970s and 1990s. But to develop these versions of the problem systematically, in a manner attentive to Latin America as a whole while respectful of country-to-country variations, would expand this essay to an impossible scope. For similar reasons, I cannot undertake a systematic discussion of the non-Hispanic Caribbean or of European countries with notable clusters of Latin Americanists. It is pertinent to note, of course, that transnational reverberations of intellectual thought—fostered not only by circulation of published material but also by teaching appointments, graduate education, symposia, lectures, personal identities, and friend-ships that cut across national borders—render the distinction between the political in Latin American history writings in the United States and those in Latin America relative rather than absolute. Indeed, from time to time this essay will, of necessity, blur or set aside such boundaries. But for reasons of feasibility, the focus here is on U.S. scholarly writings. Given the prominence and scale of scholarly production by the U.S. academy on Latin American history, this is a subject worth exploring in its own right.[3]

Second, the essay focuses on scholarship informed by center-left and left sensibilities, rather than center-right and right sensibilities. The purpose here is neither to imply an absence of politically informed or engaged writing from conservative perspectives, nor to imply that such scholarship has had little to offer for complex and insightful understandings of Latin American history. On the contrary. Elsewhere I have written about the ways conservative political sensibilities have served to advance knowledge.[4] In the last section of this essay, I will argue for the necessity of more pro-found scholarly dialogues with conservative sensibilities to achieve a well-integrated rendering of recent Latin American history.

The reason for the political parameters drawn in this essay—aside from the obvious fact that my own sensibilities lean toward the Left—is that in the period under discussion, center-left and left sensibilities defined much of what was new and influential in the remaking of the political in Latin American history writing. To be sure, political nomenclatures and sen-sibilities, for reasons we shall explore later, shifted notably. Yesterday's "radicals" may become today's "progressives." Yesterday's confident dec-laration of political faith may give way to today's ironic self-reflection. In addition, and as we shall see, a thesis of exuberant intentionality—as if only self-consciously political authors contributed to visions of the political in Latin American history—is unwarranted. But precisely for these reasons, the continuous remaking of "the political" in Latin American history, in a period of significant center-left and left sensibilities in scholarship, becomes an all the more interesting problem for analysis.

The Politics of Social History: The 1970s and early 1980s

The generation of historians who came of age intellectually during the 1960s and 1970s joined the U.S. historical profession during a time of profound intellectual and political turbulence. We need not review here the domestic and international political upheavals that, in conjunction with an expanding university system, yielded intellectual storms.[5] For our purposes, three points suffice. First, within the U.S. historical profession in general, the social history movement broke with the elitism and narrowness of a history focused largely on formal political life and on the men who wielded large influence over public life. The turn toward social history redirected the focus of inquiry toward commoners rather than elites, everyday life rather than high politics, blacks rather than whites, women rather than men, the non-Western rather than the Western, and so on. The writing of Latin American history bore witness to this larger trend. One could fairly say that in the late 1960s and early 1970s, the new scholarship in social history, for Latin America as well as other world regions, tended not so much to challenge customary political history on its own ground as to sidestep it. Understandably, the challenge was indirect, embedded within the choice of topics now deemed worthy of research rather than negligence.[6]

Second, by the mid to late 1970s a great deal of new research, especially by radical graduate students who would publish books by the late 1970s and early 1980s, found theoretical inspiration in the concepts of "agency" and "hegemony." A related but not identical scholarly approach was that which explored the tension between "agency" and "structure." (We shall explore the implications of the latter point later.) These inspirations opened the door to a genre of writing that sought to integrate the problems of power and social experience, a kind of fusion of "political history" and "social history" from below.[7] On the one hand, new works in social history sought not simply to document the lives of the hitherto neglected majorities of human history, but to take seriously E. P. Thompson's insistence on the agency of the defeated within the making of their own societies. Exploring the agency of the powerless and the victimized rendered them something more than powerless and victimized: it opened the door to the study of struggles that challenged or perhaps even constrained the political and economic options of dominant classes, and of cultural values that contended for legitimation within regional or national political cultures. On the other hand, Gramscian notions of hegemony held in check the impulse to overstate the implications of agency. Resistance by the socially powerless rarely inverted or demolished structures of power. Even more sobering, the life strategies of the poor and downtrodden often seemed to include accommodations to the realities of power—definitions of one's social rights and strategies of struggle to achieve them that perpetuated a framework of rule by elites. The hegemony concept pioneered by Gramsci—understood as combinations of coercion and consent that secured participation of the subaltern in their own domination, notwithstanding struggles that evinced resistance to abuse and affirmations of rights—offered a corrective lens. Using a Gramscian sensibility, one could hope to write a history that balanced human agency and struggle with structures of power, complicity, and constraint.[8]

Third, the twin sensibilities of agency and hegemony—or alternatively, agency and structure—defined a genre of historical writing by radical or progressive scholars that gave specific shape to "the political" in critical historical analysis. The political meant a history of "politics and society" that rendered visible the social life, creativity, adaptations, and resistance of the oppressed and the downtrodden, while setting these phenomena within wider contexts of elite rule, power, and responses to challenges from below.[9]

Several characteristics of this approach deserve mention here. Regional case studies served as the characteristic unit of analysis in this genre of historical writing. To move beyond formulaic theoretical assertions of human agency or of ruling-class hegemony required close study of social relationships—not only relatively horizontal relationships within and among distinct kinds of subaltern communities, but also vertical relations between the oppressed and their social superiors. Narrowing the unit of analysis down to a specific region or locale enabled one to explore the problems of human agency and domination historically and specifically: to name names; to chart changing labor and property relations; to evoke the textures, struggles, and aspirations of everyday life in subaltern communities; and to gauge dynamics of alliance, division, and hierarchy among subalterns as well as between them and their superiors.[10]

Significantly, the region or locale was rarely considered a "world unto itself," but rather a world integrated within a wider field of power and political economy. Awareness of this wider field was indispensable if one were to evaluate the successes and limits of agency within a wider structure of domination, or to understand the ways "resistance" and "accommodation" often constituted a complex adaptive interplay rather than a set of mutually exclusive alternatives, or if one were to harness social history research to sharp historical critique of the politics of elite rule. Awareness of this wider field was also indispensable because of the influence of "dependency" ideas as a framework of critical thought and politics in Latin America in the 1950s and especially the 1960s. The new literature emerged in dialogue with an earlier dependency-oriented cycle that had emphasized the dangers and conservatism of seeing "backward" Latin American regions as worlds unto themselves in need of "modernization."[11] Finally, given the backdrop of dependency discussions, the importance of renovated marxian traditions of critical thought in the turn toward agency, hegemony, and structure as themes of analysis, and the influence of the French Annales school as a historiographical movement that had broken apart earlier boundaries of "great man history" in Europe, the new writings devoted considerable attention to the material dimensions of life. Analysis of the material geography and political economy of human life often served as a point of departure for the assessment of social experience, struggle, and aspiration. As I have argued elsewhere, for historians of Latin America and Africa, considerable attention flowed to such themes as the historical construction and impact of the capitalist world system; the contentious organization and struggles over labor, in grand design and in everyday life; and the analysis of peasants and colonized indigenous peoples as agents in history. E. P. Thompson's notion of "moral economy," as adapted to peasant studies by James Scott, seemed to provide tools that linked analysis of material life and moral consciousness.[12]

Of course, the characterization above is too neat. Hindsight provides extra measures of clarity to issues that were more dimly or ambiguously perceived at the time, and it provides a heightened sense of order to trends and intentions that unfolded as a more contradictory and fragmentary experience. Several colleagues and I have argued elsewhere that such movements in scholarship constituted imperfect intellectual conversations, echoes, and trackings across research projects and across specialized fields—"reverberations" that provided a partial counterpoint to scholarly fragmentation. Such reverberations yielded unplanned yet patterned convergences in the flow of scholarship rather than a unified intellectual march. The metaphor of reverberation refers to the making of an intellectual climate and its characteristic dialogues, not to the making of an organized intellectual project.[13]

In short, the remarks above resort to a kind of Weberian ideal type that exaggerates the intellectual balance, intentionality, and unity of purpose that defined radical and progressive scholarship of the late 1970s and early 1980s. Two caveats are especially important. First, we need to acknowledge the ambiguities and limits of scholarly "radicalism." The scholarly circles of historiographical renovation and political radicalism overlapped, but only partially. Not every social history of the marginalized or downtrodden proclaimed a political objective or stance by the author. To adapt the terms of a trenchant essay by Claudio Lomnitz, one can produce history as ethno-centric history, professional history, theoretical history, or history as imma-nent critique. Politically "radical" historians built bridges, to one degree or another, between the latter three forms of doing history. As Thomas Skid-more has recently observed, the young generation of radical historians did graduate field research in Latin America in the 1960s and 1970s—times of tremendous political conflict, leftist intellectual influence and theoretical effervescence, and repression. In the United States, as well, these were times of sharp political controversy and critique, linked in good measure to the horrors of the Vietnam War. Under these circumstances, some young scholars proved receptive to the interplays of intellectual and political radi-calism, engagement of theory, and sensibilities about class, social conflict, and U.S. power they experienced in their fieldwork.[14]

Other researchers of history, however, remained more squarely within a tradition of professional history that eschewed dialogue with theoretical history and history as immanent critique. They were "radicals" or renova-tors in a more strictly historiographical sense, as professional participants in the social history movement that broke away from elite-oriented tradi-tions of historiography. The historiographical shift and the influence of a politically and intellectually critical climate shaped the kinds of questions these scholars asked and the analytical tools they found useful. One result is that these authors—who would not necessarily have aligned themselves as "political" or "radical," although they may have had center-left or liberal political inclinations—also contributed fine studies to the new genre de-scribed above. Their regional analyses also sought to understand the hu-man initiative and agency "from below" that contended with structures of power and constraint "from above." However ironically or ambiguously, they participated significantly in the emerging meaning of the political in critical historical analysis.[15]

A second caveat recognizes the difficulties, compounded by specific circumstances of historiographical production, of achieving a dialectical analysis that brought into balance the dynamic interrelations of agency and hegemony, agency and structure, or—to use the generational nomenclature preferred by Emilia Viotti da Costa—freedom and necessity. In truth, not every history that sought to uncover or explore human agency avoided the impulse to overestimate its reach through a sober analysis of power and hegemony. On the one hand, in a large, sprawling undertaking whose practitioners included radicals and nonradicals, only some of whom dialogued explicitly with social theory or sought as radicals to underscore structures of domination, a number of works in social history focused mainly on ferreting out the experiences or initiatives of the downtrodden. From this emphasis one need not walk many steps to arrive at an exaggerated historiography of agency that marginalizes problems of power and politics.

In this sense, and especially when we consider practice of social history as a whole in the United States, rather than the Latin Americanist branch of it, Viotti da Costa's observation of a "gradual shifting from necessity to freedom" has a great deal of truth. I think her observation is somewhat exaggerated, however, if taken as a vision of Latin Americanist historiography specifically. (To put it another way, when one turns to Latin Americanist historiography specifically, I see the glass half full, and she perhaps sees it half empty.) Precisely because problems of power and social domination were so forcefully and visibly a part of Latin America's political life and intellectual climate of radical critique for the generation that did its fieldwork in the 1960s and 1970s, researchers in Latin American history, especially but not exclusively radical scholars, found themselves drawn back to questions of power, structure, and hegemony even if they sought to uncover initiative and agency from below.[16]

On the other hand, the difficulties of achieving a well-integrated dialectical analysis were compounded when regionally or thematically specific historiographies had so emphasized "structure," as a determinant of social relations and social change, that innovation and debate seemed to require an emphatic focus on human initiative from below. A good example is the debate between Rebecca Scott and Manuel Moreno Fraginals on the abolition of slavery in Cuba. Both scholars contributed tremendously to a multifaceted understanding of slavery and abolition in Cuban history. But the weight of the historiographical past, and the monumental contribution of Moreno Fraginals within that tradition, had emphasized the structural crisis of slavery in Cuba's sugar economy during the era of industrial and politico-ideological revolution in the Atlantic world. Challenging that view almost inexorably set up subsequent intellectual conversation (especially the historiographical consumption that widens the circle of conversation, at the risk that an author's caveats or cognizance of patterns that partly counteract the main argument may drop out) as a dichotomous contest. Structure *versus* agency (i.e., Moreno Fraginals versus Scott) might prevail over dialectical synthesis (i.e., Moreno Fraginals and Scott). Given the tremendous weight of structures of domination in Latin American history, and in the dependency-oriented cycle of radical critique in the Latin America of the 1960s and early 1970s, it is not surprising that some historiographical renovation could take the form of an overemphasis on agency to undermine an overemphasis on structure.[17]

In short, not every practitioner of the turn toward history from below sought to balance and interrelate agency and hegemony, or agency and structure. And, even among those cognizant of the combined and interrelated roles of freedom and necessity in history, achieving a dialectical synthesis could be elusive. Even under the best of circumstances, one might lose one's balance and fall off the tightrope, only to get up and try again.

Notwithstanding these caveats, a certain genre of historical writing caught hold and defined a politics of writing Latin American history. The "politics" of historical writing would rest not only on a dramatic expansion of themes fit for inquiry, but also on a sense that in varied ways, regions, and time periods, oppressed social groups had implicitly or explicitly challenged, or at least modified, the rules and designs of power and political economy fashioned from above during the history of capitalism and colonialism. The rewriting of intellectually conservative political history would take place through regional studies of social power and resistance that revealed the partial frustration of elite projects by peoples subject to domination; or the partial appropriation by Indians, peasants, laborers, or other oppressed groups of institutions such as the market, the legal system, or colonial Catholic religion theoretically designed to suppress or control them; or the role of subalterns in molding or revising the major political events and turning points of national or regional life; or the repression of alternative political projects or values that had garnered support from below.

By the early to mid-1980s, evidence of the influence of such an approach was unmistakable. The Social Science Research Council organized major projects on Andean history and Mexican history that took cognizance of the new social history scholarship and sought to harness it to long-term reconsiderations of Mexican political history and Andean political, economic, and cultural history. In 1985 William B. Taylor's contribution to a retrospective project on social history scholarship observed, for the case of Latin America, the emergence of the region as a unit of analysis that bridged "global process" and "local knowledge," thereby allowing for considered assessment of human agency from below.

Although the new approach had developed most quickly in agrarian studies, its influence would soon be felt in urban and labor studies as well. In 1989 Viotti da Costa published an astute assessment of trends in Latin American labor history, a thematic field where the weight of a structuralist historiographical past had been quite heavy. She warned that historiographical renovation of working-class history that focused on "experience" (linked to notions of agency) had gone too far in marginalizing structuralist insight and explanation, rather than achieving a healthy synthesis between these approaches. Significantly, however, even as Viotti da Costa issued a cautionary critique, she could also point to historical scholarship—especially works by Peter Winn, Florencia Mallon, and Charles Bergquist—that bridged these analytical camps. In the forum on Viotti da Costa's critique, Barbara Weinstein observed that the most influential new works in the field—by Winn, Daniel James, Bergquist, and John French—"are already following her excellent advice" and had "integrated structural variables into their broader arguments." What had been discarded was structural determinism—and the notion that structure could be understood as analytically apart from experience—rather than structural variables or levels of analysis.[18]

Politics as Cultural Formation (I): Toward the 1990s

Ten years after the publication of Viotti da Costa's essay, however, the politics of writing Latin American history has acquired new meanings. (In some ways, one might say that these new meanings have given a prescient and more generalizable cast to Viotti da Costa's 1989 warnings about labor history.) New sensibilities have not so much displaced the earlier genre of writing and its conceptualization of politics in history, but have instead added new and complicating dimensions to it. At the cost of some simplification, we may gloss the transformation as a transition from studies of "politics and society" to studies of "politics and culture." The former placed a premium on the contradictory interplays of agency and structure within the unfolding political economy of regions, while the latter asked how people constructed their political imagination within the process of state formation. The answers to the latter question place a premium on integrated study of the cultural meanings and constructions of political discourse at several layers of society—from the infrastructural and "offstage" relationships and discourses that define the subaltern politics of everyday local life, community, and mediation, to participation in regional and supraregional projects of cultural and political formation that implied mutual constructions of a political imagination from above and below. A comparison of first books and subsequent research themes by scholars who came of age intellectually during the 1970s bears clear witness to this transition.[19]

For the purposes of this essay, the significant question is: how did we get to this new state of understanding "the political" in Latin American history writing? My argument is that a satisfactory answer must bring together two levels of analysis: the internal dynamics of historical research and discovery that inspired new questions and approaches, and transformations in the wider political and intellectual environment that also unleashed new sensibilities and questions.

Let us begin with the internal dynamics of historical research and discovery. Perhaps inevitably, the new genre of historical writing raised unexpected questions. The new writings focused on empirically rich, careful study of social experience and struggle in particular regions rather than a reworking of metanarratives at the national level. Moreover, politically engaged historians who dialogued with theory tended to use the latter not for its own sake, nor as models of determination that prescribed a narrow range of "relevant" empirical data, but as a way of framing questions, illuminating findings, or setting regions within wider contexts.

Careful regional research and rather indeterminate uses of theory fostered open-ended methods of empirical inquiry into regional social and political experience. One result was that studies of the social history of power presented as many questions as answers. Once one took seriously the agency of Indians, peasants, mine laborers, smallholders, or other subaltern groups as real and potential agents within history, new problems emerged. Beyond documenting the adaptations and struggles of the downtrodden within the context of regional political economy, property, and labor, how could one come to "know" and assess, based on the scraps of (always tainted and mediated) evidence in historical documents, the ideas and consciousness that infused their experience and adaptations? Beyond a certain point, universalizing allusion to theories of moral economy pioneered by E. P. Thompson and James C. Scott could not provide sufficiently convincing, thick answers.

Moreover, the new genre of social history encouraged dialogues with historically minded anthropologists. Consider, for example, the Andean field, where such dialogues became quite intense. Despite the ethnographers' criticism of their field's earlier tendency toward an ahistorical, essentialist vision of lo andino, their insistence on the specificity of native Andean cultural understandings and achievements also warned against easy allusion to universalizing theories of peasant moral consciousness as a solution. As Brooke Larson has recently pointed out, already in the 1980s such concerns about recovering and elucidating the intersections of peasant politics, consciousness, and culture had led to a heightened self-consciousness about methodology and language that in some ways foreshadowed the linguistic turn of the 1990s.[20]

In addition, the empirical findings of Andean historians and anthropologists had uncovered a dizzying variety of political expressions by native Andean peoples since the times of Spanish conquest. These phenomena were not easily reducible to explanatory visions based on peasant moral economy. The combination of millenarian movements, local peasant rebellions, Indianist supraregional insurrection, peasant nationalism, peasant pacts with radicals and populists, and periods of apparent political quiescence had shaped the political contours of rural history in Peru and Bolivia and seemed to present a conceptual challenge to theory-derived visions of consciousness.

In short, the turn to historical agency in the Andean field had opened up a series of knotty and exciting questions, both historical and conceptual. One result of this state of affairs was the 1983–86 project by the Social Science Research Council (hereinafter, SSRC) to bring historians and anthropologists together to map out new approaches for a long-term vision of Andean history and culture. (For the sake of accuracy, it should be added that the SSRC's planning groups and conferences integrated scholars from Latin America, Europe, and the United States. This is a case where the U.S.-centered boundary drawn at the outset of this essay weakens.) Significantly for our purposes, the project included but went beyond the parameters of regional political economy that had defined the politics of social history research in the late 1970s and early 1980s. The SSRC project not only aimed to present a new, anthropologically informed history of native Andean participation and incorporation of market-based adaptations since the sixteenth century. It also aimed to probe strategies of social reproduction and ethnogenesis within colonial contexts. Most important for the purposes of this essay, the project sought to chart a new approach to the history of Andean rebellions ("political" history) that placed moments of collective violence within long-term frames of reference that included periods of apparent political quiescence, and within a vision of Andean political consciousness that broke with the narrow confines of structurally derived, imputed characterizations of peasant politics. The newer approach would problematize peasant politics and consciousness in its own right rather than have the theme spin off as a by-product or epiphenomenon of resistance and adaptation to regional regimes of political economy.[21]

The SSRC project on Andean rebellions is but one example of how the process of historical research itself generated new questions that reframed the meaning of the political in social history research. A spiral of conceptual questions seemed to emerge from research that had taken the agency of the historically defeated seriously, as a matter of painstaking regional research. As an organization concerned with emerging trends and problems in intellectual life, the SSRC responded with a collaborative project to formulate and address the new questions. Individual historians also illustrate the internal dynamics of research evolution. Their open-ended inquiries in specific regional research projects seemed to yield unexpected or conceptually troubling empirical findings. As historians receptive to the unexpected finding or the unresolved mystery, yet drawn to try to understand it, individual scholars embarked on projects that problematized politics and consciousness in new ways.

The trajectories of Florencia E. Mallon and Gilbert M. Joseph illustrate these more-specific research dynamics. Mallon's first book, *The Defense of Community in Peru's Central Highlands* (1983), had uncovered an apparent case of peasant nationalism during the turbulence of the Chilean invasion of Peru during the War of the Pacific. She had not originally designed her regional research project, a study of "peasant struggle and capitalist transition," as an inquiry on peasant politics as such, or as a social history of the War of the Pacific. Moreover, the empirical discoveries of peasant nationalism in the central highlands seemed to belie ready-made theories on nationalism and its relationship to peasantries. Yet the particular story of the ways particular peasants came to conceptualize themselves as nationalist, patriotic citizens proved too important to an understanding of the regional history of peasant struggle and capitalist transition to dismiss out of hand. Mallon gave this counterintuitive finding a prominent place in the narrative and ended up drawing the predictable critiques. The evidence was too thin to support the contention of peasant nationalism; rigorous theoretical analysis made it difficult to imagine that the peasants could have been nationalist; even if these particular peasants evinced a nationalist political consciousness, they constituted exceptions that proved the general rule, and comparative historical research would no doubt underscore the anomalous character of the region and its peasants.[22]

In short, the specific dynamics of case study research and critique had unleashed a new set of questions that reframed the meaning of "the political" that had inspired the original case study. Intellectually, Mallon would either have to let go of the original finding and the debate it sparked, or embark on new research that would problematize the meaning of the original finding in a more systematic, methodologically self-conscious, and comparative perspective. Mallon's 1987 essay on nationalist and anti-state coalitions in Junín and Cajamarca during the War of the Pacific may be read as a kind of midway point in a search for theoretical and historical answers—an effort to rethink the problem in the light of a "negative" as well as "positive" case study of peasant nationalism, and in the light of new, less orthodox theoretical readings related to nationalism and political consciousness. Of course, her 1995 book on *Peasant and Nation* in the making of postcolonial Mexico and Peru is the more fully developed historical and theoretical response to the questions unleashed by her original finding. By this point, the politics of the history had to be conceptualized differently. The politics was now as much a problem of the culture and consciousness that gave meaning to social action and conflict as it was a narrative of the social actions and conflicts that drove regional life. It was now as much a creation mutually and contradictorily constructed from above and below as it was an expression of grassroots sentiment unto itself. It was as much an outcome of tension, mediation, and hegemonic processes within internally heterogeneous subaltern communities as it was an expression of communal consciousness. And the conceptualization of "hegemony" itself had evolved: from a more wooden emphasis on outcomes-of-dominance influential in the late 1970s and early 1980s, toward a more fluid view of ongoing interplays between hegemonic process and hegemonic outcome.[23]

Gilbert M. Joseph's trajectory also illustrates the specific dynamics, internal to the process of professional research and reflection, that redefined the political in history writing. The empirical findings in his first book, *Revolution from Without* (1982), presented a conundrum. Joseph's incisive study of Yucatán during the Porfiriato and Mexican Revolution demonstrated the alliances of local, national, and international elites in a regional political economy of henequen production that subjected Maya peasants to increasingly harsh and exploitative life conditions during the late Porfiriato. His analysis of oligarchical wealth, power, and social abuse provided a certain backdrop of explosiveness and poignancy for the "revolution from without" brought to Yucatán by the revolutionary leaders Salvador Alvarado and, especially, the radical Felipe Carrillo Puerto, during 1915–24. Yet the explosiveness seemed hollow at the roots, in the sense that the place of Maya peasants in the story seemed an enigma. Tight social control perhaps explained why neither free nor estate-bound Maya could mount an effective challenge to the regional plantocracy during the early years of the Mexican Revolution. But once Alvarado and Carrillo Puerto embarked on projects of revolutionary and (in the latter case) socialist mobilization, why could they not count on a more impressive base of support to defend the revolution? Put another way, why did they not find themselves pressed along by a revolutionary groundswell from below? The book saw a tragic (and understandable) fatal flaw in Carrillo Puerto's dependence on local caciques to mobilize a revolutionary following, but the relationships between caciques and their followers and the related problems of political consciousness and aspiration remained shadowy and elusive. In short, the empirical findings of *Revolution from Without* high-lighted the importance of pre-existing political bands and intermediaries in shaping the course of regional revolutionary politics, and in explaining the perhaps counterintuitive fragility of the revolution's base strength. But they also bequeathed an enigma: the textures of subaltern political consciousness and strategies before and during the years of upheaval seemed both important and mysterious.[24]

Joseph's subsequent research in Mexican political and social history may be read, in part, as a journey to unravel the mystery of subaltern political consciousness in his beloved Yucatán. As in the case of Mallon, one sees both theoretical and empirical dimensions in this journey. On the one hand, Joseph embarked on projects that signified a heightened method-ological and conceptual self-consciousness and an effort to reformulate our questions and theoretical frameworks. Joseph's book (coedited with Daniel Nugent) on *Everyday Forms of State Formation* (1994), along with his 1990 essay on bandits, mapped out a more complex conceptualization of the ways subaltern political consciousness and action must be understood as a cultural creation that was mutually and continuously constructed from above and below and in between, in ways that drew subalterns and elites into dynamics of state formation that were both complicit and conflictual. On the other hand, Joseph also pursued thick empirical research that might lessen the original enigma. His recent book (cowritten with Allen Wells) on *Summer of Discontent, Seasons of Upheaval* (1996) takes up the problem of Maya rebelliousness and consciousness in the crucial early years of the revolu-tion, *before* Alvarado and Carrillo Puerto imposed a "revolution from with-out." Careful study documents a pattern of rebelliousness that forces us to analyze rather than take as a given the maintenance of oligarchical control before 1915; that draws us subtly into a world of political mobilization, leadership, and grievance, thereby rendering the contours of Maya political action, consciousness, and dilemmas more accessible; and that suggests a modified reading of the politics of the revolution from without launched by Alvarado and Carrillo Puerto.[25]

In each of the examples cited—the SSRC project on Andean history and culture, and the research trajectories of individual scholars such as Mallon and Joseph—the internal dynamics of research moved the politics of his-tory writing in new directions. As mentioned earlier (and with some sim-plification because the transition was partial, more a matter of focus or emphasis than absolute contrast), regional studies of "politics and so-ciety," as seen from below and as framed by analysis of political economy, gave way in part to case studies of "politics and culture," as seen from above and below and in between simultaneously, and as framed by analysis of the ways people construct political languages of meaning and dispute. As Mallon has observed, this transition drew together Gramscian and Foucauldian theoretical genealogies and sparked interest in the work of the Subaltern Studies scholars of South Asia—a point to which we shall return later.[26] Just as important, in each of the three examples cited, partly driving the new approaches were the unexpected empirical findings and enigmas encountered through open-ended historical inquiry. A dialectic of the conceptual and the empirical sparked new questions and new research necessities.

This review of the inner research dynamics that redefined the politics of historical writing matters in part because it exposes the shallowness of Stephen Haber's recent critique of the "new cultural" history of Mexico. Haber's critique, which especially targets the work of Mallon and Joseph, argues that the epistemological framework of the writers of the new cultural history of Mexico abandons serious scrutiny of empirical research for verification or falsification of the authors' preconceived ideas. The new writers, in his view, ask questions for which facts cannot be established, and adopt a postmodern stance that questions the existence of facts that might prove or disprove one's hypotheses. The result is that the rules of logic and evidence that once governed historical-legal argumentation no longer apply.[27]

Haber's critique is intellectually superficial in several key respects. First, he conflates the most extreme versions of postmodern skepticism with the position of the historians he critiques, despite explicitly drawn differences between the more "historical" and "literary" proponents of subaltern studies.[28] Second, and more important, he defines the "falsificationist epistemology" he favors so narrowly that he cannot see openness to the unexpected empirical finding, or the profound research enigma, among the authors he critiques. In a curious irony, his critique does not measure up to his own self-stated criteria.[29] The other side of the same coin is his lack of engagement of the history of scientific thought and philosophy. Ever since the debates among historians and philosophers of science launched by Thomas Kuhn's *The Structure of Scientific Revolutions* (originally published in 1962, and enlarged significantly in 1970), the ability to "see and respond" to the unexpected—to the anomalies that potentially unsettle a scientific community's "paradigm" or "disciplinary matrix," to use Kuhn's vocabulary—has become a far more complex historical problem than that acknowledged in Haber's modeling of valid epistemology and method.[30]

Haber's preferred conception of truth verification relies on a straightforward sequence: explicitly defined hypotheses and expectations are "tested" through empirical data that confirm or disconfirm the expectation. For some purposes, of course, such a procedure is entirely appropriate, a feasible and useful form of historical argument.[31]

But equally important are historical inquiries less bounded by the framing and testing of formal hypotheses, and more defined by a research design that poses theoretically informed "questions" for study, defines a space-time and set of sources and methods that might illuminate the questions, and engages in rather open-ended empirical explorations of evidence—interrogations that generate hypotheses, answers, enigmas, and new questions. This more open-ended process of interrogating evidence, and the unexpected empirical discoveries and conceptual challenges it generated, defined research and argument by the SSRC's Andean project and by the scholars he criticizes.[32]

Politics as Cultural Formation (II): Toward the 1990s

The internal dynamics of historical research and discovery, however, do not suffice to explain the changing meaning of "the political" in the writing of Latin American history. As mentioned earlier, a second level of analysis must refer to transformations in the wider political and intellectual environment that redefine the sensibilities, questions, and publics that render historical research meaningful. Despite the research surprises and enigmas mentioned above, the turn toward the more culturalist, meaning-oriented visions of the political described above would be difficult to imagine in the absence of these wider changes.

In my view, three major—and related—changes in the political and intellectual environment of the 1980s and early 1990s proved fundamental. First, women's movements and the consolidation of gender as a fundamental category of historical knowledge had a profound decentering effect on prior understandings of the political. The burst of interest in women's experience and in gender gave vitality to Foucault's insistence that questions of power and politics pervaded all spheres of social life, and that study of the political could not be confined to analysis of the state or high politics alone. Once "domestic" as well as "public" spheres became realms of political analysis, critical study of the off-stage organization of power and authority in subaltern life became more inescapable. The fault lines of gender, generation, and factionalism that shaped subaltern life and its languages of community and politics became necessary themes of study and complicated enormously the depictions of "community" and "moral economy" that had defined an earlier historiographical moment.[33]

Second, the emergence of "new social movements" and "ethno-identity politics" also exerted a transforming effect on understandings of the political. For students of Latin America, in particular, the new social movements were initially seen as a point of political rupture, an alternative to and critique of understandings of politics that had been anchored in party-led mobilizations on the Left or Center-Left, or in paradigms of social change based on class identities and marxian-influenced theories of history and political economy. To witness multifarious protest movements that waved the banners of women's needs, indigenous rights, Christian liberation, and human rights, among other revindications, and to observe that often these protest movements took the lead in challenging repressive regimes or pressing for democratization, raised new questions. Such movements, whether initially idealized as sites of near-autonomous agency or subsequently subjected to a more sobering analysis of their limits and their reabsorption into power dynamics defined from above, pushed for more-diversified and -decentered views of politics, a closer interrogation of meaning and consciousness, and a stronger effort to scrutinize politics from above and below simultaneously.[34]

Finally, the collapse of paradigms of inspiration played a role in redefining the political in historical writing. Florencia Mallon put it well in the ironic opening of her article on the "promise and dilemma of subaltern studies" for Latin Americanists. The agonizing denouement of the Cuban Revolution and the triumph of the capitalist West in the Cold War, the defeat and internal disarray of the Sandinista project, the erasure of the legitimacy of the quest for social justice and state responsibility that had once inspired a Chilean politics of populism and democratic socialism, the nightmare of Shining Path as a Left so totalitarian and irresponsible that it alienated peasants, workers, and the urban poor and set the stage for the political triumph of neoliberalism: when so many potentially inspiring narratives had collapsed, she asked, "what is a progressive scholar to do?" The collapse of inspiration set the context for her examination of the ways a dialogue with the Subaltern Studies Group—particularly an appreciation of the creative tension between a Gramscian axis concerned with political hegemony and subaltern initiative, and a postmodernist axis concerned with deconstructing the language of historical texts—could prove useful for Latin Americanists. The uncertainties bequeathed by the political disasters of the 1970s and 1980s—the political discourses of emancipation in the 1960s and 1970s had yielded not liberation, but polarization and repressive dictatorship in South America, and the experiments with political change and grass-roots social movements in Central America and South America in the 1980s unraveled and gave way to neoliberalism—opened the door to a rethinking of the political in the writing of subaltern history.[35]

I have emphasized here, of course, the collapse of political certainties and inspiration as manifested in a Latin Americanist context, but one must acknowledge that the phenomenon had a worldwide dimension and paradoxically embraced the triumphant West.[36] For our purposes, what matters is the way the new uncertainties encouraged a politics of writing Latin American history that would be more self-consciously aware of the difficulties of "knowing" the subaltern, and more decentered in its understandings of the social arenas, relationships, and languages through which power is constructed and contested.

Taken together, the turn toward gendered readings of politics, society, and history, the burst of "new" social movements that unsettled preconceived categories of political action and consciousness, and the collapse of basic referents and ways of knowing that had once inspired faith in bottom-up emancipation redefined political and intellectual sensibilities. These new sensibilities gave a certain priority and legitimacy to the enigmas and questions described above as consequences of the inner dynamics of historical research. Arguably, thick historical research and the process of knowledge production always produce a series of loose ends, anomalies, surprises, and dilemmas whose resolution would lead knowledge in new directions. But researchers select which of these enigmas to pursue energetically as a central point of departure for new research and thinking, and which to let slide as uninteresting or inconsequential. The selection process cannot be convincingly explained only through a tracing of the internal process of research discovery and enigma. In the absence of wider changes in the political and intellectual environment, and their impact on scholarly networks and communities, the research findings and enigmas that provoked new approaches to the meaning of "the political" might have been neglected, or the theoretical handles used to peruse and explain them might have been different.[37]

Between Tragedy and Promise: Toward the Twenty-first Century

If one steps back to consider the period of the 1970s–90s as a whole, one can see continuities as well as changes in politically engaged writing of Latin American history. Throughout the period, the writers of such history did their research on a terrain between tragedy and promise.[38] On the one hand, there was promise. The turn toward a history from below that traced the dignity, creativity, aspirations, and agency of common people—as well as their sufferings and subordination—was inspired by the charged mix of discontent, idealism, and hopefulness that redefined so much of political life in Latin America and other world regions in the 1960s and early 1970s. On the other, too many things went wrong for promise to remain untarnished. Too often, potentials seemed to remain just that—potentials. In Mexico, idealistic protest gave way to massacre in Tlatelolco in 1968. In South America during the 1960s and 1970s political polarization culminated in new kinds of military regimes in Brazil and the Southern Cone. The new regimes—determined to root out once and for all the dissident ideas and people considered to stand in the way of national unity, order, security, and progress—violently crushed the Víctor Jaras who had sung of hope, and the political activists, workers, peasants, and youths who had dared to find inspiration in the music.

(Given the origins of this book at a Yale University conference of former graduate students to honor Emilia Viotti da Costa, it is appropriate to note that the nightmare brought an ironic double edge. Given the role of Latin American youths and intellectuals in the subversive discontents of the age, university intellectuals who inspired a critical rethinking of national mythology and dogma became redefined as subversives, fit for harassment, surveillance, reassignment to marginal jobs, imprisonment, voluntary or involuntary exile, or worse. The Brazilian version of this repressive scenario drove Viotti da Costa—a leader among the historians and social scientists who were rewriting the history of slavery, abolition, and race relations in Brazil—to take up residence in the United States. Thus her graduate students ended up in a paradoxical double role: we were at once beneficiaries and critics of the political nightmare that swept over South America.)

At first, perhaps, such nightmares could simply be denounced as outrages. The flame of popular agency could be kept alive and celebrated in solidarity movements that chanted a historical proclamation of faith: "El pueblo, unido, jamás será vencido." Eventually, however, the deeper sense of tragedy—What had gone spectacularly wrong and why? In what ways was ritual proclamation of popular unity and strength a dangerously misleading myth?—could not be so easily banished. The pueblo had not been so united, and it had indeed been bloodily defeated. Even more sobering, dictatorships did not fall so quickly, and they garnered unanticipated bases of social complicity and support, even subaltern complicity and support. To negotiate the treacherous and often heart-wrenching terrain between historical promise and historical tragedy, historians of dominated groups would have to bring the inspiration of "agency" and the hard-headedness of "hegemony" (or "structure") into balance.

As should be obvious from the discussion above of changes in the political and intellectual environment, a similar mix of hope and disappointment could be described for the periods of struggle against dictatorship and for the defense and democratization of life in a variety of Latin

American regions in the late 1970s and 1980s. On the one hand, post-Tlatelolco Mexico witnessed the rise of "new" urban social movements, and antihero leaders such as Superbarrio and grassroots activist women. (Intellectually, the period also witnessed the flowering of regional history by Mexicans and Mexicanists who decentered or undermined officialist narratives.) On the other hand, the PRI once again demonstrated, in the 1980s and early 1990s, an amazing capacity to weather political storms, impose election results, and advance Mexico's turn to neoliberalism. Similar counterpoints shaped the political and intellectual milieu of other countries. In the prefatory and editorial remarks that frame the politics of "progressive" scholarship in the 1990s, one continues to discern a mixed sensibility, caught between the hope that a respectful tracing of subaltern history, consciousness, initiative, and constructions of political meaning offers a vision of historical dignity and promise, and the sobering realization that often and persistently, historical tragedy has overtaken, deflected, or dashed such hopes.[39]

Continually caught between promise and tragedy, we have continually remade the meaning of "the political" in Latin American history. To reclaim the political is not to rediscover it so much as to trace its evolution, particularly the inner logics of scholarly research and the wider shifts of political and intellectual life that inform the writing of history. To reclaim the political is also to trace "toward the future"; that is, to imagine ways that historical, political, and intellectual experience may shape future directions for politically meaningful writing of Latin American history.

For this reason, I wish to conclude with the imagining of some future tasks in the remaking of the political. My plea for new directions is not made in the spirit of mutually exclusive displacements of one genre of writing or one set of themes by another. On the contrary. One cannot program research passions (although foundations sometimes seem to pretend otherwise) or achieve clairvoyance, and it would be foolish to slide over the varied, idiosyncratic, and deeply personal paths to original and creative research. In any event, a healthy future lies in a rather eclectic building of complementary paths to politically meaningful, socially inclusive and sensitive understandings of the history of the oppressed. Moreover, I believe that the future of the political must continue to include a prominent place for regional social histories of subaltern life and struggle that balance a potentially emancipating sense of "agency" with a hard-nosed analysis of "hegemony," and that relate the contradictory balance to an analysis of political economy that includes awareness of "structure." The future of the political must also continue to include ample place for the interrogations of consciousness, and the simultaneous constructions of political language, meanings, and authority from above and below and in between, that have characterized recent literature.

At the same time, it does not suffice simply to proclaim the continuing validity or necessity of the approaches we have constructed thus far. Without intellectual restlessness, we risk sliding into a complacency that renders us mediocre and stale, intellectually as well as politically. Why not also imagine and debate, therefore, some of the necessary twists and turns that lie ahead?

In a spirit that values complementary and idiosyncratic paths to politically meaningful knowledge of history, and with some trepidation, I offer three themes worth considering and debating as tasks for the remaking of the political in the early twenty-first century. A first task or priority is to step back to consider the tumultuous 1960s–90s period as a whole and to ask how the period will or ought to be remembered. The ongoing bursts of political and cultural convulsion that one sees around issues of "memory versus forgetting" in Argentina and Chile; the burst of truth commissions and memory issues that have emerged out of more-recent episodes of war and repression in Central America; the aging of the generations that experienced directly the transitions from the revolutionary romance of Ché, Allende, and the idea of politics itself to the nightmares of "dirty war" and "disappeared" people, to the simultaneous triumphs of democracy, neoliberalism, and a certain depoliticization—all augur a future in which the shaping of collective memory of the cycle from the 1960s to 1990s, a period when "promise" and "tragedy" were scripted in amazingly strong colors, will become a key cultural, political, and generational battleground in Latin American life. Our role as historians will be to write serious and politically sensitive histories of the period as a whole, and to participate in methodologically self-conscious study of the problem of collective memory itself, seen as a cultural and political dynamic and a legacy of the age.[40]

A second and related suggestion, as we remake the political, may seem more problematic and controversial. Progressive scholars, I think, ought to achieve the tolerance required to understand our political "antagonists" without fear that such a stance implies abandoning our basic values. We must achieve the confidence that one can carve out a terrain of "understanding" that stops short of uncritical identification with the powerful and oppressive "winners" of history. For obvious reasons, the elites who benefited from an oppressive status quo and tried to manage it or defend it; the political conservatives, reactionaries, wafflers, and pragmatists who have inhabited a variety of social strata; the centrists and conservatives who supported repressive counter-revolutions in the face of real or perceived leftist "revolutions"—these have not often been our preferred objects of complex analysis. Yet unless we accept antagonistic social actors or political stances as truly authentic voices and inhabitants of the Latin American world, to be treated not as one-dimensional foils but as subjects worthy of analysis from "within" as well as "without," we will self-restrict our ability to understand and analyze the political history of Latin America and its subaltern peoples. Indeed, one of the implications of the new literature that explores mutual constructions of the political imagination from above, below, and in between is precisely that we must achieve greater tolerance of political ambiguity and antagonism if we are to understand the consciousness, struggles, and potentials that have defined subalterns and their history. A certain tolerance that expands our vision of the authentic is necessary if we are to write a convincing history of the tragedy of our own times, the cycle that unfolded between the 1960s and 1990s.[41]

Let us refine this point by admitting some difficulties and introducing necessary caveats. To expand our vision of the authentic to include political conservatives and antagonists without fear of losing a critical edge is personally, politically, and intellectually demanding. To pretend otherwise is perhaps innocent or disingenuous. Analytical critique "from without" safely preserves one's proclaimed values and critique of power—in other words, it provides a morally comfortable stance. Narratives that approach an understanding of distasteful power wielders and antagonists "from within" may seem to draw us closer to excusing or justifying the unjustifiable, even when one stops short of apologetic history.

To avoid misunderstanding, therefore, it may be wise to recognize some limits, to specify what this suggestion does *not* imply. Granting an authentic place to complex understandings of antagonists from within, in the corpus of works we collectively write, does not imply that each and every work must adopt a kind of equal-time rule to achieve valid insight on large historical problems. Nor does it imply, in a kind of perverse contradiction, that reclaiming or remaking the political in historical scholarship requires a stance of Olympian detachment that places the historian above the fray as a neutral—fundamentally valueless and unengaged—arbiter. Arguably, more is learned about history, especially its political dimension, from the juxtaposition of intensely but diversely "engaged" works than from bloodless narratives that fail to engage profoundly the particular values, people, and controversies that infused a given space-time with significance and passion.[42]

Finally, diversifying our sensibilities of authenticity in ways that include new subjects for complex understanding from within does not deny that some kinds of antagonists lie so far beyond the pale of the acceptable that they defy one's capacity (regardless of intellectual intention or personal desire) "to understand." It is one thing, for example, to try to understand from within the people—whether subaltern, middling, or elite—who supported the 1973 overthrow of Allende in Chile, or to recognize that elites and powerful people experience their own versions of the tension between freedom and necessity.[43] It is quite another thing to try to understand torturers or master architects of "radical evil" such as Augusto Pinochet or Manuel Contreras. Inevitably, we will draw a line beyond which the dash of sympathy required for profound historical understanding proves impossible, pointless, or perverse. The problem is more intractable than one's intentions. As Hannah Arendt pointed out long ago, "radical evil" brings into history moral transgressions so extreme that they seem to "transcend the realm of human affairs and the potentialities of human power, both of which they radically destroy wherever they make their appearance." Under the circumstances, not only issues of punishment and forgiveness (themes emphasized by Arendt), but also issues of historical understanding and representation, seem to lie beyond the outer limits of our capacities. As historians, we perch ourselves on the edge of the abyss and come face to face with our inadequacy.[44]

In short, a variety of difficulties and limitations attend the task of expanding our vision of the authentic to include political conservatives and "antagonists," not to mention opportunists, pragmatists, and less than heroic subalterns. But these difficulties, while challenging, in no way diminish political and intellectual necessity. Given the mutual constructions of political imagination and strategies from above, below, and in between, until we learn to analyze the political Other at all levels of society, and in his or her varied human dimensions, our ability to understand the experience and political imagination of those who suffered exploitation and abuse will also suffer.[45]

A third task, as we remake the political for a new public, is to confront the necessity of analyzing youth culture and generational politics as historical problems in their own right. What gives urgency to this task is not simply awareness of an important and often neglected social category—a sense that the demographic and educational dynamics of Latin America in the second half of the twentieth century generated an expansive youth population and culture.[46]

Just as important, the problem of youth culture will be fundamental for politically sensitive understandings of history in the next century. On the one hand, given the prominence of youth culture and rebelliousness in the revolutionary effervescence of Latin America in the 1960s and 1970s, and the struggles against dictatorship and the Central American wars of the 1980s, it is difficult to imagine a convincing history of the 1960s–90s cycle that fails to explore the politics of youth and generations. On the other, the triumph of neoliberalism in Latin America has failed to generate widespread social optimism or satisfaction. It rests in part on a perceived absence of political alternatives, has generated potentially explosive concentrations of wealth and resentment, and has fostered a consumerist culture of individual winners and losers. These problems have become an engine of youth alienation for a significant fraction of society. Moreover, the alienation has been felt at distinct levels of society. For youth in the bottom 40 percent of income distribution, or living in shantytowns marked by serious crime, drug, and gang problems, alienation may take the form of hopelessness, a sense that one must live by the code of a fundamentally predatory society, or a profound desire for anaesthesia. For a minority of more fortunate youths in university settings, whether from the squeezed middle classes or from more prosperous strata, the alienation may take the form of disgust with the ethics of a rampant egotism that destroys a sense of common belonging or higher values. In short, the problem of youth alienation and generational dynamics may emerge as a powerful cultural and political theme in the early twenty-first century.[47] These forces will create new intellectual needs and sensibilities. The shaping of an adequate collective memory of Latin America's tragic cycle between the 1960s and 1990s, in societies caught ambivalently and conflictively between the desire to forget and the necessity to remember, will require a turn toward the problem of youth culture.[48]

One can already see some movement in the directions advocated here. A few examples, taken from the research of scholars who have been active in exploring the earlier meanings of the political in Latin American history writing, will suffice. A team of Peruvian and U.S. scholars has already undertaken an effort to trace the dynamics that turned Peru's mix of political mobilization, experiment, hope, and authoritarianism in the 1960s and 1970s into a narrative of gruesome political nightmare and unexpected subaltern initiatives in the 1980s and 1990s. In addition, the SSRC has launched a major fellowships project to facilitate research by younger scholars in the Southern Cone countries and Peru on the problem of collective memory, repression, and democratization bequeathed by the 1960s–90s cycle. One sees self-conscious exploration of the problem of historical memory in new research by Daniel James on Argentine working-class culture, in Florencia Mallon's interpretation of the "bones" that serve as artifacts of the French intervention in Mexico, or in my own current research on memory struggles in the making of a "new" Chile since 1973. Barbara Weinstein's recent book on the efforts of Brazilian industrialists to promote an industrial and working-class culture of social peace signifies a turn toward serious, complex histories of the conservative Other as a vital, authentic task for a critical history of the political imagination in subaltern life and society at large.[49]

It is perhaps for the question of youth culture that U.S. examples of emerging scholarship are as yet difficult to identify. Significantly, however, Peruvian scholars who have sought to understand the history of radicalism and Shining Path have begun to map out a compelling portrait of youth and generational politics as historical problems. Political scientist Katherine Hite has also contributed a methodologically pioneering and historically illuminating study of leftist leaders of Chile's "sixties generation."[50]

My effort to imagine new layers in future meanings of the political in Latin American history writing is one part prediction, four parts advocacy. It is tempered by awareness that paths to meaningful knowledge (including politically meaningful knowledge) are plural and often unpredictable. It is tempered, too, by awareness that in Latin America, where the inheritance of the distant past seems in many respects an "unclosed chapter" of contemporary life, the chronological proximity or distance of a study theme does not correlate neatly with political proximity or distance.[51] What is safe to predict, however, is that to reclaim and remake the political, on terms that aspire to an emancipatory and empathic vision of subaltern history, requires a continuing will to walk the terrain between tragedy and promise. The walk is an acquired taste, for it is bittersweet. But like the Brazilian music that moved Emilia Viotti da Costa's generation, the saudade of the walk can inspire beauty and creativity.

Notes

This essay originated in a paper presented at a conference at Yale University in May 1998 to honor Professor Emilia Viotti da Costa. For discussions, criticisms, and suggestions that helped me rethink and improve the essay, I wish to thank participants in several critical discussions: at the Yale conference, at a panel of the 2000 American Historical Association convention, and in a research seminar meeting at the University of Wisconsin, Madison. For specific suggestions, I am grateful to Leo Garofalo, Gilbert Joseph, Catherine LeGrand, and Gladys McCormick.

I wish to clarify that in the citations of historiography below, I have cited with ruthless selectivity for purposes of illustration and basic documentation. To keep the reference list from burgeoning to an impossible scope, I have been forced to exclude many superb studies; I trust that authors will understand that no slight is intended and that the circumstances of the original conference meant that I emphasized Yale's former graduate students in some of the illustrative material.

Finally, I wish to acknowledge a long-standing debt that is both personal and collective. Many of the scholars mentioned in the argument and notes studied with Professor Viotti da Costa. Emilia, in addition to her important research and publications, has been an enormously generative intellectual in her role as a graduate teacher who both challenges and supports her students. This essay constitutes both a reflection about history and a deeply felt thank-you.

1   The examples mentioned are not hypothetical, but reflect direct participant-observation experiences.

2   I am aware, of course, that there are exceptions to the general rule—occasions when the timing and argument of a scholarly work grant it a larger than usual political significance in public culture. Two well-known examples are Woodward 1974 (1955; 2d rev. ed. 1966), in relation to civil rights ferment in the United States, and Paxton 1972, in relation to French debate about the Vichy experience.

3   For essays on specific historical themes that consider the evolution of Latin American and U.S. writings jointly, see Roseberry 1993; Stern 1988; cf. Skidmore 1998, esp. 117–23. On the "reverberations" concept as a counterpoint that relativizes and refines ideas of scholarly fragmentation, see Stern 1993; cf. Mallon 1993. For new essays that examine Latin American relations with the U.S. in terms of mutual cultural constitutions that blur rigid dichotomies between the "foreign" and the "local," thereby setting intellectual reverberations within a broader framework, see Joseph, LeGrand, and Salvatore 1998.

4   See Stern 1992, esp. 27 and n. 37.

5   For a review of these changes and their implications in some detail—and a critique of conservative arguments about scholarly hyperfragmentation and declining standards, with citation of relevant literature—see Stern 1993; cf. Roseberry 1993; Skidmore 1998; Stern 1987a. The outstanding starting point for an assessment of the U.S. historical profession as a whole is Novick 1988.

6   For the general characterizations of historiography, see the sources in note 5 above. An early trio of articles by James Lockhart, Frederick P. Bowser, and Karen Spalding in *Latin American Research Review* in 1972, on the social history of Spaniards, Africans, and Indians, respectively, are illustrative of the new trend and its "indirect challenge" for the case of Latin America; cf. Lockhart 1968; Bowser 1974; Spalding 1976.

It is worth noting, however, that even the early social history literature for Latin America developed connections to political analysis that partly belie the idea of social history as a parallel field whose political history dimension was at most indirect and undeveloped. See, for example, the partial fusions of political and social analysis evident in Lockhart 1972a and Spalding 1970, 1973. When one considers the rapid movement toward partial fusions of "social" and "political" history evident in the works cited in notes 7 and 8 below, articles in the late 1970s and early 1980s that decried the political crisis of social history seem, from the perspective of Latin American scholarship, to be overstated and shallow—somewhat outdated when they began to circulate. See Fox-Genovese and Genovese 1976; Judt 1979; Stearns 1983.

7   It is important to note that studies of social experience in contexts of power that integrated the sensibilities of agency and hegemony were not limited to graduate students. Slavery studies were critical and widely influential in historiographical thought in the 1970s, both for scholars of U.S. history and Latin American history. Significantly, the outstanding works on slavery and abolitionism by leading senior historians of the United States in the mid-1970s were clearly influenced by the problems of agency and hegemony, and by E. P. Thompson (1963, 1967, 1971) and Antonio Gramsci (1971), the foundational thinkers associated with agency and hegemony, respectively. See Genovese 1974; Davis 1975; Morgan 1975; cf. Wood 1974. In addition to these influences, one should note that within the Latin Americanist field of writings on slavery, Stanley J. Stein

(with Barbara H. Stein's collaboration) produced an outstanding and conceptually pre-cocious revisionist study in the 1950s. The vision of slave and plantation life in Stein 1957 in many ways anticipated the integrated conceptual analysis and sensibilities that blended agency and hegemony, even though such terms were not yet in wide usage in historiography. Studies of slavery and abolition in Brazil yielded additional volumes that succeeded in coordinating an eye on human agency on the one hand, and structures of hegemonic power on the other: see esp. Viotti da Costa [1966] 1982 and Schwartz 1985. For agency and structure as influential languages of theoretical analysis, an excellent starting point is Giddens 1981–1985; cf. 1979.

8   Some of these observations and those in subsequent paragraphs have an autobiographi-cal aspect insofar as they are based on my own dissertation research in the 1970s, and on the intellectual environment at Yale University among graduate students in Latin Ameri-can history and other fields, especially U.S. southern history, who subsequently pub-lished influential books based on their dissertation research. See Stern 1982; Hahn 1983; Mallon 1983; Weinstein 1983; cf. Joseph 1982; RHR 1983; Klein 1990; and for Eastern Africa, Cooper 1977, 1980.

These observations, however, extend well beyond writings by graduate students at Yale University in the mid to late 1970s. For examples of influential writings on Latin Ameri-can history marked by similar intellectual sensibilities and timing of graduate study, and involving graduate study at settings as diverse as Columbia University, Princeton Univer-sity, Stanford University, the University of Texas, Austin, Cambridge University, and the University of Wisconsin, Madison, see, respectively, the following authors: Larson 1979, 1980, 1983a, 1988 (for perspective on timing, see 1998: chap. 10); R. Scott 1985; LeGrand 1986; Tutino 1986; James 1988; Andrews 1985; cf. Roseberry 1983, 1989; Gutiérrez 1985; RHR 1983. Influential works that contributed to these trends, but whose authors were marked by somewhat earlier timing of graduate study, include Farriss 1984; Spalding 1984; Taylor 1972, 1974, 1979; Winn 1986; see also Knight 1986. None of these scholars were graduate students at Yale (although Spalding and Winn subsequently taught gradu-ate courses at Yale). For overviews that provide additional context, see, for agrarian history trends, Bauer 1979; Roseberry 1993; Taylor 1985; Van Young 1983; cf. the essays in labor history by Skidmore 1979; Viotti da Costa 1989.

Of course, subsequent cohorts of graduate students wrote important works that built on (i.e., both extended and revised) this emerging intellectual tradition. For several examples from a variety of periods and regions within Latin America, see Cope 1994; Diacon 1991; French 1992; Gould 1990; Helg 1995; Klubock 1998; Schroeder 1998; Tinsman 1997; Wolfe 1993; see also note 19 below.

9   The characterization of a genre of "progressive" or "radical" writing that gave shape to the meaning of "the political" is based largely on the kinds of works cited in note 8 above. Four caveats must be made, however. First, not all works that contributed mean-ingfully to a literature that illuminated problems of agency and/or structure "from below" were written by authors whose political sensibilities publicly associated them with "radical" or "progressive" history—a point that will be taken up later in more detail. (Aside from prefatory or other statements in books, an added marker of public sensibilities for graduate students in the late 1970s and early 1980s was publication of articles in the journals *Radical History Review* and *Latin American Perspectives*. Among those mentioned in note 8 above, Andrews, Gutiérrez, Joseph, Larson, Mallon, Stern, and Weinstein all published essays in one or both journals.) For outstanding studies rooted in graduate study in the mid to late 1970s that serve as examples of works by authors

either more "apolitical" or more discreet, see De Shazo 1983; Martin 1982, 1985; Wightman 1990.

Second, one cannot reduce all works of politically engaged "progressive" scholarship anchored in graduate study and field research in the mid to late 1970s to the explorations of agency and hegemony or structure discussed here. Some outstanding studies of race, women's experiences, and gender, for example, do not fit as readily as other works within the genre described here. See, for example, Andrews 1980; Arrom 1985; Gutiérrez 1985; cf. Andrews 1991; Lavrin 1989, some of whose authors may be identified with graduate study in the 1970s. In addition, works focused mainly on political economy could have extremely important implications for a progressive or radical rewriting of history. Consider, for example, the impact of the rediscovery of plantation slavery and race hierarchy as central to the making of Puerto Rico in pathbreaking studies such as Scarano 1984.

Third, given the political and intellectual changes (which shall be discussed later in this essay) and the crises of grand paradigms—including leftist paradigms—that would take hold over the course of the 1980s, labels and political stances changed. Scholars or writings might be identified or self-identified as part of a "radical" current of thought in the late 1970s and early 1980s, but such political labeling might seem pointless by the late 1980s and early 1990s. To the extent that political nomenclature still applied to leftist or center-left writing, a more elastic descriptive label ("progressive") might seem more pertinent.

A fourth caveat is that works in the emerging genre described here did not always hold agency and hegemony (or alternatively, agency and structure) in neat balance. This point will be discussed in more detail below.

These caveats serve to remind us of the complicated messiness of intellectual writings and trends in the 1970s and 1980s. The scale of production and study, and the diversity of people and specialized themes and subfields that contributed to scholarship, meant that trends emerged out of a series of imperfect intellectual conversations and echoes, beset by countercurrents and fragmentary dynamics, rather than from a "meeting of the minds" within a small club of like-minded individuals. For this very reason, it is helpful to use metaphors of imperfect conversation, such as "reverberation" or "dialogue across fragments" (see Stern 1993; Mallon 1993) to characterize intellectual trends and communication.

10 Cf. Roseberry 1993, esp. 341–61. Lest we slide into too complacent a view, however, note the discussion below of the flaws that marred balance between agency and structure or hegemony in politically engaged social history, and Van Young's critique (1990) of ongoing tendencies in historical studies to impute consciousness based on supposed group characteristics when writing about subalterns.

11 Historically minded anthropologists, particularly William Roseberry, have contributed importantly to the idea of regional or local power fields within wider power fields. See Roseberry 1989, 1994 (in which he adopts E. P. Thompson's "field of force" metaphor as a point of departure); cf. O'Brien and Roseberry 1991; Mintz 1974, 1985; Wolf 1982, 1986. For the key role of Latin American anthropologists Sidney W. Mintz and Eric R. Wolf in anticipating and developing such approaches, see Roseberry 1993: 337–38, 341–45; cf. the discussion of Mintz's life history of Don Taso in Scarano 1988. The connection of this approach to intellectual dialogue between historically minded anthropologists and anthropologically minded historians also comes through in the discussion of "resistant adaptation" in Stern 1987a. For background and bibliography on the origins and fate of

the dependency-oriented cycle of intellectual critique, and its relation to earlier discussion of "modernization," see Klarén and Bossert 1986; Cooper et al. 1993.

12 Brooke Larson's retrospective writings—on the shape of the field of Andean history and anthropology, and on her own agrarian history of Cochabamba—are especially perceptive about the role of material life and political economy in the genre of writings depicted here, and about some of the intellectual problems and tensions connected to that conceptualization. See Larson 1995, 1998: chap. 10; cf. Larson 1991, 1983b. On the capitalist world system, labor, and peasants as themes that drew wide attention in Latin Americanist as well as Africanist scholarship, see Cooper et al. 1993. On "moral economy," see Thompson 1971; J. Scott 1976; Larson 1991.

13 On reverberations as imperfect yet meaningful forms of intellectual conversation, echo, and partial convergence, see Stern 1993.

14 Lomnitz 1999, esp. 378–83; Skidmore 1998: 111–15. In my own case, dissertation field research in Peru during 1976–78 coincided with leftist influence and social mobilizations strong enough to become a kind of cultural "common sense," and a source of new historical questions and meanings in innovative scholarly research and writings by historians as diverse as Heraclio Bonilla, Manuel Burga, Wilma Derpich, Alberto Flores Galindo, Lorenzo Huertas, Pablo Macera, Nelson Manrique, Scarlett O'Phelan Godoy, and Ernesto Yepes, among others, and among young historically minded anthropologists such as Marisol de la Cadena and Carlos Iván Degregori.

15 Examples of outstanding studies by historians trained in the 1970s and whose work may fairly be construed in these terms include De Shazo 1983; Martin 1982, 1985; and Wightman 1990. Among an earlier generation, outstanding examples include Schwartz 1978, 1985; and Taylor 1972, 1979.

16 The quote is taken from the chapter by Viotti da Costa in this volume. One might add that in instances where the sheer weight of hegemonic power and the intensity of popular mobilization and upheaval are both formidable, achieving a convincing integration of both perspectives becomes especially difficult. Within the historiography of the Mexican Revolution, for example, the difficulty of striking a balance between an emphasis on popular agency and an emphasis on hegemony and constraint comes out in interesting ways in the debate between populist and revisionist interpretations of the Mexican Revolution. See, for example, the contrasts between Womack 1968, 1986; cf. Knight 1986. For new efforts to supersede such debates, see Joseph and Nugent 1994b; Wells and Joseph 1996; and Knight 1994, which shrewdly connects such issues to the distinct sides of peasant politics developed in J. Scott 1976, 1985, 1990.

17 See R. Scott 1985; Moreno Fraginals 1978. Latin American labor history serves as another example where the weight of structuralist explanation was heavy; see Viotti da Costa 1989; Weinstein 1989.

18 See Katz 1988; Harris, Larson, and Tandeter 1987 (significantly revised and updated as Larson and Harris, with Tandeter 1995); Stern 1987b; Moreno Y. and Salomon 1991; Taylor 1985; Viotti da Costa 1989; Weinstein 1989: 25. For the works from the labor history discussion mentioned above, see Winn 1986; Mallon 1986; Bergquist 1986; French 1986, 1988; James 1988. Several years later, Viotti da Costa (1994) herself contributed a study of slaves, planters, and missionaries that related agency and hegemonic structure in superb balance. As she eloquently put it (1994: xviii), the history of human action is "the point at which the constant tension between freedom and necessity is momentarily resolved."

19 Compare Joseph 1982 with 1990, and with Joseph and Nugent 1994b, Wells and Joseph

1996; Stern 1982 with 1987, 1995; Mallon 1983 with 1995; Weinstein 1983 with 1996; Scarano 1984 with 1996; R. Scott 1985 with 1994, 1998; James 1988 with 1997a, 1997b, 2000; French and James 1997; Larson 1988 with 1998: xix–xxii, 322–90; Van Young 1981 with 2001 (cf. 1990, 1992, 1993, 1999); Vaughan 1982 with 1997. The off-stage metaphor comes from J. C. Scott 1990.

First books (and early research articles) by scholars whose timing of graduate study and field research placed them within the transition described here are important as markers of, and decisive contributions to, the shift toward the "politics and culture" approach. See, for example, Becker 1995; Cope 1994; Diacon 1991; Ferrer 1999; Gould 1990; Findlay 1999; Guardino 1996; Guerra 1998; Klubock 1998; Walker 1999 (cf. Serulnikov 1999; Thomson 1999); Wolfe 1993; and chapters by younger historians in French and James 1997 (essays by Ann Farnsworth-Alvear, Thomas Klubock, Deborah Levenson-Estrada, Heidi Tinsman, and Theresa Veccia); and in Joseph, LeGrand, and Salvatore 1998 (essays by Lauren Derby, Seth Fein, Eileen Findlay, Thomas Klubock, Steven Palmer, Eric Roorda, Michael Schroeder, and María del Carmen Suescun Pozas).

20 Larson 1998: 328–29; cf. Larson 1995: 17–21.

21 The 1983–86 period refers to the years when the Social Science Research Council (SSRC) sponsored three major international conferences to chart new research and conceptual directions in Andean history and anthropology. Discussion and planning of the collaborative research project actually began in 1981, when Brooke Larson and I drafted a proposal for discussion in New York by an interdisciplinary planning committee, convened by the SSRC in October. The other members of the planning committee were Carlos Sempat Assadourian, José María Caballero, Magnus Mörner, John V. Murra, Silvia Rivera, Karen Spalding, and Enrique Tandeter. Out of our discussions emerged a framework and more specific planning for working conferences on market participation (see Harris, Larson, and Tandeter 1987; Larson and Harris, with Tandeter 1995); on social reproduction and transformation (see Moreno Y. and Salomon 1991); and on resistance, rebellion, and consciousness (see Stern 1987b).

22 See Mallon 1983: chap. 3, for the original version of the peasant nationalism argument; cf. Manrique 1981. I base the description of objections not only on Bonilla 1987 (cf. 1978), which is an excellent summation of them, but also on critiques I witnessed in conference and seminar discussions in Peru in 1978, and on personal communications from Mallon regarding unpublished reader responses to early articles she wrote.

23 See Mallon 1987 (cf. 1988 for another "mid-way point" statement), 1995. For insight on the shifting meaning of hegemony, see also Knight 1994; Roseberry 1994; and the critique of a wooden (if somewhat caricatured) version in J. C. Scott 1985. I am grateful to Gladys McCormick for alerting me that the shifting meaning of "hegemony" is itself a marker of the broader shift discussed here.

24 See Joseph 1982, esp. 70–89, 115–21, 185–227, 270–73; see also the prefatory remarks by Joseph and by Alan Knight to the second edition (1988). It is worth noting that during the years Joseph was preparing the book for publication, David Brading (1980) coordinated and published an important collaborative project that focused special attention on the caciquismo phenomenon within the Mexican Revolution.

25 See Joseph and Nugent 1994a; Joseph 1990, 1991, 1994a; Wells and Joseph 1996, esp. chaps. 6–10.

26 Mallon 1994.

27 See Haber 1997a, 1997b; cf. 1999. The conference paper version (1997a) is virtually identical with the published version in Mexican Studies/Estudios mexicanos (1997b), and as a courtesy to readers citations will come from the latter. The most recent version (1999)

reproduces much of the material in the earlier essays, but one minor change, relevant to this essay's theme, should be noted to avoid confusion. The 1997 versions refer to the body of criticized work as both the "new cultural" and "new political" history of Mexico, but the 1999 version refers to "new cultural" history only. For a thorough and illuminating airing of the issues related to Haber's critique, see the forum in HAHR 1999.

28 The conflation comes through in the ways Haber's narrative strategy relies on generalizations about the "New History" as if the largely literary scholars in boundary 2 1993 and the historians associated with the "new" cultural history—Mallon 1995, and the authors in Joseph and Nugent 1994b and Fowler-Salamini and Vaughan 1994—adopt virtually the same approaches toward historical narrative and methodology, and its empirical foundations. See esp. Haber 1997b: 370–71 (cf. 1999: 317–18), where Haber moves seamlessly from Mallon to Seed and the mainly literary scholars of the Latin American Subaltern Studies Group; 373–74, where he sees in Joseph and Nugent 1994b, Mallon 1995, and the literary subalternists in boundary 2 1993 (he uses the 1995 edition of the same collection) a shared indeterminacy of terms such as "subaltern" and "nationalism." Such conflations pass over lightly the explicit evidence of serious intellectual differences on these points in the works by the historians he critiques. For explicitly drawn differences, see the critique of the more literary subalternist enthusiasts and of Patricia Seed for not having done their empirical homework—for overlooking historical research, mischaracterizing historiography, and sidestepping the Gramscian part of the Subaltern Studies school's genealogy—in Mallon 1994: 1500–1507; cf. Mallon 1999: 350.

29 It is worth noting that a number of years ago, Mallon (1987) presented the case of Cajamarca as one where peasant nationalism failed to take hold; in effect, she provided an early answer to Haber's rhetorical question about empirical "disproof" (1997b: 374). See also the careful discussion of classic historical problems of evidence, sources, and methodology in Joseph's discussion of the necessity to go beyond the discursive categories of state-generated documents, and to set discourses in their material contexts, in the debate sparked by his 1990 essay on bandits (1991: 171 incl. n. 31, 172–73). The original 1990 essay (see 15–25, esp. 15, 24–25) carefully discussed issues of empirical evidence, cross-checking of sources, and historical method, especially as applied to difficult issues of consciousness, while also indicating a certain openness to insights associated with the linguistic turn in history. The balance and caveats that marked this approach (cf. Van Young 1992 for a similar receptivity mixed with historical caution and balance) are not easy to confuse with the more one-dimensional textual analysis associated with the more militantly "literary" scholars of subaltern and cultural studies. Note, as well, that evidence of openness to empirical "disproof" comes through in the partial modification of the "revolution from without" thesis (originally presented in Joseph 1982) in Wells and Joseph 1996: 285–90.

In view of the evidence of critique and partial distancing from the more "literary" proponents of subaltern studies, the careful methodological discussions and adjustments of argument in view of evidence including negative evidence, and the body of argument and evidence presented in Mallon 1995, Joseph 1994, and Wells and Joseph 1996 and in many ways aligned with the traditional historical-legal reasoning Haber describes and approves, Haber's conflation of the historians and literary postmodernists seems deeply ironic. It exposes a tendency to use selective excerpts—often lifted from theoretical, methodological, or prefatory discussions—to confirm a preconceived idea rather than to test the idea through systematic and open-minded examination of the relevant evidence. For a detailed reconstruction in one key case, see Mallon 1999: 336.

30 See Kuhn 1962, 1970; the critiques in Shapere 1964 and in Lakatos and Musgrave 1970

(esp. the essays by Popper, Masterman, and Lakatos, and Kuhn's response); and the additional reflections in Kuhn 1977; Horwich 1993 (esp. the essays by Earman, McMullin, Cartwright, and Hacking); and Bird 2000.

I am not arguing here that Haber's favored approach (what he calls "social scientific standards of proof" and "falsificationist epistemology and methodology" [1997b: 382]) is "wrong" or unuseful, but that he has framed it too narrowly and too naively. His is not the only useful approach to the development of historical knowledge that works seriously and rigorously with evidence. In addition, his discussion of method rests on two conceptual fallacies. On the one hand, rigorous application of the hypothesis testing procedure common in the social sciences does not constitute the kind of logical pathway to convincing, accurate scholarship free of preconceived wrongheadedness implied in Haber's concluding paragraph (1997b: 383). As Florencia Mallon has recently observed (1999: 331–32; cf. Fogel and Engerman 1974; David et al. 1976), the intellectual fate of *Time on the Cross*, the work coauthored by Haber's apparent scholar-hero, Robert Fogel, should offer some humbling caution on this point.

On the other hand, the discussions of paradigms, observation, and scientific process sparked by Kuhn, and the twentieth-century history of natural science, especially physics and astronomy, warn against simple assumptions, easier to sustain in the Newtonian era of physics, that science can literally observe objective evidence in the process of testing hypotheses and thereby advancing science. (The historical validity of this idea seems now to have a "sometimes yes, sometimes no" aspect, depending on the scientific problem or experiment.) The twentieth-century history of science also casts doubt on the epistemologically comforting idea of unifying laws of logical determination of matter. For a lucid discussion of these points in relation both to Einstein's revolutionary reconceptualization of space-time and to the development of subatomic particle physics, see Hobsbawm 1994: 534–42, 548. For Einstein's own unease with the implications of quantum physics, which transformed scientific certainty into mathematical equations of probability and uncertainty, and which entangled the observer and the observed in a mutually constituting relation that undermined the objective, independent reality of the observed and pushed scientists further down the slippery slope of inferential (indirect) observation and reasoning, a useful introduction is White and Gribbin 1994: 212–26 (see also 248–60).

31 For those familiar with my critique of Wallerstein's world-system paradigm as applied to Latin America and the Caribbean, it should be evident that I think it quite useful, when a historical field has developed sufficient empirical richness, to organize a narrative that formally sets out a significant paradigm and hypothesis which are then rigorously "tested" against directly pertinent historical evidence and case studies. See Stern 1988.

32 Indeed, Cooper et al. (1993) show how this unfolding research process—cycles of dialogue and confrontation with paradigms—undermined within twenty years the initial paradigms of radical critique (strongly influenced by dependency and world-system ideas) that had defined a foundational intellectual moment in the late 1960s and early 1970s.

33 Obviously, the historical scholarship on women and gender has become too huge for a full listing in this note. For key panoramic statements from the perspective of Europe and Western civilization, excellent starting points are J. W. Scott 1986, 1988; and Lerner 1986. On Foucault's thought and influence in the emergence of a "new" cultural history, superb starting points are Foucault 1984 (especially the introduction by Rabinow) and Hunt 1989; see also Stoler 1995. For a vivid sense of the ways gender and the new cultural

history sparked critiques of an older cultural history—more Geertzian than postmodern in its anthropological sensibilities, and vulnerable to undifferentiated views of subaltern community and moral economy—see the appreciative yet powerful critiques of E. P. Thompson (esp. 1963, 1971) and Natalie Zemon Davis (esp. 1975) in J. W. Scott 1988; Desan 1989.

For the case of Latin America, a comparison of Lavrin 1978 and 1989, supplemented by Martínez-Alier [now Stolcke] 1974 and Gutiérrez 1985, 1991, provides a feel for the ways attention to women, gender, and youth, and an openness to Foucauldian sensibilities, ended up decentering our social categories. I have developed a more systematic review and appreciative critique of the historiography on women and gender for Latin America, and a reflection on the ways gender redefines the ways we examine subaltern political culture and community, in Stern 1995, esp. 11–20, 142–50, 189–213, 299–308.

34 It should be pointed out that the "new social movements" literature has been written mainly by social scientists, not historians. An excellent starting point for a sampling and critique of this literature is Escobar and Alvarez 1992; cf. Eckstein 1989; Fox and Starn 1997; Alvarez, Dagnino, and Escobar 1998. For the connections of the literature on social movements and on women, see also Alvarez 1990; Massolo 1992; Valdés and Weinstein 1993.

35 Mallon 1994; quote on 1491. For country overviews as well as general analysis of the Latin American Left during the period of collapsing narratives of inspiration, see Carr and Ellner 1993; Castañeda 1993.

36 Hobsbawm (1994) offers an impressively multidimensional treatment of the collapse of certainties and inspiration in the West within a world context.

37 I am grateful to Florencia E. Mallon for a discussion in which she observed that the wider political and intellectual environment gave her "permission" to take up systematically and rigorously, in a new research project, the enigma that had emerged in her 1983 book and the scholarly responses to her findings.

38 Readers will understand, I hope, that since I was an active researcher and writer in the cycle discussed in this section, many of the comments that follow have an autobiographical aspect. Of course, they also constitute a reflection on the influences, contexts, and spirit evident in many of the works cited above—especially works cited in notes 8, 12, 18, 19, and 21. I hope readers will also understand that since the recent and contemporary events mentioned below will be familiar to any informed scholar, I have considered them common knowledge and have eschewed detailed explication and annotations. Younger students unfamiliar with the events may find succinct review and context in Skidmore and Smith 1997, a fine textbook that emphasizes twentieth-century history.

39 For a particularly eloquent example, see Larson 1998: 389–90, xx–xxi; cf. Joseph and Nugent 1994b: xvi; Mallon 1995: 329–30, 9–20; and the sobering blend of tragedy and hope in the conclusion to a collaborative study of Peru during the Shining Path era (Stern 1998).

40 The prominence and explosiveness of these issues will be evident to anyone who follows contemporary Latin American affairs or read the international news coverage related to the detention of Augusto Pinochet in London from October 1998 to March 2000. For a good introduction that includes the Southern Cone, Central America, and Peru, see NACLA 1998b; for an assessment and initiative by the SSRC, see Hershberg 1999.

41 In my current research on memory issues and struggles in the remaking of Chile between 1973 and 1998, I have found that I could not fully appreciate the tragedy and injustices of the period, and the reshaping of political culture, until I had learned to

"listen" to the memories of those whom I might have implicitly dismissed as less "authentic" or "truthful" voices during the heated political struggles of the 1970s. One must underscore, in addition, that one important benefit of greater tolerance of ambiguity and political antagonism is an ability to confront more squarely subaltern social movements and forms of consciousness that do not fit neatly into heroic narratives. See, for example, the treatments of worker and campesino consciousness in Weinstein 1996, Wells and Joseph 1996, and Starn 1999.

42 For a specific example and more detailed argument along these lines, see the discussion of the quincentennial of 1492 in Stern 1992.

43 I wish to thank Catherine LeGrand for this formulation, and for insisting on the point, which had been left implicit in an earlier version of this essay.

44 For the "radical evil" concept as applied to problems in international jurisprudence and philosophy, and to the specific case of the trials of the Argentine generals in 1985, soon after the transition to civilian rule, see Nino 1996; a compelling example of the trickiness and value of understanding even murderers "from within," and the ways such inside vantage points also yield critical exposure of evil, may be found, again for the case of Argentina, in Verbitsky 1996. For Arendt's formulation (in a historical context quite different, of course, from Immanuel Kant's original discussion of the concept) of the radical evil problem, see Arendt 1959: 212–23, esp. 215–18 (quote on 217); cf. Arendt 1964, a controversial but profoundly important and chilling depiction of Eichmann's mental social world, where banality becomes the paradoxical handmaiden of monstrosity. I do not wish to imply, of course, that "radical evil" is found only on the Right. The war philosophy of Abimael Guzmán, leader of Shining Path, is a chilling example that radical evil can arise in many quarters.

45 At a theoretical level, this is one of the most important implications, I think, of Joseph and Nugent 1994a.

46 By the mid-1990s, for the nineteen countries of "Latin America" (I have included Spanish America and Brazil, but not Haiti nor the rest of the non-Spanish Caribbean), the estimated population of those nineteen years old or under amounted to nearly half (44.5 percent) the total population; the population of those 24 or under was a majority (53.9 percent). By 1980, school enrollment rates for those between the ages of 12 and 17 had already reached 60 percent in ten countries and 50 percent in fourteen countries. See CEPALC 1995: 66, 176–77.

47 The observations on neoliberalism and youth alienation are partly based on personal observations and conversations between July 1996 and July 1997 while I lived in Chile, and during shorter visits to Peru and Chile between 1996 and 1999. A number of discussions with residents of *poblaciones* in Santiago were quite revealing in this regard. I have also found helpful Murphy 1998, an illuminating and sensitive study based in part on social work with youth in Renca in need of drug- and violence-related therapy; cf. NACLA 1998a.

For explicit and revealing concern about the problems of youth alienation and political alienation in Chile, see the discussions by political elites, intellectuals, and media reporters about historically high voter abstention and null ballot rates (the combined abstention and protest vote rate reached 31.5 percent) in the parliamentary elections of December 1997, as reported in newspapers such as *El Mercurio*, *La Epoca*, *La Segunda*, and *La Tercera* in December 1997 and January 1998. Good starting points are *La Tercera*: electronic ed., www.tercera.cl, 13–XII–97; *La Epoca*: electronic ed., www.laepoca.cl, 13–XII–97, 21–XII–97; and for intelligent analysis, Riquelme 1999. An additional symptom of alienation and/or elite concern about alienation is the fact that Moulian 1997, a stinging critique of Chile in the neoliberal age, was a best-seller through the second half of 1997 and received substantial and favorable media attention. This was the case even though the book went against the grain of the vision of the ruling Concertación coalition.

Although I have been most exposed to recent youth alienation in a Chilean context and drafted this essay before the crisis of the UNAM in Mexico in 1999–2000, the issue cuts across national borders. For a discussion, see NACLA 2000, cf. 1998a.

My reference to the "bottom 40 percent" is based on poverty statistics for Latin America published by CEPALC (Comisión Económica para América Latina y el Caribe), which show that for Latin America as a whole, the poor—defined as households whose incomes amount to less than twice the cost of a basic food basket—amounted to 39 percent of the total population in 1990. Within this category, the "indigent poor"— defined as households whose incomes amount to less than the cost of a single basic food basket—amounted to 18 percent. It is sobering to note that these figures are virtually the same as those for 1970 (40 percent and 19 percent for the poor and the indigent poor, respectively). Obviously, the figures for specific countries will vary from the figures for Latin America as a whole. The Chilean figures, for example, were 35 percent and 12 percent for poverty and indigence, respectively, in 1990, and had improved to 28 percent and 7 percent, respectively, in 1992. Given this relatively favorable profile, within the Latin American context, the symptoms of youth alienation in Chile are all the more striking and warn us not to assume a simple mechanical connection between economic condition of life and politico-cultural alienation. For the figures cited, see CEPALC 1995: 46–47.

48 For perceptive reflection, sensitive to intergenerational issues, on the problems of *memoria* and *desmemoria*, the work of Elizabeth Jelín is a fundamental starting point. See Jelín 1995; Jelín and Kaufman 1998.

49 For the examples mentioned, see Stern 1998; James 1997a, 1997b, 2000; Mallon 1995: chap. 9 (cf. her discussion of memory-related themes in her essay in this volume); Weinstein 1996. For a brief summation of the SSRC project, with which I am also familiar through personal collaboration, see Hershberg 1999; beginning with the fellows cohort of 2000, a Peruvian component has been added to the memory project. The current research on Chile that I mentioned refers to a book project that aims to write a history of memory about the 1973 political collapse and the problem of political violence as these contentious issues unfolded in Chilean political, cultural, and personal life between 1973 and 1998.

50 See Hite 2000; and for Peru, Chávez de Paz 1989; Degregori 1990, 1991, 1998; Lynch 1990; Ansión et al. 1992; Alarcón 1994; Portocarrero 1998.

51 An obvious example is the problematic and sometimes charged sensibility about the "colonial inheritance" in much of Latin America. For recent discussion and interpretation, see Adelman 1999.

Works Cited

Acuña, Carlos H., et al. 1995. *Juicio, castigos y memorias: Derechos humanos y justicia en la política argentina*. Buenos Aires: Ediciones Nueva Visión SAIC.

Adelman, Jeremy, ed. 1999. *Colonial Legacies: The Problem of Persistence in Latin American History*. New York: Routledge.

Alarcón, Walter. 1994. *Ser niño: Una nueva mirada de la infancia en el Perú*. Lima: Instituto de Estudios Peruanos/UNICEF.

Alvarez, Sonia E. 1990. *Engendering Democracy in Brazil: Women's Movements in Transition Politics*. Princeton: Princeton University Press.

Alvarez, Sonia E., Evelina Dagnino, and Arturo Escobar, eds. 1998. *Cultures of Politics, Politics of Cultures: Re-visioning Latin American Social Movements*. Boulder, CO: Westview Press.

Andrews, George Reid. 1980. *The Afro-Argentines of Buenos Aires, 1800–1900*. Madison: Univ. of Wisconsin Press.

———. 1985. "Spanish American Independence: A Structural Analysis." *Latin American Perspectives* 12, 1 (winter): 105–32.

———. 1991. *Blacks and Whites in São Paulo, Brazil, 1888–1988*. Madison: University of Wisconsin Press.

Ansión, Juan, et al. 1992. *La escuela en los tiempos de guerra*. Lima: CEAPAZ.

Arendt, Hannah. 1959. *The Human Condition: A Study of the Central Dilemmas Facing Modern Man*. 1958. Reprint, New York: Doubleday Anchor.

———. 1964. *Eichmann in Jerusalem: A Report on the Banality of Evil*. Rev. ed. New York: Viking Press.

Arrom, Silvia M. 1985. *The Women of Mexico City, 1790–1857*. Stanford: Stanford University Press.

Bauer, Arnold J. 1979. "Rural Workers in Spanish America: Problems of Peonage and Oppression." *Hispanic American Historical Review* 59, 1 (Feb.): 34–63.

Becker, Marjorie. 1995. *Setting the Virgin on Fire: Lázaro Cárdenas, Michoacán Peasants, and the Redemption of the Mexican Revolution*. Berkeley: University of California Press.

Bergquist, Charles. 1986. *Labor in Latin America: Comparative Essays on Chile, Argentina, Venezuela, and Colombia*. Stanford: Stanford University Press.

Bernhard, Virginia, ed. 1979. *Elites, Masses, and Modernization in Latin America, 1850–1930*. Austin: University of Texas Press.

Bethell, Leslie, ed. 1986. *The Cambridge History of Latin America*. Vol. 5. New York: Cambridge University Press.

Bird, Alexander. 2000. *Thomas Kuhn*. Princeton: Princeton University Press.

Bonilla, Heraclio. 1978. "The War of the Pacific and the National and Colonial Problem in Peru." *Past and Present* 81: 92–118.

———. 1987. "The Indian Peasantry and 'Peru' During the War with Chile." In Stern 1987b: 219–31.

boundary 2. 1993. *boundary 2: an international journal of literature and culture* 20, 3 (fall). Thematic issue on "The Postmodernism Debate in Latin America," eds. John Beverley and José Oviedo.

Bowser, Frederick P. 1972. "The African Slave in Colonial Spanish America: Reflections on Research Achievements and Priorities." *Latin American Research Review* 7 (spring): 77–94.

———. 1974. *The African Slave in Colonial Peru, 1524–1650*. Stanford: Stanford University Press.

Brading, David A., ed. 1980. *Caudillo and Peasant in the Mexican Revolution*. New York: Cambridge University Press.

Carr, Barry, and Steve Ellner, eds. 1993. *The Latin American Left: From the Fall of Allende to Perestroika*. Boulder, CO: Westview Press.

Castañeda, Jorge. 1993. *Utopia Unarmed: The Latin American Left After the Cold War*. New York: Vintage.

CEPALC (Comisión Económica para América Latina y el Caribe). 1995. *Anuario estadístico de América Latina y el Caribe; Statistical Yearbook for Latin America and the Caribbean, 1994*. Santiago: United Nations.

Chávez de Paz, Dennis. 1989. *Juventud y terrorismo: Características sociales de los condenados por terrorismo y otros delitos*. Lima: Instituto de Estudios Peruanos.

Cooper, Frederick. 1977. *Plantation Slavery on the East Coast of Africa*. New Haven: Yale University Press.

———. 1980. *From Slaves to Squatters: Plantation Labor and Agriculture in Zanzibar and Coastal Kenya, 1890–1925*. New Haven: Yale University Press.

Cooper, Frederick, et al. 1993. *Confronting Historical Paradigms: Peasants, Labor, and the Capitalist World System in Africa and Latin America*. Madison: University of Wisconsin Press.

Cope, R. Douglas. 1994. *The Limits of Racial Domination: Plebeian Society in Colonial Mexico City, 1660–1720*. Madison: University of Wisconsin Press.

da Costa: see Viotti da Costa.

David, Paul, et al. 1976. *Reckoning with Slavery: A Critical Study in the Quantitative History of American Negro Slavery*. New York: Oxford University Press.

Davis, David Brion. 1975. *The Problem of Slavery in the Age of Revolution, 1770–1823*. Ithaca: Cornell University Press.

Davis, Natalie Zemon. 1975. *Society and Culture in Early Modern France*. Stanford: Stanford University Press.

Degregori, Carlos Iván. 1990. *Ayacucho, 1969–1979: El surgimiento de Sendero Luminoso*. Lima: Instituto de Estudios Peruanos.

———. 1991. "Jóvenes andinos y criollos frente a la violencia política." In Urbano 1991: 395–417.

———. 1998. "Harvesting Storms: Peasant Rondas and the Defeat of Sendero Luminoso in Ayacucho." In Stern 1998: 128–57.

Desan, Suzanne. 1989. "Crowds, Community, and Ritual in the Work of E. P. Thompson and Natalie Davis." In Hunt 1989: 47–71.

DeShazo, Peter. 1983. *Urban Workers and Labor Unions in Chile, 1902–1927*. Madison: University of Wisconsin Press.

Diacon, Todd. 1991. *Millenarian Vision, Capitalist Reality: Brazil's Contestado Rebellion, 1912–1916*. Durham: Duke University Press.

Eckstein, Susan, ed. 1989. *Power and Popular Protest: Latin American Social Movements*. Berkeley: University of California Press.

Escobar, Arturo, and Alvarez, Sonia, eds. 1992. *The Making of Social Movements in Latin America: Identity, Strategy, and Democracy*. Boulder: Westview Press.

Farriss, Nancy. 1984. *Maya Society under Colonial Rule: The Collective Enterprise of Survival*. Princeton: Princeton University Press.

Ferrer, Ada. 1999. *Insurgent Cuba: Race, Nation, and Revolution, 1868–1898*. Chapel Hill: University of North Carolina Press.

Findlay, Eileen J. Suárez. 1999. *Imposing Decency: The Politics of Sexuality and Race in Puerto Rico, 1870–1920*. Durham: Duke University Press.

Fogel, Robert, and Stanley Engerman. 1974. *Time on the Cross: The Economics of American Negro Slavery*. 2 vols. Boston: Little, Brown.

Foucault, Michel. 1984. *The Foucault Reader*. Ed. Paul Rabinow. New York: Pantheon.

Fowler-Salamini, Heather, and Mary Kay Vaughan, eds. 1994. *Women of the Mexican Countryside, 1850–1990: Creating Spaces, Shaping Transition*. Tucson: University of Arizona Press.

Fox, Richard G., and Orin Starn, eds. 1997. *Between Resistance and Revolution: Cultural Politics and Social Protest*. New Brunswick: Rutgers University Press.

Fox-Genovese, Elizabeth, and Eugene D. Genovese. 1976. "The Political Crisis of Social History." *Journal of Social History* 10 (winter): 204–20.

French, John D. 1986. "Industrial Workers and the Birth of the Populist Republic in Brazil, 1945–1946." Paper presented at Latin American Studies Association convention, Boston, 23–25 October.

——. 1988. "Workers and the Rise of Adhemarista Populism in São Paulo, Brazil, 1945–1947." *Hispanic American Historical Review* 68, 1 (Feb.): 1–43.

——. 1992. *The Brazilian Workers' ABC: Class Conflict and Alliances in Modern São Paulo.* Chapel Hill: University of North Carolina Press.

French, John D., and Daniel James, eds. 1997. *The Gendered Worlds of Latin American Women Workers: From Household and Factory to the Union Hall and Ballot Box.* Durham: Duke University Press.

Genovese, Eugene D. 1974. *Roll, Jordan Roll: The World the Slaves Made.* New York: Pantheon.

Giddens, Anthony. 1979. *Central Problems in Social Theory.* London: Macmillan.

——. 1981, 1985. *A Contemporary Critique of Historical Materialism.* 2 vols. Berkeley: University of California Press.

Gould, Jeffrey. 1990. *To Lead as Equals: Rural Protest and Political Consciousness in Chinandega, Nicaragua, 1912–1979.* Chapel Hill: University of North Carolina Press.

Gramsci, Antonio. 1971. *Selections from the Prison Notebooks.* Ed. Quintin Hoare and Geoffrey Nowell Smith. New York: International Publishers.

Guardino, Peter F. 1996. *Peasants, Politics, and the Formation of Mexico's National State: Guerrero, 1800–1857.* Stanford: Stanford University Press.

Guerra, Lillian. 1998. *Popular Expression and National Identity in Puerto Rico: The Struggle for Self, Community, and Nation.* Gainesville: University of Florida Press.

Gutiérrez, Ramón. 1985. "Honor Ideology, Marriage Negotiation, and Class-Gender Domination in New Mexico, 1690–1846." *Latin American Perspectives* 12, 1 (winter): 81–104.

——. 1991. *When Jesus Came, the Corn Mothers Went Away: Marriage, Sexuality, and Power in New Mexico, 1500–1846.* Stanford: Stanford University Press.

Haber, Stephen H. 1997a. "The Emperor's New Clothes: Dependency Theory and the New Cultural History of Latin America." Paper presented at the Mexican Studies Committee panel on "Trends and Transformations in Mexican History: The New Cultural History," American Historical Association Convention, 2–5 January.

——. 1997b. "The Worst of Both Worlds: The New Cultural History of Mexico." *Mexican Studies/Estudios mexicanos* 13, 2 (summer): 363–83.

——. 1999. "Anything Goes: Mexico's 'New' Cultural History." *Hispanic American Historical Review* 79, 2 (May): 309–30.

Hahn, Steven. 1983. *The Roots of Southern Populism: Yeoman Farmers and the Transformation of the Georgia Upcountry, 1850–1890.* New York: Oxford University Press.

HAHR. 1999. *Hispanic American Historical Review* 79, 2 (May): Thematic issue on "Mexico's New Cultural History: ¿Una lucha libre?" eds. Susan Deans-Smith and Gilbert M. Joseph.

Hanagan, Michael, and Charles Stephenson, eds. 1986. *Proletarians and Protest: The Roots of Class Formation in an Industrializing World.* Westport, Conn.: Greenwood Press.

Harris, Olivia, Brooke Larson, and Enrique Tandeter, eds. 1987. *La participación indígena en los mercados surandinos.* La Paz: CERES.

Helg, Aline. 1995. *Our Rightful Share: The Afro-Cuban Struggle for Equality, 1886–1912.* Chapel Hill: University of North Carolina Press.

Hershberg, Eric. 1999. "Collective Memory of Repression: Comparative Perspectives on Democratization Processes in Latin America's Southern Cone." *Items* (bulletin of the Social Science Research Council) 53, 1 (Mar.): 9–12.

Hite, Katherine. 2000. *When the Romance Ended: Leaders of the Chilean Left, 1968–1998.* New York: Columbia Univ. Press.

Hobsbawm, Eric. 1994. *The Age of Extremes: A History of the World, 1914–1991.* New York: Pantheon.

Horwich, Paul, ed. 1993. *World Changes: Thomas Kuhn and the Nature of Science.* Cambridge: MIT Press.

Hunt, Lynn, ed. 1989. *The New Cultural History.* Berkeley: University of California Press.

James, Daniel. 1988. *Resistance and Integration: Peronism and the Argentine Working Class, 1946–1976.* New York: Cambridge University Press.

———. 1997a. "Meatpackers, Peronists, and Collective Memory: A View from the South." *American Historical Review* 102, 5 (Dec.): 1404–12.

———. 1997b. "'Tales Told out of the Borderlands': Doña María's Story, Oral History, and Issues of Gender." In French and James 1997: 31–52.

———. 2000. *Doña María's Story: Life History, Memory, and Political Identity.* Durham: Duke University Press.

Jelín, Elizabeth. 1995. "La política de la memoria: El movimiento de derechos humanos y la construcción democrática en la Argentina." In Acuña et al. 1995: 101–46.

Jelín, Elizabeth, and Susana G. Kaufman. 1998. "Layers of Memories: Twenty Years After in Argentina." Paper presented at conference on "Legacies of Authoritarianism: Cultural Production, Collective Trauma, and Global Justice," University of Wisconsin, Madison, 3–5 April.

Joseph, Gilbert M. 1982. *Revolution from Without: Yucatán, Mexico, and the United States, 1880–1924.* New York: Cambridge University Press.

———. 1988. *Revolution from Without: Yucatán, Mexico, and the United States, 1880–1924.* Rev. ed. Durham: Duke University Press.

———. 1990. "On the Trail of Latin American Bandits: A Reexamination of Peasant Resistance." *Latin American Research Review* 25, 3: 7–53.

———. 1991. "'Resocializing' Latin American Banditry: A Reply." *Latin American Research Review* 26, 1: 161–74.

———. 1994. "Rethinking Mexican Revolutionary Mobilization: Yucatán's Seasons of Upheaval, 1909–1915." In Joseph and Nugent 1994a: 135–69.

Joseph, Gilbert M., Catherine C. LeGrand, and Ricardo Salvatore. 1998. *Close Encounters of Empire: Writing the Cultural History of U.S.–Latin American Relations.* Durham: Duke University Press.

Joseph, Gilbert M., and Daniel Nugent. 1994a. "Popular Culture and State Formation in Revolutionary Mexico." In Joseph and Nugent 1994b: 3–23.

———. 1994b. *Everyday Forms of State Formation: Revolution and the Negotiation of Rule in Modern Mexico.* Durham: Duke University Press.

Judt, Tony. 1979. "'A Clown in Regal Purple': Social History and the Historians." *History Workshop* 7: 66–94.

Katz, Friedrich, ed. 1988. *Riot, Rebellion, and Revolution: Rural Social Conflict in Mexico.* Princeton: Princeton University Press.

Klarén, Peter F., and Thomas J. Bossert, eds. 1986. *Promise of Development: Theories of Change in Latin America.* Boulder: Westview Press.

Klein, Rachel. 1990. *Unification of a Slave State: The Rise of the Planter Class in the South Carolina Backcountry, 1760–1808.* Chapel Hill and Williamsburg: University of North Carolina Press and Institute of Early American History and Culture.

Klubock, Thomas Miller. 1998. *Contested Communities: Class, Gender, and Politics in Chile's El Teniente Copper Mine, 1904–1951.* Durham: Duke University Press.

Knight, Alan. 1986. *The Mexican Revolution.* 2 vols. New York: Cambridge University Press.

———. 1994. "Weapons and Arches in the Mexican Revolutionary Landscape." In Joseph and Nugent 1994b: 24–66.

Kuhn, Thomas S. 1962. *The Structure of Scientific Revolutions*. Chicago: University of Chicago Press.

———. 1970. *The Structure of Scientific Revolutions*. 2d (enlarged) ed. Chicago: University of Chicago Press.

———. 1977. *The Essential Tension: Selected Studies in Scientific Tradition and Change*. Chicago: University of Chicago Press.

Lakatos, Imre, and Alan Musgrave, eds. 1970. *Criticism and the Growth of Knowledge*. Cambridge: Cambridge University Press.

Larson, Brooke. 1979. "Caciques, Class Structure, and the Colonial State in Bolivia." *Nova Americana* (Turin) 2: 197–235.

———. 1980. "Rural Rhythms of Class Conflict in Eighteenth-Century Cochabamba." *Hispanic American Historical Review* 60, 3 (Aug.): 407–30.

———. 1983a. *Explotación agraria y resistencia campesina: Cinco ensayos históricos sobre Cochabamba (siglos XVI–XIX)*. Cochabamba: CERES.

———. 1983b. "Shifting Views of Colonialism and Resistance." *Radical History Review* 27: 3–20.

———. 1988. *Colonialism and Agrarian Transformation in Bolivia: Cochabamba, 1550–1900*. Princeton: Princeton University Press.

———. 1991. "Explotación y economía moral en los andes del sur andino: Hacia una reconsideración crítica." In Moreno Y. and Salomon 1991, II: 441–79.

———. 1995. "Andean Communities, Political Cultures, and Markets: The Changing Contours of a Field." In Larson and Harris with Tandeter 1995: 5–53.

———. 1998. *Cochabamba, 1550–1900: Colonialism and Agrarian Transformation in Bolivia*. Rev. ed. Durham: Duke University Press.

Larson, Brooke, and Olivia Harris, with Enrique Tandeter, eds. 1995. *Ethnicity, Markets, and Migration in the Andes: At the Crossroads of History and Anthropology*. Durham: Duke University Press.

Lavrin, Asunción, ed. 1978. *Latin American Women: Historical Perspectives*. Westport, Conn.: Greenwood Press.

———. 1989. *Sexuality and Marriage in Colonial Latin America*. Lincoln: University of Nebraska Press.

LeGrand, Catherine C. 1986. *Frontier Expansion and Peasant Protest in Colombia, 1850–1936*. Albuquerque: University of New Mexico Press.

Lerner, Gerda. 1986. *The Creation of Patriarchy*. New York: Oxford University Press.

Lockhart, James. 1968. *Spanish Peru, 1532–1560: A Colonial Society*. Madison: University of Wisconsin Press.

———. 1972a. *The Men of Cajamarca: A Social and Biographical Study of the First Conquerors of Peru*. Austin: University of Texas Press.

———. 1972b. "The Social History of Colonial Spanish America: Evolution and Potential." *Latin American Research Review* 7: 6–45.

Lomnitz, Claudio. 1999. "Barbarians at the Gate? A Few Remarks on the Politics of the 'New Cultural History of Mexico.'" *Hispanic American Historical Review* 79, 2 (May): 367–83.

Lynch, Nicolás. 1990. *Los jóvenes rojos de San Marcos: El radicalismo universitario de los años sesenta*. Lima: El Zorro de Abajo.

Mallon, Florencia E. 1983. *The Defense of Community in Peru's Central Highlands: Peasant Struggle and Capitalist Transition, 1860–1940*. Princeton: Princeton University Press.

———. 1986. "Labor Migration, Class Formation, and Class Consciousness among Peruvian Miners in the Central Highlands from 1900 to 1930." In Hanagan and Stephenson 1986: 197–230.

———. 1987. "Nationalist and Antistate Coalitions in the War of the Pacific: Junín and Cajamarca, 1879–1902." In Stern 1987b: 232–79.

———. 1988. "Peasants and State Formation in Nineteenth-Century Mexico: Morelos, 1848–
1858." *Political Power and Social Theory* 7: 1–54.

———. 1993. "Dialogues among the Fragments: Retrospect and Prospect." In Cooper et al.
1993: 371–401.

———. 1994. "The Promise and Dilemma of Subaltern Studies: Perspectives from Latin American History." *American Historical Review* 99, 5 (Dec.): 1491–1515.

———. 1995. *Peasant and Nation: The Making of Postcolonial Mexico and Peru.* Berkeley: University of
California Press.

———. 1999. "Time on the Wheel: Cycles of Revisionism and the 'New Cultural History.' "
Hispanic American Historical Review 79, 2 (May): 331–51.

Manrique, Nelson. 1981. *Campesinado y nación: Las guerrillas indígenas en la guerra con Chile.* Lima:
CIC-Ital Perú.

Martin, Cheryl English. 1982. "Haciendas and Villages in Late Colonial Morelos." *Hispanic
American Historical Review* 62, 3 (Aug.): 407–27.

———. 1985. *Rural Society in Colonial Morelos.* Albuquerque: University of New Mexico Press.

Martínez-Alier, Verena. 1974. *Marriage, Class, and Colour in Nineteenth-Century Cuba: A Study of
Racial Attitudes and Sexual Values in a Slave Society.* London: Cambridge University Press.

Massolo, Alejandra. 1992. *Por amor y coraje: Mujeres en movimientos urbanos de la ciudad de México.*
Mexico City: El Colegio de México.

Mintz, Sidney W. 1974. *Caribbean Transformations.* Chicago: Aldine.

———. 1985. *Sweetness and Power: The Place of Sugar in Modern History.* New York: Penguin.

———. 1988. *Taso, trabajador de la caña.* Río Piedras: Ed. Huracán.

Moreno Fraginals, Manuel. 1978. *El ingenio.* 3 vols. Havana: Editorial de Ciencias Sociales.

Moreno Y., Segundo, and Frank Salomon, eds. 1991. *Reproducción y transformación de las so-
ciedades andinas, siglos XVI–XX.* 2 vols. Quito: ABYA-YALA.

Morgan, Edmund S. 1975. *American Slavery, American Freedom: The Ordeal of Colonial Virginia.* New
York: Norton.

Moulian, Tomás. 1997. *Chile Actual: Anatomía de un mito.* Santiago: LOM-ARCIS.

Murphy, Edward L. 1998. "Surviving Development: *Pobladores* and Social Identity in Santiago,
Chile, 1967–1997." M.A. thesis, Georgetown University.

NACLA (North American Congress on Latin America). 1998a. *NACLA Report on the Americas* 32,
1 (July–Aug.): Thematic issue on "Latin American Youth."

———. 1998b. *NACLA Report on the Americas* 32, 2 (Sept.–Oct.). Thematic issue on "Unearthing
Memory: The Present Struggles Over the Past."

———. 2000. *NACLA Report on the Americas* 33, 4 (Jan.–Feb.). Thematic issue on "The Crisis of the
Latin American University."

Nino, Carlos Santiago. 1996. *Radical Evil on Trial.* New Haven: Yale University Press.

Novick, Peter. 1988. *That Noble Dream: The "Objectivity Question" and the American Historical Profession.* New York: Cambridge University Press.

O'Brien, Jay, and William Roseberry, eds. 1991. *Golden Ages, Dark Ages: Imagining the Past in
Anthropology and History.* Berkeley: University of California Press.

Paxton, Robert. 1972. *Vichy France: Old Guard and New Order, 1940–1944.* New York: Columbia
University Press.

Portocarrero, Gonzalo. 1998. *Razones de sangre: Aproximaciones a la violencia política.* Lima: Pon-
tífica Universidad Católica del Perú.

Rabinow, Paul. 1984. Introduction. In Foucault 1984: 3–29.

RHR. 1983. *Radical History Review* 27. Thematic issue on "Colonialism and Resistance," ed. Brooke Larson.

Riquelme, Alfredo. 1999. "Voting for Nobody in Chile's New Democracy." *NACLA Report on the Americas* 32, 6 (May–June): 31–33, 44.

Rodríguez O., Jaime E., ed. 1992. *Patterns of Contention in Mexican History.* Wilmington, De.: Scholarly Resources.

Roseberry, William. 1983. *Coffee and Capitalism in the Venezuelan Andes.* Austin: University of Texas Press.

——. 1989. *Anthropologies and Histories: Essays in Culture, History, and Political Economy.* New Brunswick: Rutgers University Press.

——. 1993. "Beyond the Agrarian Question in Latin America." In Cooper et al. 1993: 318–68.

——. 1994. "Hegemony and the Language of Contention." In Joseph and Nugent 1994b: 355–66.

Scarano, Franciso. 1984. *Sugar and Slavery in Puerto Rico: The Plantation Economy of Ponce, 1800–1850.* Madison: University of Wisconsin Press.

——. 1988. "Las huellas esquivas de la memoria: Antropología e historia en *Taso, trabajador de la caña.*" In Mintz 1988: 9–48.

——. 1996. "The Jíbaro Masquerade and the Subaltern Politics of Creole Identity Formation in Puerto Rico, 1745–1823." *American Historical Review* 101, 5 (Dec.): 1398–1431.

Schroeder, Michael J. 1998. "The Sandino Rebellion Revisited: Civil War, Imperialism, Popular Nationalism, and State Formation Muddied Up Together in the Segovias of Nicaragua, 1926–1934." In Joseph, LeGrand, and Salvatore 1998: 208–68.

Schwartz, Stuart B. 1978. "Indian Labor and New World Plantations: European Demands and Indian Responses in Northeastern Brazil." *American Historical Review* 83 (Feb.): 43–79.

——. 1985. *Sugar Plantations in the Formation of Brazilian Society: Bahia, 1550–1835.* New York: Cambridge University Press.

Scott, James C. 1976. *The Moral Economy of the Peasant: Rebellion and Subsistence in Southeast Asia.* New Haven: Yale University Press.

——. 1985. *Weapons of the Weak: Everyday Forms of Peasant Resistance.* New Haven: Yale University Press.

——. 1990. *Domination and the Arts of Resistance: Hidden Transcripts.* New Haven: Yale University Press.

Scott, Joan Wallach. 1986. "Gender: A Useful Category of Historical Analysis." *American Historical Review* 91, 5 (Dec.): 1053–75.

——. 1988. *Gender and the Politics of History.* New York: Columbia University Press.

Scott, Rebecca J. 1985. *Slave Emancipation in Cuba: The Transition to Free Labor, 1860–1899.* Princeton: Princeton University Press.

——. 1994. "Defining the Boundaries of Freedom in the World of Cane: Cuba, Brazil, and Louisiana after Emancipation." *American Historical Review* 99, 1 (Feb.): 70–102.

——. 1998. "Race, Labor, and Citizenship in Cuba: A View from the Sugar District of Cienfuegos, 1886–1909." *Hispanic American Historical Review* 78, 4 (Nov.): 687–728.

Serulnikov, Sergio. 1999. "Customs and Rules: Bourbon Rationalizing Projects and Social Conflicts in Northern Potosí during the 1770s." *Colonial Latin American Review* 8, 2 (Dec.): 245–74.

Shapere, Dudley. 1964. "The Structure of Scientific Revolutions." *The Philosophical Review* 73: 383–94.

Skidmore, Thomas E. 1979. "Workers and Soldiers: Urban Labor Movements and Elite Responses in Twentieth-Century Latin America." In Bernhard 1979: 79–126, 141–56.

———. 1998. "Studying the History of Latin America: A Case of Hemispheric Convergence." *Latin American Research Review* 33, 1: 105–27.

Skidmore, Thomas E., and Peter H. Smith. 1997. *Modern Latin America.* 4th ed. New York: Oxford University Press.

Spalding, Karen. 1970. "Social Climbers: Changing Patterns of Mobility among the Indians of Colonial Peru." *Hispanic American Historical Review* 50, 4 (Nov.): 645–64.

———. 1972. "The Colonial Indian: Past and Future Research Perspectives." *Latin American Research Review* 7, 1 (spring): 47–76.

———. 1973. "Kurakas and Commerce: A Chapter in the Evolution of Andean Society." *Hispanic American Historical Review* 53, 4 (Nov.): 581–99.

———. 1976. *De indio a campesino: Cambios en la estructura social del Perú colonial.* Lima: Instituto de Estudios Peruanos.

———. 1984. *Huarochirí: An Andean Society under Inca and Spanish Rule.* Stanford: Stanford University Press.

Starn, Orin. 1999. *Nightwatch: The Politics of Protest in the Andes.* Durham: Duke University Press.

Stearns, Peter. 1983. "Social and Political History." *Journal of Social History* 16, 3: 366–82.

Stein, Stanley J. 1957. *Vassouras, A Brazilian Coffee County, 1850–1900: The Role of Planter and Slave in a Changing Plantation Society.* Cambridge: Harvard University Press.

Stern, Stern J. 1982. *Peru's Indian Peoples and the Challenge of Spanish Conquest: Huamanga to 1640.* Madison: University of Wisconsin Press.

———. 1987a. "New Approaches to the Study of Peasant Rebellion and Consciousness: Implications of the Andean Experience." In Stern 1987b: 3–25.

———. 1988. "Feudalism, Capitalism, and the World-System in the Perspective of Latin America and the Caribbean." *American Historical Review* 93, 4 (Oct.): 829–72.

———. 1992. "Paradigms of Conquest: History, Historiography, and Politics." *Journal of Latin American Studies* 24 (quincent. supp.): 1–34.

———. 1993. "Africa, Latin America, and the Splintering of Historical Knowledge: From Fragmentation to Reverberation." In Cooper et al. 1993: 3–20.

———. 1995. *The Secret History of Gender: Women, Men, and Power in Late Colonial Mexico.* Chapel Hill: University of North Carolina Press.

———, ed. 1987b. *Resistance, Rebellion, and Consciousness in the Andean Peasant World, Eighteenth to Twentieth Centuries.* Madison: University of Wisconsin Press.

———, ed. 1998. *Shining and Other Paths: War and Society in Peru, 1980–1995.* Durham: Duke University Press.

Stoler, Ann Laura. 1995. *Race and the Education of Desire: Foucault's History of Sexuality and the Colonial Order of Things.* Durham: Duke University Press.

Taylor, William B. 1972. *Landlord and Peasant in Colonial Oaxaca.* Stanford: Stanford University Press.

———. 1974. "Landed Society in New Spain: A View from the South." *Hispanic American Historical Review* 54, 3 (Aug.): 387–413.

———. 1979. *Drinking, Homicide, and Rebellion in Colonial Mexican Villages.* Stanford: Stanford University Press.

———. 1985. "Between Global Process and Local Knowledge: An Inquiry into Early Latin American Social History, 1500–1900." In Zunz 1985: 115–90.

Thompson, E. P. 1963. *The Making of the English Working Class.* New York: Vintage.

———. 1967. "Time, Work-Discipline, and Industrial Capitalism." *Past and Present* 38 (Dec.): 56–97.

———. 1971. "The Moral Economy of the English Crowd in the Eighteenth Century." *Past and Present* 50: 76–136.

Thomson, Sinclair. 1999. " 'We Alone Will Rule . . . ': Recovering the Range of Anticolonial Projects among Andean Peasants (La Paz, 1740s to 1781)." *Colonial Latin American Review*, 8, 2 (Dec.): 275–99.

Tinsman, Heidi. 1997. "Household *Patrones*: Wife-Beating and Sexual Control in Rural Chile, 1964–1988." In French and James 1997: 264–96.

Tutino, John. 1986. *From Insurrection to Revolution in Mexico: Social Bases of Agrarian Violence, 1750–1940.* Princeton: Princeton University Press.

Urbano, Henrique, ed. 1991. *Poder y violencia en los andes.* Cuzco: Centro 'Bartolomé de las Casas.'

Valdés, Teresa, and Marisa Weinstein. 1993. *Mujeres que sueñan: Las organizaciones de pobladoras en Chile, 1973–1989.* Santiago: FLACSO.

Van Young, Eric. 1981. *Hacienda and Market in Eighteenth-Century Mexico: The Rural Economy of the Guadalajara Region, 1675–1820.* Berkeley: University of California Press.

———. 1983. "Mexican Rural History Since Chevalier: The Historiography of the Colonial Hacienda." *Latin American Research Review* 18, 3: 5–61.

———. 1990. "To See Someone Not Seeing: Historical Studies of Peasants and Politics in Mexico." *Mexican Studies/Estudios mexicanos* 6, 1 (winter): 133–59.

———. 1992. "Mentalities and Collectivities: A Comment." In Rodríguez O. 1992: 337–53.

———. 1993. "The Cuautla Lazarus: Double Subjectivities in Reading Texts on Popular Collective Action." *Colonial Latin American Review* 2: 3–26.

———. 1999. "The New Cultural History Comes to Old Mexico." *Hispanic American Historical Review* 79, 2 (May): 211–47.

———. 2001. *The Other Rebellion: Popular Violence and Ideology in the Mexican Struggle for Independence, 1810–1821.* Stanford: Stanford University Press.

Vaughan, Mary Kay. 1982. *The State, Education, and Social Class in Mexico.* DeKalb: Northern Illinois University Press.

———. 1997. *Cultural Politics in Revolution: Teachers, Peasants, and Schools in Mexico, 1930–1940.* Tucson: University of Arizona Press.

Verbitsky, Horacio. 1996. *The Flight: Confessions of an Argentine Dirty Warrior*, trans. Esther Allen. New York: The New Press.

Viotti da Costa, Emilia. 1982. *Da senzala à colônia.* (1966). 2d rev. ed., São Paulo: Livraria Editora Ciências Humanas.

———. 1989. "Experience versus Structures: New Tendencies in the History of Labor and the Working Class in Latin America—What Do We Gain, What Do We Lose?" *International Labor and Working-Class History* 36 (fall): 3–24.

———. 1994. *Crowns of Glory, Tears of Blood: The Demerara Slave Rebellion of 1823.* New York: Oxford University Press.

Walker, Charles F. 1999. *Smoldering Ashes: Cuzco and the Creation of Republican Peru, 1780–1840.* Durham: Duke University Press.

Weinstein, Barbara. 1983. *The Amazon Rubber Boom, 1850–1920.* Stanford: Stanford University Press.

———. 1989. "The New Latin American Labor History: What We Gain." *International Labor and Working-Class History* 36 (fall): 25–30.

———. 1996. *For Social Peace in Brazil: Industrialists and the Remaking of the Working Class in São Paulo, 1920–1964.* Chapel Hill: University of North Carolina Press.

Wells, Allen, and Gilbert M. Joseph. 1996. *Summer of Discontent, Seasons of Upheaval: Elite Politics and Rural Insurgency in Yucatán, 1876–1915.* Stanford: Stanford University Press.

White, Michael, and John Gribbin. 1994. *Einstein: A Life in Science.* New York: Penguin/Dutton.

Wightman, Ann M. 1990. *Indigenous Migration and Social Change: The Forasteros of Cuzco, 1570–1720.* Durham: Duke University Press.

Winn, Peter. 1986. *Weavers of Revolution: The Yarur Workers and Chile's Road to Socialism.* New York: Oxford University Press.

Wolf, Eric R. 1982. *Europe and the People without History.* Berkeley: University of California Press.

———. 1986. "The Vicissitudes of the Closed Corporate Community." *American Ethnologist* 13, 2 (May): 325–29.

Wolfe, Joel. 1993. *Working Women, Working Men: São Paulo and the Rise of Brazil's Industrial Working Class, 1900–1955.* Durham: Duke University Press.

Womack, John, Jr. 1968. *Zapata and the Mexican Revolution.* New York: Alfred Knopf.

———. 1986. "The Mexican Revolution, 1910–1920." In Bethell 1986: 79–153.

Wood, Peter H. 1974. *Black Majority: Negroes in Colonial South Carolina from 1670 through the Stono Rebellion.* New York: Knopf.

Woodward, C. Vann. 1974. *The Strange Career of Jim Crow.* 1955; 2d rev. ed. 1966. 3d rev. ed., New York: Oxford University Press.

Zunz, Olivier, ed. 1985. *Reliving the Past: The Worlds of Social History.* Chapel Hill: University of North Carolina Press.

II

The Contestation of Historical Narratives
and Memory

▼

Barbara Weinstein

The Decline of the Progressive Planter and the
Rise of Subaltern Agency: Shifting Narratives
of Slave Emancipation in Brazil

▼

The central themes in the historical narrative of Brazilian abolition have
shifted dramatically over the past two decades. One only has to compare
the chapter in Emilia Viotti da Costa's *The Brazilian Empire* (1985) on "Masters and Slaves" (which both drew on and refined arguments first articulated in *Da senzala à colônia*, 1966) with George Reid Andrews's chapter on
abolition in his *Blacks and Whites in São Paulo, Brazil* (1991) to appreciate the
striking changes in emphasis.[1] Groups that figure prominently in Viotti da
Costa's narrative—new urban social classes attracted to abolitionism and
new sectors of the planter elite—barely appear at all in Andrews's account.
Instead, Andrews, on the one hand, follows the work of José Murilo de
Carvalho, emphasizing the role of the emperor and his advisers.[2] On the
other hand, he draws on monographs by Robert Brent Toplin and Warren
Dean to highlight the role of the slaves, who increasingly are portrayed as
"freeing themselves."[3] Furthermore, this trend parallels similar developments in the historiography of Cuban emancipation, as exemplified by
Rebecca Scott's thoroughgoing critique of Manuel Moreno Fraginals's materialist explanation of abolition in Cuba, and her emphasis on the slaves'
roles in accelerating the process of emancipation.[4]

This new interpretive trend in Brazil typically positions itself as a two-
part critique of the marxist historiography produced in the 1960s. One
object of criticism is that historiography's alleged tendency to focus on the
role of the slaveholding elites and to retain the notion that a progressive
segment of the planter class voluntarily embraced abolition. The other is
the implicit or explicit view that the slaves themselves could not develop the
necessary consciousness to seek their own liberation. Thus there is the oft-

cited (and oft-reproached) contention by Fernando Henrique Cardoso, in *Capitalismo e escravidão*, that "the real and profound nature of slavery would remain inaccessible to the consciousness of the slave."[5] Later historians of slavery and emancipation have been quick to take their predecessors to task for such views, but rarely acknowledge that Viotti da Costa, Cardoso's contemporary, was the first to describe in detail the massive escapes by slaves during the final years of slavery, and the role these protests played in dismantling the slave system.[6]

What also tends to be lost in these critiques is a careful differentiation of the 1960s literature from an earlier and resolutely apologetic or self-congratulatory historiography. Prior to the marxist-inflected works of Viotti da Costa, Cardoso, Florestan Fernandes, Octávio Ianni, and others, there were two deeply rooted scholarly and popular narratives of Brazilian abolition. One was an extension of the argument that Brazilian slavery was unusually benign and humane (compared to the U.S. South or the Caribbean), and therefore the gradual, peaceful process of abolition was all of a piece with the nature of Brazilian slavery itself. The humanitarian gesture of Princeza Isabel, the Brazilian Emperor's daughter and signer of the Golden Law that abolished slavery, was foreshadowed in the mildness and flexibility of the master-slave relationship.[7] The other—an extension of São Paulo's *bandeirante* mythology that informed the construction of *paulista* identity during the early twentieth century—celebrated the progressive, entrepreneurial spirit of the São Paulo coffee planters, portrayed as reluctant slaveholders, eager to free themselves and their slaves from the burdens of such a backward institution.[8]

The marxist-influenced historiography of the 1960s, in contrast, specifically challenged the persistent notion that Brazilian slavery was mild or humane compared to slavery elsewhere. The studies of Viotti da Costa et al. emphasized and detailed the exhausting work routines, physical abuses, and psychological pain that Brazilian slaves suffered, and also chronicled various forms of slave protest that counter persistent images of slave passivity.[9] Clearly, in these works abolition could not be understood as a logical extension of the slaveholder's humanity. Perhaps even more important for the historiography of Brazilian abolition, these scholars reconceptualized the figure of the progressive planter. While Viotti da Costa and Cardoso did identify certain slaveholders as more disposed toward making the transition from slave to free labor than others, they did not attribute this to a particularly moral disposition or a peculiarly enlightened mentality. Instead, their emphasis was on structural and conjunctural factors.[10] Long-term shifts in technology, demography, markets, and social structure made slavery either incompatible with new production processes (in the case of Cardoso, and Moreno Fraginals for Cuba) or less economically attractive (in the case of Viotti da Costa). The ostensibly progressive behavior of the *paulista* planters reflected not the *bandeirante* spirit, but the historical context and moment in which they entered the coffee export economy.

A subsequent generation of historians would fault such structuralist approaches for their tendency to make historical processes the result of impersonal forces, to separate the economic sphere from the social realm, and to occlude the issue of agency.[11] Yet that was precisely a feature of this interpretation that made it attractive to a generation of critical, left-wing Brazilian scholars. It allowed them to explain the relatively unconflictual emancipation process in Brazil without recapitulating the story of a humanitarian emperor or an enlightened planter class. Rather, from this structuralist perspective, to the extent that planters embraced the abolitionist cause, it was to advance a new set of class and material interests. It was the amoral (if not immoral) forces of capitalist development, not moral compunctions about slave labor among elite Brazilians, that prepared the ground for the "peaceful" abolition of slavery.[12]

As noted above, much of the recent historiography of Brazilian abolition has taken this interpretation to task on several counts. I would here cite three separate but interlocking arguments regarding abolition that have characterized this latest wave of slavery studies. Warren Dean, in his influential study of slavery in São Paulo, *Rio Claro*, argued that *paulista* coffee planters continued to purchase slaves whenever available, virtually up to the moment when slavery was definitively abolished. In other words, even the supposedly progressive planters only stopped resorting to slave labor when they were forced to do so, an argument that closely echoes Rebecca Scott's findings with regard to the western sugar plantations in Cuba.[13] A second argument is found in the work of José Murilo de Carvalho, and especially in his volume of essays *Teatro de sombras*. Murilo de Carvalho contends that the planter class (and its spokespersons) remained resolutely committed to slavery well into the 1880s, and that the gradual abolitionist process was the consequence of foreign (i.e., British) pressure and the monarchy's growing commitment to ending slavery. In Murilo de Carvalho's view, it was precisely because the imperial government maintained a relative autonomy from the planter class that it was able to implement a process of gradual abolition despite planter opposition.[14]

Finally, there is the increasingly popular argument that the slaves themselves were active and important agents in the process of abolition. Recent works have both highlighted the massive desertions of coffee plantations in São Paulo during the final years of slavery—a phenomenon that certainly helped to accelerate the process of abolition—as well as the more micro-level struggles of slaves to exploit the evolving legal apparatus to secure individual freedom and intensify the pressure on slaveholders. In *Rio Claro*, Warren Dean conjectured that the effective closing of the slave trade in 1850, and the consequent increase in the proportion of Brazilian-born slaves, meant that the slaves began to formulate a notion of themselves as citizens with certain legal rights.[15] Sidney Chalhoub, Hebe Mattos de Castro, Maria Helena Machado and others have then cited this new identity as the basis for struggles by slaves, both within and outside the existing juridical structure, to secure their emancipation.[16]

The appeal of this new narrative of slave emancipation is so obvious as to hardly require explanation.[17] For a generation of historians raised on "history from the bottom up," and on social and cultural histories that privilege resistance, transgression and contestation, there is a predictable preoccupation with showing that slaves were not passive beneficiaries of abolition but actively asserted their aspirations for freedom and autonomy.[18] In constructing this argument, historians have not only foregrounded the often courageous and sophisticated strategies of enslaved Brazilians during the final decades of slavery, but have also bolstered their claims about slave agency by insisting on the continual resistance of the slaveholding elites to abolitionist initiatives. Thus abolition, far from occurring in a peaceful and consensual fashion, is now portrayed as involving various forms of conflict—both juridical and violent—during the decades prior to the end of slavery.[19]

To be sure, for historians still interested in the enterprise of explanation, this emphasis on slave agency can be problematic since it can help us understand the acceleration of the emancipation process, but not the entire course of gradual emancipation in Brazil. In that sense, Murilo de Carvalho's contention about the role of the emperor and imperial bureaucrats in the process of abolition perfectly complements the narratives that emphasize slave agency. Both support a historical interpretation that removes any and all credit for abolition from the planter elite and instead emphasizes the obdurate resistance of the slaveholding classes to emancipation.

Not only have the historians who emphasize slave agency tacitly articulated their arguments to those of Murilo de Carvalho regarding the positive, autonomous role of the imperial government, but they have also implicitly or explicitly sought to diminish the significance of the (white) abolitionist leadership in the antislavery movement. Abolitionists are portrayed in recent studies as intimately linked to the slaveholding elite. They are criticized for a self-congratulatory view of emancipation that tended to conceal the active role of slaves in antislavery struggles and exaggerate slave dependency, and they are scorned for racist biases that led them not only to see slavery as a backward institution, but the (black) slaves themselves as a cause of backwardness and disorder.[20] Sidney Chalhoub, for example, ends a recent article on epidemics and public health in nineteenth-century Rio with a quote from Ruy Barbosa, a leading abolitionist and participant in the first Republican government, that demonstrates Ruy's strong prejudices against the Afro-Brazilian population and in favor of promoting (white) European immigration.[21] From this perspective, the abolitionists are associated more strongly with the transition to explicitly "scientific" racist modernizing attitudes under the First Republic (founded a mere eighteen months after the passage of the Golden Law) than with the glorious emancipation of the slaves.

In most respects I would heartily agree with this new perspective on abolition and its meanings. But I would like to raise two objections or reservations, one briefly and the other at greater length. First, the brief objection. As I have argued elsewhere, there has been a growing (and I would say disturbing) tendency among historians of postcolonial Brazil to rehabilitate, or even romanticize, the condition of subaltern groups under the Empire.[22] This questionable tendency is certainly encouraged by a narrative of slave emancipation that attributes the abolitionist impulse "from above" to the imperial government and consistently identifies the republican movement with diehard slavocrats and racists. The result is to bolster a view of the First Republic as an era when conditions for subaltern groups deteriorated when compared to Brazil under the Empire.[23]

To be sure, the history of the Old Republic is replete with episodes that attest to its authoritarian, racist, and repressive character, and one would hardly want to return to an older narrative of Brazilian history that regarded the transition from monarchy to republic as an inevitable and laudable step forward in the march of national progress. But the notion of imperial Brazil as somehow a golden age for the popular classes seems to imply either that slavery, as an institution, was a marginal aspect of that society, or that Brazilian people of color were so devastated by the forces of modernity that they were somehow better off living in a slave society.[24] Instead of making this rather tortuous argument, I think it would be more interesting to consider in greater detail what it meant—socially, politically and culturally—for Brazil to cease being a slave society, and what impact the end of slavery had, not only on ex-slaves, but on the subaltern classes in general.[25] In any case, one need not rehabilitate the Empire, an era when slavery was the central institution in Brazilian society, in order to highlight the failings of the First Republic.

Now for the more elaborate objection, which has to do with the recent historiography's deconstruction of the myth of the progressive planter, and this figure's transformation from a cautious but rational champion of gradual emancipation to a stalwart defender of slavery. Gone is the implication, present in most of the comparative slavery literature, that this progressive planter was quite different from his counterpart in the antebellum (U.S.) South. For example, David Brion Davis, in his most recent discussion of this question, declared that "until 1887, when the slaves took matters into their own hands, the Paulista fazendeiros were as hostile as Mississippi planters to the most moderate antislavery proposals."[26] True, he does admit a few lines earlier that "unlike American planters of the Old [U.S.] Southwest, [the paulistas] were not ideologically committed to slavery as a permanent system." But the subsequent conclusion of the paragraph indicates that Davis regards this as a trivial qualification.

While I by no means wish to resurrect the stereotype of the progressive paulista planter, I do want to argue that this qualification is not entirely trivial, and that drawing equivalencies between paulista fazendeiros and Mississippi planters renders the history of abolition in Brazil unintelligible. Moreover, the distinctions that I propose to draw between Brazilian slavocrats and Southern planters cannot be reduced to a question of timing. Rather, I would argue that for much of the nineteenth century, Brazilian slaveholders, or their spokesmen, adopted a very different set of justifications for slavery and consistently indicated that slavery should not constitute a permanent feature of the emerging Brazilian nation. While it might be tempting to dismiss this difference as trifling since it hardly resulted in the rapid abolition of slavery in Brazil, I do think it had significant consequences, including the absence of massive armed conflict over the slavery question, and the construction of racial hierarchies that were less rigid and less fraught with violence than in other white-supremacist societies.[27]

Obviously, the very way in which I am posing the problem is comparative in nature. And by doing this I am, to some extent, bucking the current tide in the field of slavery studies. Recent years have seen a decline in explicitly comparative research on slavery as historians have become more critical of the literature's structuralist orientation and its tendency to create normative and anomalous historical cases.[28] And as our histories of slavery become richer and more detailed, it has become ever more difficult to control the variables across different societies. Not that the study of slavery has become more parochial—the conspicuous and salutary influence of Rebecca Scott's research on Cuba among Brazilian scholars indicates otherwise.[29] But as historians have shifted their emphasis to micro-studies of slave agency, and have collapsed the various slaveholding elites into a unitary figure who only foreswears slave-ownership under great duress (Mississippi planters = *paulista fazendeiros*), one of the key objectives of comparative slavery research—to draw contrasts across different slave-holding societies—has become obsolete. My point, then, is that we have overhomogenized the slave-owning elites and their political representatives, and the best way to counteract this is to resurrect the comparative method. I also contend that we can dispense with the enhanced and apologetic image of the Brazilian planter class without denying all differences between the spokesmen for Brazilian slaveholders and those of the antebellum U.S. South who led their region into an insanely bloody civil war rather than give up slavery.

In a classic work of comparative slavery, *The World the Slaveholders Made*, Eugene Genovese casually raised an issue that directly relates to the central concern of this essay. He cited as an important distinction between Southern planters and Brazilian slaveholders the absence of what has been called a "positive-good" pro-slavery argument among the latter. Despite seeing this difference as significant, Genovese wasted little time in trying to puzzle out its causes; instead, he briefly speculated that it was due to the influence in Brazil of Catholicism, which always associated enslavement with sin, thereby supposedly preempting any notion of slavery as a positive good.[30]

A few years after reading Genovese's provocative study, I had occasion to read the 1826–27 slave trade debates in the Brazilian Chamber of Deputies. Among the most startling aspects of these debates was the almost complete consensus on the evils of the slave trade, as well as widespread commentary on the evils of slavery itself (indeed, many of the speakers slipped in the course of their speeches from referring to the slave trade to referring to slavery).[31] Even the few vigorous defenses of the slave trade/slavery (which, for obvious reasons, were much more likely to be elided in Brazil than in the United States) were made on purely pragmatic/materialist grounds. At no point was there any sort of moral or philosophical defense of the slave trade and slavery, despite the very real threat to slave-owners' interests posed by the imperial treaty with Britain.

Instead, Raymundo José da Cunha Matos, secretary in perpetuity of the Sociedade Auxiliadora da Indústria Nacional (an agricultural association), protested that the impending abolition of the slave trade would "cause enormous harm to national commerce," would "destroy agriculture, the vital foundation of our people's existence," would be "a cruel blow to state revenues," and would be "premature."[32] To be sure, these were all serious concerns for the Brazilian elites, but not the basis for a permanent commitment to a slave-based economic and social order or a compelling moral vision for an emerging Brazilian nation.[33] Moreover, Cunha Matos felt obliged to preface these objections with the following statement: "I am in no way proposing to defend the justice and eternal convenience of the commerce in slaves for the Brazilian Empire: I would not fall into the unpardonable absurdity of supporting in today's world and in the midst of the top-ranking intellects of the Brazilian nation, a doctrine that is repugnant to the enlightened men of this century, and that contradicts generally accepted philanthropic principles."[34] Cunha Matos is referring to the slave trade, not slavery, but it is impossible to read this description of the trade without hearing implications for slavery itself—and this from one of the few avid defenders of the slave trade in the Chamber of Deputies.

Of course, such attitudes did not imply that these deputies (with a few interesting exceptions) were contemplating the abolition of slavery in the near future. After all, the imperial minister, José Bonifácio, had recently been forced into exile for pressing the issue of abolition.[35] And it might be argued that the 1820s were an unusual period that reflected the liberalizing impulses of a recently independent nation (analogous to the brief period following U.S. independence when Southern slaveholders expressed relatively critical views about slavery).[36] Just a decade later, in response to widespread political turbulence and social unrest, there was a marked conservative turn in Brazilian politics which, together with the coffee boom that began in the 1840s, served to harden the defense of slavery. (Thus, for example, Bernardo Pereira de Vasconcelos went from being a liberal, mildly antislave trade deputy to a deeply conservative and vocal apologist for slavery).[37]

Yet even in the midst of this conservative turn, pro-slavery advocates resorted to what seem, in comparative terms, to have been "weak" arguments. Pereira de Vasconcelos and his ilk argued that slavery was, at least for the time being, crucial to Brazil's increased participation in the world market and to the maintenance of the country's precarious social order. And while much has been written about the slaveholders' use of liberal notions of property to defend their ownership of slaves, this is an even weaker argument given the recent abolition of slave property in the resolutely liberal British Empire, and the widespread acknowledgement that property rights were not absolute.[38] The private property argument was a strong basis on which to claim indemnification, but a shaky basis for defending slavery as a permanent, or even long-term, institution. Finally, while it is well known that intense British pressure bore most of the responsibility for the effective termination of the slave trade in 1850, it should still be noted that no Brazilian deputy attempted to mount a moral defense of the slave trade (or slavery itself) in the debates that led to the passage of

the Queiróz Law.[39] From the mid-nineteenth century on, those public figures still actively supporting slavery in Brazil treated it as a necessary evil.[40]
As Eugene Genovese argued, in Brazil "slavery was defended as economically necessary and traditionally sanctioned, but no one argued with any
discernible conviction that it was a good thing in itself or the proper
condition of the laboring classes." Or as Robert Brent Toplin put it, "the
major arguments expressed to support slavery in Brazil in the era of the
abolitionist campaign aimed not to defend the institution as a positive
good but to extend its life."[41]

The contrast between these "weak" justifications and the "strong" arguments expressed by the Southern slaveholders from the 1820s on is difficult
to exaggerate. Far from defending their ownership of slaves through a
recourse to liberal notions of property rights or a forecast of economic
collapse, the Southerners based their claims on the alleged immorality of
free-market capitalism and the inhumanity of a labor system in which
relations between employer and employee were mediated solely by the
profit motive. Slavery, in contrast (argued the Southern slavocrats), assured
propertyless dependents of a master's protection and created a harmonious relationship between capital and labor. To take one of many such
comments from the writings and speeches of John C. Calhoun: "Many in
the South once believed that [slavery] was a moral and political evil; that
folly and delusion are gone; we see it now in its true light, and regard it as
the most safe and stable basis for free institutions in the world."[42]

In a similar vein, James Hammond, a leading politician and planter in
South Carolina, favorably compared the status of slaves in the South with
that of free laborers in the North: "The difference between us is that our
slaves are hired for life and well compensated; there is no starvation, no
begging, no want of employment among our people, and not too much
employment either. Yours are hired by the day, not cared for, and scantily
compensated, which may be proved in the most painful manner, at any
hour in any street in any of your large towns. Why, you meet more beggars
in one day, in any single, street of the city of New York, than you would
meet in a lifetime in the whole South."[43] In short, these men were publi-
cists, not apologists, for slavery and had crafted notions of race and status
that created a permanent place for slavery in Southern society.

It is not that Brazilian slaveholders and politicians were immune to
concerns about the new forms of poverty or social conflicts that a fully
capitalist society might entail. But such concerns were usually manifested
in calls for a very gradual and orderly transition to free labor, rather than in
claims that slavery was the best possible foundation for the construction of
the Brazilian nation.[44] There were, to be sure, the occasional, partial excep-

tions. As late as 1870 Peixoto de Brito published a tract that portrayed slavery as a "beneficent tutelage," and argued that the slave "knows nothing of the bitterness of misery and begging."[45] Similarly, during the slavery debates in the Brazilian parliament, one deputy declared himself a "slavocrat to the core" and suggested that "slavery ought to be maintained for the love of the slaves themselves." Yet, the very same deputy also avowed that "no one reputes slavery to be a good and virtuous institution," while another leading pro-slavery politician publicly declared slavery "a cancer" on Brazilian society.[46] In Brazil, unlike the U.S. South, even slavery's most vigorous defenders rarely managed to express their support in unambiguous terms.

When social history was all the rage, many historians were likely to dismiss such comments as empty rhetoric, but in the current era, when scholars tend to take language very seriously, it makes sense to consider more carefully the origins, and the ramifications, of these discursive differences. Some of the implications seem relatively straightforward. For example, in contrast to the U.S. South, there was never any significant effort in Brazil to restrict or roll back the process of manumission.[47] Whereas free blacks increasingly signified a potential challenge to the political order in the South, as well as an implicit criticism of slavery, manumission was perfectly compatible with a defense of slavery as a "necessary evil." Furthermore, steady rates of manumission helped to bolster the Brazilian slaveowners' claims that theirs was a moderate and humane form of slavery.

The "weak" defense of slavery also created a political climate in which experiments with sharecropping and other non-slave-labor arrangements could be applauded rather than denounced for encouraging abolitionist sentiment. Senator Nicolau Vergueiro's efforts to substitute immigrant workers for slaves on his coffee estates in São Paulo, beginning in the 1840s, might have proved unsuccessful but were generally met with praise and occasional public subsidies. These failures may well have reinforced the "necessary evil" argument, as planters concluded that free immigrant brokers were less adaptable to the plantation work routine than slaves, but they did not foreclose all discussion of alternative sources and forms of labor.[48]

Again, questions of manumission and experiments with free labor are concrete and tangible manifestations of the divergent discursive tendencies of slaveholders in Brazil and the U.S. South. Exploring the origins and broader ramifications of their discursive differences requires a greater degree of speculation, and perhaps even counterfactual reasoning. As noted earlier, Genovese casually attributed the absence of a "positive good" argument in Brazil to the influence of Catholicism, since Catholic doctrine associated slavery with sin and the freeing of slaves with Christian charity. One might also conjecture that the less-rigid racial attitudes of the Brazilian elite, and the more fluid racial categories that characterized Brazilian society, complicated any attempts to create formal, permanent distinctions between whites and blacks in the manner that the "positive good" argument implied.[49]

I think a more compelling and historically specific factor, however, was the appeal of modernity to Brazilian elites, and the strong association between slavery and backwardness in the Brazilian intellectual milieu from the early nineteenth century on. While the concept of underdevelopment would not appear for another century, Brazilian politicians and essayists in the first half of the nineteenth century already characterized their homeland as backward in terms of technology, culture, wealth, and power compared to those societies where mechanization and industrialization were advancing productivity, efficiency, and national prestige. This close and persistent association between progress and free labor, reinforced by Brazil's own apparent backwardness and repeated subjection to Britain's will, made it extremely difficult for defenders of slavery to find a position from which to construct positive arguments for building a nation on the basis of slave labor.[50]

The appeal of modernity, however, could cut more than one way. After all, the quickest route to Brazil's full insertion in the modern world economy, to "progress," was the expansion of export-oriented production—a process that, in the short run, seemed to make slavery an even more necessary evil. Some echoes of our contemporary scholarly confusion over whether to regard slavery as a precapitalist social formation or as a labor system that was modern and industrial in character can be found in the planter discourse of the nineteenth century.[51] Thus the dominant discursive tendency was to argue pragmatically for a slave-labor regime until the conditions were ripe for a transition to free labor. While such arguments did not serve to uncouple slavery from backwardness, they did help the slaveholding interests to postpone the actual transition from slave to free labor.

A full discussion of why nineteenth-century Brazilian elites tended to regard their society as backward is beyond the scope of this chapter. There are many possible factors to explain this perspective, including the preponderance of non-whites in the population, the depression in plantation agriculture in the decades following independence, the noncompetitiveness of certain economic sectors, notions about the degenerative effects of tropical climates, their derisive view of the former metropolis (Portugal) on the one hand, and their rapid subordination to British commercial hegemony on the other.[52] In any case, this sense of backwardness, and the strong association of free labor with progress, made it difficult, and perhaps impossible, to construct a vision of their nation's future in which slavery constituted a permanent (and positively good) feature of Brazilian life.

Again, this is an argument that can only be sustained within a comparative framework. Thus, I am contending by implication (as Genovese did many years ago) that the "positive good" argument was the *sine qua non* of emergent Southern (U.S.) nationalism.[53] It both fortified the Southern planter class with an anticapitalist worldview that shielded it from mounting abolitionist criticism and increasingly hegemonic liberal notions of progress, and made them more confident in their appeals to non-slaveholding whites. Southern planters, politicians, and intellectuals also had the luxury of constructing an antimodernist (and anti-Northern) discourse even as they enjoyed the technological, financial, military, political, and commercial resources created by a rapidly modernizing nation. It has become a commonplace to explain the Southerner's extreme pro-slavery sentiment as a response to intensifying attacks from abolitionist Northerners. The contiguous presence of a modernizing, non-slaveholding society supposedly made it all the more pressing for the Southern planter class to erect a strong defense of slavery. But one could argue, in a different vein, that the South's association with the North (indeed, their common national boundaries until the outbreak of the Civil War) also enabled the formation of an aggressive pro-slavery worldview by masking or minimizing certain backward features of other slave-plantation societies.[54] This unusual set of circumstances made it possible for white Southerners to imagine a national community that had slave-ownership as one of its foundational characteristics.

In the late 1860s, as Brazil began to consider concrete measures for the gradual abolition of slavery, Senator José Tomaz Nabuco de Araújo inquired of his colleagues in the Brazilian parliament, "How can Brazil, isolated and the only one of its kind on the globe, resist the pressure of the entire world?" Yet another senator declared, "The eyes of the world are upon us, judging us barbarians, savages."[55] Two more decades would pass before Brazil would finally and definitively abolish slavery, but these statements vividly illuminate the failure of the Brazilian elites to construct an alternative national identity that would allow for a vigorous defense of human bondage. Unlike the antebellum Southern planters (who clearly did not rely on references to Brazil and Cuba to defend slavery as a normative institution), the Brazilian elites could not "resist the pressure of the entire world," either discursively or politically. Indeed, by the 1860s, slavery in Brazil was so thoroughly identified with backwardness in some circles that a senator could invert the usual association of slaves with barbarity and rhetorically label the slaveholders as barbarians.

Let me reiterate that this association of slavery with backwardness intensified even as the coffee planters were eagerly buying up additional slaves for their highly profitable plantations. As noted above, several recent works have cited this continuing enthusiasm for slave purchases as unimpeachable proof that the *paulista* planters were just as anxious to defend and retain slavery as their antebellum Southern counterparts. But the issue here is not whether slavery continued to be profitable at the micro-level, which it surely did, but whether the outlook of the *paulista* planters can be determined simply by summing up their individual economic decisions.[56] I have argued elsewhere that the identity of a social class is not equivalent to the sum of its parts, and this argument would surely hold for the *paulista* planters, whose numbers included a significant cohort of politicians and essayists who were increasingly self-conscious about, and critical of, their region's position within the Brazilian nation. For these men, the question was not only whether slavery was profitable, but whether it could form a firm and enduring basis for a prosperous, progressive, and cohesive society. Even before the Rio Branco Law (1871) made abolition inevitable, many of these men would have answered the question in the negative.

Yet if the association of slave labor with backwardness, and free labor with progress, did not prevent Brazil from being the very last nation in the Western Hemisphere to abolish slavery, what significance can I claim for this argument? Why not just endorse the politically satisfying scenario of slaves acting as agents of their own liberation in the face of stubborn resistance from reactionary slavocrats? After all, we are living in an intellectual age when few historians would regard themselves as engaging in scientific inquiry or in discovering something we could call objective truth. So why should I bother with this argument unless it has some significant interpretive value?

There are many different perspectives from which to answer this question about significance. One is explicitly counterfactual. That is, we might consider the weak ideological defense of slavery as accounting, in part, for the *relatively* nonviolent course of emancipation in Brazil. While virtually every study attributes the definitive abolition of the African slave trade to British pressure, it is worth speculating whether Britain would have declared a full-scale war against Brazil had Brazilian elites chosen to defy the British on this matter. Their rapid acquiescence to the British, despite the widespread conviction that the end of the traffic would inexorably lead to the end of slavery, certainly tells us something about the attitudes of Brazilian elites on this question a full decade before the outbreak of the U.S.

Civil War. In a similar vein, there were no concerted efforts by slaveholding elites to organize violent campaigns against abolitionists or to suppress all abolitionist opinions in their midst. One student of Brazilian abolitionism has contended that many of the leading abolitionists had intimate ties to the planter class—a point she makes to underscore the limited potential for radical social critique among Brazilian abolitionists.[57] But we could also reverse her contention to underscore the relative tolerance of Brazilian slaveholders for abolitionist activities (relative, of course, to the much more repressive southern U.S. planters).

I do not, however, want to make too much of this counterfactual conjecture; it is not my intention to add "Why was there no Civil War in Brazil?" to such hoary questions as "Why was there no French Revolution in Britain?" or "Why is there no socialism in the United States?" For I believe my argument gives us insight into what did happen, as well as what did not. I would claim, for example, that the relatively weak pro-slavery sentiment laid the groundwork for rapid transition to free labor in São Paulo, rather than a resort to some form of quasi-slavery or apartheid-like labor system. At the same time, it reinforced racist notions that associated free, efficient labor with European immigrants rather than with African, Afro-Brazilian, or Chinese workers.[58]

This very qualified rehabilitation of the progressive planter also helps us to understand the overlap in ideas between the *paulista* republicans, with their roots in the regional agrarian elites, and the *jacobin* republicans of the urban areas. While it is well known that the more-radical republicans were extremely critical of the *paulistas'* failure to take an early, forceful stance on the abolition question, this did not necessarily indicate dramatically different notions of what had to be done to modernize Brazil. From this perspective, it becomes much more difficult to reduce the fall of the monarchy and the installation of the First Republic to a reactionary impulse on the part of *paulista* planters, bitterly resentful of the emperor's failure to protect their property rights—an odd argument, but one that has gained some currency in the recent literature.[59]

Again, most of the historians who have foregrounded the slaves' role in the process of abolition have argued, as a corollary, that earlier claims about the elites' cooperation in the abolitionist process have been false or exaggerated. Yet we hardly need to construct an image of the Brazilian planters as uniformly committed slavocrats to admire the creative and courageous maneuvers of Brazilian slaves to gain their freedom. Even more important, unless we take into account the declining credibility of slavery as an institution even among the most powerful segments of Brazilian society, we cannot explain why slave agency was so often successful rather than suicidal.[60] And we might also want to reconsider what has become for some historians a "natural" sympathy among the "grateful" ex-slaves for the benevolent monarchy.[61]

My last point has to do with the broader historiography of slavery and abolition. As I noted at the outset, the structuralist or materialist explanation for the decline of slavery (exemplified in its more extreme form by the work of Manuel Moreno Fraginals and Fernando Henrique Cardoso) has been roundly criticized and shown in several respects to be incompatible with the empirical evidence. Instead, historians have tried to understand the process of abolition within specific geographic and societal contexts, and have revived the idea of abolition as a sociopolitical process. But it is useful to recall that one of the features of the structuralist approach that gave it credibility to an earlier generation of historians was its apparent ability to explain a process that was occurring in many different places at once. After all, abolition did not just occur in one or two locations; chattel slavery, which had been a significant feature of every New World society, had become by the late nineteenth century an illegitimate and illegal institution in every corner of the hemisphere. Yet the fine-grained political and social narratives that we find in studies such as Rebecca Scott's or Sidney Chalhoub's provide us with little means to understand the near simultaneity of the decline of slavery throughout the New World.

To be sure, scholars have suggested alternative arguments to explain this global trend, including Britain's international antislavery campaign (prompted by the hegemonic pretensions of British liberals) and rising demands for citizenship and democratic rights inspired by the French and Haitian revolutions.[62] To these factors I would add the emergence of the modern nation-state, an entity widely imagined in a way that made it incompatible with the institution of slavery. In this respect I think we should regard the U.S. South as anomalous: the antebellum Southerners were uniquely successful in crafting a national imaginary that legitimated slavery as a permanent institution. Elsewhere in the hemisphere, the rise of nation-states seems to have been a powerful force in undermining slavery, and we might say the same about serfdom in Europe.[63] Moreover, if we shift away from Benedict Anderson's elite-centered view of how nations are imagined and take into account popular visions as well, we have an approach that allows us to ask how the abolition of slavery could encompass both elite yearnings for modernity and progress, and subaltern aspirations for greater rights and dignity.[64]

Notes

1 Emilia Viotti da Costa, *Da senzala à colônia* (São Paulo: Ciências Humanas [1966] 1982); "Masters and Slaves," in *The Brazilian Empire: Myths and Histories* (Chicago: University of

Chicago Press, 1985), 125–71; George Reid Andrews, *Blacks and Whites in São Paulo, Brazil, 1888–1988* (Madison: University of Wisconsin Press, 1991), 25–53. *The Brazilian Empire* is the revised English edition of *Da monarquia à república: Momentos decisivos* (São Paulo: Ed. Grijalbo, 1977).

2 See, especially, José Murilo de Carvalho, "A política da abolição: O rei contras os barões," in *Teatro de sombras: A política imperial* (São Paulo: Edições Vértice, 1988), 50–83.

3 Robert Brent Toplin, *The Abolition of Slavery in Brazil* (New York: Atheneum, 1971); Warren Dean, *Rio Claro: A Brazilian Plantation System, 1820–1920* (Stanford: Stanford University Press, 1976).

4 Rebecca Scott, *Slave Emancipation in Cuba* (Princeton: Princeton University Press, 1985). Scott directly influenced a new generation of historians of slavery in Brazil when she was a visiting Fulbright lecturer at the University of Campinas in 1986. For a marxist-structuralist approach to Cuban emancipation, see Manuel Moreno Fraginals, *The Sugarmill* (New York: 1979).

5 "O sentido real e profundo da escravidão teria, contudo, de permanecer inaccessível à conciência escrava." Fernando Henrique Cardoso, *Capitalismo e escravidão: O negro na sociedade escravocrata do Rio Grande do Sul* (São Paulo, 1962), 219. See also Octávio Ianni, *As metamorfoses do escravo: Apogeu e crise da escravatura no Brasil meridional* (São Paulo: 1962), and Florestan Fernandes, *A integração do negro na sociedade de classes*, 2 vols., 3d ed. (São Paulo: Ed. Atica, 1978). Viotti da Costa's *Da senzala à colônia* would usually be included in this historiographical tendency, but I would argue that it provides a more complex portrait of slaveholders, abolitionists, and the slaves themselves than the comparable works by Cardoso, Fernandes, and Ianni (who were not trained as historians). For a brief discussion of this "school" of slavery studies, see Suely Robles Reis de Queiróz, "Escravidão negra em debate," in Marcos Cezar de Freitas, org., *Historiografia brasileira em perspectiva* (São Paulo: USF/Contexto, 1998), 106–7.

6 Viotti da Costa, *Da senzala à colônia*, 311–19.

7 The classic text for this narrative is, of course, Gilberto Freyre, *The Masters and the Slaves: A Study in the Development of Brazilian Civilization* (New York: Knopf, 1946), first published in Portuguese in 1933.

8 The *bandeiras* were expeditions that departed from São Paulo to the interior of Brazil during the 17th century to capture Indians for enslavement and to search for precious minerals. In the early twentieth-century, *paulista* historians began portraying the men who participated in these colonial expeditions, the *bandeirantes*, as risk-taking proto-entrepreneurs, and as the source of São Paulo's "difference" from the rest of Brazil. For examples of the *bandeirante* myth, see Paulo Prado, *Paulística: História de São Paulo* (São Paulo, 1925) and Alfredo Ellis Jr., *Raça de gigantes* (São Paulo: Novíssima, 1926). For a critique, see Barbara Weinstein, "Region vs. Nation: São Paulo and the Formation of Brazilian National Identity" (forthcoming, Duke University Press).

9 See, especially, Viotti da Costa, *Da senzala à colônia*, 219–313. The most stalwart defense of the structuralist school is Jacob Gorender, *A escravidão reabilitada* (São Paulo: Ed. Atica, 1990), but his insistence on treating slavery almost exclusively as a "mode of production," and his preposterous attack on recent studies of slave community and subjectivity, sharply reduce the value of his work for serious scholars. Indeed, Gorender actually ends up underestimating the value and impact of the "structuralist" school he so vigorously defends. It was precisely the structuralists' effective dismantling of the notion of Brazilian slavery as unusually benign that has allowed subsequent historians of slavery the luxury of exploring more nuanced, ironic, and complicated aspects of the master-slave relationship.

10 Viotti da Costa, "Masters and Slaves," 159–61.

11 Viotti da Costa, however, emphasized that human beings make history, even though "they do it within determined conditions." *Da senzala à colônia*, xxvii. For a careful discussion of this historiography which recognizes certain crucial contributions made to slavery studies by these scholars while critiquing the structuralist tendency to treat the economic and the social separately, see Sílvia Hunold Lara, *Campos de violência: Escravos e senhores na capitania do Rio de Janeiro, 1750–1808* (Rio de Janeiro: Paz e Terra, 1988), chap. 4.

12 Indeed, Viotti da Costa discerns a broad consensus among *paulista* planters that slavery should be eliminated rather than prolonged only beginning in the mid-1880s. It is then that she notes that "the adherence of this group to the idea of free labor made the final victory of abolition possible in Parliament and explains in great part the relatively peaceful character of the movement" ("Masters and Slaves," 161).

13 Dean, *Rio Claro*; see also Andrews, *Blacks and Whites*, 38–39. The debate between Viotti da Costa and Dean over the early experiments with free labor (in the 1840s–50s) is not merely reflective of different statistical calculations. Viotti da Costa's emphasis on the structural conditions (high transport costs, low prices) that made wage labor unfeasible at that moment mirrors her assumption that planters would have embraced whichever system of labor was most profitable. Dean's claim that a more prolonged commitment on the planters' part would have eventually yielded higher profits reflects his contention that the planters irrationally clung to slave labor even when free labor would have been more lucrative. See Dean, *Rio Claro*, 106; and Viotti da Costa, "Sharecroppers and Plantation Owners: An Experiment with Free Labor," *The Brazilian Empire*, 94–124.

14 Murilo de Carvalho, *Teatro de sombras*. Illustrative of his tendency to locate the state outside of the planter class is the following quote: "Abolition, understood as the combination of public policies which gradually led to the extinction of slavery, constitutes a privileged vantage point from which to examine the relations between the government, i.e., the King and his bureaucrats, and the class of rural landowners. . . . At no other moment, and on no other issue, was the opposition between the motives and interests of the bureaucratic pole of power [the state] and the interests of the social and economic pole of power [the planters] so clear." Cited in Andrews, *Blacks and Whites*, 274 n. 20. For a different view of the relationship between planters and the state, see Richard Graham, *Patronage and Politics in Nineteenth-Century Brazil* (Stanford: Stanford University Press, 1990).

15 According to Dean, by the 1860s slaves "had absorbed the rhetoric of egalitarianism and citizenship" (*Rio Claro*, 127).

16 Sidney Chalhoub, *Visões da liberdade* (São Paulo: Companhia das Letras, 1990); Hebe M. Mattos de Castro, *As cores do silêncio: Os significados da liberdade no sudeste escravista* (Rio de Janeiro: Arquivo Nacional, 1995); Maria Helena Machado, *O plano e o pânico: Os movimentos sociais na década da abolição* (Rio/São Paulo: Editora UFRJ/Edusp, 1994); Keila Grinberg, *Liberata: A lei da ambiguidade* (Rio de Janeiro: Relume-Dumara, 1994); Maria Angélica Zubarán, "Slaves and Contratados: The Politics of Freedom in Rio Grande do Sul, Brazil, 1865–1888," Ph.D. diss., SUNY at Stony Brook, 1998. For a study of Peruvian emancipation that emphasizes slave agency (even in the title), see Carlos Aguirre, *Agentes de su propia libertad: Los esclavos de Lima y la desintegración de la esclavitud, 1821–1854* (Lima: PUC/Fondo Editorial, 1993).

17 In her conclusion to *O plano e o pânico*, published in 1994, Maria Helena Machado laments that "abolition, as a rule, has been, in recent years, treated exclusively as an event produced solely by the elites and for the elites, with no participation by the interested

parties, that is, the slaves, the freedmen and the poor freemen." I'm not sure that was even accurate in 1994; certainly today, no reputable scholar would portray abolition as exclusively an elite project.

18 Here I would cite the influence of Stuart Schwartz's studies of slavery. Although his main works focus on the colonial period, and therefore do not deal with emancipation, they have had a major impact on new approaches to issues of slave resistance and negotiation. See, especially, "Resistance and Accommodation in Eighteenth-Century Brazil: The Slaves' View of Slavery," *Hispanic American Historical Review* 57, 1 (Feb. 1977), 69–81.

19 See especially Célia Marinho de Azevedo, *Onda negra, medo branco: O negro no imaginário das elites* (Rio de Janeiro: Paz e Terra, 1987).

20 Célia M. Marinho de Azevedo, "On Hell and Paradise: Abolitionism in the United States and Brazil, a Comparative Perspective," Ph.D. diss., Columbia University, 1993, and "Brother or Enemy: Views of the Slave by American and Brazilian Abolitionists," paper presented at the eighth Jornada de Estudos Americanos (ABEA), Rio de Janeiro, June 20, 1998. This latter paper drew a dramatic contrast between the North American abolitionists, portrayed as involved in a constant effort to empathize with the slaves, and the Brazilian abolitionists, who are dismissed as having "hardly any sentiment of empathy toward the slave." So what should we make of the following passage from Joaquim Nabuco's classic text *O abolicionismo?*: "The worst side of slavery is not its great abuses and passions, nor its terrible retributions, nor even the death of the slave. It is, rather, the daily pressure which slavery imposes on the slave: his constant fear for himself and his family; his dependence upon the goodwill of the master, the spying and treachery which surround him, forcing him to live forever shut up in a prison of Dionysius, whose walls repeat every word, each secret confided to another, and, even worse, each thought which he may unintentionally reveal in the expression of his face. It is said that among us slavery is mild and the masters are good. The truth is, however, that all slavery is the same, and the goodness of the masters depends upon the resignation of the slaves." Personally, I find it hard to imagine a more empathetic (and less condescending) passage written by a white abolitionist. This is not to deny that Nabuco elsewhere expressed racist attitudes toward the slaves, but it does prompt one to ask why Marinho de Azevedo would be so eager to characterize virtually all Brazilian abolitionists as so much more racist, and so much less empathetic, than their U.S. counterparts.

21 Sidney Chalhoub, *Cidade febril: Cortiços e epidemias na corte imperial* (São Paulo: Cia. das Letras, 1996), 57; also, "The Politics of Disease Control: Yellow Fever and Race in Nineteenth-Century Rio de Janeiro," *Journal of Latin American Studies* 23, 3 (Oct. 1993): 441–63. Ruy lamented the impact of yellow fever, which devastated European immigrant communities but left Brazilians of African "blood" almost untouched, "giving us, in the eyes of the civilized world, the air of a slaughterhouse for the white race" (Ibid., 463).

22 Barbara Weinstein, "Not the Republic of Their Dreams: Historical Obstacles to Political and Social Democracy in Brazil," *Latin American Research Review* 29, 2 (1994): 262–73.

23 Dain Borges, at the November 1997 BRASA meetings (Washington, D.C.), during a panel on key conjunctures in Brazilian history, gave an intriguing presentation on the transition from monarchy to republic. He argued, in effect, that most popular groups (artisans, people of color) experienced a worsening in their quality of life with the transition from empire to republic. But this contention implies, at the very least, that the existence of slavery during all but the last eighteen months of the Empire was inconsequential for subaltern groups except, perhaps, for the slaves.

24 The classic study of the impact of slavery on free non-slaveholders is still Maria Sylvia de Carvalho Franco, *Homens livres na ordem escravocrata* (São Paulo: Ed. Atica [1969] 1974).

25 One interesting attempt to do this for São Paulo is the chapter "Immigration" in Andrews, *Blacks and Whites in São Paulo*, 54–89.

26 David Brion Davis, *Slavery and Human Progress* (Oxford: Oxford University Press, 1984), 292, emphasis added.

27 While Anthony Marx makes a similar argument, I think he got his causality backwards. He claims that Brazil never developed an apartheid-like regime because there were no major violent conflicts within the white population (in comparison to the Civil War in the United States and the Boer War in South Africa). But I would argue that there were no major conflicts in Brazil precisely because white attitudes about race and the social order were already different. See Anthony W. Marx, *Making Race and Nation: A Comparison of South Africa, the United States, and Brazil* (Cambridge: Cambridge University Press, 1998).

28 A few recent exceptions are Steven Hahn, "Class and State in Postemancipation Societies: Southern Planters in Comparative Perspective," *American Historical Review* 95, 1 (1990): 75–98; Azevedo, "On Hell and Paradise"; Marx, *Making Race and Nation*.

29 Among recent works on Brazilian slavery that reveal some influence from Scott's work, I would cite Chalhoub, *Visões da liberdade*, and Machado, *O plano e o pânico*.

30 Eugene D. Genovese, *The World the Slaveholders Made* (New York: Pantheon, 1969).

31 On Brazilian antislavery writings in the decades following independence, see Viotti da Costa, *Da senzala à colônia*, 325–40, and Azevedo, *Onda negra, medo branco*, 37–42.

32 *Anais da Camara*, July 3, 1827, p. 21.

33 A knee-jerk response might be that slavery could not be made compatible with a moral vision, but both slaveholding and non-slaveholding whites in the U.S. South would have disagreed. On non-slaveholders' support for the slave order, see Stephanie McCurry, *Masters of Small Worlds: Yeoman Households, Gender Relations, and the Political Culture of the Antebellum South Carolina Low Country* (Oxford: Oxford University Press, 1995).

34 Ibid., 12.

35 See Viotti da Costa, "José Bonifácio de Andrada e Silva: A Brazilian Founding Father," in *Brazilian Empire*, 24–52.

36 On post-independence liberalism in Brazil, see Viotti da Costa, "Liberalism," in *Brazilian Empire*, 53–77; and Roderick Barman, *Brazil: The Forging of a Nation, 1798–1852* (Stanford: Stanford University Press, 1988).

37 Alfredo Bosi, "A escravidão entre dois liberalismos," *Estudos Avançados* 2, 3 (1988): 6–8. On the conservative turn in Brazilian politics in the 1840s, see Ilmar Rohloff de Mattos, *O tempo saquarema* (São Paulo: Hucitec, 1987).

38 Bosi ("A escravidão entre dois liberalismos") makes a sharp distinction between the oligarchic liberalism (with its emphasis on property rights) of the early nineteenth century and the reformist liberalism of the later nineteenth century, but I think his approach understates the continuities.

39 The classic study of this is Leslie Bethell, *The Abolition of the Brazilian Slave Trade: Britain, Brazil, and the Slave Trade Question, 1807–1869* (Cambridge: Cambridge University Press, 1970). Even more than in the 1820s, the rapid growth of the coffee economy, and the continued inability of slaves to reproduce their numbers, meant that the abolition of the slave trade would ineluctably move Brazil to other sources of labor besides African slaves. Again, the slave trade and slavery are not easily separable issues in Brazil. Maria Stella Bresciani observes that in the state of the province speeches delivered by the presidents of São Paulo from 1850 to 1858, slavery "shifted from being an accepted and practiced labor arrangement to a condemned and practiced one" ("Liberalismo: Ideologia e controle social," Ph.D. diss., University de São Paulo, 1976, 1: 123).

40 Toplin, *Abolition of Slavery*, has an entire chapter, "The Defense of Slavery" (131–44), that

echoes many of the points I raise here. But he insists that the Rio Branco Law of 1871 (also known as the Law of the Free Womb) was the event that derailed the formulation of a "positive good" argument in Brazil, whereas my contention is that at no point in the nineteenth century were the climate and conditions in Brazil conducive to such an argument.

41 Genovese, *World the Slaveholders Made*, 131; Toplin, *Abolition of Slavery*, 131.

42 Eric L. McKitrick, ed., *Slavery Defended: The Views of the Old South* (Englewood Cliffs, N.J.: Prentice-Hall, 1963), 81.

43 Ibid., 123.

44 Viotti da Costa, in "Masters and Slaves," notes: "Contrary to what happened in the United States, no one dared to make an outright doctrinaire defense of [Brazilian] slavery in the second half of the nineteenth century" (163).

45 Cited in Viotti da Costa, *Da senzala à colônia*, 349–50.

46 Toplin, *Abolition of Slavery*, 132.

47 On the increasing restrictions, and even elimination, of legal manumission in the antebellum South, see Ira Berlin, *Slaves without Masters* (New York: Random House, 1974).

48 Viotti da Costa, "Sharecroppers and Plantation Owners."

49 While we need to be careful not to overstate the fluidity of race relations in nineteenth-century Brazil, the French traveler Charles Expilly (in the 1860s) commented that the Brazilian slaveholders "do not feel themselves obliged, like their American colleagues, to invent for the Negro a new original sin, nor to erect a system of absolute distinction between the races, nor to place an insurmountable barrier between the offspring of descendants of slaves and those of free men" (*Le Brésil tel qu'il est* [Paris: Charlieu et Huillery 1862]). This carefully measured assessment of racial attitudes in Brazil hardly identifies it as a racial democracy, but does point out some important contrasts with the U.S. South.

50 Viotti da Costa (*Da senzala à colônia*, 340) emphasizes that the concern (in these early critiques of slavery) was not so much with the slave as a human being, but with the problem of slavery from the perspective of the dominant class. See also Iraci Galvão Salles, *Trabalho, progresso, e a sociedade civilizada* (São Paulo: Hucitec, 1986).

51 On the tension between slavery as a premodern/precapitalist system and as a modern/proto-industrial system, see Paul Gilroy, *The Black Atlantic: Modernity and Double Consciousness* (Cambridge, Mass.: Harvard University Press, 1993), 220–22.

52 It should be noted that had Brazilian elites constructed their national self-image purely with reference to other emerging Latin American nations, the conclusions might have been different given Brazil's relative stability and prosperity during the first half of the nineteenth century. But I would argue that North America and western Europe (minus Iberia) already functioned as normative categories. On Brazil's technological backwardness, see Richard Graham, "Slavery and Economic Development: Brazil and the United States South in the Nineteenth Century," *Comparative Studies in Society and History* 23, 4 (1981): 620–55.

53 See, particularly, the essay on George Fitzhugh, "The Logical Outcome of the Slaveholders' Philosophy," in Genovese, *World the Slaveholders Made*, 118–244. Also on proslavery ideology and southern nationalism, see Drew Gilpin Faust, *The Creation of Confederate Nationalism: Ideology and Identity in the Civil War South* (Baton Rouge: Louisiana State University Press, 1988), and Faust, ed., *The Ideology of Slavery: Proslavery Thought in the Antebellum South, 1830–1860* (Baton Rouge: Louisiana State University Press, 1981).

54 On the relative modernity of southern U.S. agriculture, see Richard Graham, "Slavery and Economic Development."

55 Cited in Toplin, *Abolition of Slavery*, 42.

56 There is considerable disagreement over the profitability issue. Some historians argue that slavery was less profitable than free labor, but that autocratic habits prompted planters to continue buying slaves; others argue that slavery was indeed more profitable than free labor under the circumstances. See Viotti da Costa, "Masters and Slaves," 266 n. 36.

57 Azevedo, "On Hell and Paradise."

58 On the rejection of Chinese immigrants as replacements for slaves, see Jeffrey Lesser, *Negotiating National Identity: Immigrants and the Struggle for Ethnicity in Brazil* (Durham: Duke University Press, 1999), 13–39. This widely shared negative attitude toward Chinese laborers contrasts with the more pragmatic view of Cuban slaveholders, who first confronted this issue as a colonial elite with few nationalist aspirations. Evelyn Hu-DeHart, "Neither Black nor White, Neither Slave nor Free: Chinese Coolie Workers in Ninteenth-Century Cuba," unpublished paper.

59 Murilo de Carvalho, *Teatro de sombras*, 78–79; Andrews, *Blacks and Whites*, 52. José Murilo de Carvalho traces his argument back to Stanley Stein's *Vassouras: A Brazilian Coffee County, 1850–1900* (New York: Atheneum, [1958] 1970) which describes former slaveholders rushing to join the Republican Party once slavery was abolished. But the relationship between abolition and the fall of the Empire is much more complex, especially since many of the leading figures in the overthrow of the monarchy were longtime supporters of abolition. See Viotti da Costa, "Fall of the Monarchy," in *Brazilian Empire*, 202–33.

60 Here I am echoing Viotti da Costa's often reiterated point that human beings may make history, but they cannot make it any way they please. See, for example, "Experience versus Structures: New Tendencies in the History of Labor and the Working Class in Latin America—What Do We Gain? What Do We Lose?" *International Labor and Working-Class History* 36 (fall 1989): 3–24, and *Da senzala à colônia*, xxvii. My argument about the openings created for slave agency with limited violent retaliation by planters would also apply to the Cuban case.

61 Andrews, *Blacks and Whites*, 43–45.

62 See David Brion Davis, *The Problem of Slavery in the Age of Revolution, 1770–1823* (Ithaca: Cornell University Press, 1975); Robin Blackburn, *The Overthrow of Colonial Slavery, 1776–1848* (London: Verso, 1988); Seymour Drescher, "Brazilian Abolition in Comparative Perspective," *Hispanic American Historical Review* 68, 3 (1988): 429–60.

63 Benedict Anderson, *Imagined Communities* (London: Verso, 1983). Here I would disagree with Prasenjit Duara, who cites southern (U.S.) nationalism to underscore his claim that scholars have erroneously associated the nation with modernity. But I think this is problematic in its underestimation of the modern aspects of Southern society, which, I argue, made it possible to imagine a nation with slavery as a permanent institution. Duara, "Historicizing National Identity, or Who Imagines What and When," in Geoff Eley and Ronald Grigor Suny, eds., *Becoming National* (New York: Oxford University Press, 1996), 171–72.

64 For a study of slave rebellion that examines the intricate relations between slave consciousness and reformist discourses within the white community, see Viotti da Costa, *Crowns of Glory, Tears of Blood: The Demerara Slave Rebellion of 1823* (New York: Oxford University Press, 1994).

Mary Ann Mahony

A Past to Do Justice to the Present:
Collective Memory, Historical Representation,
and Rule in Bahia's Cacao Area

▼

Elite identity and concerns about legitimacy have influenced discussions of
the history of Bahia's cacao area strongly during the twentieth century.
Over the course of the century, they have helped to shape and reshape a
narrative about the founding and early growth of the cacao area, and about
the origins of the cacao elite. Briefly, this narrative tells the story of hardworking men struggling to farm the frontier in the nineteenth century. It
goes on to chronicle the careers of the few who succeeded in becoming
wealthy, and thus members of the elite in the twentieth century. Finally it
presents twentieth-century cacao society as a very unusual one for Brazil:
one dominated by self-made men who had never had access to slave labor
rather than by aristocratic plantation owners who had ruled over large
numbers of slaves. Portions of this narrative have been challenged, but it
remains the one most frequently found in published accounts of regional
history, and the dominant version recounted by southern Bahian elites.

This tradition is an origin myth that tells the story of the birth of the
cacao economy and the formation of its regional elite. Like most historical
myths, it is a narrative that aims to explain and to justify the past, but which
also attempts to explain and justify the present.[1] From the beginning this
myth has served as a weapon in the cacao elite's ongoing struggle for local,
regional, and national power and legitimacy. Over time it has helped to
justify horrific land and income concentration, to obscure racial dispari-
ties, to defend elite opposition to land reform, labor organizing, and rural
labor regulations, as well as to add force to elite appeals for federal assistance in troubled times.

This tradition was not invented, at least not out of whole cloth.[2] Cacao elites, government officials, scientists, and intellectuals did not make it up, although at various times they helped to shape it, to disseminate it, and to make it the dominant paradigm of regional history. It grew out of the actual experiences and concerns of a group of nouveau riche cacao elites at the beginning of the twentieth century, and it can be substantiated through documents, published studies, local tradition, or memories. But it is only a partial, exaggerated reflection of the complex history of the cacao region. It creates a false impression of the past because it focuses on one portion of the region's history and one element of the regional elite to the exclusion of others. This chapter traces the process through which this tradition developed, how it related to elite political concerns, and how, over time, it was transformed into collective memory and history.[3] As we will see, it was, and was not, a conscious process, but it was always related to the cacao elite's sense of itself and its understanding of local, regional, and national issues affecting the region.

From Timber, Staples, and Sugar to Cacao: Ilhéus to the 1880s

Throughout the colonial period and during the first two-thirds of the nineteenth century, what is today southern Bahia produced timber, food crops, and some rum and sugar, largely for consumption in Salvador, the provincial capital, but also for export. During the colonial period, Jesuits, bureaucrats, and European colonists introduced coffee and cacao, the chief ingredient in chocolate, and by about 1800, southern Bahian farmers were growing and exporting small quantities of both crops each year.[4] Over the course of the next six decades, the economy grew significantly, and by 1870 cacao had emerged as the region's most important crop. By 1890 cacao was one of Brazil's most important exports, and Bahia was the second largest cacao producer in the world. Cacao had not only supplanted sugar, food crops, and coffee, but had pushed the agricultural frontier west from the coast, expelling the region's indigenous people as it moved.

Several different groups of people were responsible for this process, including aristocratic sugar planters from the Recôncavo, European settlers, impoverished migrants from northeastern Brazil, African slaves, and residents of Ilhéus of all social classes. The sugar planters, European settlers, and some others had slaves and capital available to them in the new endeavor, but most cacao farmers did not. That, however, was the beauty of cacao in nineteenth-century Bahia: people who wanted to grow it did not need a large amount of capital or large numbers of laborers to begin. Thus, sugar planters with their capital tied up in mills and slaves, as well as farmers with a few day laborers and the rural poor, could all cultivate some:

how much they could plant depended upon the amount of labor and capital to which they had access. Therefore, of the hundreds of cacao plantations in southern Bahia by 1880, some were very large and very well established, with more than 100,000 trees, owned by wealthy families with sugar mills, sawmills, and groves of coffee. Others were in a middle group of perhaps 5,000 to 10,000 trees, while most were small and fairly marginal, with perhaps 1,000 trees and little else. Slaves labored on all of the very large estates, most of the medium-sized ones and some of the small ones as well.[5]

The few large planters with mills and slaves in Ilhéus played a much more important role in the development of the local economy during the nineteenth century than their small numbers would suggest. Their key position grew out of the refusal of Bahia's merchants to deal directly with any but the largest, most well established planters. Foreign merchants made exceptions for their compatriots, but few were willing to extend such courtesies to Brazilian planters, no matter what type of crop they cultivated. As a result, throughout Bahia, and indeed Brazil, only planters who had collateral that merchants found attractive—in other words, slaves—were in a position to trade directly with them. Since foreign merchants were also the ultimate source of agricultural credit, this meant that only planters with slaves had direct access to agricultural credit. Thus, in Ilhéus, as in other parts of Bahia, a small number of large estate owners and their relatives with investments in sugar, cacao, timber, and slaves monopolized the trade with Salvador and agricultural credit. They were the principal buyers and sellers of cacao; they provided most of the agricultural credit for cacao planters and farmers; and they were the source of most commercial goods in the region as well.[6]

The invention of milk chocolate in the 1870s, along with abolition and the reform of the debt collection legislation in the 1880s, brought major changes to the cacao region. Most particularly, these new laws broke the hold of the large estate owners over the trade with Salvador and agricultural credit, in addition to liberating labor throughout the northeast to migrate to newer areas if they chose. Merchants in Salvador began to invest more strongly and directly in cacao, no longer limiting their transactions to planters with slaves, and at the same time thousands of people moved to the southern Bahian frontier where they claimed land or went to work for already established farmers. The combination of new capital investment and population growth, along with rising cacao prices, allowed extraordinary expansion in cacao cultivation and exports. Between 1880 and 1920, the region grew from a forested territory with a settled population of some 10,000 souls, slave and free, uncounted hostile Indians, and about five hundred multipurpose agricultural properties of various sizes, to a region of two separate municipalities, more than six thousand cacao plantations, 105,000 residents, and few hostile Indians.[7] In the process, a group of small and mid-sized farmers became wealthy and joined the ranks of the well-to-do in Ilhéus, while those members of the traditional elite who had invested in cacao made a relatively smooth transition from slave to free labor.

Intra-Elite Conflict and Identity in
a Post-Emancipation Society

By 1900 there were two groups of elites in southern Bahia: one made up of aristocratic Brazilian families, and the other composed of nouveau riche families. While both groups were equally wealthy, during this period they did not share anything that might remotely be considered a common identity. Rather than a single class, they represented instead different status groups whose visions of each other were strongly influenced by the notions of social and racial hierarchy inherited from the slave society that had only recently been abolished.[8]

The aristocrats of Ilhéus belonged to some of the most prestigious families in Bahia, including Sá Bittencourt Camara, Cerqueira Lima, Gallo, and Saraiva. One of them, Pedro Augusto Cerqueira Lima, was a member of what had been the most famous slave-trading family in Bahia, if not Brazil. Another, Fortunato Pereira Gallo, was the son of one of Bahia's most important sugar mill owners. Still another, Maria Joaquina de Saraiva, was the sister of one of Emperor Dom Pedro II's most trusted advisers. Although they owned property in Ilhéus and spent some time there each year, their primary residences were in Salvador or Rio de Janeiro.[9]

Local political leadership lay with the Sá Bittencourt Camara family, the only one in the group that lived primarily in Ilhéus. Domingos Adami de Sá and his uncle Ernesto Sá Bittencourt Camara were the turn-of-the-century leaders of a family that had been prominent in Minas Gerais and Bahia since colonial times, when the family had owned gold mines and sugar mills. A great-great-uncle, Dr. João Sá Bittencourt Camara, was the royal judge responsible for overseeing the expulsion of the Jesuits from Bahia in the eighteenth century. Their great-grandfather, Dr. José de Sá Bittencourt Camara, and his brother, Dr. Manuel Ferreira da Camara, had been educated at Coimbra, had participated in the independence movement, and had been influential in the governments of the late colonial and early independence periods. Their fathers and uncles were heroes of the independence wars and had been decorated by the emperor. Their mothers and aunts had been literate, and perhaps even well-educated, at a time when few men and fewer women had such opportunities. Most of them had inherited fortunes from their parents and grandparents based on landed estates created out of the former Jesuit Engenho Santanna—one of the largest and best-capitalized sugar mills in all of colonial Brazil and the most prestigious property in Ilhéus. In the second half of the nineteenth century, some members of the family had moved strongly into cacao, as both planters and traders, while others had remained in sugar. They did not all carry the distinctive Sá Bittencourt Camara surname; they were not all extremely wealthy in the twentieth century; they might not be as well connected politically as their ancestors had been—but they all saw themselves as members of a distinguished Luso-Brazilian family.[10]

The nouveau riche planters, on the other hand, were a very different group. Manuel Misael da Silva Tavares, the son of an unmarried indigenous woman, began his working life as a muleteer and went on to become one of the richest men in Bahia. Miguel José Alves Dias, an Afro-Brazilian, had been a traveling jewelry salesman before he began to buy cacao property. Firmino Alves was a *caboclo* (a person of mixed indigenous and European descent) from the province of Sergipe who had settled on the frontier in the mid-nineteenth century. Henrique Berbert Jr. had been the son of a German immigrant turned small farmer; Ramiro Ildefonso de Araujo Castro was the descendant of colonial settlers of Ilhéus long since turned small farmers; and Virgilio Calasans had worked in his father's shop before beginning to grow cacao. Clearly these men had not been born to prestigious families. Many were of mixed racial heritage, many had been born to parents who had never married, and at least a few were the children of freed slaves. They had inherited neither great wealth, nor elite culture, nor political power.[11] They were, instead, a rougher lot, with little formal education, more comfortable on the farm with a machete and a repeating rifle than in the formal parlor of a city home.

These men did share one common characteristic, however, and that was the tendency to marry young women from well-established local families with middling farms and shops.[12] The leadership of the nouveau riche planters in Ilhéus was all connected by marriage to such women, and in particular to the granddaughters of Henrique Berbert. Born Heinrich Berbert, he had come to Brazil from his native Germany as a child, and by the end of the century he and his two sons, Henrique Jr. and Cypriano Oliveira, had acquired most of a *sesmaria* along the Cachoeira River. Henrique Jr. married the daughter of other German immigrants, while Cypriano married a Brazilian, and like many Brazilian families they developed a branch that was referred to as white and another that was considered black. By the turn of the century, Henrique Jr., his brother, and their wives were among the most important of the nouveau riche planters, and they had arranged marriages for their daughters with some of the most promising young men around: the *caboclo* Tavares for Santinha, the "black" daughter of Cypriano; and the white Ramiro Ildefonso de Araujo Castro, Leopoldo Kruschevsky, and Virgilio and João Calasans Amorim for Henrique Jr.'s white daughters, Libuça, Antonia, Adelaide, and Theodolinda.[13]

While these men became the symbols of social mobility in the region, they were not particularly representative of southern Bahia's lower classes. In 1890 they were literate when 80 percent of the local population was not.[14] They largely came from families with small properties or shops and a few slaves, while the very poor owned nothing of the sort. Yet if they were not destitute before they became rich, when we compare their backgrounds and experiences to those of the leaders of the Adamista Group, all of them begin to look like self-made men: they had not inherited great wealth, they had not owned large numbers of slaves, and they did not have family and other social connections with the other powerful families of Bahia and Brazil.

Not surprisingly, there was tension between the two groups fueled by social and cultural differences, legacies of three centuries of Brazilian slavery and its attendant social hierarchies. The central problem lay in the refusal of Ilhéus's traditional elite to treat the nouveau riche planters as equals—as members of the same social class. They considered the darker complexions, the nonstandard Portuguese, and the rough manners of the nouveau riche planters as indications of their inferiority. They found confirmation of their attitudes, as "old money" often does, in the habits of conspicuous consumption of the nouveau riche planters. To the aristocratic planters, the marks of nouveau riche wealth—the huge, ostentatious houses with monograms above each doorway, the Limoges chamberpots (deemed too pretty and elegant for their intended use) used as flowerpots on the balconies of the new mansions, the pianos in farmhouses where no one knew how to play them—simply showed that these cacao planters were crass.[15] To Bahia's aristocrats the new group might be rich, but that did not save them from being, at best, little more than *caboclo* or mulatto peasants, and at worst, upstart freed slaves with money.

The elite of Salvador shared the attitudes of their Ilhéus cousins toward the nouveau riche cacao planters. When those planters began to appear in Salvador to conduct business, to vacation, to treat their health, to educate their children, or to live, they found the doors to the mansions of Salvador's aristocrats closed. They were not invited to socialize with Bahia's traditional elite, nor were they considered suitable marriage partners for the children of the old aristocratic families. They might have had money, they might have owned new homes in the most prestigious Salvador neighborhoods, but that was not enough to gain them acceptance by Bahia's aristocracy: they had no claim to aristocratic bloodlines, they did not carry important family names, and they were not white. They were part of what elites considered the *povo*.[16]

The disdain that the traditional elite families felt for the nouveaux riches was not based on financial superiority. Many of Bahia's aristocratic families had fallen on hard times when the sugar economy collapsed after abolition. While some families had managed to diversify their holdings and thus preserve and improve their fortunes, as many if not more had been unable or unwilling to do so. But wealthy or impoverished, the members of these families saw themselves as the true Bahian aristocracy. The old city buildings and monuments, reminiscent of Salvador's days as the colonial capital, only seemed to reinforce their belief in their own superiority. By the turn of the century many were looking back with nostalgia on the good old days of slavery and sugar, and viewing progress and the nouveau riche cacao planters who had brought it with some trepidation and disdain.[17]

The nouveau riche cacao planters resented these aristocratic attitudes. They were proud of their achievements, and especially of the wealth and progress they were bringing to their state. As far as they were concerned, they were prospering in a state and in a nation where social mobility was difficult. In the process they were creating a powerful economy in a part of Bahia that the Portuguese and the sugar planters had never successfully developed. Because of their efforts southern Bahia was one of the world's largest producers of cacao, and Ilhéus now boasted mansions, a railroad line, the first elevator outside of the state capital, four movie theaters, and six cabarets. Moreover, in their view, now that sugar had collapsed, it was their cacao that kept the Salvador docks busy and the state solvent, their cacao that made possible the new government buildings, the new thoroughfares, and the new trolleys in Salvador. They believed that their hard work and sacrifice had made this possible, and that it ought to be appreciated.

Rather than push for social acceptance in this state where family alliances and political power merged, they began a campaign to have their voices heard, led by Antônio Pessoa da Costa e Silva. Pessoa, whose round face and high cheekbones suggested an indigenous ancestry, was born in 1864 in Jeremboabo, Bahia, son of a middle-sized planter. As a young man he obtained a legal education by apprenticing himself to a lawyer, never graduating from one of Brazil's prestigious law schools. He went on to practice law as a state prosecutor, first in Victoria da Conquista and Cannavieiras, Bahia, and then in Ilhéus in 1881. In 1883 he lost his position, replaced by a lawyer with a degree, and moved to Ceará for a position in the government there. After a short stint, he returned to Ilhéus to practice law as a spokesman for those individuals and families who opposed Domingos Adami and his allies. After the declaration of the Republic, he emerged as the nouveau riche planters' candidate for mayor and founded a series of newspapers as vehicles for his political ambitions.[18]

In each election between 1893 and 1911, Pessoa ran for mayor, and several of his allies ran for a city council. On at least two occasions they claimed to have won the elections; unfortunately, Adami and his friends made the same claims. It then fell to the state legislature to choose between competing municipal governments. For almost twenty years after the fall of the Empire, it continued to confirm mayors and city councils in Ilhéus associated with the aristocratic planters led by Adami, entirely ignoring the political aspirations of the nouveau riche planters.

The consequences of this political exclusion show why control of city hall was so important. Adami was able to nominate land agents, police officers, and court officials. These appointees showed clear preferences for Adami supporters in surveying lands for new title applications, in court actions over land, in attempts to judicially foreclose on debts, in carrying out postmortem inventories, and in prosecuting criminals. Adami supporters had preferential access to the limited state-sponsored agricultural mortgage program and even to municipal funds. They succeeded in manipulating the initial state plans for railway construction so that the new tracks and stations served the Adamista districts and left out the principal Pessoista planter district. They allowed their relatives in Salvador to set export taxes on cacao at an astronomical 14 percent while retaining a protectionist 1 percent tax on sugar.[19] And finally, they successfully stonewalled efforts by nouveau riche planters to carve a new municipality, Itabuna, out of territory controlled by Ilhéus. As far as the nouveaux riches were concerned, they were being exploited.

Together with the social discrimination they were suffering, this sense that they were being economically and politically abused by Bahia's traditional elites contributed to a growing nouveau riche identity and set the tone for Antônio Pessoa's political campaigns. In his legal briefs and newspaper articles, Pessoa identified his and his allies' enemies as the region's feudal, dictatorial, former slave-owning planters, led by Domingos Adami de Sá and his uncle Ernesto Sá Bittencourt Camara. He called Adami Ilhéus's Emperor Nero; he informed his readers that the Sás had owned large numbers of illegally obtained slaves; and he quipped that if Ernesto Sá was not wealthy, it hadn't been for lack of slaves or inherited resources. He particularly liked to accuse his opponents of manipulating the government on their own behalf, of attacking peaceful *posseiros* farming on the frontier, and of insulting local farmers with racial slurs. At the same time Pessoa presented himself as the defender of the small farmers and the supporter of progress. He emphasized that he and his "coreligionaries" and friends were hard workers who had struggled to earn what they had, and who had succeeded despite their lack of inherited wealth, access to government revenues, or powerful social and political connections. They were self-made men, victimized by the backward-looking authoritarian aristocrats of traditional Bahia.[20] In many ways he and his group made it a matter of pride to be a nobody, a man who worked for a living rather than an aristocrat, accepting the elite's view of them as peasant upstarts but transforming its meaning.

Pessoa's discourse was also a direct appeal for the political support of the hundreds of small and medium-sized farmers struggling to grow cacao on the Ilhéus frontier, and the thousands of impoverished northeastern migrants who were swelling the regional population looking for work. These people were of mixed race, most of them were of humble origins, and some were former slaves. All of them had been raised in northeastern states controlled by slave-owning sugar aristocrats, and all hoped to prosper in cacao. Pessoa's strategy was brilliant: what better way to recruit political support, laborers for plantations, and foot soldiers in the war against the Adamis than to tell the thousands of people from former sugar-producing areas seeking their fortunes in Ilhéus that the Pessoistas were self-made men and that the Adamis and their friends were aristocrats who had once owned many slaves? Pessoa never mentioned that several of the families in his group had once owned slaves themselves (although, granted, many fewer than the Adami group), that the fortunes of many of the self-made men in his party were founded on marriages to women from well-established families or important connections, or that many of them had expanded their holdings by expropriating small farmers in debt. Instead he offered a dream of social mobility that any man who worked hard could replicate.

It would be tempting to suggest that those small farmers and rural workers who joined the Pessoista camp were deluded. But it is more useful to see Pessoa's rhetoric as an appeal to the region's well-to-do "nobodies," and to those "nobodies" who hoped to become well-to-do, to rally against Bahia's traditional elite in the years after abolition and the declaration of the republic. Such appeals reflected the self-perceptions and, to some degree, the realities of a growing group of wealthy cacao planters and merchants who came from nonaristocratic families. It also reflected the aspirations of thousands of new arrivals in Ilhéus who believed that the changes taking place in Brazil were creating opportunities for them on the Bahian frontier.[21]

This Pessoista experience and rhetoric resounded beyond the borders of the cacao area, and even of Bahia. Throughout Brazil social groups representing new economic sectors had emerged during the nineteenth century to challenge traditional aristocrats. The members of these new groups espoused republican ideas during the decades leading up to the 1889 military coup that overthrew the monarchy. They were understandably disappointed when they found that many of the reforms they supported were not implemented, and that many imperial aristocrats had survived the transition to republican government with their privileges and power intact. This was particularly the case in Bahia, the last state to join the republic, where imperial aristocrats had been very strong, where the republican movement was one of the nation's weakest, and where social, racial, and political hierarchies were deeply rooted.[22]

Other elements of Pessoista discourse were not so widely shared, either in Bahia or in Brazil. Pessoa did not explicitly refer to race when describing his supporters, but there was a statement about race in his rhetoric, and his readers and listeners would have understood it. About 80 percent of Ilhéus's population was mestiço, caboclo, or black, and more than two-thirds of the residents of Bahia and other northeastern states were black or mestiço. Although there was no strict color division by class in the northeast, it was generally true that whites and light-skinned mulattos or mestizos tended to belong to the upper classes, while dark-skinned mestiços, mulattos, Indians, or blacks belonged to the lower classes. In the first decades of the 1900s, as today, to speak of northeastern migrants or humble Bahians was by definition to speak of people with dark complexions.[23]

This racial message made Pessoa's rhetoric quite different from that common in Brazil at the time. Supporters of republican reforms did not necessarily believe in racial equality: the intelligentsia of the early republican period was heavily influenced by the tenets of positivism and social Darwinism. Intellectuals and other elites, whether supporters of the monarchy or the republic, believed that Brazil's mixed-race and African population was holding the nation back. To solve the problem, Brazilian planters hoped to encourage European immigrants to come and "whiten" the population. We know a great deal about Paulista efforts to do so; it is less well known that the Bahian sugar elite had the same goals. Their efforts were largely unsuccessful, but their lack of success in drawing thousands of white foreigners to Bahia should not be equated with a lack of interest in such a policy, or taken as evidence that they held more tolerant attitudes toward Afro-Brazilians or other non-whites.[24]

When Pessoa began writing in his newspaper that some of the richest men in Bahia were "products of their own efforts," the Bahian state militia had just finished executing thousands of northeastern peasants who were followers of Antônio Conselheiro.[25] These people were all of mixed Indian, African, and European heritage and came from the same geographic areas as the migrants who went to the cacao area. While there may have been some differences among them, the migrants to Ilhéus, the migrants to Canudos, and the rural poor native to Ilhéus all shared a similar racial heritage.[26] Pessoa's rhetoric, arguing that people of nonaristocratic and, by extension, nonwhite origin had created the most important economy in Bahia, took Bahian, and Brazilian, attitudes about race and class and turned them upside down. Non-whites and poor people had not dragged the state down. To the contrary, they were raising it up.

The Nouveau Riche Planters in City Hall, 1912–30

By 1911, the power of traditional elites in Bahia was eroding, and Pessoa succeeded in winning election to the Bahian Chamber of Deputies. The following year, he and the nouveau riche planters and merchants finally gained control of city hall in Ilhéus when J. J. Seabra, Pessoa's friend and political ally, succeeded in winning the election for governor. Pessoa was elected president of Bahia's Chamber of Deputies, but also took over as mayor. After several years of holding simultaneous local and state office, Pessoa was replaced in city hall by Manuel Misael da Silva Tavares, followed by other supporters, but he remained in the city council and state legislature. The nouveau riche planters did not completely displace the aristocrats, however, since João Mangabeira, the husband of one of Adami's nieces, had been elected to the federal legislature and remained there. Moreover, various members of the Cerqueira Lima clan, although never formally involved in politics, were working hard from Salvador to influence state and national policies affecting their state and their region through the Bahian Agricultural Association.[27] For the first time, both aristocratic and nouveau riche planters had access to political power.

Pessoa's close ties to Bahian governor J. J. Seabra helped him to obtain resources for his district. He used his new influence to obtain a loan for urban improvements in the city of Ilhéus, installing sewers; paving and lighting streets; building parks, schools, and a hospital; and renovating the city slaughterhouse. To showcase these improvements, and to highlight the role of the nouveau riche cacao planters in bringing them, Pessoa commissioned a history of Ilhéus that would "endow the municipality . . . with an index of its most important events in the History of Brazil."[28] The *Memória sobre o município de Ilhéos*, by Francisco Borges de Barros, recounted the early colonial struggles of the Portuguese against the Indians in Ilhéus and the difficulties in establishing a valuable economy there. Most of the text, however, described the substantial progress that cacao had made possible in Ilhéus and the contributions of the nouveau riche planters to cacao cultivation. According to the author, a traveling European had left the first cacao plants with a Cannavieiras planter in 1746. No one had recognized the plant's potential until a group of German settlers began to cultivate it. Later waves of northeastern migrants continued to plant it, such that there had been significant growth in cacao during the nineteenth century. But cacao had only become important after 1890. Because of the vision and hard work of these planters, Ilhéus was now a thriving city with a bustling port and many urban improvements.[29]

This was a political text in a political battle. Throughout the text, progress was associated with cacao, and cacao was associated with the nouveau riche planters and their ancestors. Jesuits, colonial administrators, aristocrats, and slaves had nothing to do with introducing or developing cacao in southern Bahia. Instead, a foreign planter in another town had first planted it, and cultivation only spread when the German colonists and the northeasterners arrived. Among these German settlers, everyone was aware, were the Berberts; among the northeasterners were the Calasans Amorims. Pessoa and Misael Tavares were introduced as "products of their own efforts" and advocates of progress. Domingos Adami and Ernesto Sá were described as men from traditional families who had owned large numbers of slaves. Although many of the more prominent Pessoistas had owned slaves as well, this was never mentioned, and Pessoa was placed at the head of an Ilhéus abolitionist campaign, about which I have been able to find no documentation.[30]

It is hardly surprising that a Bahian historian, contracted by a Bahian mayor to write a history of a Bahian town, should produce work amenable to his patron. It is surprising, however, that the same vision should appear in the work of biologists, agronomists, bureaucrats, and social scientists from other parts of Brazil, from Europe, and from the United States who wrote about southern Bahian cacao in the twentieth century. But just that began to occur when Dutch agronomist Leo Zehntner, the world's foremost expert on cacao at the time, came to southern Bahia to study its cacao farms. Zehntner spent one hundred days between 1909 and 1911 in southern Bahia, contracted by the state of Bahia and the Bahian Commercial Association. The book he wrote based on his research is an informed source on the cacao area around 1910, but its historical section leaves something to be desired, based as it was on interviews with local elites and one text published in 1852. He noted that cacao had been introduced to the region in the middle of the eighteenth century, but by whom he was not sure. He did not think, however, that it had been by Domingos Adami's ancestors. The extended Sá family had made important contributions to the region, but according to his reading, German settlers had played the most significant role in developing cacao in early-nineteenth-century Ilhéus. In another section he noted that most cacao plantations had been founded with no other capital than sweat and hard work.[31] When the text was finally published in Berlin, it was distributed to libraries throughout Europe and North America.

Zehntner began to be quoted almost immediately. In 1917 Brazilian minister of agriculture Miguel Calmon quoted him in a government-sponsored study of cacao, arguing that men with no other capital than the "strength of their arms and the sweat of their brows" had pushed back the hostile forest and established the cacao economy.[32] Calmon was the descendant of generations of Bahian slave owners, and a member of the Bahian Agricultural Association. It is inconceivable that he was unaware of the role that traditional Bahian families with slaves had played in the development of the cacao area, but he failed to mention anything about them. In 1923, while Calmon was still minister of agriculture in the federal government, Affonso Costa, director of the ministry's information section, wrote simply that the cacao economy was the result of tenacious work. Certainly he knew that Bahians from wealthy families had invested in cacao, because some of his data on the cacao trade came from the Cerqueira Lima clan, but he chose not to mention it. Pessoa must have been pleased.

Pessoa's growing influence did not mean that tension between the two groups dissipated. If anything, it became worse in the years after the nouveau riche takeover. Political violence, which had been sporadic in the region since the 1880s, became a regular feature of cacao area life as aristocratic and nouveau riche planters, as well as ambitious newcomers, fought each other as well as the small producers. Disputes over foreclosures, property lines, control of railroad stops, municipal appointments, elections, and family honor boiled over into murders and gun battles. In 1919 a disagreement between two clans based near Siqueiro do Espinho, one associated with the Pessoistas and the other with the Adamistas, erupted into full-blown war when Basílio de Oliveira and the Badaró brothers sent their hired guns and political allies against each other. Small farmers, workers, and bandits joined the armies, and many seem to have taken advantage of the violence to settle old scores growing out of the process of expropriation that had been taking place. Eventually the Ilhéus Commercial Association prevailed upon the governor to send the state militia to put down the violence and occupy the region. By the time the fighting was over, members of both Pessoista and Adamista groups had lost thousands of dollars worth of property.

The battle for Siqueiro Grande, as it came to be known, was a turning point in regional history. The rage of unemployed rural workers and expropriated small farmers that had been unleashed by the clash between elites shocked both groups into realizing that they had common enemies. Given that high interest rates and unstable international prices for cacao were combining to put pressure on all cacao planters at the same time,[33] cacao planters were being forced to recognize that their inability to get along could lead to financial ruin. Increasingly, cooperation rather than competition seemed to be required.

This developing class consciousness was aided by the gradual easing of social tensions. While the first generation of cacao elites came from vastly different worlds, their children did not. The sons of both types of families attended the same boarding schools in Salvador and obtained their law or medical degrees from the same universities, while daughters attended the same convent schools. They all ran into each other on vacation in Rio, in São Paulo, and in Paris. Slowly, nouveau riche families began to intermarry with old planter families, whether from Ilhéus or elsewhere. All in all, the stark social differences between the nouveau riche elites and the traditional elites were fading.[34] This growing alliance did not mean that there were no differences of opinion among them, or that all vestiges of the old rivalry had disappeared. But the new money/old money split was beginning to fade. Cultured sons and daughters of both groups made fun of the behavior of their provincial parents. Pessoa may have begun to accuse Tavares of usury, and any number of people despised Pessoa, but for the most part they had stopped trying to kill one another.

A 1924 publication sponsored by Ilhéus's city government, O livro de Ilhéus: A contribuição do município de Ilhéus ao progreso geral do Estado da Bahia, reflected the new situation. Along with discussions of Ilhéus's social development, agriculture, industry, commerce, and transportation in the 1920s, and pictures of prominent men of both groups, were two essays on regional history. One told of the contributions of Jesuits, colonial administrators, sugar planters, Germans, and northeastern migrants in establishing the cacao area. The other left out all mention of this history except to remind readers that the Sás had stolen two elections from Pessoa. But both agreed that cacao and progress were linked, and neither mentioned that slaves had once planted cacao on southern Bahian plantations and farms.[35]

An Era of Cooperation

By the 1930s, the development of a common elite identity was well under way, encouraged by the most severe economic crisis the planters had yet encountered and by the passing of the generation that had come of age in the years leading up to the declaration of the Republic. Adami and Ernesto Sá were dead, and while Pessoa still carried enormous local influence, increasingly he left day-to-day affairs to his sons and sons-in-law. Moreover, the world market, once the source of great wealth, now seemed bent on destroying them. Overextended planters became rapidly overwhelmed with debt, and the courts filled with foreclosure cases. Rural workers suddenly found their wages cut or their jobs eradicated. They began to organize to change the terms of employment in the countryside, while Indians on the western frontier began to band together to oppose the further expansion of cacao farming.[36]

During this difficult time for cacao planters, a new political alliance brought the university-educated sons of the traditional and nouveau riche planters, particularly the Lavignes and the Berberts, together under one umbrella. Their program, outlined by Ramiro Berbert de Castro and Eusínio Lavigne in several publications, advocated bringing the rule of law to the region; advancing rural and urban education and health care; improving infrastructure, agricultural research, and extension programs; lobbying on behalf of Bahian cacao in foreign capitals; establishing a commodity exchange for cacao with complete information on daily transactions in foreign markets; introducing tax reform; establishing farming cooperatives to handle the purchase and sale of cacao; and encouraging cocoa and chocolate manufacture locally.[37] It was a comprehensive and thoughtful reform program.

Dr. Eusinio Gaston Lavigne emerged as the group's political leader. He was the descendant of French immigrants who had come to Brazil with the Taunay expedition on one side and the Sá family on the other. He had been born in 1883, just before abolition, and received a law degree from the prestigious university at Recife in 1908. Yet, despite his ancestry, he was a very different kind of politician from Domingos Adami and Ernesto Sá. Like other populists of the era, he saw himself as the friend of the common man and the defender of regional sovereignty against the aggression of foreign capital. He believed that enlightened leadership and cooperation among classes could bring important benefits to his region and his nation. But he and his allies were faced with the problem of how to present themselves as legitimate reformers. After all, Pessoa had effectively labeled his ancestors as slave-owning aristocrats, a legacy neither Lavigne nor the Berberts were interested in emphasizing. As bad, if not worse, the creditors foreclosing against small farmers, and the planters laying off large numbers of rural workers tended to be friends or even members of their families. Lavigne's marriage to Odília Teixeira, an accomplished woman of mixed race, helped symbolically, but when Vargas named Lavigne *intendente* in 1931, new opportunities presented themselves.[38] Taking his cue from Pessoa, Lavigne also turned to history to bolster his political aspirations. Two texts sponsored by his administration help to show the direction he took.

As part of the celebrations marking the fiftieth anniversary of the creation of the city of Ilhéus, Lavigne invited Epaminondas Berbert de Castro, the foremost intellectual of the nouveau riche families, to speak on regional history.[39] The speech was a sophisticated rendition of the nouveau riche tradition. In it Berbert de Castro argued that Ilhéus had grown slowly, but was "like those villages that, as if they were touched with a magic wand, grow quickly, finished and perfect, in the hinterlands of North America or São Paulo." Ilhéus had a history as old as any in Brazil; if it wasn't as prestigious a history, it was not the fault of its residents. Ilhéus had not fulfilled its potential during the colonial period because it had not been well served by the colonial government. But streams of settlers, first from Germany and then from other Brazilian states, slowly but surely began to replace the virgin forest with a forest of cacao. Finally the village of Ilhéus began to grow, and in 1881 the Province of Bahia rewarded its residents by making it a city. In the following years, cacao fulfilled its promise, and in 1931 Ilhéus was "a splendid reality" made possible by the cacao planters.[40]

Lavigne also commissioned João da Silva Campos, the most important Bahian historian of the period, to write a history of Ilhéus. A crônica da Capitania de São Jorge dos Ilhéos was not published until 1938, but it is the work of several years and clearly outlines Lavigne's ideas about regional history. The text voluminously chronicles the period from 1500 to 1936 and includes references to slavery, slave trading, aristocratic planters, and frontier farmers, as Silva Campos mentioned every primary and secondary source about Ilhéus that he uncovered in extensive research in local, state, and national archives. Yet the text contains no clear narrative argument, sources are not contextualized, nor contradictions explained. It is possible, therefore, to sustain a number of arguments based on the text. Still, Lavigne's position emerges clearly from the pages if one reads the entire chronicle. In Silva Campos's view, Lavigne's ancestor Manuel Ferreira da Camara—graduate of Coimbra, friend of the Portuguese emperor, and founding father of the nation—had been an enlightened colonial administrator largely responsible for the introduction of cacao to the region. The Sás, Lavignes, Cerqueira Limas, and other local plantation owners had been forward-thinking planters, largely responsible for the spread of cacao in the nineteenth century. People of humble origin, especially German colonists and northeasterners, had made important contributions as well, such that by the 1880s there had been significant economic growth in the cacao area involving both small farmers and large estate owners. All of these people had contributed to the development of Ilhéus, although at various times and in various ways. They had often been bitter rivals, but Eusinio Lavigne's selection as *intendente* had ushered in a new era of cooperation and hard work.[41]

Arguments like these made a powerful appeal for regional pride and unity at a time when the cacao area was suffering the effects of severe economic crisis. They also linked the cacao area's past and present to notions about Brazilian development and nationalism at a time when the entire nation was suffering the effects of international economic crisis, and social conflict was intensifying. Further, the emphasis on frontier farmers and progressive planters made the cacao area's planters and their ancestors seem more like the heroic *bandeirantes* and progressive planters of São Paulo than the aristocrats of Bahia's depressed sugar industry.[42] In such a light, saving Bahia's cacao planters from economic collapse brought by low cacao prices might seem like a good investment.

By June 1931, important segments of the Bahian and Brazilian leadership had been convinced that was the case. This was not solely because of the lobbying efforts of Lavigne and Berbert de Castro, but they played an important part in garnering support for the planters' plight. Upon taking over city hall, Lavigne immediately sent a delegation of cacao planters to Rio to meet with Vargas. The new head of state granted the cacao delegates ten minutes, but they so impressed him that he kept them talking for an hour, after which he sent them to meet the minister of agriculture. Shortly thereafter, Vargas announced a moratorium on foreclosures against indebted cacao properties and created the Bahian Cacao Institute, a research and development program as well as a commercial and credit cooperative, funded by an initial government grant of 10:000$ and a tax on cacao exports.[43]

Given the desperate straits in which the region and Brazil as a whole found themselves, convincing the national government that the cacao planters *needed* help was not difficult. Persuading the national government that they *deserved* to be helped was undoubtedly not so easy. Many groups were demanding assistance, and by the 1930s southern Brazilians perceived northeasterners, and Bahians in particular, as backward and a drag on Brazilian progress. Exactly how the representatives of the cacao area convinced Vargas, from the southern state of Rio Grande do Sul, that these Bahians and northeasterners deserved aid is not clear, but presenting themselves as the descendants of hardworking frontiersmen surely helped.[44]

The institute was an ambitious and comprehensive program for the "defense of the planter class."[45] Despite the idealism of its initial program, however, it never lived up to expectations and ultimately exacerbated land concentration. There were several problems inherent in the program. The first was that no single planter class existed. Rather, cacao planters belonged to at least three classes: the elite, composed of enormously wealthy planters who also had investments in commerce and a group of wealthy merchants with investments in cacao; a middle group made up of mid-sized farmers who did some trading in cacao; and a group of small farmers whose children and siblings supplemented family incomes by working for other planters. The second problem was that Bahia's cacao aristocrats, the Cerqueira Limas, appear to have been influencing institute policy from behind the scenes. Octavio Moniz Barreto, married to a granddaughter of Pedro Augusto Cerqueira Lima, had been involved in preparing the plan for the institute presented to the Bahian government in March 1931, and he was probably involved in the selection of Ignacio Tosta Filho as the institute's first executive director. Another member of the family, Amando de Lemos Peixoto, a Portuguese merchant-planter married to another grand-daughter of Pedro Augusto Cerqueira Lima, became one of the associate directors of the institute. The experimental farm where the institute techni-cians began to conduct their experiments bordered Cerqueira Lima prop-erty and was probably carved out of it. Finally, the extended family held a very large number of shares in the cooperative that the institute formed. Whether they were setting institute policy is not clear, but it is one pos-sible explanation for the muddle of contradictions that it became by the late 1930s.

Certainly something went wrong despite Tosta Filho's and Lavigne's best hopes. Tosta Filho had been an excellent choice to direct the institute, although Lavigne was not very happy with him. He came from a very well to do Brazilian coffee family and had studied agricultural cooperativism in the United States. He was, in fact, the son of the man who had instituted Brazil's coffee valorization program in the 1910s, and he had learned from his father's mistakes. Moreover, he was brimming with ideas about what was possible in the cacao area. Yet the most socially progressive aspects of his program, those directed toward small farmers, quickly fell by the way-side. Participation in the institute's debt-forgiveness and credit programs required land titles, but most planters did not have them, and Tosta did not consider helping planters acquire land titles to be central to the program. Moreover, he allowed exporters who owned cacao property to join the institute and become some of its largest shareholders, even though the institute had been conceived as a way to protect planters against the ex-porters. In hindsight, it appears that the institute was designed to help the largest planters and drive the smaller or more ill prepared producers out of business.[46] "Good" government had actually combined with the depression to reduce the number of farmers growing cacao.

Given what happened, it is ironic that the institute implicitly endorsed the growing discourse about frontier farmers. In two influential studies of the region, Tosta Filho argued that the small farm had given way to large estates because of a combination of international price cycles, land fraud, the lack of land titles, the informal credit and commercial networks, and the psychology of Bahia's planters. Neither those analyses nor the annual reports of the institute that he prepared and distributed to libraries around the United States and Europe mentioned the period prior to 1890. It was as if the cacao economy was born with abolition and the Republic as a community of small farmers who later lost their land.[47]

Gregório Bondar, the Russian entomologist and director of the Cacao Institute's experimental station, did turn his attention briefly to cacao area history. But in *A cultura de Cacao na Bahia* in 1938 he reiterated the tradition of the frontier farmers. "It was not," he argued, "the efforts of foreign arms, nor the gold of well-to-do pockets, nor the support of strong government, but the constancy of humble men, the boldness of the national worker, whose arms constituted their only capital, who made it [the cacao economy] triumphant."[48] He worked on an experimental farm neighboring the Cerqueira Lima plantation, but he insisted that the roots of the cacao economy lay with the small farmers of the nineteenth century. Like Zehntner's, his book was distributed to libraries throughout Brazil, Europe, and the United States.

A Voice Raised in Dissent

All members of the cacao elite did not accept this vision of regional history and politics. One young man, Jorge Amado, saw things quite differently. Amado was born on a Bahian cacao *fazenda* in 1911, and his family was part of Ilhéus's nouveau riche elite. Like many other sons of the nouveau riche planters, Amado was sent to boarding school in Salvador and spent vacations on the farm. But instead of producing appropriate conservative, elitist attitudes in the boy, this combination of education and experience pushed him to the left. In his twenties, he quit law school, joined the Communist Party, and began to write novels. The second one, *Cacau*, was published in Rio de Janeiro in 1933. In it he "tried to tell . . . with a minimum of literature and a maximum of honesty, the life of the workers on the cacao plantations of southern Bahia." On the plantation Fraternity, he wrote, workers were treated like slaves. The plantation owner, Manuel Misael da

Souza Telles, was a nouveau riche planter who had begun with nothing and struck it rich in the early days of cacao. His name closely resembled that of the man people were calling the "King of Cacao," self-made millionaire Manuel Misael da Silva Tavares.[49] His workers would not share his experience, however, since out of every thousand people who tried to plant cacao, only one made good. Hard work was not enough: theft, violence, and stinginess were also required. The workers acknowledged their understanding of their situation by calling their boss "Mané Miseravé Saqueia Tudo" (Miserable Manny who Steals Everything), or "Merda Mexida Sem Tempero" (Mixed Shit without Seasoning), or "Mané Frajelo" (Miser Manny). Communism alone would save them.[50]

In a situation like the one in the cacao area of the 1930s, one might have expected a discourse like this to lead to further rural violence or political organizing, especially since the Communist Party was gaining adherents among urban and rural workers and some sons of the elite. It did not, however, because Vargas declared the Estado Novo in 1937, repressing dissent in the city and the countryside alike. Advocates of communist reforms were arrested, rural workers who had been organizing were fired and sometimes jailed, and the militia arrived to put down an Indian insurrection on the Catarina Paraguaçu reservation. *Cacau* was banned, and existing copies were burned in Salvador. Amado was forced into exile in Uruguay. Even Eusínio Lavigne wound up in jail.

In exile, Amado wrote two more novels attacking the progressive frontier farmer view: *Terras do sem fim*, published in English as *The Violent Land*, and *São Jorge dos Ilhéus*, published in English as *The Golden Harvest*.[51] Yes, he wrote, the cacao planters had begun as poor men and were nouveau riche. Some people had been able to strike it rich, but they had gotten their start in the early days of cacao.[52] Horacio da Silveira, from *Terras do sem fim*, like Horatio Alger for whom he was named, was one of these men who had gone from rags to riches. Beginning as a muledriver for another plantation owner, in the early years of cacao cultivation he had acquired a bit of land and, through personal bravery, hard work, violence, chicanery, and perhaps a devil pact, had turned his small plot into one of the largest plantations in southern Bahia.[53] Newly wealthy, although crude, he had gone in search of a wife and married a refined merchant's daughter, educated in a convent school in Salvador, and installed her on the *fazenda* deep in the forest, with a piano for her entertainment. The character, like the planter in *Cacau*, clearly resembled Manuel Misael da Silva Tavares.

Silveira and his counterparts were feudal lords, not modern capitalists. They cared more about honor than about profit. They stole their land and ordered hired guns to murder their enemies. They treated the workers like slaves, and as in the days of slavery, they believed they had rights to the sexual favors of any woman or girl who lived on their land.[54] Abolition had brought no changes. As one old man said, "I was a lad in the days of slavery. My father was a slave, my mother also. But it wasn't any worse then than it is today. Things don't change; it's all talk."[55] For all their power, however, the planters were ultimately buffoons. Their wives cuckolded them, and the exporters outwitted them. They had brought neither progress nor modernity to the region. Modernity and capitalism arrived in the area with the exporters who used their international connections to rob the planters of their land. And all this took place in the shadow of the Bahian Cacao Institute, which was of no use at all.[56]

Amado's work captivated readers throughout Brazil and around the world as critical acclaim and his membership in the Communist Party facilitated the rapid and extensive publication and translation of his work. *Terras do sem fim*, the most successful of his early cacao novels, was translated into twenty-one languages and by 1987 had gone through eighty-seven Portuguese editions.[57] By the early 1950s Amado was the most widely known source of information on southern Bahia. Cacao-area elites were rather ambivalent about this. On one hand, they did not appreciate being called backward, clientelist, exploitative, murdering cuckolds. On the other, they recognized that Amado loved his *terra natal*, shared their views about the exporters, and never contradicted the basic points of their emerging origin story. After all, in many ways the novels are studies of the nouveau riche planters, their roots, their methods, their attitudes, and, especially, their pretensions. They are populated by nouveau riche planters and *grapiúnas*, people who migrated from the northeast to the cacao area and settled the western frontier.[58] His frontier farmers were feudal lords who behaved like slave owners when they became wealthy, but they had been poor when slavery had actually existed. It was possible to agree with Amado and still subscribe to many elements of the dominant narrative about regional history.

A Life of Its Own

In the postwar period, the tradition about frontier farmers developed a life of its own as a wide variety of technicians and scholars from Brazil and the United States took an interest in Bahian cacao. They were professionals connected with major government or international organizations or universities, whose work appeared in prestigious publications. As professionals, they read the best work they could acquire on the cacao area, giving preference to the arguments of scientists and bureaucrats like themselves. Zehntner and Bondar found special favor with them, and they repeated, nearly word for word, arguments about impoverished men farming the frontier with no other capital than their muscle and sweat. Thus the nouveau riche planter origin story was legitimized by the *Revista Brasileira de Geografia*, the Pan American Union, and Columbia University, among other institutions.[59]

This period saw the beginnings of another serious economic crisis in the region. Prices had declined after the highs of World War II, and the trees planted at the beginning of the century were aging. Ilhéus still had no port for oceangoing vessels, and many cacao planters still had no land titles. Planters were in debt, and agricultural unemployment was high. The Cacao Institute, although still functioning, was now completely moribund, having degenerated into a road-building program and a mechanism for enriching its directors. Rural organizing had begun again, led by the Brazilian Communist Party (PCB), and in 1957 the Brazilian Labor Ministry recognized the Rural Workers Union of Ilhéus and Itabuna, the only rural union in Bahia to carry such a distinction. By the early 1960s, peasant leagues were actively demanding radical agrarian reform.[60] Once again the cacao elite felt threatened by enemies from within and without.

In the midst of these trying times for planters, Jorge Amado published another book about the cacao area. Many Brazilian intellectuals criticized *Gabriela, Clove, and Cinnamon* because it did not fit into the genre of socialist realism. The cacao elite hated it for a different reason: it criticized and made fun of them at the same time, just when they were trying to present themselves to the federal government in a positive light. Amado did not devote much attention to rural conditions in *Gabriela*. What he did say, however, labeled the cacao elites as murderers who had stolen their land and treated their workers no differently from the way that planters had treated slaves prior to abolition. He then went on to ridicule their pretensions. They had nothing in common with the sophisticated, modern coffee planters. All they were interested in was local gossip, illicit sex, and parties. They were so tied to their old ways that they could not support the changes that the cacao area needed to progress, especially a deepwater port in Ilhéus. Some younger local planters advocated the improvements that modern technology could bring, but most believed that there was no need to change. Slowly but surely capitalism was dragging them into the modern world, but outside influences brought the changes, not the cacao planters.[61]

Eusinio Lavigne was furious with Amado over *Gabriela*. In his view Amado had betrayed his homeland in writing a novel that showed that cacao's wealth had created a rotten society (*sociedade podre*), a land of adventurers, charlatans, and loose women. Others were enraged by Amado's treatment of Ilhéus's women. Others disliked being called land-grabbing exploiters of their workers and being compared to nineteenth-century slave owners. Others were scandalized that he seemed to be airing the dirty laundry of several cacao area families in public. *Gabriela* was controversial elsewhere in Brazil for other reasons, but in Ilhéus the members of the cacao elite believed it to be a specific attack on specific people and their way of life when, as Lavigne said, it was the responsibility of cacao area intellectuals to work for the good of their region.[62]

Despite *Gabriela*, the cacao planters received significant assistance when Kubitschek was elected. He would not, however, build a deepwater port in Ilhéus—and perhaps that is why Lavigne was so angry with Amado. Nevertheless, in 1957 the administration forgave the cacao planters' debts once again, declared a moratorium on foreclosures, and created the Commisão Executiva do Plano da Lavoura Cacaueira (CEPLAC), the largest research and development program devoted to cacao in the world, as part of the federal Ministry of Fazenda.[63] The planters soon found that CEPLAC was not the Cacao Institute of Bahia. Tosta Filho had planned the new development institute, but he had learned from his mistakes. Experts came from all over Brazil to work at CEPLAC on every aspect of the cacao area except its history and culture. Influenced by Tosta, many of the sociologists and agronomists saw helping the small farmers to acquire land titles for their properties as central to their mission. It did not take long before the elite came to see those technicians as threats.

It was in this atmosphere that a local pharmacist and amateur historian, Carlos Pereira Filho, published a history that argued that the cacao economy had been founded by aristocratic families who owned large estates and many slaves. He dismissed the notion that the roots of the cacao economy lay with obscure workers farming the frontier. "On the contrary," he wrote, "the cacao economy was born alongside the sugar mills, on the Almada, Castello Novo and Provisão fazendas, owned by the Cerqueira Lima, del Rei, and the Adami families, who dominated those areas with their properties."[64] Some salaried workers or *desbravadores* had made good, he believed, but the most important developments in the production and commercialization of cacao resulted from actions of noble families whose influence continued to be significant until the 1930s.

Pereira Filho may as well have saved his energy and his paper: no one paid any attention to him, even though the story he told approaches the one told in nineteenth-century documents. As much as anything this was because a new generation of cacao elites had emerged, generally the children and grandchildren of the early-twentieth-century planters, who had never heard about slaves growing cacao on large estates belonging to aristocrats. Having been brought up on stories about life on the frontier, according to Odette Rosa da Silva, they believed the early cacao planters to have been pioneers who had conquered the forest despite a great many difficulties. And they saw themselves as the heirs of those early regional heroes, struggling to grow cacao despite tremendous difficulties.[65] Estórias da história de Ilhéus, published in 1970, demonstrated their pride in what Rosa da Silva called a "heroic" past. The book's pages are filled with descriptions and pictures of early-twentieth-century planters and their late-twentieth-century descendants. Both Pessoista and Adamista families are represented among the vignettes, but there are no aristocrats among them. Their ancestors, whether large or small planters, were all referred to as desbravadores, or frontier farmers, the equivalent of São Paulo's bandeirantes, and Misael Tavares, the self-made King of Cacao, received special attention.[66]

The brief biography of Odilon Pompílio de Souza is illustrative of their ideas. Originally from the northeast, Souza had arrived in Ilhéus as a child accompanied by his father and other relatives. They spent three years working for a planter at Vai Quem Quer (Go Who Wishes), during which one of his brothers died of fever. In 1915, Souza established himself as a merchant, stocking the store with merchandise he had acquired on credit, and married Clarina, "whom he always called his right arm in the construction of his patrimony." Eventually he acquired the mid-sized Providence plantation. His father died in 1920, just after the battle of Siqueiro do Espinho, leaving many debts. Charged with dealing with the problem, Souza went to his father's creditors and said, "Let me work. What I owe you, I don't know if I'll be able to pay. But the debts of my father, Teotônio Leolino de Souza, will be religiously paid, with interest." Five years later, according to the story, he had paid off the debt and had a credit of 43:000$ with the export house Wildberger and Company, as well as a considerable stock of merchandise. He was, the authors continued, the definition of an honest man.[67]

By the 1970s, the cacao elite were insisting that their ancestors had worked hard to earn what they had. The planters felt the need to show that their families had earned their money the hard way because they felt under constant threat from the international market, from rural labor organizing, from idealistic technicians at CEPLAC, and from Jorge Amado. The military coup in 1964 took care of some of their problems when the generals closed the PCB-controlled unions, repressed the peasant leagues, and purged CEPLAC of researchers and technicians deemed to be too radical.[68] While the military was in power, the planters finally obtained the deepwater port they had been lobbying for, but they could not control either the international market for cacao or Jorge Amado, who spent most of his time in Paris.

Shortly after the military began to ease censorship in 1976, Teve Globo syndicated *Gabriela* for television. The series remained quite faithful to the original novel and therefore chronicled the transition of Ilhéus from a violent, feudal frontier town to a sophisticated, capitalist city during the roaring twenties. The show ran during prime time for six months, six nights a week and was watched by an estimated 70 percent of Brazilian households. So people all over Brazil learned about the ruthless murdering planters, the hired guns, the exporters, the politicians, the northeastern migrants, the prostitutes, the loose women, and the well-to-do, proper, but boring elite ladies of Ilhéus. They also learned about land theft, domestic violence, and the struggle of a few visionaries to build a deepwater port in Ilhéus despite the opposition of the old planters. The marketplace where rural workers were hired was called the "slave market," just as it was in Ilhéus, and eerily, one of the actors looked just like Antônio Pessoa. People all over Brazil loved *Gabriela*, but it made a lot of people in Ilhéus angry.[69]

Denying Slavery

The cacao elite and its institutions began to respond to the televised *Gabriela* almost immediately. In 1976 Adonias Filho, the region's other internationally acclaimed novelist, took up Amado's challenge and wrote a historical essay called *Sul da Bahia, chão de cacau (Uma civilização regional)*, published by Civilisação Brasileira and distributed throughout Brazil. In the essay Adonias presented a very different picture of southern Bahia from the one Amado painted. He argued that the region's special history had produced a democratic rather than an exploitative society. Hostile Indians had prevented the Portuguese from establishing themselves in southeastern Bahia, and it had taken a new, stronger man, the Brazilian-European peasant, to create a valuable export economy there. These peasants were the "legendary *desbravadores*, who conquered the forest with fire, gunpowder, and machetes" in the nineteenth century. Such men had not had slaves, or if they did, they were in such small numbers as to be insignificant. They did not order things done; they did them themselves. And if they ordered other people to work, they worked alongside them. The cacao area's twentieth-century elite had its roots in this group of humble men who had challenged the frontier. They had not engaged in a violent struggle for land: they were too busy taking care of their businesses. Not all frontier farmers had become wealthy, he was careful to point out, but the frontier farmer had left an important legacy of democracy for the cacao elite of the twentieth century. This non-aristocratic past had created a regional culture that was completely different from those in the sugar, cattle, or coffee regions, where slave labor had been the norm.[70]

CEPLAC also joined the fray over the portrayal of the cacao region. They contracted two graduate students at the Universidade Federal da Bahia in Salvador, Angelina Nobre Rolim Garcez and Antônio Fernando Guerreiro de Freitas, to research and write the history of the region. The two publications these social scientists prepared followed the already established trend: the first, CEPLAC's "Diagnóstico histórico," argued that the cacao area had begun as an area of small farmers, that family labor had been most common on the cacao plantations, and that large estates had begun to form after 1890. Their *Bahia cacaueira: Um estudo de história recente* began in 1930.[71] This is perhaps not surprising for Bahian intellectuals contracted by a Bahian institution, especially given that the military was still in power. What is perhaps more surprising is that they both did serious research in primary documents, both uncovered materials that called the dominant tradition into question, and both incorporated the material into their unpublished master's theses. As Guerreiro implied in the introduction to his thesis, it was difficult to do first-rate scholarly work on history when associated with cacao area research institutions: "the commented 'folklore' of the cacao [planters]," he wrote, "may have transferred itself to these institutions, which fundamentally demonstrates the victory of the cacao elite in its struggle for hegemony."[72] In the midst of military rule, two graduate students were in no position to challenge that tradition.

Bahian graduate students were not the only people who found it difficult to challenge what was now a well-established narrative. Angus Wright, an American Ph.D. candidate who was outside of the system of support and politics of the cacao area, noted in his dissertation the presence of a "modest oligarchy" with some slaves and political connections to the provincial government. But he also ended by arguing that these families were ultimately not very important in the overall development of the economy.[73] He was not alone. Historians of Bahia and Brazil who were not working principally on the cacao area but who wished to comment briefly on cacao also found themselves repeating portions of the dominant tradition.[74]

Three sociologists, Selim Raschid Asmar, Amilcar Baiardi, and Gustavo Falcon, took that tradition a step further in the mid-1980s: they began to argue that cacao had been a free-labor crop in Bahia—that slaves had never worked in cacao at all. They drew on Adonias Filho, local tradition, and the various texts that spoke of the rural poor farming cacao in the nineteenth century.[75] Baiardi and Falcon appear to have believed that the cacao elites were violent exploiters, but they never questioned the overall narrative. There was no need to: by the 1980s, everyone knew the fundamentals of regional history, and they did not include slave labor.

Amado only reinforced the dominant narrative in 1986 when he published *Tocaia grande: A face oscura*, translated as *Showdown* in English, but perhaps better rendered as "Ambush: The Dark Side." There is little new in the book, which is not one of his masterpieces. Still, it is full of men who used violence and patronage networks to get rich.[76] Once again, he critiqued the hardworking frontier farmer myth, but he never offered an alternative historical narrative.

Questioning the Narrative

Several people began to question this historical tradition in the late 1980s. Mauricio Puls, a graduate student at the University of São Paulo, argued in the first draft of his master's thesis that slavery and large estates had been fundamental to the formation of the cacao economy, basing his arguments on obscure nineteenth-century secondary sources and Pereira Filho. Shortly thereafter, Agenor Gasparetto, a Gaucho sociologist at CEPLAC, devoted one of his bylines to Puls's argument, included them in a new CEPLAC-sponsored pamphlet on cacao area history, and tried to get Puls a job at CEPLAC. The response was telling: there was no job for Puls, who wound up leaving his degree program and finding work as a journalist in São Paulo, and Gasparetto's article was attacked in the press by Selem Raschid Asmar, his superior at CEPLAC.[77] Gasparetto persisted, but he was among the first researchers to be dismissed when Brazilian president Fernando Collor cut the CEPLAC budget in 1990. He had made too many enemies, and his refusal to follow the official history of the region had played a role in the process.[78]

While Gasparetto was fighting with his CEPLAC colleagues, I was researching cacao area history for my dissertation and coming to similar, although not identical, conclusions. As I was completing that research, I was asked to give a talk on my work at a symposium on the region's history at what is today the Universidade Estadual da Santa Cruz in Ilhéus. More than a hundred people turned out for a 7 A.M. lecture that dealt specifically with the topic of slave labor in cacao. In the audience were students and faculty from the college, and researchers from CEPLAC. Some had come to watch the foreigner make a fool of herself.

I presented a short paper that focused on the empirical evidence for slaveholding among early cacao planters, and the implications of that evidence for regional history. When I finished the talk, Asmar stood and began to speak. Until now, he said, he had always believed that cacao had begun as a small farming crop in Bahia and that it was therefore very different from other Brazilian agricultural crops. There was no local tradition about slavery in cacao, and he had never heard that local blacks claimed to be the descendants of slaves who worked in cacao. But the documentary evidence that I had presented made it clear that he had been wrong. The next thing I knew, a television camera had been thrust in my face, and a reporter was asking me if it was true that there had been slaves working in cacao in the nineteenth century. I said yes, and the story went out on the evening news. The next day several people stopped me in the street to say that they had known it was true, and they offered to show me cacao trees planted with slave labor or postmortem estate inventories listing both cacao trees and slaves.

Since that time my colleagues in Bahia and I have been working to incorporate this tradition about slaves and aristocratic families into the history of cacao in southern Bahia. The issue is extraordinarily polemical, so although we are meeting with some success, it is not without a struggle. We encounter constant resistance from southern Bahian elites, especially from those who consider themselves descendants of the frontier farmers. Descendants of slave owners prefer to avoid the topic altogether, but when pressed will admit that their families once owned slaves. They go on to insist, however, that those slaves were well treated. Despite the opposition and the official silence on the question, however, we have found a few rural workers who remember stories of the slaves who participated in turning the sugar estates into cacao plantations in the nineteenth century. We have also found the physical ruins of sugar mills under groves of cacao. Those men and women, and these silent stones and cauldrons, tell a very different story about the past than the one usually told in the cacao area.

Conclusion: How Identity Became History

As we have seen, narratives about the history of the cacao area have been entwined in the political struggles of the local elite since the beginning of the twentieth century. Whether written by local residents, internationally acclaimed novelists, or scientists and historians from other parts of the world, whether by people on the left or the right, texts dealing with regional history largely conform to a narrative about the origin of the cacao economy that is integral to cacao elite identity and politics. The striking thing about the dominant narrative of southern Bahian history is that so many elites and intellectuals, southern Bahians and people from elsewhere, people on the left and the right, have come to believe it. They may not believe that southern Bahia is democratic, nor that the wealthy nouveau riche planters of the early twentieth century came by their money honestly, but they do believe that the first farmers emerged from the rural poor, and that some of them struck it rich.

To some degree, people believe this because it does reflect the experience of some people who live or lived in the region. The Berberts, the Castros, the Tavareses, the Alveses, as well as many others, still own property in the region, and they have been raised on stories about small-farming frontier life at the turn of the century. Those stories are, in turn, repeated in homes, schools, bars, and offices all over the cacao region. Visitors to the region, whether tourists, scientists, or historians, are introduced to those same stories almost immediately upon their arrival—and directed toward sources like Amado, Bondar, Zehntner, and Garcez for confirmation.

Moreover, the physical landscape retains vestiges of small farms, even though most of them are gone. The most-traveled roads in the region traverse the area originally settled by small farmers. The road from Ilhéus to Itabuna travels through the former German colony, and although the estates on the left bank of the river look to be quite large, those on the right (those most easy to see) appear to be narrow and long. The old houses on these farms are quite simple: nothing like those on the sugar plantations of the Recôncavo or the coffee estates of the Paraiba Valley of Rio de Janeiro. Bills of sale still carry the names of all the previous owners of the farm's property, and so the numerous small farms that were expropriated to form big ones are always listed there. The residents of much of southeastern Bahia's cacao area have good reason to believe that small farmers were important in their area and to forget, if they ever knew, that large estates date from Ilhéus's earliest history.[79]

Further, neither intellectuals nor the public are usually confronted with concrete evidence that the dominant narrative is false. Nearly all the physical evidence of the colonial and nineteenth-century sugar mills, sawmills, and coffee and sugarcane fields has disappeared. Most of the mills themselves have been destroyed, and the land is now covered with cacao trees. At the Engenho Santanna, which remained a sugar plantation, all that is left of the most important sugar mill in southern Bahia is a restored sixteenth-century Jesuit chapel, an enormous cauldron, and a small village of the descendants of the plantation's former slaves. It is still a large estate, and it still produces cane, but the old mill is covered in brush, and the surrounding area produces cacao. A grove of cacao trees now covers the ruins of the big house and the sugar mill of the Engenho Santo Antônio das Pedras, which even has a new name. The Almada cemetery, where the slaves and neighbors of the Cerqueira Limas were once buried, is now abandoned and covered in brush. No big sign marks the entrance to the largest single property in Ilhéus, the Engenho turned Fazenda Almada, nor to the two other plantations, Santa Rita and Bomfim, that were created out of it in 1894 when the first Pedro Augusto Cerqueira Lima died. Some local residents know, however, that what appears to be nine kilometers of forest punctuated by a few buildings along the Ilhéus-Urucuca road is actually the border of the Almada, Santa Rita, and Bomfim plantations, located on land granted by the Portuguese emperor before independence.

All of this suggests that collective or social memory has been at work in southern Bahia. As Maurice Hawlbachs argued several decades ago, "The individual calls recollections to mind by relying on the frameworks of social memory."[80] By this he meant that our memories are tied to those of the social group of which we are a part. Roger Bastide, in theorizing about social memory and the experiences of African slaves in Brazil, adopted Hawlbachs's ideas, but went on to argue that the survival of the social group is key to the maintenance of social memory and that changes to social groups will contribute to changes in social memory.[81] From this perspective we can see that the tradition that developed in Ilhéus is clearly related to the character of the elite in twentieth-century southern Bahia: we remember the planters who came, lived, died, and left family there. We also remember the ones that Jorge Amado wrote about. Thus, we remember neither the aristocrats from elsewhere who bought property, came to visit, and went home to Salvador or Rio, nor the slaves who worked their property, who took off on May 13, 1888.

This is not to say that active forgetting, or the repression of memory, has not been involved in the development of this historical tradition in southern Bahia.[82] In the twentieth century neither the descendants of slaves nor slave owners have advertised their antecedents, at least not publically. Many of the descendants of the slaves have not had access to media that would allow them to tell their stories. Even if they did, they might not wish to discuss the bondage of their ancestors in a Brazil in which all people are created equal, at least in theory. The descendants of slave owners who still own plantations, on the other hand, have no reason to be interested in acknowledging their slaveholding past. Owning slaves now carries the connotation of having abused people—of having beaten men and raped women—certainly not the kind of legacy Brazilian elites wish to acknowledge when labor organizers are accusing them of exploiting their current labor force and they need government assistance.

Although we must remember that an active process of forgetting has been at work in southern Bahia, that does not really explain why writers studying the history of southern Bahia conformed to, and even contributed to, an elite historical myth. Certainly some people were paid to cooperate, and others felt pressured to do so. But others honestly looked at the sources valued within their respective disciplines and concurred with the elite's vision of itself. This suggests that it is the coincidence of arguments about the cacao area's history, in the absence of visible contradictions, that makes the conventional wisdom so powerful. The mythology about cacao's history works so well because it is not imposed but rather, by now, part of regional traditions confirmed by historical and technical studies, and literary works published by Brazilians and foreigners alike over the course of the entire twentieth century.

Notes

I wish to thank Emilia Viotti da Costa, Daniel James, Gilbert M. Joseph, Janaína Amado, Hendrik Kraay, Stuart Schwartz, and Barbara Weinstein for helpful and constructive comments on this essay in its various stages. I would also like to thank the Yale Council on International and Area Studies, the Albert J. Beveridge Grant Program of the American Historical Association, and the Institute for Scholarship in the Liberal Arts of the University of Notre Dame for financial assistance in carrying out the research on which this essay is based.

1 For this discussion of myth I found the following texts particularly helpful: Emilia Viotti da Costa, *The Brazilian Empire* (Chicago: University of Chicago Press, 1985); Janaína Amado, "Construindo mitos: A conquista do Oeste no Brasil e nos EUA," in Sidney Valadares Pimentel and Janaína Amado, organizers, *Passando dos limites* (Goiânia: Editora UFG, 1995); and Janaína Amado, "Míticas origens: Caramuru e a fundação do Brasil," *Actas dos IV cursos internacionais de verão de Cascais (7 a 12 de julho de 1997)*, vol. 3 (Cascais: Camara Municipal de Cascais, 1998), 175–209; David Cohen, *The Combing of History* (Baltimore: Johns Hopkins University Press, 1994); Jeffrey Gould, *To Die in This Way: Nicaraguan Indians and the Myth of Mestizaje, 1880–1965* (Durham: Duke University Press, 1998); Lowell Gudmondson, *Costa Rica Before Coffee: Society and Economy on the Eve of the Export Boom* (Baton Rouge: Louisiana State University Press, 1986); Allesandro Portelli, "O massacre de Civitella Val di Chiana (Toscana, 29 de junho de 1944): Mito e política, luto e senso comun," in Marieta de Moraes Ferreira and Janaína Amado, eds. *Usos e abusos da história oral* (Rio de Janeiro: Fundação Getúlio Vargas Editora, 1996), 103–30; Raphael Samuels and Paul Thompson, *The Myths We Live By* (New York: Rutledge, 1990); Joanne Rappaport, *The Politics of Memory* (Cambridge: Cambridge University Press, 1990); Rolph Trouillot, *Silencing the Past: Power and the Representation of History* (Baltimore: Johns Hopkins University Press, 1995).

2 On invented traditions, see, especially, E. J. Hobsbawm and Terence Ranger, eds., *The Invention of Tradition* (New York: Cambridge University Press, 1983).

3 For fundamental discussions of the concept of collective memory, see Maurice Halbwachs, *On Collective Memory*, ed., trans., and with an introduction by Lewis A. Coser (Chicago: University of Chicago Press, 1992); Roger Bastide, *The African Religions of Brazil: Toward a Sociology of the Interpenetration of Civilization*, trans. Helen Sebba (Baltimore: Johns Hopkins University Press, 1960), 240–59; Nathan Wachtel, "Memory and History, Introduction," *History and Anthropology* 2 (October 1986): 207. For an excellent example of

memory as a social process, see Daniel James, "Meatpackers, Peronists, and Collective Memory: A View From the South," *American Historical Review* 102, 5 (December 1997): 1404–13.

4   On the manioc trade and manioc farming, see B. J. Barickman, *A Bahian Counterpoint* (Stanford: Stanford University Press, 1999). The history of the cacao area is drawn from Mary Ann Mahony, "The World Cacao Made: Society, Politics, and History in Southern Bahia, Brazil, 1822–1919," Ph.D. diss., Yale University, 1996.

5   Durval Vieira de Aguiar, *A província da Bahia*, 264–66.

6   This system was essentially the one described by Stuart Schwartz for the Recôncavo. Stuart Schwartz, *Sugar in the Formation of Brazilian Society: Bahia, 1550–1835* (Cambridge: Cambridge University Press, 1985), 204–11.

7   On the commercial legislation, see E. Ridings, *Business Interest Groups* (Cambridge: Cambridge University Press, 1994) 149; on the changes in the population and farming, see João da Silva Campos, *A crônica da Capitania de São Jorge dos Ilhéos*, Edição commemorativa de sua elevação a categoria de cidade (Rio de Janeiro: Ministerio da Educação e Cultura, Conselho Federal de Cultura, 1981), 262; Brazil Ministerio da Agricultura, Industria, e Commercio, Directoria Geral de Estatísticas, *Recenseamento realizado em 1 de setembro de 1920* (Rio de Janeiro: Typografia da Estatística, 1928), 3: 2, pp. 26–27.

8   On class consciousness as a necessary element in class formation, see E. P. Thompson, *The Making of the English Working Class* (New York: Vantage Books, 1966); on status groups, see Max Weber, *Economy and Society* (New York: Bedminster Press, 1968).

9   Pierre Verger, *Notícias da Bahia, 1850* (Bahia: Editora Corrupio, 1981), 45; Antônio Loureiro de Souza, *Baianos ilustres: 1567–1925*, 3d ed., revised (São Paulo: Instituição Brasileira de Difusão Cultural, 1979), 103–4; Arquivo Público do Estado da Bahia (hereafter APEB), Secção Judiciaria (hereafter SJ), Testamento, Salvador, 05/2177/2646/04, Pedro Cerqueira Lima, 1881; Inventory, Ilhéus, no. 03/1010/1479/08, Maria Joaquina Saraiva Carvalho, 1890; Foro Epaminondas Berbert de Castro, Primeiro Cartório da Vara Civil (hereafter FEBC/PCVC) Ilhéus, Inventory, Pedro Augusto Cerqueira Lima, 1894; Registro de Testamentos, vários escrivões, 1847–1939.

10 APEB, SJ, Inventories, Ilhéus, no. 03/1406/1285/22, Maria Piedade Mello e Sá, 1876; no. 03/757/1224/06, Luiza Theodolinda Sá Adami, 1882; FEBC/PCVC, Acção de demarcação, Engenho Santanna, 1936; Marcos Carneiro de Mendonça, *O intendente Câmara: Manuel Ferreira da Camara Bethencourt e Sá, intendente geral das minas e dos diamantes, 1764–1835* (São Paulo: Companhia Editora Nacional, 1958); Kenneth Maxwell, *Conflicts and Conspiracies: Brazil and Portugal, 1750–1808* (Cambridge: Cambridge University Press, 1973), 116 n. 3, 178–79, 196; F. W. O. Morton, "The Conservative Revolution of Independence: Economy, Society, and Politics in Bahia, 1790–1840" (Ph.D. diss., University of Oxford, 1974), 13–14, 51–56.

11 Francisco Borges de Barros, *Memória sobre o município de Ilhéos* (Bahia: Typografia Bahiana, de Cincinnato Melchiades, 1915), 15–16; Eustaquio da Souza Brito, *O livro de Ilhéos* (Ilhéus, Bahia: 1924), 61–62, s.n.; Arthur Brandão and Milton Rosário, *Estórias da história de Ilhéus* (Ilhéus, Bahia: Edições SBS, 1970) 229–33, 236–39, 318.

12 These families owned farms that were much smaller than those of the aristocrats, but that were nonetheless very well organized and maintained. They included groves of cacao and coffee, as well as sturdy, although small, homes for the family, country stores, drying and storage facilities, and sometimes a small *senzala*. Between two and ten slaves and a few free workers provided the labor. Mahony, "The World Cacao Made," 297–302.

13 FEBC/PCVC, Inventories, Henrique Berbert, 1902; Colonel Henrique Berbert, 1910.

14 Brazil Directoria Geral de Estatísticas, *Sexo, raça, e estado civil–da população recenseada em 31 dezembro de 1890* (Rio de Janeiro: Officina de Estatística, 1928).

15 Interview, Dona Alina Afonso de Carvalho, July 20, 1990.

16 On elite Bahian attitudes toward the *povo*, see Dain Borges, *The Family in Bahia, Brazil, 1870–1945* (Stanford: Stanford University Press, 1992), 17; the most insightful account of the attitudes of Salvador's traditional elite is Katia M. Queirós Mattoso, *Bahia, Século XIX: Uma província no Império* (Rio de Janeiro: Editora Nova Fronteira, 1992), 9–12.

17 Dain Borges, "Salvador's 1890s: Paternalism and Its Discontents," *Luso-Brazilian Review* 30, 2 (1993): 48–51.

18 Borges de Barros, *Memória*, 14–15.

19 Mahony, "The World Cacao Made," 471–75.

20 *Gazeta de Ilhéos*, 15 August 1901; 15 September 1901; 8 January 1903; 13 March 1904; 2 April 1905; 9 April 1905, p. 2; 21 June 1903.

21 Mary Ann Mahony, "Afro-Brazilians, Land Reform, and the Question of Social Mobility in Southern Bahia, 1880–1920," *LBR* 34, 2 (winter 1997): 59–79, anthologized in Hendrik Kraay, ed., *Afro-Brazilian Culture and Politics: Bahia, 1790s to 1990s* (New York: M. E. Sharpe, 1998), 90–116.

22 Emilia Viotti da Costa, "1870–1889," *Brazil: Empire and Republic, 1822–1930* (New York: Cambridge University Press, 1989), 206–9; *Da monarquia a república: Momentos decisivos*, 4th ed. (São Paulo: Editora Brasiliense, 1987), 336–50; Consuelo Sampaio, "Crisis in the Brazilian Oligarchical System: A Case Study of Bahia, 1889–1937," Ph.D. diss., Johns Hopkins University, 1979, 43–51.

23 Mahony, "Afro-Brazilians," *LBR*, 61–62.

24 On Brazilian, and especially Bahian, elite views about race, see Nina Rodrigues, *Os Africanos no Brasil*, 7th ed., Coleção Temas Brasileiros 40, Brasiliana 9 (Brasília: Universidade de Brasília, 1988), 5–7; Euclides da Cunha, *Os Sertões*, 4th ed., corrected (Rio de Janeiro: F. Alves, 1981), 66–75; Thomas Skidmore, *Black into White: Race and Nationality in Brazilian Thought*, with a preface to the 1993 edition and bibliography (Durham: Duke University Press, 1993); Kim Butler, *Freedoms Won, Freedoms Given* (New Brunswick: Rutgers University Press, 1998).

25 On the role of the Bahian elite's racial attitudes in the repression of the followers of Antônio Conselheiro in Canudos, see Robert M. Levine, "The Singular Brazilian City of Salvador," *LBR* 30, 2 (1993): 59–69; and *Vale of Tears* (Berkeley: University of California Press, 1992), 4.

26 On the social origins of the residents of Canudos, see Levine, *Vale of Tears*, 97–105, 132–33. On the origins of the migrants to Ilhéus, see Mahony, "The World Cacao Made," 425–27.

27 Campos, *Crônica*, 329–88.

28 Borges de Barros, *Memoria*, iii, 1–11.

29 Ibid., esp. 1–4, 15–16.

30 Ibid., 13–15, 24.

31 Leo Zehntner, *Le cacaoyer dans l'Etat de Bahia* (Berlin: Verlag R. Von Friedlander & Sohn, 1914), 22–23, 34–41.

32 Miguel Calmon, *Notas acerca da producção e commercio do cacau* (Rio de Janeiro: Typografia Journal do Commercio de Rodrigues & Cia., 1917), 4–6; Affonso Costa, *Producção, commercio, e consumo de cacao* (Rio de Janeiro: Imprensa Nacional, 1924), 13.

33 *Correio de Ilhéus*, 18 August 1923, 25 August 1923; Mahony, "The World Cacao Made," 475–84.

34　See APEB, SJ, Testamento, Salvador, no. 08/3445/21, Miguel José Alves Dias, 1946; Souza Brito, O livro de Ilhéus; Campos, Crônica, 369–427.

35　Souza Brito, O livro, 1–12.

36　Arquivo da Polícia Militar do Estado da Bahia (hereafter APBEB), EZB356–X, Comdo. Das F. O. contra a cellula communista no "Posto Indigena Catharina Paraguassu," 1936 relatorio apresentado ao Exmo. Sr. Cap. Secretario de Estado da Segurança Publica pelo Col. Cmt. Das Forças; Zander Navarro, "Movimentos sociais em areas rurais do sudeste da Bahia: As lutas sindicais no período 1955/1964," Revolucções Componesas na América Latina (São Paulo: Icone Editora, 1985), 246.

37　Ramiro Berbert de Castro, O cacau na Bahia (Rio de Janeiro: 1929), 67–69.

38　On Lavigne, see Campos, Crônica, 431–519; Angus Lindsay Wright, "Market, Land, and Class: Southern Bahia, Brazil, 1890–1942," Ph.D. diss., University of Michigan, 1976, 175; Agenor Bandeira de Mello, ed., Cartilha histórica da Bahia: A república e seus governadores, 2d ed. (Salvador, Bahia: Gráfica Central, 1978), 172–73.

39　Wright, "Market, Land, and Class," 111–14, 172–76.

40　Epaminondas Berbert de Castro, Formação econômica e social de Ilhéus (Ilhéus, Bahia: Prefeitura Municipal de Ilhéus, 1981), 11–21. From this speech, it would seem clear that Berbert de Castro had read the literature on the progressive Paulista planters which, elsewhere in this volume, Weinstein notes were emerging in São Paulo in the 1920s.

41　Campos, Crônica, 443.

42　On the progressive planters of São Paulo, see Barbara Weinstein's essay in this volume, "The Decline of the Progressive Planter."

43　Before and after the declaration of the republic, the real (pl. réis) was the basic unit of currency in Brazil. One thousand reis were referred to as one conto, and usually written as 1:000$000. 10:000$, therefore, would have been expressed as 10 contos and worth the equivalent of 5,000 to 10,000 well-producing cacao trees at the time. Eusinio Lavigne, Como nasceu o Instituto de Cacau da Bahia (Salvador, Bahia, 1974), 4; Wright, "Market, Land, and Class," chapter 4.

44　On the impression that Vargas's appointees had of the cacao region, see Juracy Magalhaes, Minha vida pública na Bahia (Rio de Janeiro: Livraria José Olympio Editora, 1957), 112.

45　Lavigne, Como nasceu, 4–5; Otto E. Seligsohn, O cacau da Bahia: História e problemática (Salvador, Bahia: Edição IPESA, 1970), 23; Wright, "Market, Land, and Class," chapter 4.

46　Instituto de Cacau da Bahia, Livro de Asociados; Seligsohn, O cacau, 23; Wright, "Market, Land, and Class," chapter 4.

47　Ignacio Tosta Filho, Reestabelecendo a verdade sobre o cacau brasileiro; Tosta Filho, Instituto de Cacao da Bahia, secção B do volume 2 do plano de ação econômica para o Estado da Bahia (Bahia: Instituto de Cacau da Bahia, 1948), 24–40; see, for example, Instituto de Cacau da Bahia, Relatório da directoria referente ao anno de 1935 (Salvador, Bahia, 1936).

48　Gregório Bondar, A cultura de cacao na Bahia, Instituto de Cacao da Bahia, Boletim Téchnico no. 1 (São Paulo: Empreza Graphica da "Revista dos Tribunães," 1938), 23.

49　Amado denies any direct correlation between his characters and actual human beings. Jorge Amado, O menino grapiúno (Rio de Janeiro: Editora Record, 1981), 11–14; and Navegação de cabotagem (Rio de Janeiro: Editora Record, 1992), 444–47.

50　Jorge Amado, O pais do carnaval, Cacau. Suor. 10th ed. (São Paulo: Livraria Martins Editora, 1961): 154–55, 187–89.

51　Jorge Amado, The Violent Land, trans. Samuel Putnam (New York: Avon, 1988), originally published as Terras do sem fim (São Paulo: Editora Martins, 1943); Jorge Amado, The Golden

Harvest, trans. Clifford E. Landers (New York: Avon Books, 1992), originally published as São Jorge dos Ilhéos (São Paulo: Editora Martins, 1944).

52 Amado, The Violent Land, 203.

53 Ibid., 32–33.

54 Amado, Cacau, 155.

55 Amado, The Violent Land, 85.

56 Amado, São Jorge dos Ilhéos.

57 Bobby J. Chamberlain, Jorge Amado, Twayne's World Author Series (Boston: Twayne Publishers, 1990), xvi.

58 Jorge Amado and Adonias Filho, A nação grapiúna: Adonias Filho na Academia, Series: Biblioteca de Estudos Literários, 2 (Rio de Janeiro: Edições Tempo Brasileiro, 1965).

59 Pan American Union, Documentary Material on Cacao: For the Use of the Special Committee on Cacao of the Inter-American Social and Economic Council, Washington, D.C., 1947; Inês Amélia Leal Teixeira Guerra "O cacau na Bahia," Revista Brasileira de Geografia 14 (1952): 81–99; Carlos de Castro Botelho, "Aspectos geográficos da zona cacaueira da Bahia," Revista Brasileira de Geografia 16, 2 (April–June, 1954): 161–212; Anthony Leeds, "Economic Cycles in Brazil: The Persistence of a Total Culture-Pattern: Cacao and Other Cases," Ph.D. diss., Columbia University, 1957; and Milton Santos, Zona do cacau: Introdução ao estudo geográfico, 2d ed. (São Paulo: 1957).

60 Navarro, "Movimentos sociais," 248–54; Seligsohn, O cacau, 32; Garcez and Guerreiro, Bahia cacaueira, 39–43; Amilcar Baiardi, Subordinação do trabalho ao capital na lavoura cacaueira da Bahia (São Paulo: Editora Hucitec, 1984), 62–65.

61 Jorge Amado, Gabriela, Clove, and Cinnamon, trans. James L. Taylor and William Grossman (New York: Avon Books, 1978), 22–28; originally published as Gabriela, cravo, e canela (São Paulo: Editora Martins, 1958).

62 Eusinio Lavigne, Cultura e regionalismo cacaueiro: A personalidade de Manoel Ferreira da Camara Betencourt e Sá (Rio de Janeiro: Editora Cultura Brasileira, 1967), 23–24; interview, Dona Alina Afonso de Carvalho, 20 July 1999.

63 On CEPLAC, see Garcez and Guerreiro, Bahia cacaueira, 44; Baiardi, Subordinação, 65–68.

64 Carlos Pereira Filho, Ilhéus, terra do cacau (Ilhéus, Bahia: Editora Andes, n.d.), 18.

65 Odette Rosa da Silva, "Os homens do cacau," Tese de doutoramento, Universidade de São Paulo, 1975, 289–91.

66 Brandão and Rosário, Estórias da história, 83–342.

67 Ibid., 283.

68 On the military period in the cacao area, see Bandeira de Mello, ed., Cartilha histórica, 172–73.

69 Interview, Dona Carmen Sa Steiger Queiroz, 11 April 1989; Dona Alina Affonso de Carvalho, 20 July 1990.

70 Adonias Filho, Sul da Bahia: Chão de cacau (Uma civilização regional) (São Paulo: Civilização Brasileira, 1976), 27–28, 43, 51–53, 77–80.

71 Angelina Nobre Rolim Garcez, "Mecanismos de formação de propriedade cacaueira no eixo Ilhéus-Itabuna (1890–1930)," dissertaçao apresentada ao Mestrado em Ciencias Sociais da Universidade Federal da Bahia, 1977, 15–20, 165; Antonio Fernando Guerreiro de Freitas, "Os donos dos frutos de ouro," dissertaçao apresentada ao Mestrado em Ciencias Sociais da Universidade Federal da Bahia, 1979; CEPLAC, Diagnóstico socioeconômico da região cacaueira, vol. 9 (Ilhéus, Bahia: Commissão Executiva do Plano da Lavoura Cacaueira, 1976), 17, 24; Garcez, Angelina Nobre Rolim, and Antonio Fernando Guerreiro de Freitas, Bahia cacaueira: Um estudo de historia recente (Estudos Baianos, Univer-

sidade Federal da Bahia, no. 11, Salvador Bahia: Núcleo de Publicações do Centro Editorial e Didático da Universidade Federal da Bahia, 1979.

72 Guerreiro de Freitas, "Os donos," n.p.

73 Wright, "Market, Land, and Class," 29–44.

74 Eul Soo Pang, *Bahia in the First Republic*; Dain Borges, *The Family in Bahia*, 21, 56.

75 Gustavo Aryocara de Oliveira Falcón, "Os coronéis do cacau: Raízes do mandonismo político em Ilhéus, 1890–1930," dissertação apresentada ao Mestrado em Ciencias Sociais da Universidade Federal da Bahia, 1983, 21; Baiardi, *Subordinação*, 57; Selim Rashid Asmar, *Economia da microregião cacaueira* (Ilhéus, Bahia: CEPLAC 1985).

76 Jorge Amado, *Showdown*, trans. Gregory Rabassa (New York: Bantam Books, 1988), originally published as *Tocaia grande: A face oscura* (São Paulo: Editora Record, 1986).

77 Personal communication, Agenor Gasparetto, June 1989. For further debates between Gasparetto and Asmar, see Gasparetto, *Cacau mitos e outras coisas mais* (Itabuna, Bahia: Proplan, 1986).

78 See CEPLAC, *A socioeconomia rural da região*.

79 The importance of monuments and the physical landscape in the creation of our ideas about the past is explored in David Lowenthal, *The Past Is a Foreign Country* (Cambridge: Cambridge University Press, 1990).

80 Hawlbachs, *On Collective Memory*, 182.

81 Bastide, *African Religions*, 240–48.

82 For a very insightful discussion of forgetting, see Cohen, *The Combing of History*; see also Jeffrey Gould's fascinating essay in this volume on memories of La Matanza in El Salvador.

Jeffrey L. Gould

Revolutionary Nationalism
and Local Memories in El Salvador

▼

In January 1998 a ceremony took place in Nahuizalco, El Salvador, in commemoration of one of the bloodiest repressions in modern Latin American
history. The 1932 massacre occurred after a peasant uprising, and on
January 22, government troops executed at least ten thousand people,
mostly Indians, including more than a third of the region's adult male
population. A local human rights group loosely affiliated with the Frente
Farabundo Martí de Liberación Nacional (FMLN) organized the event,
which was to include indigenous dance, musical performances, and oral
testimonies of La Matanza. Despite the organizers' assurances, however,
no old-timers recounted their stories at the event. Instead, a historian from
the capital offered a traditional leftist narrative of a heroic peasant uprising
crushed by brutal repression. Other speakers called La Matanza ethnocide,
pointing to the prohibition of the Nahuatl language and indigenous dress.
Listening in the audience were elderly folks who in 1932 had been children
or adolescents.

Both the Left and the Right have long regarded the events of 1932 as
pivotal in modern Salvadoran history. When President Francisco Flores
kicked off his recent campaign in Izalco, he did so because, "Here we
buried communism!" Since 1932, the governing elites have successfully
placed anticommunism at the center of their nationalist discourse. Yet for
the Left, the meaning of 1932 has shifted quite dramatically from a heroic
class struggle that revealed the brutality of the ruling elite to an ethnocidal
massacre. The manifestos and analyses of the revolutionary Left in the
1970s and early 1980s are silent about indigenous participation in 1932.[1]
During the past decade, however, responding to the impact of the anti-

quincentenary campaign and the activities of local indigenous activists, those rebellious *campesinos* and workers have became "*indígenas*."

In this chapter I offer some perspective on why the indigenous militants could not find an "available" or "useful" testimony about 1932 and, in so doing, probe the disjunctures and silences of revolutionary nationalist discourse. We will attempt to listen to the reverberations of the silenced voices of indigenous witnesses of the massacre, recognizing the fragmentary, localized, and re-created nature of such memories. Whether conditioned by a massacre followed by sixty years of military rule, as in El Salvador, or lesser forms of coercion, as in Nicaragua, those memories, constituents of indigenous identities and guides to collective practice, have not been assimilable by revolutionary nationalist discourse.[2] This essay is a meditation on this tragic irony: revolutionary nationalists fought throughout the century to create a socially and politically inclusive form of the nation, yet in so doing often silenced its indigenous dimension.

Central American nationalisms involve *mestizaje*, understood as a nation-building myth of race mixture and as a cultural process of "de-Indianization" that conditions subaltern consciousness. *Mestizaje* formed a key dimension of nationalist ideology in Central America because it expanded the power and reach of liberalism by allowing for more inclusive forms of national identity in two ways. First, it allowed progressive intellectuals, particularly during the 1920s, to take an active role in nation building by forging anti-imperial images. Sandino and his supporters throughout the region achieved the maximum expression of this in their declaration of struggle for the "indo-hispanic" race.[3] Second, the particular images of the mestizo nation allowed for a greater inclusion of subaltern groups (I am referring to peasants, artisans, workers, semiproletarians, and petty-trades people) through the forging of a version of liberalism shorn of its most egregious racism and elitism. For many of these people, *mestizaje* in its various national permutations offered a positive and ennobling identity. Yet, as we probe the subaltern, in particular the indigenous responses to *mestizaje*, we will uncover some of the hidden political and cultural costs of this component of nation building in the twentieth century.

The impact of the emergence of *mestizaje* on the indigenous people may be better appreciated with recourse to the notion of "the unthinkable." Michel-Rolph Trouillot cites Bourdieu's remark that the unthinkable of an epoch is so not only for ethical and political inclinations, but also because of a lack of conceptual instruments. Trouillot then adds, "The unthinkable is that which one cannot conceive within the range of possible alternatives, that which perverts all answers because it defies the terms under which the questions were phrased."[4] This notion is relevant in two respects. First, the

Sites of Rebellion, 1932.

traumatic events of 1932 and the subsequent military regimes made it largely unthinkable for indigenous people to conceive of their own agency in the period of mobilization. Second, the construction of myths of *mestizaje*, dominant views of society as ethnically homogenous, made it unthinkable to conceive of indigenous cultures that re-created themselves without reference to ethnic emblems such as language and dress.[5] In contrast to colonial or postcolonial situations, in several Central American cases over a century after the end of colonial rule, class and ethnic oppression often took the form of "invisibility," a failure to recognize indigenous people as culturally distinct and autonomous cultural groups. Indeed, I would argue that phenotypical or linguistic similarities between ladino (non-Indian) and indigenous peasants—typical of the contemporary cases of indigenous peoples in the western portions of Nicaragua, Honduras, and El Salvador—creates the possibilities or even the likelihood of deep misunderstandings between emerging revolutionary nationalists and indigenous groups.

The bulk of the Salvadoran indigenous population, representing perhaps 20 percent of the population in 1930, resided in a geographically contiguous area of western Salvador, in the departments of Ahuachapán, La Libertad, and Sonsonate.[6] Not surprisingly, however, the term "indigenous" referred to many different kinds of identities. Often in the 1920s in the same indigenous *cantón* (a village-sized unit within a municipality) there would be some who wore traditional dress and spoke Nahuatl (although males were usually bilingual) and others who dressed as ladinos and were monolingual Spanish speakers. Such marked differences often corresponded to a pattern of social geography whereby those areas most directly dominated by coffee plantations were the least identifiably indigenous. A failure to account for this internal differentiation of indigenous groups has led to confusion about the ethnic and class dimensions of the 1932 rebellion.

It is also important to consider the unique characteristics of the Salvadoran agrarian elite. The coffee plantation owners played an extraordinarily powerful role within the national elite (indeed, they were often synonymous). The power of the regional coffee elite and its geographical coincidence with a cohesive indigenous community allowed it to dictate the ethnocidal events of 1932.

Memories of La Matanza

Following the 1921 failure of the Central American unionist experiment, an emerging nationalist intelligentsia consciously strove to create a Salvadoran identity draped in specifically "Cuzcatlecan" indigenous origins. Indigenous folklore became a key part of the nationalist movement, and the study of the indigenous language, Nahuatl, briefly gained importance.[7] Similarly, a group of nationalist historians invented an indigenous cacique, Atlacatl. The same group persuaded the government to pay for a statue which was in fact a self-portrait of the sculptor, and then baptized it as a statue of Atlacatl, "part of the national patrimony, representative . . . of the Salvadoran nationality."[8]

The Salvadoran strand of *mestizaje*, like the Mexican and Nicaraguan counterparts, strongly valorized the indigenous contribution. In the 1920s the writer Miguel Angel Espino expressed his understanding of the roots of Salvadoran nationalism in the following terms: "The de-Hispanization of the continent is . . . one of the problems that has modified the life of the continent, albeit in hidden and latent forms. By demonstrating this, we are Indians. Of five liters of blood that we possess, only one cup of Spanish blood flows within; the rest is American . . . out of the mixing of Spain and America derived a new race; to believe that the race was (mostly) Spanish was an error."[9]

Rebels about to be shot. National Archives of Canada.

These nationalist intellectuals developed a reasonably strong sense of group identity, as revealed by the folklorist and ethnomusicologist María de Baratta, writing about the late 1920s:

> The year 1931 was a year of an abundant spiritual harvest of Salvadoran folklore and for the dignity and redemption of some aspects of our Indian, of lo indio; in other words, of something that still beats with great strength and force to the impulse of the autochthonous sediment that still vibrates within us, in order to mark the road of their needs and rights.
>
> There is a group of youthful spirits who are seeing . . . the sun rise of a new day that will light up the tremulous race. There was a great spirit of work, research, and improvement in this group.[10]

These introductory sentences to her two-volume study, published in 1952, are curious. First, although she uses the past tense to specify the year 1931, the use of the present tense at the start of the second paragraph throws off the reader's sense of time, especially since the publication was the result of twenty-eight years of research. Undoubtedly her silence on La Matanza distorts the temporal dimension of the study; in more than seven hundred pages of writing on Salvadoran Indians, she makes only one passing reference to La Matanza: "In this same town that witnessed the fratricidal struggles between ladinos and naturales during that unforgettable January!"[11]

De Baratta's reference to 1931 does raise potentially important questions about the relationship of this cultural movement and the concrete struggles of Indians for their "necessities and rights" during that year. Although it is doubtful this cultural movement was directly involved with the popular mobilizations of that year, it does seem likely that to a limited degree they enabled each other: the cultural movement, and especially the university students attached to it, responded to and vaguely supported the movement for social justice, and the Indian labor activists took advantage of the limited discursive and political opening. La Matanza, of course, closed off any possibility for the maturation of such a relation between national intellectuals and the western Salvadoran Indians.

Following La Matanza, Salvadoran *mestizaje* continued to gather force. The ennobling of the Indian past accompanied anticommunism as fundamental components of the emerging national identity. The regime popularized the "day of the Indian," when city dwellers would dress up as Indians. Similarly, at elite "coffee balls," guests wore Indian costumes. The real Indians, of course, became increasingly marginalized.[12]

La Matanza must be understood in the context of the ideological blossoming of *mestizaje*, the simultaneous ennobling of the indigenous past and the creation of a nonoligarchic, popular national identity. None of these examples suggest that the discourse of *mestizaje* had reached a level approaching that in Mexico or Nicaragua. Rather, we must rethink the view of La Matanza as a logical outcome of a virulently racist political culture. Tentatively, we suggest that from the 1920s onward the oligarchy had to compete with other ideological currents and that its classical liberal racism did not predominate in the formation of national-level discourse. In this regard, we need to focus more on the political and cultural relationships between local Indians and ladinos, and the relationship between local and national elites (including the army).[13] After La Matanza the army and what was left of the intelligentsia attempted to reinsert the surviving (and dead) Indians into the preexisting discourse and policy of *mestizaje*. How that reinsertion took place in discourse and in political/cultural practice needs to be studied closely. Although strongly shaped by La Matanza, that process in no way can be reduced to a paradigm of forced acculturation and cultural ethnocide.

The 1932 Rebellion

The repression of an increasingly powerful communist-led labor movement played a major role in creating the conditions for the rebellion of January 1932.[14] The economic crisis, combined with a wave of land dis-

Executed Indians inside Sonsonate barracks. National Archives of Canada.

possession over the previous decade, helped to spark an impressive labor-organizing drive. By 1931, 50 percent wage cuts drove the increasingly land-poor rural folk in the coffee zone below subsistence levels. In the words of a newspaper editor, "When the rural worker had food he put up with his bad treatment. But now the *finquero* needs to reduce the number of *mozos* he employs and to cut the already low daily wage. The repressed discontent breaks out.[15] Labor organizers mobilized around the wage cuts and increased their membership from a tiny minority of the workforce to at least 25,000 members (concentrated in the coffee zone of central and western Salvador) out of a total national population of 1.5 million.[16]

Since 1927, a democratic opening had allowed for the growth of social democratic and communist parties. In 1931, in the first free elections in Salvadoran history (and the last until the 1980s), Arturo Araujo, a reform-ist, was elected president. Significantly, the Araujo campaign raised hopes of land reform among the rural poor, and the failure to meet that promise provoked further discontent. One U.S. embassy observer commented on "all kinds of election promises which led many farmers and laborers to think that the millennium was likely once Araujo was elected. There was rumored . . . that the big coffee estates would be divided and every family given its acre of ground . . . the unrest of the last few days may be laid partially to the rural population's somewhat hastily drawn conclusion that the president has turned his back on them."[17]

There was also a cultural dimension to the mobilization. The majority of the inhabitants of the coffee-producing departments of Ahuachapán and Sonsonate were self-identified Indians, many of whom spoke Nahuatl and dressed in a distinctive style. Notwithstanding, many of their neighbors spoke only Spanish and dressed in the ladino style. For several decades, but especially since the political opening of 1927, Indian factions, often in alliance with ladinos, battled for control over the region's municipal governments. Previously, indigenous political control had often been assured through an alliance with the governing party. During the administration of Pío Romero Bosque (1927–31), but especially following the electoral campaign of 1930–31, that alliance crumbled, at least in the important indigenous barrio of Izalco. There, the indigenous cacique, Feliciano Ama, following the electoral defeat of the officialist candidate, pushed his *cofradía* (lay confraternities that often combined religious and political functions) into an alliance with the Communist Party.[18] The combination of this alliance, sharp ethnic polarization in the municipalities, and the union activism of many Indians gave a strongly indigenous cast to the mobilization and rebellion.[19] However, in the important coffee region of the department of La Libertad, the large majority of the people involved in the mobilization neither identified themselves as indigenous nor were identified as such by others. In the coffee region south of Atiquizaya, another important base of rural activism, people clearly identified as ladinos formed the main element of the movement.

On December 2, 1931, a military coup overthrew Araujo and installed his vice president, General Maximiliano Hernández Martínez, as president. One of the first actions of the military government was to postpone the municipal and congressional elections until early January. The Left has generally posited that the regime consciously used the elections to provoke an uprising and then repression. Surely the regime was aware that Communist slates could triumph in Ahuachapán and Sonsonate, and perhaps in San Salvador. Similarly, they were aware that particularly in western Salvador, given the bitter labor conflicts, peasants and workers would respond violently to any attempt to tamper with the votes.[20] On January 13, the British chargé d'affaires reported on strikes that combined economic demands and political protest: "The Communist agitation among plantation labourers is steadily increasing in seriousness. . . . It has already given rise to serious affrays between the national forces and the Communists, and the loss of life has been considerable . . . the large body of armed strikers . . . move about in the west intimidating the plantation workers and obliging them to leave their employment. These men are armed with revolvers.[21]

Whether the elections involved a conscious provocation or not, two points are worth bearing in mind: the Communist activists did believe that the Martínez government had thwarted probable Communist electoral victories in western Salvador and had directly provoked the violent strike movements in the countryside. Political resistance to the electoral fraud in conjunction with intense union agitation on the plantations sparked spontaneous revolts and violent confrontations with the National Guard. Referring to the strikes during the first two weeks of January, an internal Communist Party document written in 1934 stated:

The strikes in the western zone had been combated by the military and the general strike could not be carried out; the higher body sent a commission to meet with President Martínez with the object of reaching agreements but the (government) people that met with them told them that since the country people had machetes and the government had machine guns, they were not going to accept any kind of truce. When the *occidentales* became aware of what happened they threw themselves into battle and that is how the insurrection was provoked.[22]

Other accounts differ in minor respects but similarly underscore that the decision to plan an insurrection came directly after the government's refusal to negotiate a peaceful solution to the crisis.[23] The Communist Party, in part inspired by the "Third Phase" revolutionary program of the Communist International, and in part fearing a significant loss of legitimacy among the peasantry if they did not respond to the government provocation by leading the workers and peasants in battle, reluctantly opted for an insurrectionary adventure. The insurrection failed before it began: the government arrested the Communist leadership and some key supporters in the military several days before the scheduled insurrection on January 22. Poor communication, exacerbated by the military alert, impeded apparent attempts to call off the insurrection.

On January 22 and 23 thousands of rebels, armed mostly with machetes, assaulted government buildings and looted stores in a dozen municipalities in central and western Salvador. Although the rebels harassed ladinos, including forcing them to perform menial labor, only sixty were killed or executed in the uprising. The rebels targeted mayors, in particular, for execution. It is difficult to identify the makeup of the rebel bands except to note that many of those who attacked Ahuachapán and Juayua were probably the same people (mostly nonindigenous) involved in the roving strikes cited by the British official. Indians from the barrio of Asunción in Izalco and Indian and Ladino plantation workers from the outlying *cantones* of that municipality participated in the failed attack on the Sonsonate barracks. Finally, coffee workers from the Cumbre de Jayaque staged the attack on Santa Tecla (eight miles west of San Salvador).

The rebels, when successful, occupied the municipal buildings and then broke into the town's stores (and some mansions), inviting the town residents to participate in the looting. An American Protestant minister in Juayua wrote immediately after the event: "The 'reds' distributed the spoils with a lavish hand; in fact they wanted all those who were not otherwise lined up with them, to share in their ill-gotten gains, in order that they be thus identified with their cause . . . men clothed in rags carrying off fine clothes, bright colored, woolen blankets, hats, implements; women bearing proudly on their heads sheets of corrugated iron, measures of corn, bolts of cloth; children with their pockets full of candies, handkerchiefs and toys. . . . Thus was the town of Juayúa sacked."[24]

In Nahuizalco, indigenous people from the suburbs, known as *las afueras*, participated in similar activities. The military arrived within three days and immediately crushed the insurrection, although the rebels held out a few days longer in the isolated village of Tacuba. Then the killing began in earnest, and government troops and civil guards began executing thousands of people in central and western Salvador.

Memories of Cause

None of the more than seventy testimonies of witnesses of 1932 that we have recorded narrate the events in a way that resembles the above account. Most significantly, indigenous agency is suppressed in these testimonies. A typical account runs as follows: "The ladinos were behind *el robo* [the robbery]. The looters included Indians but the Communist leaders came from Turín and Atiquizaya [predominantly ladino towns]. Some of the ladino leaders tricked the Indians and then when the troops came the ladinos escaped and the Indians died. *Pagaron los justos por los pecadores* [the just paid for the sinners]."[25]

All accounts are highly fragmentary. What narrative coherence does exist hinges upon the interrelated tropes of anticommunism ("ladino" is often interchangeable with "Communist") and *el robo*. The interchangeability is all the more intriguing since, at the time, the ladino elite identified Indians with Communists. One hacendado exclaimed: "There is not an Indian who is not a Communist."[26] Beyond the need to invert this aspect of the dominant discourse, there seem to be several causes for the high level of fragmentation and its rightist hue. The large majority of the eyewitnesses were children or young adolescents at the time of La Matanza. They were less likely to have comprehended the causes of the rebellion and relied for such interpretations on post-Matanza familial, communal, or official explanations.[27]

Moreover, the terror associated with the events conditioned the suppression of agency in indigenous memories. Fear of state or local ladino reprisal undoubtedly led survivors to avoid implicating their kin and neighbors. Since the military-oligarchic alliance remained in power until the 1980s, the passage of time did nothing to diminish the traumatically induced fear. This fear can be seen in the manner of speaking itself: some informants' lips barely moved when speaking. Similarly, only one informant could recall any song about the insurrection or the massacre, other than one lamenting the death of Emilio Redaelli, hacendado and former mayor of Juayúa. The consequent omission of indigenous subjects at the very least confuses the narrative and certainly affected generational transmission.

Finally, the social geography of the rebellion and of interethnic relations strongly shaped the memory of particular informants. After interviewing people in some twenty distinct locations, it has become clear that the particular social history of a rural cantón colored the particular emphases, tones, and textures of guilt, mourning, and resentment. Those often profound differences further complicated the collective transmission of stories; they also made them largely inaccessible to outside groups, such as the Left or the intelligentsia.

It is important to note that in the most traditional areas, where most people spoke Nahuatl, there was little or no participation in the insurrection, and indigenous agency is thus suppressed dramatically. In Santo Domingo de Guzmán and Santa Catarina de Masahuat, people recall that divine intervention saved their communities: people recall that an archangel stopped the insurrectionists as they were about to enter their communities. With a slight variation on the theme, the elders of Cuisnahuat, another Nahuatl-speaking village, recall that San Lucas saved both the village and a local Communist leader. Similarly, in Salcoatitán, people remember that when the insurrection was under way, San Miguel appeared and called a halt to it, thus supposedly saving ladino lives and property.[28] In another village, Apaneca, people tell the story of three saints who intercepted the rebels and caused water and volcanic ash to fall on their heads, thus driving them away.[29]

A more significant site of memories of 1932 is Izalco, where indigenous inhabitants living in several ethnically segregated barrios formed a substantial minority of the town's population. Ladinos and indigenous people inhabited the cantones. Somewhat surprisingly, the Indians of the cantones were apparently more ladino-ized than those of the barrio, and there was apparently little contact between the two groups. The Indians and ladinos of the cantones who worked as jornaleros on haciendas such as San Isidro and Los Lagartos were among the first recruits to the labor movement in Sonsonate.[30]

Although memories of the rebellion's causes in Izalco were weak, they do offer a glimpse of what may have been salient in the local mobilization, the rebellion, and the repression—ethnic polarization that paralleled, incorporated, and intensified class conflicts. Local ladinos are the ubiquitous antagonists in all of the testimonies, as the "Communists" who tricked and deceived the Indians, as rebels from ladino towns, and especially as those local leaders who denounced Indians to the murderous civil guards. In short, regardless of the specific role assigned to ladinos, it is charged with negativity and activity as opposed to indigenous innocence and passivity.

Virginia Tilley and Erick Ching have recently offered important empirical data that substantiates the notion that a military-Indian political alliance emerged in Izalco.[31] In the months following La Matanza, the military regime provided food for the survivors and protected them against the vengeance of local ladinos. Over the following decade, pro-Indian policies continued, including special schools for orphans of the massacre, support for Indians in land and water disputes, and official recognition of the indigenous civil-religious hierarchy that local ladinos attempted to abolish. Given the severe disruption of family life and the asymmetrical power relations that followed La Matanza, this emerging alliance surely influenced local memories of the mobilization and the repression.

Not surprisingly, the military version of events entered into the local narrative. The military immediately developed an explanation of the revolt that blamed previous governments and absolved itself from a decisive role in the massacre: "The history would have been very different if those in power had been inclined to listen to the just demands."[32] Stories also circulated throughout the region about Martínez's indigenous origins and his sympathies for the pre-insurrection labor struggles. A typical account suggested that Martínez wanted the rural poor to engage in nonviolent protests so that he could use their mobilization as a political weapon against the oligarchy.[33] Others suggest that he personally was not to blame for La Matanza. In short, many elderly indigenous people in Izalco and elsewhere have favorable recollections of the Martínez regime.[34]

In the municipality of Nahuizalco, however, the narratives—without unraveling the threads of anticommunism, looting, and ladino agency—more visibly tie the Indian/ladino opposition to the prevailing levels of class conflict. In Nahuizalco, some informants recall specific demands of the mobilizations: land, higher salaries, decent housing, and medicine. They recall village union meetings, leaflets, and the felt desire to "work together." Some informants recall the key role of elders in organizing to reappropriate the land lost by their parents and grandparents.

According to several informants in Nahuizalco, the nefarious role of the ladino plantation owners was more determinant than a sense of rekindled outrage about the loss of land: they provoked the rebellion in response to the growing power of the rural union movement. According to one informant, Gabino Mata, a major landholder, "called his workers to explain to them about the red leaflets. He said, 'Well, these are good for you and pretty bad for me since the land is going to belong to the poor people.' "[35] A common version of the story about how Mata took advantage of the first wave of terror states that "Gabino Mata called together his workers in order to give them a *salvaconducto*. But he turned them over to the military."[36] Similarly, Raimundo Gómez, ten years old at the time, recalls that "the foreman called my father and the other workers to give them a *contraseña*, but the password was bullets."[37]

Most of the rural indigenous informants in Nahuizalco explain this mortal betrayal as a consequence of the landlords' fear of losing the land. The story comes quite close to forming a coherent thread of collective memory of those survivors of the northeastern *cantones* of Nahuizalco. The nine informants, including eyewitnesses, all tell roughly the same tale of betrayal.[38] The British consul did report a similar event that took place three weeks after La Matanza in the town of Nahuizalco.

> There was a bad affair at Nahuizalco last Friday. About a thousand Indians drifted into town that morning, ostensibly with the object of procuring from the Mayor the new *boleto de identidad* to show that the bearer is not a communist. The mayor became alarmed when he saw how many were coming and he telegraphed urgently, twice, for help. Troops were sent from Sonsonate, Juayúa and Izalco. They surrounded the town, lined up the Indians and searched them. Then it was found that many of them had concealed knives and a notice calling them to Nahuizalco for the "day of vengeance." The troops shot 388. . . . Many planters are still afraid to go back to their estates.[39]

Directly responsible for this atrocity was the town's mayor, who had survived rebel efforts to capture and kill him. It is difficult to ascertain the role of *terratenientes* like Mata in this last act of La Matanza. According to one testimony, Gabino Mata, a congressional deputy, along with his brother, was also complicit in this last atrocity in Nahuizalco. Regardless of their ulterior motives, there seems little doubt that planters did encourage their workers to obtain the identity papers, and that accounted for the large turnout. The possibility that the Nahuizalqueños were planning a "day of vengeance" is remote.[40] It is striking, however, that there is so much clarity and unanimity about Mata as opposed to previous moments in the mobilization and repression. We could argue that the collective nature of this memory derives from the unambiguous moral position of the murdered Nahuizalqueños. Both Mata's victim in the cantón El Canelo and those murdered while awaiting their *boleto de identidad* were innocent victims who had not been implicated in *el robo*. Indeed, the three weeks that separated the uprising from the last round of killing may have removed not only the victims but also the military and elite perpetrators from the more ambiguous categories of actors that were involved in the mobilization and immediate repression. In other words, rather than Communists, looters, and ladinos, the relevant categories became deceitful landlords, the military, and (implicitly indigenous) plantation workers.

In the Nahuizalqueño memories, then, the temporal separation of the February killings from *el robo* allowed for a more pronounced emphasis on elite antagonists and the class roots of the mobilization than in Izalco.[41] Probably of more importance was the relative weakness of the military-Indian organizational alliance in Nahuizalco, due to the growing disarticulation of the local civil-religious hierarchy before and after La Matanza.[42]

These hints of a counter-discourse in Nahuizalco did not crystallize but rather fragmented at the margins of memories unified by *el robo* and by anticommunism. The violent transformation of power relations and the trauma of collective annihilation explain, to a certain extent, the emergence of these contradictory memories. Those forms, in turn, allowed the communities to mitigate their collective grief and terror, emotions compounded by their complete impotence against the repression and by their difficulty in mourning their loved ones.

Long after La Matanza, local folks refused to touch pork since hogs had feasted on the rotting corpses. Similarly, one informant recalls stumbling across human bones, and his elders telling him, "There are your brothers."[43] Particularly tragic in their memories was their inability to provide a decent burial. Some survivors claim that the fear of repression blocked the possibility of proper mourning. Said the daughter of one survivor, "The mourners were afraid to have a wake for fear of the authorities.[44] Yet, at some mass grave sites, people put crosses and left flowers annually for a few years. It is unclear why that practice ceased, and why the crosses were not maintained. Some informants suggest that a lack of assurance that their loved ones were actually buried at the site dissuaded the survivors from continuing to leave flowers.[45] That, in turn, suggests a growing individualization of commemorative practices as these collective graves became inadequate sites for mourning. After less than a decade they became rarely mentioned historical reference points, apparently devoid of spiritual significance.

The testimony of Paulino Galicia, the son of a former indigenous municipal official, provides additional insight about the failure for a counter-narrative to emerge in the Nahuizalco region. Galicia's testimony points to the high level of the preceding mobilization and the state's repressive response as the key determinants of the insurrection. He vividly recalls that on two different Sundays (in 1930 or 1931) the National Guard broke up large open-air union meetings in Nahuizalco and hauled off hundreds of Indians from the *cantones* in trucks. He also reveals something of the class fissures within the community that the mobilization exacerbated. Several local indigenous leaders, all former *regidores* (councilmen), had asked his father to participate in the movement. The former mayor refused to aid the movement. Both Galicia and his father were working on their small farm when the insurrection broke out and were thus spared harm by either side. Galicia's father had a small laboring force that worked his cane field. He vividly recalls when a laborer told his father: "What a shame! You folks are going to disappear because whoever doesn't want to join is going to disappear and whoever wants to join is going to appear."[46]

This testimony suggests two aspects of the revolt that warrant further research. First, the unmistakable millenarian ring to "whoever doesn't join will disappear" is echoed in other testimonies in Nahuizalco that often include the refrain "The last shall be first." In addition, there is documentary evidence of a millenarian dimension of the rebellion. An eyewitness to the repression, Commander V. G. Brodeur, commanding officer of the Canadian destroyer the *Skeena*, reported the following:

> Another interesting and illuminating fact observed was the very peaceful look on the faces of those dead, this fact is specially noticeable in the case of the Indian Chief. . . . In fact it was proved that all the Indians executed were apparently glad to sacrifice their lives in the hope that this martyrdom might bring a brighter future for the next generation . . . the case of a young pregnant married woman who was informed her husband had just been executed by troops, her only answer being that she did not care as she was carrying his avenger and future rebel against society.[47]

This millenarian aspect, however, should not be exaggerated. Rather, given its lack of an explicit religious imagery, on one hand, and its immediate origins in rather prosaic wage demands, we should analyze millenarianism in a subordinate role within the broader movement.[48]

Galicia's testimony also reveals indigenous agency; yet, in so doing, it underscores class fissures within the community that were not visible in other testimonies from the indigenous campesinos. We might argue, then, that class divisions, in addition to others such as those between more-traditional and more-assimilated groups of Indians (for example, the absence of rebellion in Santo Domingo and Santa Catarina), contributed to the weakness of the movement. Those divisions also contributed to the fragmentation of indigenous memories.

To conclude this discussion of memories of causes, let's briefly consider the testimony of Fabián Mojica, a ladino carpenter and pro-Communist union activist, who was twenty-seven years old in 1932. At the moment of the uprising, Mojica was in a San Salvador prison along with several hundred political prisoners from the department of Sonsonate. His recollections of union organizing in the countryside minimize the importance of cultural difference. Union activists recruited acquaintances in neighboring Indian and ladino *cantones* who, in turn, would persuade the other villagers to join the union to fight for demands about salary and working conditions. For Mojica, there was no communication difficulty across ethnic barriers because the Indians readily understood the need to fight for such demands. Following a classic Leninist script, Mojica's version highlights the constant repression of that struggle, which drove the union activists, Indian and ladino, toward more militant positions.[49]

Mojica's testimony shares certain characteristics with those of other leftist ladinos.[50] On the one hand, he expresses great admiration for *indios comprensivos* and *indios arrechos*; he manifests enormous respect for Indians as militants capable of great intelligence, courage, and commitment. Yet, at the same time, for the union militant, all proletarians, ladinos or Indians, had the same basic concerns and interests. That view, revalidated in his daily activities, led him to dismiss the importance of cultural differences between ladinos and Indians, or within the indigenous communities. Mojica's lack of interest in ethnic identity reflects I would argue a degree of cultural difference, a gap that would become important in posterior reconstructions of the events.

Memories of Consequences

There is a significant gulf between contemporary leftist and indigenous activist (often the same people in western Salvador) narratives on one hand, and oral testimony of Matanza survivors on the other. There are, however, also small bridges between the two, across which the militants have appropriated selective memories to support their theses. Although activists and local informants both recognize that La Matanza accelerated the process of cultural *mestizaje* in western Salvador, leftists and Indian activists argue that La Matanza involved ethnocide: specific state attacks on indigenous language and dress. For indigenous activists, forced assimilation involving the elimination of the most important ethnic markers is a politically useful concept because it transforms a complicated process of state assaults and coercion against their people into powerful, convincing tropes: the state prohibition of Nahuatl and *el refajo* (female indigenous dress) in 1932. In the testimonies of survivors, those ethnic markers possess extraordinary importance. Similarly, younger Indians and ladinos of all political tendencies often conflate them with indigenous identity itself. At the very least, they represent a strongly salient image of authenticity.

The most important political documents of the Left produced in the late 1970s and 1980s share two characteristics: they cite 1932 as a founding moment of their revolutionary movement, and they omit any mention of the indigenous component of that movement or the repression.[51] The notion that state repression eliminated ethnic markers makes the Left's adherence to a strict language of class much more comprehensible. In other words, by eliminating the ethnic dimension of 1932, it was easier to establish their identity with the proletarianized campesinos who had become the protagonists of the popular struggle in the 1970s.

The class-based narrative—campesinos as the subject of the mobilization and as the object of repression—was acceptable to some indigenous youths in the 1970s because many of them had rejected the surviving ethnic markers of their parents and grandparents. By 1992, the continent-wide campaign against the exaltation of the figure of Columbus affected many local people who became increasingly interested in their indigenous roots.[52] In addition to the anti-quincentenary campaign, nongovernmental organizations tended to offer support for indigenous organizations, thus stimulating indigenous identification in western Salvador. The detailed ethnocide narrative that emerged in the 1990s met the needs of this small group of leftist indigenous activists and eventually came to form a key component of the ideological arsenal of all indigenous groups.

Oral and documentary sources, however, contradict the leftist and Indian activist view that governmental policies following La Matanza directly caused the accelerated process of *mestizaje* in the 1930s and 1940s; the loss of ethnic signs in this account had endogenous causes. In one poignant encounter, a thirty-eight-year-old indigenous communal leader asked a blind octogenarian about the prohibition of Nahuatl following the matanza. The elderly man faced the communal leader and seemed to stare at him quizzically. "What do you mean, prohibition? There was no prohibition. People just stopped talking 'Nahuatl' because the ladinos didn't understand it and we had to deal with them a lot."[53]

Several informants signaled a corner of a submerged edifice of linguistic domination as they recalled when coffee plantation owners or foremen came upon Nahuatl conversations and scolded them with the words "hable bien . . . no hable chapeado" (speak well . . . don't speak all chopped up).[54] Another informant from the *cantones* of Nahuizalco recalled the admonition "Deje de hablar esas babosadas!" (Stop speaking that foolishness).[55] Those relatively mild rebukes were, of course, far from ethnocidal acts. Yet in combination with numerous similar gestures and policies—such as the unofficial prohibition of Nahuatl in schools that educated town Indians before 1930 and village folk after 1950—it surely had a profound effect on the disappearance of Nahuatl in El Salvador.

The informant's view that increased contact with ladinos brought about the language shift should be evaluated in terms of the evolving cultural context. More research needs to be done to understand how the increased frequency of contact and the greater asymmetry of that linguistic exchange provoked the shift from bilingualism to monolingual Spanish usage. But oral testimony does point to a fairly obvious pattern that emerged well before 1930: Nahuatl was weakest in those areas of greatest contact with ladinos (with the apparent exception of Izalco).

Public education in the town centers of Juayua, Nahuizalco, and Izalco before 1932 had a pronounced negative effect on Nahuatl usage. Most Indians in town and in the immediate surroundings born between 1890 and 1910 did not converse in Nahuatl with children or friends, and only did so on special religious occasions or with monolingual parents. Following La Matanza, with many adult males gone, there were even fewer opportunities or incentives to speak or listen to Nahuatl. Similarly, in those regions where coffee plantations bordered or absorbed villages, Nahuatl was only spoken by the eldest generation (born before 1880). Those who were young adults in 1930 were not at all conversant in the language. As in the towns, the repression accelerated a process that was already well advanced.

There were several areas, however, where bilingual or even monolingual Nahuatl speakers predominated: Cuisnahuat, Santo Domingo de Guzmán, and several *cantones* of Nahuizalco. The first two municipalities were well outside of the coffee zone and largely cut off from ladino centers. Nahuatl was the dominant language in the contiguous Nahuizalco *cantones* of Anal, Pushtan, Tajcuilulaj, and Sábana San Juan. Although village residents worked seasonally on coffee plantations, they were not *colonos*. Their household economy was largely based on subsistence economic activities (*milpa* farming and *petate* weaving). It was in these *cantones* where the events of 1932 probably accelerated the decline of Nahuatl as people were thrust into greater contact with ladinos as the spaces of subsistence economic activities closed down and state surveillance increased. Testimony from these *cantones* echoes that cited above. Ramón Aguilar, of Cusamuluco, stated, "No I wasn't interested in speaking Nahuatl. What was the point?

People couldn't understand it."[56] Rosario Lué, originally of Anal Abajo, stated, "No we didn't speak Nahuatl because it was impolite to speak it in front of outsiders. They could be offended."[57]

The outsiders in these testimonies were by no means exclusively ladinos, as more and more town-based Indians could not understand the language. Various elements seem to intermingle in the collective memory of language loss. At the most elemental level, in those *cantones* most affected by La Matanza, Nahuatl had become a language of familial intimacy, and after 1932 that particular linguistic community had become drastically reduced. The fear of offending people cut both ways. Ladinos and non-Nahuatl-speaking Indians could easily have taken offense at conversations that they could not understand (and indeed may have been mocking them), and outsiders scorned Nahuatl speakers. There is also some evidence that authorities around the time of La Matanza cast a threatening glance at anyone who spoke the language, considering it a possible form of subversive activity (particularly in Izalco). Finally, bilingualism is not easy to maintain either individually or collectively in a reduced linguistic community, and people may have seen little point in expending extra energy in an exhausting life when the payoffs seemed so paltry.

Nevertheless, as late as the 1970s, Nahuatl continued as an underground idiom among some families in the *cantones* and especially in Cuisnahuat and Santo Domingo (both largely unaffected by 1932). Linguists and anthropologists were convinced that many families throughout the region spoke Nahuatl at home but denied knowledge to outsiders. It is difficult to estimate the number of Nahuatl speakers in the *cantones* of Nahuizalco, but there is little doubt that as in Cuisnahuat and Santo Domingo, during the sixties and seventies many indigenous youths rejected and even mocked the language of their parents.[58]

There are similar stories about el *refajo*, the other salient ethnic marker of the Salvadoran Indians. Scholars and leftists have viewed the disappearance of el *refajo* (really the decline) as a direct consequence of La Matanza. According to that version, the racist repression drove women to wear ladino clothes. A few testimonies from Izalco and from the coffee zone of Nahuizalco offer some evidence to support that contention. Undoubtedly some women shed the indigenous garb out of fear, and it seems that one group of indigenous village patrolmen right after the first wave of repression ordered women in El Canelo and Sábana San Juan Arriba (neighboring *cantones* in Nahuizalco, bordering on Gabino Mata's plantation) to stop wearing indigenous garb.[59] There is ample documentary and testimonial evidence that the most significant decline in the use of el *refajo* came at least two decades later. A *National Geographic* article in 1944 offers visual and textual evidence that indigenous dress still predominated in the region:

"Women dress in a wrap-around sarong type of skirt and loose blouse. . . . Women of even the more modernized villages cling stubbornly to their sarong skirts. 'I will not put on a round skirt,' they say, speaking of the conventional women's dress."[60]

Salvadoran indigenous women and men, as in the Nicaraguan highlands, offer several different explanations about the demise of indigenous garb. Most emphasize the fact that the best fabric, imported from Guatemala at least since the 1940s, eventually became more expensive than ladino clothes. Others suggest that el refajo is not suitable for field or factory labor. One refajada claimed that her daughters did not want to wear it because it was "too hot."[61] Yet these arguments are contradicted by those who underscore how much longer it lasts than ladino dress, and how indigenous women dressed in el refajo have always performed all manner of field and market labor.

Regardless of the validity of such arguments, their children, male and female, also subtly and not so subtly pressured their mothers to plegarse (to change to ladino clothing).[62] Interviews and documentary sources point to the coincidence of expanded educational opportunities and increased pressure on parents to shed their refajos, and there is little doubt that the pressure derived from a sense of shame about their mother's dress. Consider this dialogue. In response to my question about his generation's ethnic identity, Carlos Shul, a forty-year-old Frente activist, replied, "No, I was never ashamed of my parents' Indian identity. On the contrary, I've always been proud of them."[63]

Shul had grown up in a cantón. When he was twelve, an uncle who lived in town brought him to live and work with him. He also allowed Carlos to go to school, where he encountered what he terms "social discrimination" at the hands of ladinos. After many playground fights, hard labor, and studying, Shul managed to go on to secondary school in Sonsonate. At some point along the journey, he became ashamed of his indigenous roots and tried to "pass" as a ladino. After dredging up this difficult past, he corrected his earlier remarks: "Well, I guess that's not true. Maybe I was ashamed of my mother. I do remember asking her to stop wearing el refajo."[64] Several days later, we visited Shul's mother, and she confirmed this painful moment in the past. Still wearing a refajo, she bitterly recalled in front of her embarrassed son, "You begged me to stop wearing el refajo!"

Gender, Generation, and Mestizaje

The cultural genocide thesis has preempted a difficult, if necessary reflection on post-1932 patriarchy and sexuality. Preliminary research suggests that el refajo became associated to some extent with filth (it could not be washed daily, and women apparently did not wear undergarments). One informant recalls how ladina market women used to insult indigenous venders with the following slur, metonymically linking the Indian woman, piglike filth, and indigenous dress: "India, cochina, refajada."[65] The use of *el refajo* could also symbolize indigenous women's modesty and faithfulness, as can be seen from the following excerpt from a song: "No me plegaré, me dijo, al irse a San Salvador, y ayá se quitó el refajo, y de al tiro me olvidó" (I won't change to ladino dress, you told me when you went to San Salvador, but there you took off your *refajo* and left me in a flash).[66]

Much more research needs to be done on both the indigenous and the ladino (the military and the leftist) gendered constructions of women and masculinity and their impact on the indigenous communities. The focus here is limited to underscoring the role of gender in undermining indigenous patriarchy, which accompanied the internal challenging of indigenous symbols in the 1960s and 1970s.

It seems clear that the sexuality of Salvadoran indigenous women was an extremely charged issue in two related respects. First, hacendados, as elsewhere, exerted their power sexually. Salarrué, a ladino of Sonsonate and a leading figure of Salvadoran letters, wrote the following in his novelistic rendition of *La Matanza*, published in 1933:

> The Indian women in the street or on the road still turn their backs when cars pass for they carry (according to the Indians) the enemies, the whites, the ladinos, the damned, the bad, the ugly. But, just as before the battle, the Indian woman will once again (impelled by a magnetic force in great part of pure necessity that is even greater today) become *el petatillo* in a black market of slavery; she will once again deliver herself, to allow herself to be possessed by the white and the mestizo and become the mother of that unsuspecting and discolored offspring.[67]

This contemporaneous view of a sympathetic ladino blames the "whites and mestizos" for what he suggests was a very widespread phenomenon. Yet he also echoes a common ladino and indigenous perception that the economic power of *los ricos* and the impoverishment of the Indians turned the latter into *petatillos* (literally, small grass sleeping mats). In short, the sympathetic observer (and informants today) insinuated that misery compelled many Indian women to prostitute themselves. The products of such unions, which he called *descolorida* (but whose color might have been pleasing to the mother), carried a heavy emotional load. Consider the following testimony of a child born in Nahuizalco in 1932:

My grandmother was a servant for Gabino Mata [the man who ordered the massacre of his workers]. My mother used to visit her at the hacienda. So then I was born. Three years later, my mother died. Then my grandmother started to take me to the hacienda so don Gabino could get to know me. He embraced me and told me that I was his child and he gave me his name. When I was ten years old, my grandmother died and I was left alone. I got a job at a sawmill at another hacienda. Then I was sent to don Gabino's hacienda to work cutting trees. My father remembered me, you know. He embraced me, "My son, my son!" But I came there barefoot and I left barefoot.[68]

It does not stretch the imagination to assume that those numerous children of hacendado/indigenous sexual relations have been similarly tormented by such memories (even without the intrusive probing of academics) and that anguish of origins and identity has caused much shame and resentment as well as provided additional evidence of the eclipse of the indigenous population.

It is still hard to assess the impact of La Matanza on the procreation of Indian/ladino offspring. We can ascertain, however, that the coming of age of those people born around 1932 coincided with the decline of the more severe forms of indigenous patriarchy. As in the highlands of Nicaragua, in Salvadoran collective memory, the decline of indigenous patriarchy is treated as a crucial moment in the loss of indigenous identity. Some thirty or forty years ago, arranged marriages, a key institution of patriarchy and endogamy, began to die out. Not coincidentally, the new generation of 1960s and 1970s pushed away the last vestiges of arranged marriage practices at the same time young women were rejecting el refajo.

Beyond these questions of gender and identity, Carlos Shul's remarks about his mother's refajo indicate something about his generation's experience, which involved the simultaneous distancing from indigenous identity and awakening to the possibilities of political and social change. The 1970s generation seems to have challenged not only their parents' counsel of political passivity, but also many aspects of their culture.[69] The questioning of traditional indigenous cultural forms seems to have become particularly intense during the 1960s and 1970s and went beyond language and dress, ranging from their elders' religious beliefs to their deep suspicion of everything ladino.

Often inspired by progressive priests, this generation exhibited a relatively high level of militancy during the 1970s and early 1980s, thus breaking with decades of regional political passivity. Indeed, activism should shatter the portrait etched by both the Left and the Right that the indigenous people were still too terrorized by the memories of 1932 to participate in any popular movements. However, military repression in the early 1980s conjured up again those memories of terror and reinforced the relative passivity that had reigned in the region from 1932 until the 1970s. Most strikingly, the state's repressive forces carried out small-scale massacres in El Carrizal (1980), El Canelo (1980), Santo Domingo (1980), Los Gramales (1980), and Las Hojas (1983), in addition to countless political assassinations in the region.[70]

Conclusion

Research in Central America has at times made me despair at making sense of the great micro-regional diversity of historical experience. Like the cool air but a few hundred feet above the steaming heat of a valley, the clarity of some ethnographic or historical insight is quickly blurred in a neighboring village. In this chapter, I have attempted to both embrace the temptation of local detail and, at the same time, develop a comparative discussion of collective memory, social struggles, and revolutionary nationalism.[71]

The local memories, however contradictory, allow us some ethnographic insight into the events themselves. Recent trends in historiography have stressed the strong indigenous element of the 1932 uprising and the racism of the repression. Héctor Pérez Brignoli and Erik Ching, in particular, emphasize the different social and cultural worlds inhabited by the Communist activists and the Indians, suggesting high levels of misunderstanding and manipulation.[72]

As noted in this chapter, there was a significant amount of cultural variation among those groups considered Indian in western Salvador: people identified as Indians by ladinos and other Indians ranged from monolingual Nahuatl speakers to monolingual Spanish speakers, from those who wore Western dress to those who wore native dress, and from those who participated in indigenous cofradías to those who did not. Union activists, insurrectionists, and looters occupied a large range of assigned and expressed identities. Western Salvadoran communities all suffered from conflicts between traditionalists and modernizers as well as from divisions by class and gender. But we cannot deduce participation in the movement from any particular position within those communities: all groups were represented in the insurrection and the massacre. Finally, it is obvious that local ladino artisans played crucial organizational roles, as did rural Indians and ladinos who had worked as union activists since 1930.[73] Thus an interpretation that stresses the cultural gulf between urban Communists and rural Indians, and stresses the autonomy of the latter's movement is somewhat partial and misses a story that would include conversations across these multiple, murky cultural divides. Indeed, a remarkable story yet to be told is of the organizers who managed to create a unified movement out of so much cultural difference and conflict.

Similarly, the repression was less a culmination of a strictly racist discourse than a moment—albeit a horrifying, anomalous one—in a broader process of *mestizaje*. In El Salvador, unlike in Nicaragua, the ladino conquest of local power and the marginalization of Indians were punctuated by the naked terror of 1932. Yet despite their radically different content, the narrative forms of Nicaraguan and Salvadoran indigenous memories are similar.[74] In both countries it has been that element of complicity and shame interwoven into the narrative of indigenous resistance that has proved incompatible with the discourse of *mestizaje* and revolutionary nationalism. To the nationalists of both countries, the stench of colonial complicity relegates that indigenous memory to a recycling bin marked "artifacts of the past."[75]

Listening to the reverberations of 1932, we can reconstruct some elements of shame and complicity that have blocked communication with new generations or with potential allies. First, it seems that the decisive cultural changes that took place since 1932 depended far less on state coercion and more on extremely unequal power relations. Those relations, in turn, conditioned what social psychologists call chains of shame and anger.[76] Thus, indigenous people felt shame at speaking Nahuatl in front of ladinos and at the same time despised those ladinos for making them feel that way. Second, the pace of ethnic marker loss accelerated in the 1960s and 1970s primarily through their rejection by a new generation who saw them as emblems of submission.

The fear of ladino power has suppressed indigenous agency and fragmented collective memories of 1932. This has permitted the elite-imposed silence to remain largely uncontested. Moreover, it has allowed the Left to avoid accepting any responsibility for its role in the catastrophe.[77] The discursive transformation of an indigenous into a mestizo people during the 1970s perhaps helped it establish an alliance with some of the region's younger generation. The generational conflict also created the conditions for the emergence of a mestizo identity, in which youths rejected their parents' Indian-ness while still recognizing their own indigenous heritage. Similar to the process that I uncovered in Nicaragua, this form of *mestizaje* would be a precondition for an alliance with the Left.[78] In Nicaragua, my recent study noted, the Sandinistas could relate to both the memories of primitive accumulation and the notion that Indian-ness was in the past. They had a far more difficult time relating to the moral and narrative complexities in the *cañadas* of Matagalpa.[79] In the Nicaraguan highlands, those sharp symbols of complicity with ladino authority—even the identification of Indian with deference—broke up the narrative of indigenous resistance. Those deferential markers and detours rendered the narrative incompatible with the discourse of *mestizaje* and revolutionary nationalism.

The criticism of my colleague Charles R. Hale is relevant to this discussion of revolutionary nationalism and ethnicity. He faulted my recent book for criticizing Sandino and latter-day Sandinistas for failing to embrace pro-Indian policies when new political and cultural possibilities were opening for people who abandoned identification with indigenous communities.[80] On one level, the critique is valid. After all, why shouldn't revolutionary nationalists find common ground with emerging generations of indigenous people who have embraced new identities, rejecting their parents' cultural baggage? How could they possibly critique that process without falling victim to essentialism? This critique goes to the heart of the postmodern dilemmas about the role of historians and ethnographers. In a tentative response, I would argue that there are realms of subaltern history and experience whose silence has a powerfully distorting effect on social analysis and action. It did matter that the Sandinistas did not take seriously the existence of the *Comunidades Indígenas*, regardless of their state of decay, if only because their failure to do so converted the Sandinistas into an alien and alienating force in the eyes of the *indígenas*. Yet this process of mestizaje and the related disarticulation of indigenous communities are by no means the only such realm of silencing.

In Nicaragua, local folks and actors operating on a national plane often share vocabularies but inflect them with different resonances and meanings. This process, often effective in periods of mobilization, eventually led to breakdowns in communication and alliances. Here I am referring to the experience of those Chinandegan campesinos (whom I studied in my first book) who fought alongside the Sandinistas but after ten years broke with them, angered that their goals, embodied in their own histories, were simply not taken seriously.

In a certain sense, then, this inquiry into the memories of *mestizaje* touches upon one facet of the larger problem of the relationship between local consciousness and memories and national discourse. Whether or not these disjunctures are inevitable, they need not have lethal consequences. Perhaps, then, the committed scholar, at the dawn of the millennium, might pursue the modest goal of helping to create conditions for a more even and just discursive field.

Let us close by glancing at what might be a hopeful counter-tendency. In western Salvador, the local rebirth of the Left coincides with the reforging of indigenous identities linked, in turn, to small groups of community activists. Thus Frente Farabundo Martí para la Liberación Nacional (FMLN) activists have joined with others to engage in activities ranging from teaching Nahuatl to children, to founding an Indian radio station. Notwithstanding, there is relatively little synergy between the two (potential) movements. Although the Left in the region wins many indigenous votes, it does not grow organizationally. Similarly, the indigenous movement, per se, remains relatively weak and fragmented.

The lack of synergy between the two movements derives from the history of conflictual relations between the Salvadoran Left and the Indians since La Matanza. This relation can be glimpsed in the following vignette from an FMLN campaign rally in January 1999. At this rally in a small Indian *cantón*, all but one of the speakers were ladinos from town. The village activists were not asked to give speeches, even though one of them was an elected councilperson. A claim of common indigenous roots allowed the ladinos to speak for the Indians. The one activist of indigenous origin who did speak was Carlos Shul, a town resident for thirty years. He exclaimed, "I'm poor just like you. My mother's a *refajada* [wearer of indigenous dress]. We know what those ARENA people think of us. The FMLN is my party because it's the party of the poor."[81]

For Indian village activists, their exclusion from the podium was something to be expected from ladinos. That is depressing enough in this age when even (or should we say, especially) neoliberals embrace multiculturalism.[82] But Shul's comment, taken in the context of his previous confession of shame about his mother's *refajo*, is indicative of a broader problem. Admittedly, it takes an overbearing outsider to insist that Shul should have publicly acknowledged his former embarrassment and his own transformation from viewing his mother's *refajo* as an emblem of shame into one of pride. Yet the masking of previous assimilationist attitudes contributes to the silencing of previous local ethnic and class histories, with important political consequences. The reluctance of Indians and ladinos on the Left to interrogate the problematic origins of contemporary indigenous identity—an identity that Indians rejected and ladinos scorned a generation ago—contributes to the silencing of those bitter ethnic divisions so vivid in the memories of their elders. That silencing, in turn, allows ladinos claiming shared indigenous roots to continue to speak for the Indians.

I would suggest that the failure of the Left and the indigenous movement to engage with collective memories of the process of *mestizaje* and La Matanza will continually thwart their efforts to chart a participatory democratic path that allows Indians and ladinos to emerge from six decades of fear, distrust, and silence. The movement toward indigenous pride should not come at the expense of the elders' memories.

There may be poetic justice in the Left's electoral victories in Nahuizalco, where so many were massacred in the name of anticommunism, and in the sudden ennobling of Nahuatl, the language of the scorned. Yet these symbolic reversals of history's death sentences will not necessarily become a solid foundation for social change; these signs of hope can easily be dashed on the hard rocks of economic reality and political rigidity. As a first step, the Left must overcome its particular forms of bad faith, whether that means that an indigenous leftist should acknowledge his earlier shame at his mother's dress, or that a ladino leftist should recognize that his group has been doing the talking for an awfully long time.

Notes

The first stage of the research on El Salvador was carried out with Patricia Alvarenga in 1998. It forms part of a larger project on *mestizaje* in Central America since the early 1900s. This project, supported by NEH Collaborative Grant #RO 22827-95, is directed by me and Charles R. Hale, and involves twelve Central American scholars. Hale has been an exceptionally engaged critic of my work, including this article. Although he will remain unsatisfied with this product, I am indebted to him for his encouragement and criticism. Indeed, since my apprenticeship with Emilia, my ideas and writing have not suffered such merciless interrogation as that proffered by Charlie. I am also deeply indebted to Peter Guardino, whose every read of this manuscript has immediately led to its improvement. I also wish to thank Patricia Alvarenga, Erik Ching, Danny James, Gilbert Joseph, Miguel Huezo Mixco, Aldo Lauria-Santiago, and Iván Molina for their comments and suggestions. Carlos Henriquez Consalvi, Carlos Lué, and Reynaldo Patriz provided invaluable help during the research for this article.

1 "Perspectiva histórica del movimiento campesino revolucionario en El Salvador," published by the Federación de Trabajadores del Campo," August 1979 (NACLA, El Salvador, File 95) devotes ten pages to an analysis of the 1932 events without any mention of "*indígenas*" citing the protagonists as "*jornaleros*" and "*campesinos.*" Fermán Cienfuegos, "El Salvador: La revolución inevitable" (NACLA, File 89) devotes nine pages with the same use of language. An examination of all other manifestos and documents produced by people and organizations connected to the Frente Farabundo Martí para la Liberación Nacional (FMLN) reveal the same use of the terms *pueblo, campesinos,* and *jornaleros* to describe the protagonists of the revolt, and no use of the term "Indian." Anthropologists who sympathized with the Left, such as the martyred Segundo Montes, *El compadrazgo: Una estructura de poder en El Salvador* (San Salvador: Editores UCA, 1987) during fieldwork in 1977 or Alejandro Dagoberto Marroquín, *Panchimalco,* 2d ed. (San Salvador: Ministerio de Educación, 1974), and, in particular, "El problema indígena en El Salvador," *América Indígena* 35, 4 (1975), did make clear the indigenous component of the rebellion. I would argue that their contribution makes the Left's formal omission of Indians all the more significant.

2 See Jeffrey Gould, *To Die in This Way: Nicaraguan Indians and the Myth of Mestizaje, 1880–1965* (Durham: Duke University Press, 1998).

3 Ibid., 134–76.

4 Michel-Rolph Trouillot, *Silencing the Past: Power and the Production of History* (Boston: Beacon Press, 1995), 822.

5　See Emilia Viotti da Costa, *The Brazilian Empire: Myths and Histories* (Chicago: University of Chicago Press, 1985). I would like to note Professor Viotti da Costa's chapter in this volume implicitly questions and criticizes this article's reliance on oral historical sources and its insistence on the importance of the study of memory to gain some access to popular consciousness (in the present and, less directly, in the past). Nonetheless, I would argue that my chapter and others have been inspired by Viotti da Costa's thought and methodology: "In the last instance, what matters is the way people interact, the way they think about the world and act upon it, and how in this process they transform the world and themselves" (Viotti da Costa, *Crowns of Glory, Tears of Blood: The Demerara Slave Rebellion of 1823* [New York: Oxford University Press, 1994], xix).

6　Rodolfo Baron Castro, *La población de El Salvador* (Madrid: Consejo Superior de Investigacion, Cientílijcas, 1942); Richard Adams, *Cultural Surveys of Costa Rica, El Salvador, Guatemala, Honduras, Nicaragua, and Panama* (Washington, D.C.: Pan American Health, 1957), 487.

7　In 1924 the government commissioned a Panamanian schoolteacher to study Nahuatl in Nahuizalco. See the pamphlet by Tomas Fideas Jimenez, "Idioma Pipil o Nahuat de Cuzctlan," San Salvador, Ministerio de Educación, 1937. Also see, Inés Masín, "El Pipil de Izalco," *Revista de Etnología, Arqueología, y Lingüística* 1, 5 (1927).

8　*La Epoca*, 17 June 1931. See Carlos Gregorio López Bernal, "El proyecto liberal de nación en El Salvador (1876–1932)," 166.

9　Miguel Angel Espino, *Prosas escogidas* 6th ed. (San Salvador: UCA Editores, 1995), 20.

10　Maria de Baratta, *Cuzcatlán típica: Ensayo sobre etnofonia de El Salvador* (San Salvador: Ministerio de Cultura, 1952), 9.

11　de Baratta, *Cuzcatlán típica*, 2: 225. *Cuzcatlán típica*, published in 1952, was the result of a twenty-eight-year-long study. The silence on La Matanza poses a problem in other post-1932 writings about Salvadoran Indians, pushing the narrative into a nebulous sense of time and thus converting living indigenous populations into a timeless entity. For an important example of this amnesia, see Adolfo Herrera Vega, *El indio occidental de El Salvador y su incorporación por la escuela* (Santa Ana: Tipografía Comerica de Duarte, 1935). Written three years after La Matanza by a ladino of Izalco, this study of western Salvadoran Indians contains not a single statement about La Matanza.

12　Luis Marden, "Coffee Is the King in El Salvador," *National Geographic Magazine* 85, 5 (November 1944): 604–5. Already in 1924, children would dress up as Indians in school events.

13　It is worth noting that key military officers who directed La Matanza were of local origin; Alfonso Marroquín and Tito Calvo in Izalco, and apparently a colonel in Juayúa (interviews with Juan Ama, Izalco, 1998, and with Raúl Cisneros, Juayúa, May 1999).

14　What follows is a brief account of the popular mobilization that led to la Matanza, based on primary and secondary sources. The primary sources include the Foreign Office documents in the Public Records Office (London) and the State Department files in the U.S. National Archives (USNA). The classic account is by Thomas Anderson, *Matanza*, 2d ed. (Willimantic, Conn.: Curbstone Press). Erik Ching has written an interesting account based on the Comintern archives in Moscow: "Where's the Party? The Communist Party, the Comintern, and the Peasant Rebellion of 1932 in El Salvador," *The Americas* 55, 2 (1998): 204–39.

15　*La Epoca*, 1 May 1931.

16　Such a figure is impossible to estimate with any degree of certainty. Thomas Anderson (*Matanza*, 42–45), citing secondary sources, says that 80,000 people turned out for the

May Day rally in San Salvador in 1930 (population 80,000) and 50,000 signed a labor petition in the same year. At the time of the insurrection, General Calderón estimated that the Communist Party had 80,000 members, but newspapers later dropped the estimate to 25,000.

17 Warren Robbins to Secretary of State, 27 March 1931, USNA, 816.00/801, no. 478.

18 See the interviews in Segundo Montes, El Compadrazgo, 266, 274. Two ladinos who had been close to the Izalco political elite recalled an interview between a local ally of Gómez Zárate and Ama in which the latter exclaimed: "Miré, patrón, hemos sido amigos, somos amigos y seguiremos siendo amigos, pero usted es capitalisto (sic) a un lado y nosotros trabajadores del otro, el proletariado." These interviews also attempt to portray Ama and his followers as terratenientes, with no interest in the land issue. Even with land access, the urban Indians still worked as jornaleros. Although there is no strong evidence, the large involvement of indigenous jornaleros in the movement surely helped persuade Ama to ally with the Communists.

19 Interviews with Fabián Mojica, Sonszacate, Sonsonate, January 1999; Raimundo Aguilar, Cusamuluco, Sonsonate, May 1999; Alberto Shul, Nahuizalco, May 1999.

20 Similarly, there is little doubt that the authorities would have used the public party voting lists for repressive purposes.

21 Rogers to Simon, no. 5, 13 January 1932; FO Document 75, A865/9/8, reprinted in British Documents on Foreign Affairs, ed. Kenneth Bourne and Cameron Watt, pt. 2, vol. 8, 1991.

22 Legajo de correspondencia a Julio Sánchez la noche del 20 de agosto 1934, 320, Archive of Museo de la Palabra y la Imagen, San Salvador.

23 Roque Dalton, Miguel Marmol, trans. Kathleen Ross and Richard Schaaf (Willimantic, Conn.: Curbstone Press, 1987), 239–40.

24 Rev. Roy MacNaught, "Horrors of Communism in Central America," The Central American Bulletin, March 15, 1932.

25 Interview with Rodrigo Malía, Anal Arriba, Nahuizalco, March 1998. The phrase "pagaron justos por pecadores" is a common refrain among survivors.

26 Quoted in Joaquín Méndez, Los sucesos comunistas en El Salvador (San Salvador: Imprenta Funes, 1932), 105.

27 This is especially true of orphans and fatherless children, many of whom fell into direct dependence on authorities or plantation owners. In addition, some of the young adults survived through their positions of confidence with plantation owners and the military authorities, and thus we can suppose they had a unique vantage point with which to view and recall the events.

28 Interview with Ana Cortés, Salcoatitán, June 1998.

29 Rafael Antonio Portillo, Recopilador, "Tradición oral de Apaneca," Santa Ana, 27 agosto 1996. On Santo Domingo Guzmán, I want to thank Henrik Roensbo for providing transcripts of oral testimony.

30 Interview with Fabián Mojica, Sonzacate, 1999. Mojica was a union organizer who organized in the cantones of Izalco in 1930–31.

31 Erik Ching and Virginia Tilley, "Indians, the Military, and the Rebellion of 1932 in El Salvador," Journal of Latin American Studies 30, 1 (February 1998).

32 Memoria del Ministerio de Fomento, Gobernación, etc. (San Salvador: Imprenta Nacional, 1933), 8.

33 Interviews with Paulino Galicia, Cara Sucia, January 1999; Prudencio Hernández, La Sabana, Nahuizalco, March 1998; Carlos Alarcón, Salcoatitán, May 1998.

34 The evidence for these assertions is still fragmentary, although recent work by Erik

Ching and Virginia Tilley substantiates the argument that the military often supported the Indians against wealthy ladinos during the 1930s. Memory studies—such as Daniel James, in *Doña María's Story: Life History, Memory, and Political Identity* (Durham: Duke University Press, forthcoming); Luisa Passerini, *Fascism in Popular Memory* (Cambridge: Cambridge University Press, 1987); and Alessandro Portelli, *The Death of Luigi Trastulli and Other Stories: Form and Meaning in Oral History* (Albany: State University of New York Press, 1991)—have analyzed the impact of elite domination on subaltern memory in other historical contexts.

35 Interview with Ramón Esquina, Tajcuilulaj, Nahuizalco, June 1998.

36 Ibid. Also see Patricia Alvarenga, *Cultura y ética de la violencia, El Salvador, 1880–1932* (San José: EDUCA, 1996), 334–35.

37 Interview with Raimundo Gómez, Cusamuluco, Nahuizalco, June 1998. Don Raimundo explained that his original last name was "Paez" but that the hacendado did not like it and thus forced him to change it to Gómez. Such was the power and arrogance of the hacendados after 1932.

38 The informants include: Pedro Lue, Ramón Esquina, Esteban Tepas, Raimundo Gómez, Benito Zarco, Francisco Perez, Jesús Tino, and Raimundo Aguilar from the *cantones*, and Alberto Shul from Nahuizalco.

39 D. Rogers to Grant Wilson, 16 February 1932, Foreign Office, 813/23 no. 24 238/13a.

40 Interview with Alberto Shul, May 1999. In an attempt to understand the motivations of the planters and their military allies, it would be useful to compare them with the rubber planters analyzed by Michael Taussig in *Shamanism, Colonialism, and the Wild Man* (Chicago: University of Chicago Press, 1987). Mata's massacre in El Canelo was a separate incident. We cannot be sure about the "day of vengeance" leaflet, but it is likely that it was merely a creation of the local authorities, the pretext for another mass killing. Rogers did not actually see the leaflet. Further argument for the invention of the leaflet can be inferred from a newspaper account in *El Diario del Salvador*, 17 February 1932. It claims that the minister of war confirmed that "unos trescientos indios de Nahuizalco se levantaron contra la guarnición, los que se retiraron del pueblo para esperar el auxilio de Sonsonate . . . procedieron a pacificar a los revoltosos pero como estos opusieron resistencia, hubo de hacer uso de la fuerza . . . sucumbieron en la refriega 280 comunistas." If the chargé d'affaires had taken this supposed "uprising" seriously, he would have reported it, one assumes. In addition to eliminating the particular motive of misunderstanding from this account—the *boleto*—this is a particularly clear example of how "*indio*," at least during this period, was interchangeable with "Communist."

41 For a thoughtful analysis of the temporal dimension of memories, see Alessandro Portelli, *The Death of Luigi Trastulli and Other Stories: Form and Meaning in Oral History* (Albany: State University of New York Press, 1991). Unlike in Nahuizalco, where we have recorded testimonies in "coffee" *cantones*, we have not yet recorded testimonies in the coffee *cantones* in Izalco, nor in those where many traveled distances to larger haciendas (and usually resided for two weeks at a stretch).

42 See Adams, "Cultural Surveys," 494, on the hierarchy in the 1950s, especially the independent role of the cacique. In Izalco, the civil religious hierarchy before 1932 formed a structure largely independent of the municipality and the state. In Nahuizalco, on the contrary, up until 1932 the indigenous people, over 80 percent of the population, often won control over the municipal government. That political control tied to the national state probably weakened the religious dimension of the civil-religious hierarchy. In any event, the civil-religious hierarchy did not survive the matanza.

43 Interview with Esteban Tepas, Pushtan, Nahuizalco, January 1998.

44 Interview with Angelica Lue, Tajcuilulah, May 1998.

45 On the other hand, an informant from the *cantón* Carrizal stated that the survivors converted one of these sites into a cemetery where people left flowers (interview with Manuel Acensio Pérez, Carrizal, June 1998). Other informants claim that over the years, people stopped leaving flowers because they had no assurance where their loved ones had been buried (Ramón Aguilar, Cusamuluco, June 1999). If so, the failure to practice collective forms of remembrance says something about the atomization of the community. Finally, Rosario Lué (Nahuizalco, May 1998) suggests that "when the children grew up, we stopped leaving flowers." Further research will have to pursue this enigmatic clue.

46 Interview with Paulino Galicia, Cara Sucia, Sonsonate, January 1999. Galicia was twelve years old in 1932.

47 Commander V. G. Brodeur, "Secret Report of Situation, as It Developed at Acajutla," 7 April 1932, Foreign Office Archives, FO 371/15814.

48 Without specifically referring to the millenarian aspect, Héctor Pérez Brignoli ("Indians, Communists, and Peasants: The 1932 Rebellion in El Salvador," in William Roseberry et al., *Coffee, Society, and Power in Latin America* [Baltimore: Johns Hopkins University Press 1995], 252–53) argues that the rebellion resembled rebellions of the colonial era. According to Pérez, the Communist Party played a role similar to that of native appropriations of Christian religious authority in the Chiapas Indian rebellion of 1712. In that rebellion, an apparition of a virgin, following Spanish repression of her cult, commanded Indians to rise up against the Spaniards. However, in many regards, although there is no question that beliefs in magic and redemption existed among the rebels, there were also hard-nosed material demands involved in the movement, and even the choice of targets suggests a strong degree of rational calculation; e.g., the rebels spared the properties of planters who were not particularly harsh in their treatment of workers, and there was no overt attempt to drape the movement in religious imagery. See Brodeur, "Secret Report," 4. For a useful discussion of millenarian movements, see David G. Rowley, "Redeemer Empire: Russian Millenarianism," *American Historical Review* 104, 5 (1999): 1582–1602.

49 Interview with Fabián Mojica, Sonzacate, Sonsonate, January 1999. Congruent with the above emphasis on class struggle and a lack of interest in the ethnic dimension of the revolt is Mojica's recollection about the famous Indian cacique of Izalco, Feliciano Ama, the man whose public hanging in 1932 came to symbolize the barbarity of racist repression: "Feliciano Ama came to one of our meetings here in this house. He slept through the whole meeting. I don't think he had anything to do with the movement."

50 For example, in the interviews with Ramón Vargas and Antonio Valiente, ladinos of Turín, Ahuachapán, there is a marked lack of interest in questions of ethnic identity at the time. Vargas's father was a Communist militant and himself became a labor activist in the forties. Valiente participated in union organization but apparently broke with the movement before the insurrection. Similarly, Miguel Mármol's testimony in Roque Dalton, *Miguel Mármol* (Willimantic, Conn.: Curbstone Press, 1987), similarly presents ethnic difference and conflict in a class language. Curiously, a filmed interview with Mármol reveals a much greater awareness of indigenous culture than does his recorded testimony.

51 See note 2. In a personal communication and commentary on this article, Miguel Huezo Mixco, an activist in the 1970s and 1980s, referred to a document written by Salvador

Cayatano Carpio, one of the most important figures on the Left, that involves "pro-letarizar a los indígenas e introducir la prescencia de los artesanos . . . en el levanta-miento."

52 On the anti-quincentenary campaign, see Charles R. Hale, "Between Ché Guevara and the Pachamama: Mestizos, Indians, and Identity Politics in the Anti-Quincentenary Cam-paign," *Critique of Anthropology* 14, 9 (1994): 9–39.

53 Interview with Cornelio Pátriz, Carrizal, Sonsonate, January 1998. In the Barrio Abajo of Izalco many informants insist that Nuhuatl was prohibited.

54 Interviews with Rodrigo Malía, March 1998, and Pedro Lué, Sábana San Juan, June 1998. Both informants recall the same phrase.

55 Interview with Benito Sarco, Nahuizalco, March 2000.

56 Interview with Ramón Aguilar, Cusamuluco, June 1999.

57 Interview with Rosario Lué, Nahuizalco, May 1999.

58 See Concepción Clará de Guevara, *Exploración etnográfica de Sonsonate* (Ministerio de Edu-cación, 1976). Also see Leyla Pineda Ortiz and Ana Lilliam Ramírez Cruz, "Vision socio-cultural de Nahuizalco," Licenciatura thesis, School of Social Work, Universidad de El Salvador, 1975, 95. Also see Juan José Contreras, "Monografía de la poblacion indígena de Nahuizalco," tesis doctoral, Facultad de Medecina, Universidad de El Salvador, 1963. He writes: "Durante la investigación todos negaron hablar el dialecto Nahuat . . . y que es una 'bayuncada' hablar en 'lengua.' . . . La verdad es que todos hablan el Nahuat, sólo que no lo hablaban en público porque los mestizos se burlan de ellos" (45). Lyle Camp-bell, "La Dialectología Pipil," *América Indígena* 35, 4 (1975): 833. Campbell states that "in Cuisnahuat there are about forty [Nahuatl speakers] and in Santo Domingo de Guzmán the majority of indigenous adults still know how to speak it, although there are few youths who have learned it."

59 Interview with Juan Cestino Lué, El Canelo, March 2000. This witness claimed that women who had relatively new *refajos* were afraid that they would be implicated as looters.

60 Marden, "Coffee Is the King in El Salvador," *National Geographic* 85, 5 (November 1944): 602.

61 Interview with Rosario Lué, Nahuizalco, June 1999. This argument should not be dis-missed, as it is entirely possible that temperatures did increase in the area due to deforestation.

62 The term *plegarse* is curious in that, unlike so many other forms of expression, its only figurative meaning refers to the adoption of ladino dress. The origins of this usage probably lie in the visual difference between the indigenous wraparound dress and ladino apparel. Thus *plegar* means "to fold, or double." Yet another meaning is "to submit" or "to yield." Another more remote meaning refers to submission to another force or authority. In other words, *plegarse* means to fold, to double, or to plait; to submit or to yield. It seems likely that its emergence as the only term used to describe the adoption of ladino dress derives from the secondary meaning, "to submit."

63 Interview, Nahuizalco, March 1998. The name has been changed.

64 Ibid.

65 Anonymous interview, Sonsonate, 1998. Indigenous women, the informant pointed out, responded with curses in Nahuatl. Our study of the birth records reveals a curious fact: the rate of indigenous births did not decline in 1933 as one would have expected given that the forces of repression slaughtered more than one-third of the male population in Nahuilzalco and Izalco. Several informants suggest that the reconstitution of the indige-

nous families involved at least a period of extensive polygamy. Regardless of the degree of objectivity of those accounts, we can state that as in Nicaragua, the ethnic barriers in El Salvador involved fantasies about sexual practices inspired by the reality of indigenous patriarchy.

66 See de Baratta, *Cuzcatlán típica*, 1:244. The song is about a woman who leaves her Indian *compañero* to become her patron's mistress dates from the 1920s or later (based on a reference to a contemporary Izalqueño figure).

67 Salarrué, *Cataleya luna* (San Salvador: Ministerio de Educación [1933] 1974), 172.

68 Anonymous interview, Nahuizalco, June 1999.

69 Interview with Reynaldo Pátriz, January 1999. Pátriz on several occasions has reiterated the rigid attitude of parents toward any form of participation in social or political movements. Also Rosa Hernandez, Nahuizalco, June 1998, comments on how her family "discriminated against me . . . my mother said she was ashamed that I was her daughter" because of her union activism.

70 Interviews with Reynald Patriz and Manuel Ascencio Perez, El Carrizal (1998–99); Margarito Vasquez and Manuel Vasquez, June 1998, Santo Domingo. On las Hojas, see Mac Chapin, *La población de El Salvador* (San Salvador: Ministerio de Educación, 1990). On los Gramales, see the interview with Pedro Sánchez, Tajcuilulaj, June 1998. The military gunned down and killed fifteen to one hundred people in these incidents.

71 This chapter speaks to only one aspect of a broader *desencuentro* between the Left and Indians. With the Maya and Miskitu, the Left primarily has been faced with assertions of ethnic pride that challenged it. In the context of ethnic pride, when the Left has attempted to confront those aspects of indigenous consciousness that we have called shame or complicity, then indigenous militants have accused it of racism. Personal communication of Charles R. Hale, 1999.

72 Perez Brignoli, "Indians, Communists, and Peasants," and Erik Ching, "Where is the Party?" Although these serious studies do not share a common analysis, they both stress the cultural and ideological distance between the Communist Party and the Indians. Also see Patricia Alvarenga's pioneering study *Cultura y ética de la violencia, El Salvador 1880–1932*, EDUCA, San Jose, 1996.

73 One piece of evidence for this comes from "el Libro de Ciudadanos" in Juayúa: of forty-five people marked "dead in the communist rising," ten were urban artisans. Several informants in Nahuizalco emphasize the key role of local *cantón*-based activists. Interviews with Alberto Shul, Nahuizalco, January 1999; Raimundo Aguilar, Cusamuluco, June 1999; Pedro Lue, Sabana San Juan, June 1999.

74 See Gould, *To Die in This Way*, chapter 7.

75 Gould, *To Die in This Way*, 230–31.

76 Thomas Scheff, "Emotions and Identity: A Theory of Ethnic Nationalism," in Craig Calhoun, ed., *Social Theory and the Politics of Identity* (Cambridge, Mass.: Blackwell, 1996), 277–303. Also see William Reddy, "Against Constructionism: The Historical Ethnography of Emotions," *Current Anthropology* 38, 3 (June 1997): 327–51. Reddy's following remark is worthy of consideration in the Salvadoran context: "Shame, I would argue, also derives from thoughts about how one is seen by others. . . . Thus, shame can lead to withdrawal coupled with action aimed at managing appearances; such action can, in turn, take the form of emotive utterances and behavior that drum up and intensify socially approved feelings and play down or deny deviant ones. Local varieties of shame are therefore, in many cultural contexts, a principal instrument of social control and political power" (347).

77 This is not to say that the Communist Party bears anything resembling the responsibility of the military or the elite.

78 The generational conflict in Cuisnahuat, a municipality with a large indigenous population, had a specifically political expression. Modernizers and traditionalists without specific national affiliations battled for control of the municipality in the early 1970s. See Concepción Clará de Guevara, *Exploración etnográfica de Sonsonate* (Ministerio de Educación, 1976). Since writing this essay, further research has revealed significant non-indigenous participation in the movement. Preliminary evidence suggests that in this sector there have been more linear forms of transmission to the younger generations. In other words, children and grandchildren of participants remember their rebellious forebears with pride. Undoubtedly, the more concentrated repression against specific indigenous communities accounts, in part, for the discrepancy.

79 Gould, *To Die in This Way*, 259–66.

80 See review by Charles R. Hale, *Ethnohistory* (December 1999): 268–71.

81 Speech, January 1999. Name changed.

82 On neoliberalism and multiculturalism, see Charles Hale, "Memorias de mestizaje: Un marco conceptual," paper delivered at Mestizaje Workshop, Tegucigalpa, Honduras, July 1999.

III
Articulating the Political:
The Intersection of Class, Race, Gender,
Sexuality, and Generation

▼

Diana Paton

The Flight from the Fields Reconsidered:
Gender Ideologies and Women's Labor
After Slavery in Jamaica

▼

Ever since the full abolition of slavery, in August 1838, observers and
historians of the British colonies in the Caribbean have believed that one of
the most dramatic and immediate social changes that took place upon
emancipation was women's widespread refusal to participate in wage labor
in the plantation economy—not only on sugar estates, but also on coffee
plantations and in livestock pens.[1] The phenomenon has frequently received passing comment, but for a long time historians did not consider it
to present any issues requiring explanation. Assumptions about the natural
place of women led many to imagine it self-evident that women, because
they were women, would not continue to perform the exhausting work of
the sugar estates when they could avoid it. The congruence of this view
with the perspective of the colonial officials, abolitionists, and missionaries who observed the phenomenon made women's refusal of wage labor
seem even less remarkable.

Feminist scholarship and activism have since undermined assumptions
about women's natural role, but did not initially stimulate research on
women's post-emancipation labor choices. The first wave of Caribbean
women's history was primarily concerned with slavery, and thus paid little
attention to the issue. This priority to some extent followed the traditional
emphasis on slavery in Caribbean historiography, but was also, I would
suggest, motivated by a desire to present an image of strong, resistant
women.[2] Such an image was more easily found in women such as Nanny of
the Jamaican maroons than in those who chose not to participate in wage
labor.[3] The latter, perhaps seeming at first glance to share rather too much
with their ladylike counterparts in Victorian England, provided uncomfort-

able heroines for feminist and nationalist historians. However, analysis of similar processes in other parts of the Americas and a growing sense of the need to investigate the complexity of gender relations and ideologies have led recent review essays about Caribbean emancipation to call almost ritualistically for greater study of gender issues in general, and of women's refusal of wage labor in particular.[4] Once one stops considering it obvious that women would not participate in wage labor after emancipation, many questions become pressing: To what extent did women refuse to participate in wage labor? Which women refused to do so? Perhaps most important, why did these women want to avoid wage labor? What did they do instead? Who made decisions about how women were to spend their time? How did freed people, women and men, describe and justify the decision to themselves and others?

Swithin Wilmot, Thomas Holt, and, most important, Bridget Brereton have begun the process of posing the necessary questions and providing answers.[5] Additionally, because of historians' longstanding interest in all former slaves' efforts to construct lives autonomous from the plantation economy, many detailed, although mainly ungendered, studies of postemancipation conflicts about residence and work exist.[6] This chapter attempts to answer some of the questions posed above through close attention to the competing ideologies and modes of representation mobilized in the struggle over labor in the immediate aftermath of slavery. I focus here on Jamaica, where women's refusal to become part of the paid labor force was probably the most extensive, and certainly the most contentious, in the English-speaking Caribbean.

Of particular concern are the motivations of former slaves, especially former slave women. Such a project necessarily presents methodological problems, for traces of the past come almost without exception in the form of documents produced for the purposes of the colonial state, abolitionists, missionaries, or planters, none of whose interests coincided with those of former slaves. One response to this order of problem has been to turn away entirely from the traditional goals of social history in favor of attention to the discursive strategies of colonial power. While such work has produced significant results, it also carries the risk of repositioning the majority of the population, especially in colonial societies, outside of history.[7] Sharing Sherry Ortner's sense that it is "grotesque to insist on the notion that the text is shaped by everything but the lived reality of the people whom the text claims to represent," I aim to show that former slaves, as much as those who directly produced the texts I discuss here, were engaged in a struggle over representation as well as practice.[8]

The first two parts of this essay address the effects of and reasons for women's refusal of plantation wage labor. In the first I examine the implications of that refusal, and argue that it was the crucial first step in the struggles between planters and freed slaves that led to the much-debated "flight from the estates."⁹ I argue that, rather than being studied as a separate phenomenon, women's post-emancipation nonparticipation in wage work should be placed at the heart of analyses of the building of Jamaican peasant communities. Historians and anthropologists have paid close attention to the process by which former slaves ultimately left the plantations, practicing what Jean Besson, following Sidney Mintz, calls the "resistant response" of "reconstituting" a peasantry.¹⁰ Unfortunately, this debate and the discussion of women's withdrawal from estate labor have been conducted without much reference to one another. The conflicts involved in the "flight from the estates" have been interpreted within exclusively class-oriented frameworks. For this reason, the centrality of women's actions in struggles over work and residence, and the interlocking nature of class and gender as axes of struggle have not been recognized. In practice, the class struggle over estate work and residence was played out through a struggle over gender relations.

In the second part of the essay, I ask why women refused to participate in wage labor. I agree with those historians who have interpreted women's refusal of wage work as part of freed slaves' efforts to consolidate "family," but suggest that we need to be more precise about what we mean by that term for it to be analytically useful. I also argue that it is necessary to place women's decisions in the context of an investigation of the ideologies, conventions, and material practices that generated them. After all, while the desire to sustain kinship units may well be universal, the particular steps that a group of people takes to achieve this goal are culturally determined. I interpret women's actions as demonstrating neither former slaves' ideological incorporation by domesticity, nor as a simply pragmatic response to material need, but as arising out of Afro-Jamaicans' developing understandings of gender, which partially overlapped with the assumptions of the British colonial elite.

In the final section I focus more narrowly on evidence about the ways in which women defended their decisions not to work for the plantations. Looking particularly at the controversy that arose in response to Jamaican governor Lionel Smith's proclamation in which he advised freedmen to "spare [their] wives from heavy field work," I argue that we must take seriously the reported words of freed slaves—even when those words cannot be interpreted as straightforward evidence of subaltern belief. Former slaves were aware of the overlaps as well as the differences between their understandings of gender and those embedded in colonial policy. By actively manipulating contemporary political discourse, women were able to use this knowledge as part of a consciously political strategy that enabled them effectively to justify their decisions not to work for wages.

My analysis is confined to the immediate post-emancipation period. From the abolition of slavery until the late 1840s, Jamaican workers stood in a relatively powerful economic position in relation to their former masters, who needed their labor. Compared to other Caribbean colonies, and even to Britain, wages were high. Planters were desperate to control labor, although this desperation led them to try to control workers' mobility rather than to provide them with greater incentives, as free-market theorists might expect. Thus, I assume that in this period gendered labor patterns were primarily determined by the decisions of the former slaves, in that employers would have liked all individuals to work for them.

After the late 1840s, however, the rapid decline of the sugar industry led to an economic depression lasting until the banana boom at the end of the nineteenth century. In this period we cannot necessarily conclude that gendered employment patterns resulted from the decisions of workers, for the decline of the plantation economy greatly diminished the negotiating strength of Jamaican workers: the supply of labor outstripped the demand, and employers could choose whomever they preferred to employ.[11] In addition, we do not even know the extent to which women participated in wage labor in this period, since very little research has been conducted on Jamaican labor patterns in the second half of the nineteenth century. A gap exists between studies of slavery on one hand, and studies of twentieth-century practice on the other.[12]

The Gendering of Class

Conflicts about whether or not women would perform field work for the estates predated emancipation. They were brought to the fore during the period of gradual transition from slavery to a free-labor economy known as "apprenticeship" (1834–38). In this system, devised in London for all Britain's slave colonies, slaves were declared apprentices of their former masters, for whom they were required to work forty hours each week without monetary compensation. Newly appointed and supposedly impartial stipendiary magistrates, rather than the overseer's lash, enforced labor discipline. The system was planned to last for six years, but in practice was abolished everywhere by 1838.[13]

Apprenticeship destabilized the implicit and unequal, but nevertheless long-standing, bargains between planter and slave that had governed plantation life.[14] Now, with slavery formally abolished, planters tried to avoid any expenses they were not legally obliged to incur, while attempting to extract labor from those who had previously, by custom and sometimes by law, been excused from estate work. Although these efforts affected all apprentices in some form, the burden of unaccustomed labor fell most severely on women, especially mothers.[15] During the last years of slavery older women and women with six or more living children had been excused from field labor, often being employed to look after all the children who lived on the estate. Women with small children were allowed to take time out of the day's work in the fields in order to breast-feed or prepare food for their children. As soon as apprenticeship began, planters sent the "nurses" back to the fields and refused time for breast-feeding. Women resisted the increased labor demands, often coming to the fields later than was officially required or refusing to work altogether. According to stipendiary magistrate (hereafter S.M.) William Oldrey, "When the elder females were thus discontented and the younger women also, it was no wonder that discontent prevailed. We all know very well the influence females have on mankind, and the conduct I have alluded to produced general discontent."[16]

Maggy Lewis, also known as Ann Palmer, was one of these "elder females." Thirty-nine of her descendants lived on the Orange Valley estate to which she belonged, and she had not done field work for many years. At the start of apprenticeship she was ordered to "turn trash," a relatively light form of labor, but one from which she felt she was rightfully exempted. When she refused to do the task, she was taken before a stipendiary magistrate, who sentenced her to ten days solitary confinement in the parish prison, the "house of correction."[17] There were many Maggy Lewises, and there were even more women who, while not feeling entitled to exemption from plantation work, resented the loss of particular stretches of time they had customarily devoted to looking after children. Complaints about women's late arrival in the fields were frequent throughout apprenticeship, reflecting the reluctance of such women to perform labor they felt they should not be obliged to do. As one stipendiary magistrate put it in 1836, "Offenses . . . [are] chiefly for loss of time in turning out to field labour in the morning, women particularly." Another wrote that the majority of complaints consisted of "petty thefts, loss of labour by the pickaninny mothers, and turning out too late to work."[18]

Women began to withdraw more completely from estate labor as soon as they were able to make this choice, with complete emancipation in August 1838. In September, S. M. Lyon was already writing as if it were a foregone conclusion that "married women" would not do field labor.[19] S. M. Woolfrys reported in October on three estates in St. Ann where, respectively, "many of the women refuse to do field work," "same, respecting the women," and "women refuse to work."[20] A planter with responsibility for four estates testified that "since the first of August last, only two-thirds of the men have been at work . . . and none of the women or children."[21] Similar reports continued to be produced by both planters and stipendiary magistrates over the course of the next year. According to Bridget Brereton's thorough study, "There was wide agreement [among magistrate and clergymen, as well as planters] that a significant withdrawal by married women and mothers had occurred by the middle of 1839."[22]

In early 1839, planters began to collect information favorable to themselves for presentation to the British public. The main goal was to prove the disastrous decline in available labor since emancipation, with the implication that some form of further support for the colony's planters—directly financial or through subsidized immigration—should be provided. "Committees of correspondence" in many of the parishes wrote to each attorney or overseer, asking a series of questions about employment, the labor force, and production. Some asked questions about gender. The committees then compiled reports from the results. While these reports may well have exaggerated the overall decline in available workers, there is no reason to assume that they would overstate the proportion of that decline made up of women. A proportionally higher loss of male labor would probably have attracted greater sympathy in Britain, and would therefore have provided better propaganda. The figures produced showed a much steeper decrease in the number of women available for plantation labor than of men. A report from St. James parish in February 1839 claimed that the number of women "usually at work" throughout the parish had fallen from 2,605 during the apprenticeship to 677 at the time of the report, a decrease of 74 percent. The same figures indicate that the male labor force had declined much less, from 2,310 to 1,354—a still considerable loss of 41 percent.[23] A similar report on the parish of Hanover suggested that roughly 80 percent of women were no longer doing field work. It claimed that about half of the 4,253 apprentices employed on plantations prior to 1 August 1838 had been women (ca. 2,127), whereas now between a sixth and a fifth of the 2,143 at work were female (between 357 and 429).[24]

Despite the consistency and frequency of these reports, we should not assume that all of the women concerned refused to perform any wage labor in the fields. Planters, used to an enslaved labor force, considered any effort by workers to offer their labor flexibly or variably to constitute reluctance or refusal to labor. Many of the women reported as saying they would not work may actually have told planters that they would not work on that day or that occasion, but would have been prepared to perform occasional wage work. It is nevertheless solidly substantiated that women, at a greater rate than men, refused to devote their time primarily to estate wage labor.

Planters reacted rapidly to women's actions. The collection and publication of information was one tactic in their response to the decline in their labor force; others were far more direct and coercive. Their most widespread response was what became known as the "wage-rent system."[25] In this system planters charged each adult for his or her house and provision ground, regardless of the number of people with whom these were shared. They deducted the rent from earnings if the person did wage labor for the estate, charged it to other members of his or her household, or simply presented demands for cash backed up with threats of evictions. Those who did not work regularly for the estate were often charged rent at higher rates than those who did. Notices to quit plantation property often followed the rent demands. Some individuals were presented with such eviction notices even if they had relatives performing wage work on the estate from whose wages rent could, theoretically, have been deducted. A case like this was reported by S. M. Edmund Lyon, who was visited by "several married, and some aged and decrepid [sic] females, from Gibralter Estate" who had been served with eviction notices "because they had devoted their attention to their husbands and families who are working on the same estate."[26] The purpose, admitted by planters at the time, was primarily to force people to perform wage labor rather than to generate income.

Although the wage-rent system affected anyone who shared a house with someone not doing wage labor—that is, a very large majority of freed people—its most direct targets were the individuals who had refused to work for the estates. The goal was to force family groups as units to change the way they organized their labor patterns: most of the surviving rent bills and notices to quit are addressed to a head of household, assuming his or her responsibility for all household members. However, it was those individuals who were not doing wage work who would have had to change their behavior in order to satisfy their former masters, now reconstituted as landlords. Since most non-wage-laboring adults were women, most of the individuals within household groups whose behavior the planters aimed to alter were women.[27]

Not surprisingly, women were also prominent in resistance to the wage-rent system and the attempted evictions to which it led. Swithin Wilmot has documented some of these acts of resistance in his article on women and protest in post-emancipation Jamaica. He describes incidents at Golden Grove estate in St. Thomas in the East, as well as others in Hanover and Trelawney, and at Mahoe and Spring Hill coffee plantations in St. George.[28]

One of the earliest confrontations over rent and evictions took place at Beckford's Retreat in St. Dorothy in August 1838. The bookkeeper, Mr. Scott, reported that he had been "assaulted and abused" by several women on the property to whom he was trying to serve notices to quit. According to Scott, he was first assaulted by Selena Benlay,

> who struck me a blow with her fist on my left side. Shortly afterwards another woman, named Christiana Dinont, followed me about exclaiming she would knock out my brains with stones. A little afterwards a third woman named Elizabeth Taylor, meeting me on the roads, as I was going to the overseer, caught me by the throat and held me fast until a man, who had lately been special constable separated us. Upon her letting go of me she collared the constable and tore his shirt.[29]

The next day Scott returned with policemen to try to implement the warrants, which appear to have been directed mainly at women, including Elizabeth Taylor. Although the sources do not directly state it, it is reasonable to assume that the eviction notices were meant as threats to coerce people to work. Scott and the two policemen were met by a crowd of men and women whose behavior successfully prevented both the arrest of Taylor and Benlay for assault and, for a second day running, the serving of the notices to quit. S.M. McLeod did not manage to arrest Taylor until he brought a group of policemen and planters with him the next day. At that point she was taken into custody along with her husband, Robert, and another man, John Dinont. The three were tried at the October quarter sessions parish court, where Taylor was convicted of assaulting Scott, and all three of assaulting police constables. Selena Benlay and Christiana Dinont were not arrested.[30]

The reasons behind planters' apparently irrational and counterproductive approach to labor relations in the immediate post-emancipation period are beyond the scope of this chapter. It is clear, though, that large numbers of freed people concluded from confrontations such as these that planters were not prepared to negotiate satisfactory terms for the cultivation of grounds, occupation of houses, and participation in estate wage labor, and instead would use the state's coercive forces to impose "solutions" to conflict. As a result, freed people began to establish villages and settlements away from estate-owned land. As many historians have described, freed people, in many cases with the assistance of missionaries, began purchasing land where they settled as residents of "free villages."[31]

The wage-rent system is the most significant evidence supporting the argument that the establishment of free villages was a response to the "inequities of early freedom" rather than to slavery per se. Hugh Paget argues that "the people would have preferred to continue to live in their old villages on the estates and to cultivate their old provision grounds," and would have done so had they not been subject to high rents and evictions, while Douglas Hall argues for the possibility that "had the ex-slaves been allowed to continue in free use of gardens, houses and grounds, and to choose their employers without reference to that accommodation, there would have been very little movement of agricultural labour at all from the communities apparently established on the estates during slavery."[32] Neither Paget nor Hall notes, however, that women were the main targets of the wage-rent system. Nor do they recognize that the system was a response to a concerted effort by former slaves to restructure their relationships to the plantations. Hall's argument that freed people were prepared to perform wage labor if they thought the terms offered to be fair—a position characterized by Woodville Marshall as underestimating former slaves' ambitions—simplifies the actual situation.[33] While this may have been true of male workers, it was certainly not true of women (whose nonparticipation in the estate labor force Hall simply assumes to have been natural).[34] Furthermore, as Nigel Bolland has argued, we should not try to assess freed people's actions after emancipation as if former slaves were the self-sufficient individualists of liberal theory.[35] As the following section suggests, women's decisions about what work to do were clearly taken in conjunction with the decisions of other women, and of men. Male workers' willingness to do wage work was largely predicated on their kinswomen's—their wives', but also their sisters', mothers', and cousins'—ability to avoid it.

The Formation of Afro-Jamaican Gender Conventions

As shown above, women's avoidance of wage labor preceded and was more extensive than men's, and was related to the ensuing struggles over work and residence between planters and freed people—struggles that facilitated the creation of a peasantry within the interstices of the plantation system. This still leaves open the question of why women acted as they did. What gender conventions held by the freed slaves led to this behavior by women? Were women motivated primarily by "push factors"—the conscious wish to avoid agricultural wage labor—or by "pull factors"—such as a desire to use their time for other activities—so that estate work was not a practical option?[36]

We know relatively little about the internal structure of economic life among the mass of Jamaicans who attempted to establish themselves as peasant farmers in the years after slavery. However, research on the importance of "family land," held inalienably for the use of all descendants of an original ancestor, indicates the importance of kin groups in providing the means of livelihood, at least in times of emergency, for all their members.[37] We also know that provision grounds had been worked collectively in family groups under slavery, with some division of labor by sex.[38] It is fairly certain, then, that when former slaves had the opportunity to make decisions about which economic activities to undertake, they did so in conjunction with groups of kinsfolk. Making such decisions as a group of kin was itself an activity that fostered familial solidarity, while at the same time the decisions made were taken in order to consolidate family ties.

In making this argument I follow a number of scholars who have explained women's labor decisions after slavery with reference to family life or kinship. Swithin Wilmot points out that freed women's "focus on activities beyond the confines of labouring on the plantations formed an important part of various strategies that freed people developed to provide for their families." Bridget Brereton argues that freed slaves pursued "family strategies," and that "concern for the welfare of the family unit, the anxiety to secure a degree of independence from the planter and his demands, a desire to offer protection to vulnerable women and children, and a commitment to social and religious pursuits . . . lay behind the withdrawal of females from the labour force after 1838." According to Woodville Marshall, freed slaves "expected emancipation to facilitate consolidation of family by permitting the reconstitution of units that had suffered forced separation and by enabling heads of households to redistribute domestic responsibilities and to allocate family labour." In very similar terms, Eric Foner describes the attempts of "West Indian blacks . . . to reconstruct family life by withdrawing women and children from plantation field labor." Raymond Smith likewise lists "stabilization of the family" alongside the withdrawal of women from field labor as a pan-American concern of freed slaves. Nigel Bolland, while not specifically addressing the question of women's labor, argues that former slaves had goals "connected with family life, with conceptions of the home and of domestic authority, with religious and cultural life, and with education," and notes that "insofar as slavery involved the natal alienation of the slave and his social death through the loss of kinship ties the transcendence of slavery must recover or establish such ties."[39]

This is an impressive group of scholars, and the argument they make is compelling. However, we need to go beyond the explanation that freed people wanted to consolidate their families to ask two crucial questions:

How were these families organized—that is, what did "family" mean in this context? And, why did their consolidation require women's refusal of wage labor in particular? The small number of surviving rent bills addressed to freed people in 1838 indicates the existence of a variety of coresidential familial groups. Some take a form that suggests a traditional nuclear family, such as "Robert Barkey, wife and daughter," or "Charles Williams, for self, wife, and three children." Rent bills issued on a St. Elizabeth coffee plantation indicate households composed of women and their children: bills were addressed to Ann Barrett, "for rent for you at 3s 4d per week and your children Susan, John, William, and Robert at 1s 8d each per week," and Lucy Hanson, for herself and "each of your children viz Penells, Eleanor, Rachel, and Marcus."[40] Other family forms were more complex: James Baugh addressed a bill for rent to "Grace Heywood, labourer, . . . for yourself, one child, and Sarah Douglas." According to one observer, Sarah Douglas was "an orphan girl of only nine or ten years of age," who Heywood took care of because she was "the daughter of her [Heywood's] shipmate."[41] This grouping suggests the significance of kin or kinlike relationships constructed through the experience of enslavement, and also provides an early example of the informal adoption mechanisms that have been documented in the contemporary Caribbean.[42]

This evidence confirms what we would expect from studies of West Indian and specifically Jamaican kinship during slavery and more recently; that is, that the people who were newly free in 1838 did not live only in simple kin groups of husband, wife, and children. Rather, as Bridget Brereton suggests, "there was considerable diversity of family forms among the newly freed people."[43] Some of these family forms included a male "head of household"; others were households headed by women in "visiting" relationships with men. Some households included children from more than one partner; most of their members had substantial numbers of consanguineal kin living close by, if not in the same household. Resources and labor would often have been shared or exchanged with people, frequently kin, living in the same yard but not the same household.[44] Thus, "consolidating the family" meant something rather broader than the strengthening of the relationships among a conjugal couple and their children. It implied the creation of a living situation in which broader groups of kin could live near one another and ensure the survival of all their members.

Women's refusal of wage labor was part of this broadly conceived process of consolidation of family, as well as a step in the "reconstitution" of a Jamaican peasantry, as described by Sidney Mintz. Women's refusal of wage labor prior to (and precipitating) the planters' attacks on them and on all ex-slaves lends support to those such as Marshall, who argue that the "flight from the estates" was not simply a response to the "inequities of early freedom." Clearly, the ex-slaves were prepared to continue working on the estates only if they could dramatically alter the place of that work in their lives. Within groups of kin, only a minority of the total time available would be allocated to wage work for estates: a portion of the time of adult men. In contrast, all the time of women and children would be devoted to autonomous economic activities: cultivation of crops for sale and subsistence, marketing of the surplus, looking after stock, child-care, and care of the home. Women's refusal to work as wage laborers was a decision taken by family groups to make time for what both men and women understood as "women's work." Women had the primary responsibility for the continuing cultivation of the provision grounds, as well as the marketing of the surplus (although some agricultural tasks seem to have been reserved exclusively for men). Men's labor could be spared from the cultivation of provision grounds long enough for them to go and work for wages for the estates. Women's could not. This was, in large part, a result of women's exclusive responsibility for children, who also contributed to the family livelihood through their work on the provision grounds. These men and women should not be thought of as relating to each other exclusively, or even primarily, as husbands and wives: kin groups sharing resources would have included adult sons living with their mothers, and adult women living with their brothers. Many men would have fathered children who lived in other households, but may well have felt their primary allegiance, in economic and emotional terms, to their natal household.

Although it seems likely that the decision that women should not participate in wage labor was made collectively with male and female groups of kin, we should not assume that these decisions were always easy and harmonious. They may also have involved conflicts between male and female family members who considered their interests to be divergent. Those men who embarked on wage labor may well have preferred not to have to continue working for sugar estates; their gender may have been used against them in conflicts among family members about who would earn the necessary cash. Men may also have tried to establish or consolidate patriarchal authority over other family members on the basis of their access to cash. On the other hand, some have suggested that men may have prevented their wives from working as a way of controlling them.[45] While I would not want to rule it out as a possibility, I think this latter suggestion is unlikely, given both the relative autonomy of male and female economic decisions in Afro-Caribbean gender systems, and the fact that wage work seems to have been a source of marginality more than power in post-emancipation Jamaica.[46] Newspaper reports of trials and arrests document many occasions when conflicts over gender rights and obligations led to violence—almost always committed by men on women. In these cases, violence arose repeatedly in a number of contexts, most notably conflicts about sexual infidelity; women's refusal of men's demands for domestic services such as cooking; women's greater loyalty to their families of origin than to their partners; and one partner's refusal to accept the other's decision to end a relationship. I have found none involving conflicts over wages or wage labor.[47] Obviously, such records reveal only a tiny fraction of gender conflict. The absence in this evidence of disputes about wages and wage labor does not mean that such conflicts did not take place, perhaps on a more minor scale that did not lead to violence. It does suggest, however, that the decision that men should perform wage labor and women should not was not a main axis of contention among Jamaican men and women in this period.

My interpretation of the division of labor that ex-slaves wanted to put into practice is based, it should be acknowledged, on relatively scarce direct evidence. Some evidence about what women did with the time they had previously spent working for the estates is contained in the documents from the period. Unfortunately, most of it is rather vague. Thus Edmund Lyon talks of women "devot[ing] their attention to their husbands and families" and performing "domestic duties," but does not detail what such attention and duties entail.[48] S.M.s Fishbourne and Hewitt wrote in March 1839 that women had withdrawn "from field labour, to pursue those avocations to which females usually devote themselves in other countries."[49] They assume that these "avocations" are obvious to their readers. Slightly more specific evidence comes from a planter's report of May 1839. After complaining that neither women nor children would work on the estates he had charge of, John Salmon wrote that "all these people, nevertheless, live on and cultivate, or have hitherto, your land, and take a large quantity of produce to market for their own special use and benefit."[50] In contrast, a missionary at Morant Bay wrote in June 1839 that "many young women have left the estates with the intention of obtaining situations in towns."[51]

Statements such as these imply that younger women behaved differently than mature women, and that women took part in a certain amount of provision ground cultivation and marketing. Support for the last point is provided by women's concerted resistance to efforts to evict them from provision grounds. We can also probably assume that women had primary responsibility for children. Any detail beyond this has to be filled in from what we know about the division of labor by sex in the slavery period and from ethnographic studies of twentieth-century Jamaican rural life. Although we do not know precisely which agricultural tasks were seen as men's work and women's work, we can be sure that women were actively involved in small-scale agriculture and marketing.[52]

Freed people's desire to expand what had been their "own account" activities under slavery thus explains the decision to devote only a small portion of the total time available to wage labor. But why should it have been men who continued to work for the estates? Could not family consolidation have taken place with men and women undertaking different gender roles, or without the organizing principle of gender? This question can be answered only with reference to the gendered beliefs and conventions, the worldviews or ideologies, that structured former slaves' understanding of their world. Discussions about this issue have often centered around the extent to which freed people accepted or rejected the ideology of "woman's sphere" or "domesticity" promoted by missionaries. This has led to at least two understandings of freed people's gender conventions.[53] On one hand, some scholars have reflexively used language suggesting that women's withdrawal from the fields represented a turn toward Victorian domesticity. In this scholarship, former slaves appear to accept the dominant ideology. One example occurs in Janet Momsen's article on "Gender Roles in Caribbean Agricultural Labour," which argues that "many women ex-slaves sought the private sphere hitherto denied them."[54] Momsen here naturalizes the existence of the "private sphere": slaves were denied it, former slaves could seek it, but as a phenomenon it is taken for granted. She does not acknowledge the specificity of the idea that the world is divided into public and private "spheres," an idea that developed in the specifically urban-industrial context of eighteenth-century Europe, and which, I would argue, was not widespread in the nineteenth-century Caribbean.[55] The implication of her use of the term is that women ex-slaves subscribed to the domestic ideology out of which the idea of separate spheres was constructed.[56]

Perhaps in reaction to this type of argument, other scholars have argued that ideology played no role in women's decisions not to perform wage labor, apparently assuming that the only available gender ideology was that of the Victorian middle class. For instance, Bridget Brereton argues that "ex-slave men and women were not blindly obeying hegemonic gender ideologies nor seeking to transform freedwomen into dependent housewives confined to the home. They were pursuing rational family strategies aimed at securing the survival and welfare of their kin groups, in the face of appalling odds."[57] Brereton here sets up a dichotomy between rationality on one hand and hegemonic ideology on the other, foreclosing the possibility of investigating the content and meaning of the conventions that led to the particular gendering of the family strategies pursued by former slaves.

The choice between seeing women's refusal of wage labor as indicating their submission to bourgeois hegemony on one hand or their pragmatic existence in a nonideological world on the other does not do justice to the complexity of the situation. I would suggest a third possibility: that freed women and men acted according to the conventions of a gender ideology of their own. This gender ideology was related to, but not derivative of, English middle-class mores; it drew on the multiple gender conventions through which enslaved Africans in Jamaica made sense of their new situation, and was constructed out of the experience of everyday life under slavery.[58] While this was a construct much less fully theorized than that of the English middle class, and one that no one was trying to establish as hegemonic, it was still an internally coherent set of conventions that can usefully be termed ideological.

Clearly, proponents of versions of the dominant gender ideology of the Victorian middle class—most prominently, missionaries and colonial officials—tried to promote their understanding of the proper gendered order of things among former slaves. This included the idea that women should not participate in the world of wage labor and should be dependent on their husbands or fathers. Catherine Hall has demonstrated the centrality of the promotion of Victorian gender conventions to the post-emancipation missionary project.[59] Equally clearly, missionaries and colonial officials did not succeed in their endeavors: women's active involvement in marketing, which led them to play highly "public" roles; the fact that legal marriage did not become the norm; and the maintenance of relative economic autonomy between men and women in long-term sexual and emotional partnerships—all demonstrate that the gender ideologies of former slaves were not identical to those of missionaries and colonial officials.

Probably more significant than Victorian domesticity in the formation of Afro-Caribbean gender ideologies were the West African gender conventions that newly enslaved Africans brought with them to the Caribbean. The importation of new Africans to Jamaica had ended with the closing of the slave trade in 1807. Nevertheless, a substantial minority of those freed in 1838 were African-born; a much larger, though indeterminate, proportion had at least one African parent.[60] Although slaves came from a number of different African societies with different gender conventions and ideologies that were themselves undergoing change (in part as a result of disturbances due to the slave trade itself), these societies shared many significant features, some of which clearly influenced the gender ideologies developed among slaves and freed people.[61] Some of the most fundamental characteristics of West African gender relations, most notably the centrality of lineages as a source of identification, could not, for structural reasons, have been transferred to, or even transformed in, the Americas. But other characteristics—those more easily reproduced by individuals in a new environment—could have been.[62] Most notably, women's autonomous control of property has been a noted feature of African diasporic communities in many parts of the Americas, contrasting sharply with dominant Latin American and Anglo-American patterns. Autonomous control of property by men and women, with women retaining property rights on marriage, is also characteristic of most West African peoples, including the Akan groups that dominated numerically and culturally during the formative period of the development of Afro-Jamaican culture.[63]

Even if it were possible, it would not be especially helpful to measure European against West African gender ideologies and see which comes closest to that of the former slaves. For one thing, labor in West African societies during the period of the Atlantic slave trade was structured through households, not performed by wage laborers. The question of whether or not women should do wage labor on large-scale plantations was not one that would have arisen in those societies, and thus freed people in Jamaica could not have answered it simply by reference to inherited patterns of thought. My point in noting some parallels and influences is that freed people had their own ways of thinking about gender that did not have to be either simply practical or embedded in European ideologies.

Nevertheless, freed people were in regular interaction with the European gender ideology, which was constantly being preached among them, whereas they were more removed from direct African influences (at least until the arrival of more Africans in the 1840s). How did their worldview overlap with, differ from, and interact with the gender ideologies that were promoted among them by others?

British, West African, and Afro-Jamaican ideologies of gender—each of which was itself internally divided—overlapped in many ways.[64] Crucially, all three worldviews shared a sense of gender as fundamentally significant in determining a person's nature. Former slaves, middle-class Britons, and West Africans all maintained a strong sense that women and men were different types of people who should be responsible for different kinds of activities. Likewise, Afro-Jamaicans shared with both Britons and with members of the West African societies from which their ancestors came the expectation that women should have total responsibility for looking after children. This is evident from the fact that apprenticeship-period struggles around time for child-care never involved men. It could be argued that women's responsibility for children had made their experience of slavery, and particularly of apprenticeship, harsher than that of men. After slavery ended, women continued to have exclusive responsibility for children. This responsibility lay at the heart of their desire to avoid plantation work. While theoretically it should not be more difficult to combine child-care with estate labor than with, for instance, taking crops to a market, the greater flexibility of a peasant labor process would have made the combination much easier—and women's experience of slavery and apprenticeship had not led them to expect planters to accommodate themselves to women's need for flexibility.

In significant ways, the gender conventions of the ex-slaves diverged from Victorian domestic ideology. Most obvious is the area of sexuality, which in turn relates to family organization.[65] There was no expectation that women would marry before bearing children. Nor did bearing children necessarily imply that a woman would live with and pool resources with the father of her child. She could expect support from other family members, especially her mother and the other older female relatives, but bore primary responsibility for the economic support, as well as the physical and emotional care, of her children. In a society in which many aspects of life were not commodified, the production of one's own crops and other activities that minimized the need for cash, as well as the generation of income through marketing, were economically more significant than earning wages. Women's avoidance of wage labor may, paradoxically, reflect not so much their withdrawal from work as their need to devote time to a range of other essential tasks with which wage work for estates, especially on the full-time basis demanded by planters, was incompatible.

Women's refusal to work for wages, then, derived not just from pragmatism, nor from acceptance of domestic ideology, but from an ideology quite distinct from that which was being promoted among them. Even the similarities between the two ideologies had different meanings for the different groups. While members of the English middle class could usually assume their existence as gendered beings, Jamaican former slaves had to struggle to attain and institutionalize gender. Although the labor force under slavery had been structured by gender to the extent that some positions were filled only by men and others (fewer and less prestigious) only by women, the general tendency of slavery was to reduce individuals to units of labor, pushing gendered—along with all other—aspects of differentiation among people to the margins. One might paraphrase Nigel Bolland and argue that, insofar as slavery involved the degendering of the slave, the transcendence of slavery had to involve the reassertion of gender distinction as a principle of social life. Holding fast to the idea that men and women were different types of people with different responsibilities was not merely a practical choice, it was also a politicized assertion of personhood.

English middle-class and Afro-Jamaican gender ideologies differed in myriad ways, but their assumptions led them to share one crucial aspect: freed women should devote their time to responsibilities other than wage labor. Afro-Jamaicans were able to use this partial convergence as a political weapon against planters' efforts to coerce them to work. In this final section I show how, as well as physically resisting such attempts, freed women appropriated an argument made by colonial authorities to counteract the planters' efforts to get them to work in the fields. The tension between the two worldviews, as well as the political intent involved, can be seen in the subtle way in which Afro-Jamaican women altered the English ideology.

On the eve of emancipation, the governor of Jamaica, Lionel Smith, published a proclamation to all those who were about to be freed in which he urged them to be responsible, hardworking, and respectable citizens of the new society. Part of the address included the advice to "Be honest toward all men—be kind to your wives and children—spare your wives from heavy field work, as much as you can—make them attend to their duties at home, in bringing up your children, and in taking care of your stock—above all, make your children attend divine service and school. If you follow this advice, you will, under God's blessing, be happy and prosperous."[66] Although Smith's proclamation purported to speak to all apprentices, the imagined addressee is a married man with children. He does not speak to women directly.

As well as issuing this proclamation, Smith toured the island delivering speeches that contained the same message. His address to a crowd outside the Falmouth courthouse included the following: "And you husbands, take care of your wives; let them do as little hard work as possible; I don't mean to say that they are not to work at all, but that you must lighten their labours, and give them time to take care of your houses and children. Your masters will require so many cane-holes to be dug, and they won't care who does the work, so that it is done. Let your wives therefore do light work and take care of the children. WE WANT AS MANY CHILDREN AS YOU CAN GET!"[67] According to the newspaper that reported this speech, Smith's last comment was greeted with "immense laughter and cheers."[68]

Apprentices were given similar advice by several of the stipendiary magistrates. In his newspaper the *West Indian and Jamaica Gazette*, S.M. Edward Baynes addressed an article "to the labouring population of Jamaica." He echoed Smith's call for the separation of spheres, while also emphasizing the need for legally recognized marital relations:

You must not continue to live in concubinage, but must marry according to the law of Christians, and become the husband of one wife. The time is near at hand, when a person living in fornication and adultery, will be rejected by every congregation in the Island. You must educate your children and send them to school, and not begrudge a small portion of your weekly earnings to this most essential of all purposes. I have already said a great deal on the propriety of employing your wives, as much as possible, in domestic avocations.[69]

The Jamaican stipendiary magistrate Richard Chamberlaine's imagined view of post-slavery gender relations was similar, if less directly didactic. A few days after full emancipation he spoke to a group of two thousand to three thousand former slaves assembled at the Wesleyan chapel in Manchioneal. Despite the fact that the congregation must have included many women and single men, he directed his address to married men. Insisting that "freedom brings with it no exemption from labour," he declared himself confident that they would use their "best exertions for the support of yourselves and families." He continued to present an idyllic domestic fantasy predicated on a radical split between home and work, and on the assumption that women's main responsibility would be the home.

Your wives, hitherto accustomed to be partakers in your daily toils, running to the fields with you in the morning, and returning with you down-spirited and dejected at sun set day by day, bringing no alleviations, will be enabled to remain at home, to look after your clothes, and your children's clothes—your household affairs—your stock—your comfortable dinner, so that whilst you are at work in the field, as the day advances, instead of lagging in your work, you are more cheerful, more industrious, because moving in the certainty of finding every thing comfortable when you get home. To find . . . your household affairs all clean and tidy, your children and your wife contented, receiving you with smiles, you embrace them in ecstasy. You acquire a relish for, and entertain settled notions of, domestic happiness; your meals are properly prepared; everything is decent and in order; you are comforted; you sleep soundly, and rise in the morning refreshed and invigorated, ever and anon prepared to labour for a continuance of the same happiness and comforts.[70]

Apart from the responsibility for stock, referred to also by Smith, Chamberlaine's view assumes not only that women and men will live in nuclear families in which the wife and children are dependent on the husband, but also that the whole family's needs will be entirely met through wage labor.

Incidentally, he thereby illustrates the specifically bourgeois nature of the domestic ideology, which would be very hard to fit with a way of life involving extensive peasant agriculture. Thus as they approached emancipation, apprentices had no shortage of people advising them to organize their family life and the gender division of labor within it along the lines of the Victorian middle class.

These statements, especially the governor's, became controversial very quickly. Planters complained that such advice would lead women away from wage labor when they should be told to devote themselves wholeheartedly to the sugar economy. Planters looked at the situation through a gender ideology that differed from both British domesticity and the Afro-Jamaican worldview. The planters' worldview was highly racialized, conceptualizing black women as a specific type of woman to whom the "normal" prescriptions of gender convention did not apply. When women began to refuse wage labor, planters saw their behavior as entirely negative and argued that the governor's advice was responsible. One example, of which many could be given, was written by an anonymous planter: "With regard to the females, a foolish misapprehension of the governors address to them on the 1st August calling on the men to relieve their wives from heavy labour, has had the effect of putting an end to agricultural labour on their parts."[71] Many went further than this, claiming that women only refused to participate in wage labor because of the governor's advice, and reporting that they knew this because women had told them so.

Planters clearly had an incentive to exaggerate the extent to which women presented their actions as a response to the governor. Doing so reinforced the racist view of black people as lacking the ability to make their own decisions. Perhaps more important, such an analysis transformed what was actually a deep-seated conflict of interest into an easy-to-solve problem of bad advice—one that could be resolved if the governor were only to issue another proclamation. In their discussions of the "flight from the estates," scholars have been almost totally silent about such planter claims.[72] This may be because the claims clearly fit with planter interests. Not wanting to give credence to an "outside-agitator" interpretation of class and gender relations, historians have simply dismissed reports of women claiming that they refused wage work as a result of the governor's advice. In addition, the dominance within Caribbean history (as in many other fields of history) of a paradigm in which the task of the historian is seen as establishing the "truth" of "what really happened" has led to an approach in which narratives generated by people in the past are either taken as unproblematically transparent or dismissed as false. But this is not an adequate response to the reports about women's justifications for their refusal to wage labor. The reports that focus on women's own words are too extensive to be entirely fabricated. At least some women claimed that they would not do wage labor because the governor had told them not to. This does not mean that women's primary motivation in refusing wage labor was the governor's advice; it does mean that, when asked why women would not work, ex-slaves frequently referred to the governor's words as justification for a decision taken for broader and deeper reasons. Examining how they used the governor's discourse reveals an aspect of the political claim-making that was part of the process of the post-emancipation struggle over gender.

There are rare reports in which men use the governor's advice to argue that women should not do wage labor. For instance, a reply to Smith's proclamation from the Baptist missionary Samuel Oughton's congregation at Lucea, quite likely drafted by Oughton, adopted a masculine voice. It stated that "we entertain no idea of sitting down in idleness after the first of August, on the contrary we are resolved to devote ourselves with increased industry to the discharge of our several duties, that by so doing we may provide for our wives and children as well as support our aged and infirm relatives, who are unable to labour for themselves."[73] Despite the fact that any Baptist congregation would have included many women, the "we" here is clearly male. Men assume an active role both in economically supporting and in speaking for women, who are rendered silent. The statement is thus a fitting response to Smith's proclamation, with the group that he addressed replying to him.

Oughton's congregation's statement is rare in this sense. In almost all of the reports I have found in which former slaves refer to the governor's or similar advice, it is women who make the argument. Thus, in Trelawney, planters argued that, "The refusal on the part of the women to work is general all over the Parish, and when spoken to, they invariably reply 'the Governor told us we were not to work.' "[74] Similarly, in Westmoreland planters pointed out that "a feeling exists generally on the part of the females that they would be acting contrary to the instructions of the Governor were they to engage in Field Labour."[75] Other examples included those given by clergyman Andrew Cooke and planter John Salmon. Cooke reported that "upon visiting an estate in the neighbourhood of Morant Bay, of which I have the charge, some time after the 1st of August, the women told me, 'that the Governor said they were to do no work,' and that they would be 'sinning against God' if they either worked themselves or permitted their daughters to work."[76] And Salmon wrote that "the women, except in a few instances, will not work; they have frequently replied to my urging them to labour, that his Excellency told them no."[77]

In all these examples, the dialogue is presented as taking place between the planter and the women who will not work. Ex-slave men do not come into it; the women feel no need to have men speak for them. Implicitly, then, such women challenge their advisers' assumptions about their dependence on men even while using one aspect of the advice given them. The women appropriate what is useful to them in the governor's advice— the idea that they should be "spared from heavy field labour." I have found no reference to any other aspect of the advice: the women are never said to state that their duties should be confined to the home, they do not speak of a radical disjuncture between home and work, nor do they avoid taking their own decisions or speaking for themselves. By adopting this strategy of justification, freed women were able simultaneously to deflect responsibility for their decisions away from themselves, and to enlist the symbolic support of the state for their choices. Both factors could be expected to mitigate the hostility directed toward them as a result of their transgression of planter wishes.

Women's relationship to wage work in the post-emancipation period needs to be considered in light of the total reconstruction of social relations in post-slavery society. In its extent and its impact, it was a key axis of the class struggle between planters and former slaves that ensued after slavery. Indeed, the ability to organize gender relations as they wanted was a critical component of freed slaves' goals in the aftermath of emancipation. Women's decisions about labor were taken in conjunction with male and female kin, and in the context of a gender ideology which was itself undergoing development stimulated by the new possibilities and constraints of freedom. This ideology to some extent overlapped with the ideology of "woman's sphere" promoted by missionaries and colonial officials. Recognizing this overlap does not mean that we have to understand freed people's gender ideologies as derivative of elite discourse. Rather, it opens up a space for investigating the political use to which such ideological connections could be put. Women's justifications for their refusal of wage labor underline their awareness of both the differences and similarities between their gendered ideas and those of their colonial masters, and their ability to make use of colonial discourse to suit their own ends.

Notes

1   Although the phenomenon I am discussing here is commonly referred to as "women's withdrawal" from field labor or estate labor, and I sometimes use this phrase in order to avoid repetition, I prefer to use "women's refusal of wage labor." I refer to "wage" rather than "field" labor to avoid the implication that women were no longer involved in

agriculture. I use the term "refusal" rather than "withdrawal" in order to emphasize the active nature of former slaves' decisions, and to avoid the insular implication carried by "withdrawal." To discuss a "withdrawal from estate labor" emphasizes what people stopped doing, whereas talking about a "refusal of wage labor" provokes questions about the alternatives in favor of which wage labor was refused.

2   The demonstration of women's agency was an important achievement of women's history in many fields. The pioneering work on the Anglophone Caribbean in this tradition was Lucille Mathurin, "A Historical Study of Women in Jamaica from 1655 to 1844" (Ph.D. diss., University of the West Indies, 1974). See also Lucille Mathurin Mair, *The Rebel Woman in the British West Indies During Slavery* (Kingston: Institute of Jamaica Publications, [1975] 1995); Hilary McD. Beckles, *Natural Rebels: A Social History of Enslaved Black Women in Barbados* (New Brunswick: Rutgers University Press, 1989); Barbara Bush, *Slave Women in Caribbean Society, 1650–1838* (London: James Currey, 1990). Note the way that many of these titles emphasize women's intrinsic or "natural" rebelliousness. Hilary Beckles provides a useful review of this work in "Sex and Gender in the Historiography of Caribbean Slavery," in *Engendering History: Caribbean Women in Historical Perspective,* ed. Verene Shepherd, Bridget Brereton, and Barbara Bailey (New York: St. Martin's Press, 1995), 125–40.

3   On Nanny, see Mair, *Rebel Woman,* 34–37; Barbara K. Kopytoff, "The Early Political Development of Jamaican Maroon Societies," *William and Mary Quarterly* 3d ser., 25 (April 1978): 300.

4   For instance, Kevin D. Smith, "A Fragmented Freedom: The Historiography of Emancipation and Its Aftermath in the British West Indies," *Slavery and Abolition* 16, 1 (1995): 101–30; Michael Craton, "The Transition from Slavery to Free Wage Labour in the Caribbean, 1780–1890: A Survey with Particular Reference to Recent Scholarship," *Slavery and Abolition* 13, 2 (1992): 60. For a similar call, more broadly focused, see Rebecca Scott, "Exploring the Meaning of Freedom: Postemancipation Societies in Comparative Perspective," *Hispanic American Historical Review* 68 (1988): 423 n. On similar processes in other post-slave societies, see Jacqueline Jones, *Labor of Love, Labor of Sorrow: Black Women, Work, and the Family from Slavery to the Present* (New York: Basic Books, 1985), 58–68; Tera W. Hunter, *To 'Joy My Freedom: Southern Black Women's Lives and Labors After the Civil War* (Cambridge, Mass.: Harvard University Press, 1997), chap. 2; Leslie A. Schwalm, *'A Hard Fight for We': Women's Transition from Slavery to Freedom in South Carolina* (Urbana: University of Illinois Press, 1997), 6–8, 204–14; Rebecca J. Scott, *Slave Emancipation in Cuba: The Transition to Free Labor, 1860–1899* (Princeton: Princeton University Press, 1985), 242–44; George Reid Andrews, *Blacks and Whites in São Paulo, Brazil, 1888–1988* (Madison: University of Wisconsin Press, 1991), 84; Pamela Scully, *Liberating the Family? Gender and British Slave Emancipation in the Rural Western Cape, South Africa, 1823–1853* (Portsmouth, N.H.: Heinemann, 1997), chap. 5.

5   Thomas C. Holt, *The Problem of Freedom: Race, Labor, and Politics in Jamaica and Britain, 1832–1938* (Baltimore: Johns Hopkins University Press, 1992), 151–76; Swithin Wilmot, " 'Females of Abandoned Character'? Women and Protest in Jamaica, 1838–65," in *Engendering History,* ed. Shepherd, Brereton, and Bailey, 279–95; Bridget Brereton, "Family Strategies, Gender, and the Shift to Wage Labour in the British Caribbean," in *The Colonial Caribbean in Transition: Essays on Postemancipation Social and Cultural History,* ed. Bridget Brereton and Kevin A. Yelvington (Kingston, Jamaica: The Press University of the West Indies, 1999), 77–107.

6   Perhaps the most significant is the classic article by Douglas Hall, to which the title of my paper alludes: Douglas Hall, "The Flight from the Estates Reconsidered: The Brit-

ish West Indies, 1838–1842," *Journal of Caribbean History* 10–11 (1978): 7–24. See also Hall, *Free Jamaica, 1838–1865: An Economic History* (New Haven: Yale University Press, 1959); Hall, *Five of the Leewards: The Major Problems of the Post-Emancipation Period in Antigua, Barbuda, Montserrat, Nevis and St. Kitts* (Aylesbury, Bucks.: Ginn and Company and Caribbean University Press, 1971); Alan H. Adamson, *Sugar Without Slaves: The Political Economy of British Guiana, 1838–1904* (New Haven: Yale University Press, 1972); O. Nigel Bolland, "The Politics of Freedom in the British Caribbean," in *The Meaning of Freedom: Economics, Politics, and Culture After Slavery*, ed. Frank McGlynn and Seymour Drescher (Pittsburgh: University of Pittsburgh Press, 1992), 113–46; Woodville K. Marshall, " 'We be wise to many more tings': Blacks' Hopes and Expectations of Emancipation," in *Caribbean Freedom: Economy and Society from Emancipation to the Present*, ed. Hilary Beckles and Verene Shepherd (Kingston: Ian Randle Publishers, 1993), 12–20; Sidney W. Mintz, *Caribbean Transformations* (Baltimore: Johns Hopkins University Press, 1974); Hugh Paget, "The Free Village System in Jamaica," *Caribbean Quarterly* 10, 1 (1964): 38–51; Rawle Farley, "The Rise of Village Settlements in British Guiana," *Caribbean Quarterly* 10, 1 (1964): 52–61; Michel-Rolph Trouillot, "Labour and Emancipation in Dominica: Contribution to a Debate," *Caribbean Quarterly* 30, 3–4 (1984): 73–84. The last three articles are included in Rex Nettleford, ed., *Apprenticeship and Emancipation: Reprints from Caribbean Quarterly* (Mona, Jamaica: Caribbean Studies Initiative, University of the West Indies, 1999).

7 On this point, see the comments of Sumit Sarkar in his "The Decline of the Subaltern in Subaltern Studies," in *Mapping Subaltern Studies and the Postcolonial*, ed. Vinayak Chaturvedi (London: Verso, in association with New Left Review, 2000), 300–323.

8 Sherry Ortner, "Resistance and the Problem of Ethnographic Refusal," *Comparative Studies in Society and History* 37 (1995): 188.

9 In addition to the works cited in notes 4–6 above, see Jean Besson, "Freedom and Community: The British West Indies," in *The Meaning of Freedom*, ed. McGlynn and Drescher, 183–219; and Verene Shepherd, "Alternative Husbandry: Slaves and Free Labourers on Livestock Farms in Jamaica in the Eighteenth and Nineteenth Centuries," *Slavery and Abolition* 14, 1 (1993): 41–66.

10 Besson, "Freedom and Community," 185, following Mintz, *Caribbean Transformations*, part II.

11 The decline of the sugar economy is documented in William A. Green, *British Slave Emancipation: The Sugar Colonies and the Great Experiment, 1830–1865* (Oxford: Clarendon Press, 1976), esp. chaps. 7 and 8; Hall, *Free Jamaica*, chaps. 2 and 3; Holt, *Problem of Freedom*, chap. 4.

12 On gendered labor patterns in the twentieth century, see Edith Clarke, *My Mother Who Fathered Me: A Study of the Family in Three Selected Communities in Jamaica* (London: George Allen & Unwin, 1957); Helen Safa, "Economic Autonomy and Sexual Equality in Caribbean Society," *Social and Economic Studies* 35, 3 (1986): 1–21; and Keith Hart, ed., *Women and the Sexual Division of Labour in the Caribbean* (Mona, Jamaica: Canoe Press, 1996). One suggestive, but short, study, which reaches back to the 1880s, is Erna Brodber, "Afro-Jamaican Women at the Turn of the Century," *Social and Economic Studies* 35 (Sept. 1986): 23–50, which is the main source for Holt's comments on these issues in *Problem of Freedom*, 168–76. Some points can also be gleaned from works not primarily concerned with gender: see Patrick Bryan, *The Jamaican People, 1880–1902: Race, Class, and Social Control* (London: Macmillan Caribbean, 1991); Gisela Eisner, *Jamaica, 1830–1930: A Study in Economic Growth* (Westport, Conn.: Greenwood Press, 1961).

13 On apprenticeship, see Green, *British Slave Emancipation*, chap. 5; W. L. Burn, *Emancipation*

and *Apprenticeship in the British West Indies* (London: Jonathan Cape, 1937); Holt, *Problem of Freedom*, 55–112.

14 For discussion of some of these "bargains," see Emilia Viotti da Costa, *Crowns of Glory, Tears of Blood: The Demerara Slave Rebellion of 1823* (New York: Oxford University Press, 1994), 63–74; and the essays in Mary Turner, ed., *From Chattel Slaves to Wage Slaves: The Dynamics of Labour Bargaining in the Americas* (London: James Currey, 1995).

15 W. K. Marshall makes a similar point with regard to the Windward Islands. See his "Apprenticeship and Labour Relations in Four Windward Islands," in *Abolition and Its Aftermath: The Historical Context, 1790–1916*, ed. David Richardson (London: Frank Cass, 1985), 203–24. See also Brereton, "Family Strategies," 79–82.

16 Report from the Select Committee appointed to inquire into the working of the Apprenticeship System, Evidence of Captain W. Oldrey, 292, British Parliamentary Papers (hereafter PP) 1836 (560) XV.

17 George Blythe to Nunes, 28 July 1835, enc. in Sligo to Glenelg no. 103, 6 Sept. 1835, P.R.O. CO 137/202.

18 Reports of C. Hamilton and R. Facey, enc. in Sligo to Glenelg no. 207, 2 Apr. 1836, PP 1836 (166–1) XLVIII.

19 Report of S.M. Lyon, 15 Sept. 1838, enc. in Smith to Glenelg no. 25, 24 Sept. 1838, PP 1839 (107) XXXV.

20 Report of S.M. Woolfrys, 17 Oct. 1838, enc. in Smith to Glenelg no. 29, 1 Nov. 1838, PP 1839 (107) XXXV.

21 William Forsyth before Grand Jury of Surrey Assizes, Jan. 1839, in appendix C, enc. in Burge to Normanby, 18 March 1839, PP 1839 (158) XXXV. For similar claims by planters, see Thomas McCornock to Richard Chamberlaine, 15 Oct. 1838, and Jon Drysdale to Richard Chamberlain, 19 Oct. 1838, both enc. in Smith to Glenelg No. 29, 1 Nov. 1838, PP 1839 (107) XXXV.

22 Brereton, "Family Strategies," 89.

23 Report on St. James, 25 Feb. 1839, enc. in Burge to Normanby no. 1, 7 May 1839 PP 1839 (290) XXXV. Note that women had made up the majority of the workforce during apprenticeship.

24 Report upon the state of labouring population and sugar cultivation in Hanover, to mid Jan. 1839 enc. in Burge to Normanby, 1 Apr. 1839, PP 1839 (200) XXXV.

25 For other discussions of this system, see Brereton, "Family Strategies," 90–92; Bolland, "Politics of Freedom," 120–22; Wilmot, " 'Females of Abandoned Character'?" 280–284; Hall, "Flight from the Estates."

26 Report of S.M. Lyon, 15 Sept. 1838, enc. in Smith to Glenelg no. 25, 24 Sept. 1838, PP 1839 (107) XXXV.

27 A few planters directed separate bills to individual occupants rather than household groups. Rent bills and notices to quit may be found in PP 1839, volume XXXV: in paper 109 they are enclosed in T. W. Jackson to Smith, 22 Sept. 1838, and Henry Sterne to Smith, 17 Sept. 1838, both in Smith to Glenelg no. 25, 24 Sept. 1838; and in John Gurley to Richard Hill, 27 Nov. 1838, and S. R. Rickets to Darling, 17 Dec. 1838, both in Smith to Glenelg no. 43, 25 Dec. 1838; in paper 107-II they are enclosed in J. W. Grant to Smith, 9 Jan. 1839, in Smith to Glenelg, 6 Feb. 1839.

28 Wilmot, " 'Females of Abandoned Character'?" 280–84.

29 Affidavit of William Lowe Scott, 14 Aug. 1838, enc. in Smith to Glenelg no. 37, 5 Feb. 1839, P.R.O. CO 137/237.

30 Details of this case are in Smith to Glenelg no. 37, 5 Feb. 1839, and Smith to Glenelg no. 52, 25 Feb. 1839, both in P.R.O. CO 137/237.

31 Paget, "Growth of Villages"; Mintz, Caribbean Transformations, chap. 6; Catherine Hall, "White Visions, Black Lives: The Free Villages of Jamaica," History Workshop Journal 36 (1993): 100–132.

32 Paget, "Growth of Villages," 42; Hall, "Flight from the Estates," 23. "Inequities of early freedom" is Hall's phrase.

33 Marshall, "We Be Wise," 13. See also Trouillot's comments on this point in his "Labour and Emancipation in Dominica."

34 "Obviously, there were many who with the ending of compulsion would have withdrawn from fields and factories—the old, the very young, women who wished to give their time to their own households, and others who preferred village or 'urban' to estate employment, or town life to country life." Hall, "Flight from the Estates," 60. See also Five of the Leewards, 11, where Hall makes a very similar assertion and implies that the category of "the adult able-bodied" did not include women.

35 Bolland, "Politics of Freedom," 141–42.

36 Madhavi Kale, in a work that focuses primarily on Trinidad and British Guiana, suggests that women's primary motivation for rejecting wage labor may have been that the wages offered to them were lower than those offered to men. Madhavi Kale, Fragments of Empire: Capital, Slavery, and Indian Indentured Labor Migration in the British Caribbean (Philadelphia: University of Pennsylvania Press, 1998), 58–59. I have found no reference to this possibility in the contemporary debate about Jamaica, and specific reports of Jamaican wages were always gender neutral. Anton V. Long, Jamaica and the New Order (Mona, Jamaica: Institute for Social and Economic Research, University of the West Indies, 1956), 7, claims that women and men received the same wages. Women were, however, excluded from most of the higher-paid estate jobs, in particular in sugar manufacturing and supervision, and this discrimination must have meant that women's average earnings were less than men's; this may have deterred women from wage labor more generally. Even so, it seems that men were more prepared than women were to work as general laborers.

37 Jean Besson, "A Paradox in Caribbean Attitudes to Land," in Land and Development in the Caribbean, ed. Jean Besson and Janet Momsen (London: Macmillan Caribbean, 1987), 13–45.

38 Marietta Morrissey, Slave Women in the New World: Gender Stratification in the Caribbean (Lawrence: University Press of Kansas, 1989), 57–58; Woodville K. Marshall, "Provision Ground and Plantation Labor in Four Windward Islands: Competition for Resources during Slavery," in Cultivation and Culture: Labor and the Shaping of Slave Life in the Americas, ed. Ira Berlin and Philip D. Morgan (Charlottesville: University Press of Virginia, 1993), 210; Roderick A. McDonald, The Economy and Material Culture of Slaves: Goods and Chattels on the Sugar Plantations of Jamaica and Louisiana (Baton Rouge: Louisiana State University Press, 1993), 26; Mary Turner, Slaves and Missionaries: The Disintegration of Jamaican Slave Society, 1787–1834 (Urbana: University of Illinois Press, 1982), 45.

39 Wilmot, " 'Females of Abandoned Character'?" 279; Brereton, "Family Strategies," 103; Marshall, "We Be Wise," 17; Eric Foner, Nothing But Freedom: Emancipation and Its Legacy (Baton Rouge: Louisiana State University Press, 1983), 20; Raymond T. Smith, "Race, Class, and Gender in the Transition to Freedom," in The Meaning of Freedom, ed. McGlynn and Drescher, 274–79; Bolland, "Politics of Freedom," 141–42. See also Mimi Sheller, "Quasheba, Mother, Queen: Black Women's Public Leadership and Political Protest in Post-emancipation Jamaica, 1834–65," Slavery and Abolition 19, 3 (1998): 96–98.

40 S. R. Rickets to Darling, 17 Dec. 1838, enc. in Smith to Glenelg no. 43, 25 Dec. 1838;

Henry Sterne to Smith, 17 Sept. 1838, enc. in Smith to Glenelg no. 25, 24 Sept. 1838, both in PP 1839 (107) XXXV.

41 Ibid.

42 Olive Senior, *Working Miracles: Women's Lives in the English-speaking Caribbean* (London: James Currey, 1991), 10–18; Brodber, "Afro-Jamaican Women," 25–28.

43 Brereton, "Family Strategies," 94.

44 These statements are based on the following sources, most of which draw their evidence from twentieth-century ethnographic fieldwork: Barry Higman, *Slave Population and Economy in Jamaica, 1807–1834* (Kingston: The Press University of the West Indies [1976] 1995); Raymond T. Smith, *Kinship and Class in the West Indies: A Genealogical Study of Jamaica and Guyana* (Cambridge: Cambridge University Press, 1988), esp. chap. 5; Lydia Mihelic Pulsipher, "Changing Roles in the Life Cycles of Women in Traditional West Indian Houseyards," in *Women and Change in the Caribbean*, ed. Janet H. Momsen (London: James Currey, 1993), 50–64; Karen Fog Olwig, *Cultural Adaptation and Resistance on St. John: Three Centuries of Afro-Caribbean Life* (Gainesville: University of Florida Press, 1985); Michael Mullin, *Africa in America: Slave Acculturation and Resistance in the American South and the British Caribbean, 1736–1831* (Urbana and Chicago: University of Illinois Press, 1992), chap. 7; Mintz, *Caribbean Transformations*; Clarke, *My Mother Who Fathered Me*. There are few studies of Jamaican or West Indian families in the nineteenth century, because the evidence is slim. Barry Higman, using evidence from estate censuses, has shown that the modal household was made up of an adult man, an adult woman, and the woman's child or children, but that a significant minority of households differed from this pattern, with many consisting of a woman and child or children. His evidence does not give information about changing household composition over time, nor does the evidence provide information about the fatherhood of children, which can only be inferred. Higman suggests a trend toward the development of extended (as opposed to nuclear) coresidential family units over time, as Creole families became more complex. It seems that this trend continued after emancipation. See Higman, *Slave Population and Economy in Jamaica*, 156–73. The most problematic aspect of using evidence of household structure to discuss family relationships is that it tells us nothing about relationships among people who did not live together. In order to ascertain the importance of these, we have to turn to more recent ethnographic sources as well as contemporary descriptive sources (unfortunately, almost all written by outsiders who were also usually explicitly racist). Several anthropologists have emphasized the significance of kinship relations beyond the household in West Indian family life. See especially the work of Karen Fog Olwig, who argues that the attention in Caribbean history and anthropology to the precise makeup of residential groups (especially the question of whether families are "male-headed" or "female-headed") is misplaced, because family life, at least in St. John, is better understood as consisting of "a constellation of consanguineal and affinal relationships" upon which slaves and, later, freed people, depended "for the sharing of tasks and goods that spouses, children, and parents commonly share in the nuclear family." Olwig, *Cultural Adaptation and Resistance*, 80.

45 Smith, "Race, Class, and Gender," 268.

46 On economic autonomy, see Brodber, "Afro-Caribbean Women," and Sidney Mintz, "Black Women, Economic Roles, and Cultural Traditions," in *Caribbean Freedom*, ed. Beckles and Shepherd, 238–44. Brereton comes to a similar conclusion as I do on this point, suggesting that women and men were probably "broadly agreed" on the "gendered occupational strategies" they each pursued. "Family Strategies," 100.

47 I read the court reports in the *Falmouth Post* from 1838 to 1863, and supplemented this

with some years of the *Morning Journal* and with cases reported in the Colonial Office archives, P.R.O. CO 137 series. I found a total of twenty-four cases involving violence between men and women who were identified as partners at the time of the violent incident or until shortly before it took place (by terms indicating that the couple were married, that the woman was the man's "concubine," or that the two lived together). Of these, two cases involved violence against men inflicted by women or women and men; the rest of the victims were women. Fifteen cases resulted in the death of the victim. Not all the cases provided enough information to judge the context, and all must have involved much greater complexity than can be gleaned from the newspaper reports. Nevertheless, such sources provide a rare insight into some of the issues that led to conflicts within families. I also found some cases of sexual violence committed against children, but no details were ever given of the circumstances of these cases.

48 Report of S.M. Lyon, 15 Sept. 1838, enc. in Smith to Glenelg no. 25, 24 Sept. 1838, PP 1839 (107) XXXV.

49 Report of Fishbourne and Hewitt, 20 Mar. 1839, enc. in Smith to Glenelg no. 20, 6 Apr. 1839, PP 1839 (523) XXXVI.

50 Salmon to Darling, 7 May 1839, enc. in Smith to Normanby no. 44 (no. 139), 19 July 1839, PP 1839 (523) XXXVI.

51 Benjamin Franklin to Darling, 27 June 1839, enc. in Smith to Normanby no. 42, 3 July 1839, PP 1839 (523) XXXVI.

52 On gender divisions of labor in those aspects of work controlled by slaves, see McDonald, *Economy and Material Culture of Slaves*. On the gender division of labor practiced by post-emancipation Caribbean peasants, see Janet Henshall Momsen, "Gender Roles in Caribbean Agricultural Labour," in *Labour in the Caribbean: From Emancipation to Independence*, ed. Malcolm Cross and Gad Heuman (London: Macmillan Caribbean, 1988), 141–58; Brodber, "Afro-Jamaican Women"; Mintz's analysis in *Caribbean Transformations*, 180–224, crosses both periods.

53 In criticizing the examples that I discuss below, I do not wish to imply that their authors make uniquely problematic arguments. Indeed, I see both as important contributions to the field. I present them in order to clarify my own argument by presenting what I see as the two dominant paradigms for understanding the problem in the current historiography.

54 Momsen, "Gender Roles," 145.

55 Riva Berleant-Schiller and William M. Maurer ("Women's Place Is Every Place: Merging Domains and Women's Roles in Barbuda and Dominica," in *Women and Change in the Caribbean*, ed. Momsen, 65–79) argue, based on ethnographic fieldwork, that the public/private division is unhelpful in analyzing Caribbean gender relations. See also Elizabeth Fox-Genovese's argument that the notion of public and private spheres is inappropriate when applied to the slave society of the U.S. South. Elizabeth Fox-Genovese, *Within the Plantation Household: Black and White Women of the Old South* (Chapel Hill: University of North Carolina Press, 1988), 78–80.

56 Momsen makes this claim more explicitly in "Gender Ideology and Land," in *Caribbean Portraits: Essays on Gender Ideologies and Identities*, ed. Christine Barrow (Kingston, Jamaica: Ian Randle Publishers, 1998), 115–32. On domestic ideology, see Catherine Hall, "The Early Formation of Victorian Domestic Ideology," in *White, Male, and Middle Class: Explorations in Feminism and History* (Cambridge: Polity Press, 1992); Leonore Davidoff and Catherine Hall, *Family Fortunes: Men and Women of the English Middle Class, 1780–1850* (Chicago: University of Chicago Press, 1987); G. J. Barker-Benfield, *The Culture of Sen-*

sibility: *Sex and Society in Eighteenth-Century Britain* (Chicago: University of Chicago Press, 1992); Mary Poovey, *Uneven Developments: The Ideological Work of Gender in Mid-Victorian England* (Chicago: University of Chicago Press, 1988). Davidoff and Hall's work has become controversial, in particular for its linking of the ideology of domesticity to the middle class, but their descriptions of the content of the ideology remain unsurpassed. For critiques, see Dror Wahrman, " 'Middle-Class' Domesticity Goes Public: Gender, Class, and Politics from Queen Caroline to Queen Victoria," *Journal of British Studies* 32 (1993): 396–432; Robert B. Shoemaker, *Gender in English Society, 1650–1850: The Emergence of Separate Spheres?* (London: Longman, 1998); Amanda Vickery, "Golden Ages to Separate Spheres? A Review of the Categories and Chronology of English Women's History," *Historical Journal* 36 (1993): 383–414. Vickery's article supports my argument against the use of the language of "public" and "private" and of "separate spheres" as descriptive categories rather than facets of a particular ideology.

57 Brereton, "Family Strategies," 28.

58 Scully, *Liberating the Family?* 96, makes a similar claim with regard to the Cape colony, arguing that the gender conventions of freed people "overlapped, but did not strictly accord" with missionary ideology.

59 Hall, "White Visions, Black Lives."

60 In 1817, 37 percent of slaves in Jamaica were African. Higman extrapolates from this figure to estimate that 45 percent of slaves in 1807 and 25 percent in 1832 were African. Higman, *Slave Population and Economy*, 75–80.

61 On changes in gendered behavior in precolonial West and Central Africa, see John Thornton, "Sexual Demography: The Impact of the Slave Trade on Family Structure," in *Women and Slavery in Africa*, ed. Claire C. Robertson and Martin A. Klein (Madison: University of Wisconsin Press, 1983), 39–48.

62 The question of so-called African "survivals" has been much debated among historians and anthropologists since at least the 1950s. For some of the key positions, see Melville J. Herskowitz, *The Myth of the Negro Past* (Boston: Beacon Press [1958] 1967), and Sidney W. Mintz and Richard Price, *The Birth of African-American Culture: An Anthropological Perspective* (Boston: Beacon Press [1976] 1992), and for a recent contribution to the debate which also contains a useful analysis of what is at stake, Richard D. E. Burton, *Afro-Creole: Power, Opposition, and Play in the Caribbean* (Ithaca: Cornell University Press, 1997). Recent differences between what Burton dubs the "creationists" and "Afrogenesists" have focused on whether particular cultural phenomena (prayers, musical instruments, linguistic forms), rather than general cultural principles or orientations, can be directly traced to African roots. Both sides would probably accept my points about the general African principles underlying Afro-Caribbean gender relations.

63 On gender relations and ideologies in precolonial West Africa, see Niara Sudarkasa, "The 'Status of Women' in Indigenous African Societies," in *Women in Africa and the African Diaspora*, ed. Rosalyn Terborg-Penn, Sharon Harley, and Andrea Benton Rushing (Washington, D.C.: 1987); Claire Robertson, "Developing Economic Awareness: Changing Perspectives in Studies of African Women, 1976–1985," *Feminist Studies* 13, 1 (1987): 87–136; Wilhemina J. Kalu, "Modern Ga Family Life Patterns: A Look at Changing Marriage Structure in Africa," *Journal of Black Studies* 11, 3 (1981): 349–59; T. C. McCaskie, "State and Society, Marriage and Adultery: Some Considerations towards a Social History of Pre-Colonial Asante," *Journal of African History* 22 (1981): 477–94; Claire C. Robertson and Martin A. Klein, eds., *Women and Slavery in Africa* (Madison: University of Wisconsin Press, 1983). Oyeronke Oyewumi argues that the concept of gender is inappropriate

when applied to precolonial Yorubaland, and implicitly questions its use in African history more generally. Nevertheless, her evidence, particularly with regard to ideas about motherhood, implies a strong sense of division between male and female, existing alongside important distinctions based on age-linked seniority. Oyeronke Oyewumi, "Inventing Gender: Questioning Gender in Precolonial Yorubaland," in *Problems in African History: The Precolonial Centuries*, ed. Robert O. Collins, James McDonald Burns, and Erik Kristofer Ching (New York: Markus Wiener Publishing, 1993), 244–50. On the implications of the history of African gender ideologies and practices for the study of women in the African diaspora, see Claire Robertson, "Africa into the Americas? Slavery and Women, the Family, and the Gender Division of Labor," in *More than Chattel: Black Women and Slavery in the Americas*, ed. David Barry Gaspar and Darlene Clark Hine (Bloomington and Indianapolis: Indiana University Press, 1996), 3–42.

64   My main sources for British and West African gender ideologies are cited in notes 56 and 63, respectively.

65   On post-emancipation conflicts around sexuality and "illegitimacy," see Robert J. Stewart, *Religion and Society in Post-Emancipation Jamaica* (Knoxville: University of Tennessee Press, 1992), 63–65; Persis Charles, "The Name of the Father: Women, Paternity, and British Rule in Nineteenth-Century Jamaica," *International Labor and Working-Class History* 41 (spring 1992): 4–22, and the commentaries that follow it; Norbert Ortmayr, "Church, Marriage, and Legitimacy in the British West Indies (Nineteenth and Twentieth Centuries)," *The History of the Family* 2, 2 (1997): 141–70.

66   Smith to Glenelg no. 11, 27 July 1838, PP 1839 (109) XXXV.

67   *Falmouth Post*, 1 Aug. 1838.

68   Ibid.

69   The *West Indian and Jamaica Gazette*, 23 Aug. 1838, enc. in Smith to Glenelg no. 171, 10 Sept. 1838, P.R.O. CO 137/229.

70   *Morning Journal*, 17 Aug. 1838, enc. in R. Chamberlaine to Normanby, no. 8, 27 June 1839, PP 1839 (523) XXXVI.

71   Anonymous letter from a "gentleman of property and standing," enc. in William Burge to James Stephen, 3 Oct. 1838, P.R.O. CO 137/233.

72   One exception to this is Brereton, "Family Strategies," 88, who concludes that "it is not very likely that the women were significantly influenced by [the Jamaican governor's] words," but does not consider the possibility that women may have deliberately made use of them as a political strategy. Gad Heuman also referred to these claims in an unpublished paper presented to the Institute of Latin American Studies, University of London, November 1998.

73   Samuel Oughton, on behalf of Baptists of Gurney's Mount, Lucea, to Smith, 21 July 1838, enc. in Smith to Glenelg no. 11, 27 July 1838, PP 1839 (109) XXXV.

74   Statement at meeting of freeholders, proprietors, and managers of Trelawney, held in Falmouth, 4 Feb. 1839, reported in *Jamaica Standard*, 20 Mar. 1839.

75   Statement of Westmoreland planters, reported in *Jamaica Standard*, 30 Mar. 1839.

76   Andrew Cooke to Darling, 8 May 1839, enc. in Smith to Normanby no. 6, 11 May 1839, PP 1839 (523) XXXVI.

77   John Salmon to Darling, 7 May 1839, enc. in Smith to Normanby no. 44, 19 July 1839, PP 1839 (523) XXXVI.

Greg Grandin

A More Onerous Citizenship: Illness, Race, and
Nation in Republican Guatemala

▼

Illness is the night-side of life, a more onerous citizenship.
—Susan Sontag, *Illness as Metaphor*

There is an almost irresistible temptation, as Susan Sontag pointed out
decades ago, to assign meaning to malady. Ever since European political
philosophers began to conceive of social groups as organisms, threats to
these bodies have been analogized as disease. Sontag, however, identifies
an important shift that took place around the eighteenth century, since
explored in more detail by historians of medicine, in the use of illness as
metaphor.[1] Rather than using disease to represent social "imbalances" that
could be corrected through rational administration, proactive revolutionary regimes, thinkers, and reformers came to use the rhetoric of disease to
refer to social evil. "After this point," Sontag writes, "the melodramatics of
the disease metaphor in modern political discourse assumes a punitive
notion: of the disease not as a punishment, but . . . something to be
punished."[2] This shift set the stage, to apply the metaphor here, for a more
virulent and chronic recurrence of disease imagery in the development of
modern nationalisms.

   In the nineteenth and twentieth centuries, politicians, intellectuals, and
reformers—in Europe, the United States, and Latin America—increasingly
began to use the rhetoric surrounding disease to represent not just social
disorder, but disruptions in national narratives of progress, be they disruptions caused by racial or class contradictions. Given the physical representations of both race and disease, the most explicit use of the illness metaphor has been in relation to ethnicity: disease often represented race, and
since the metaphor was easily reversible, race often represented disease.[3]

Social reformers also came to use disease to understand class relations, as they identified working-class slums and the living habits of their denizens as breeding grounds of a host of ailments thought to threaten the social order.[4] At the same time, nationalists and public health advocates have used the images associated with disease to represent threats to ideal gender relations—ideologies which often affirm national identity.[5]

Usually, these rhetorical strategies—used to interpret, represent, and confront class, racial, and gender conflicts—worked in tandem, as Donna Guy has pointed out in her study of prostitution in Buenos Aires.[6] As in other countries, Argentine reformers, politicians, and intellectuals attempted to understand the sex trade, which grew as a result of the social dislocation caused by industrialization, within an interpretative framework of nation and family. Rather than being understood as emerging from the contradictions inherent in capitalist industrialization, prostitution was represented as a blight caused by those outside the national family: single women, immigrants, homosexuals, and Jews. Public officials used medical criteria and the imagery of disease to cast those involved in the trade as marginal elements that needed to be regulated. This imagery both emerged from and helped to reaffirm ideologies governing gender, class, and ethnic relations.

In Guatemala, the language of disease has historically provided ladinos, Guatemalans not considered Indian, with a powerful metaphor with which to understand the nation's abiding ethnic divide. This metaphor has been particularly suitable in articulating a set of racial assumptions that set Guatemalan nationalism apart from that of countries with similar ethnic demographies, such as Peru, Bolivia, and Mexico.

Indians into Ladinos

Historians and anthropologists have long been stymied by Guatemalan nationalism. It purports to deny the importance of blood, yet it has been viciously racist against Mayas. On one hand, nineteenth- and early-twentieth-century national reformers have promoted the transformation of Indians into ladinos through a series of cultural, educational, and behavorial reforms.[7] On the other, Guatemalan nationalism permits nothing like what is found in Mexico, where there is a rhetorical celebration of the mestizo as representative of la raza cósmica—the genetic and cultural hybrid who supposedly bears the best of both European and American "races."[8] In Guatemala, in contrast, the term "ladino," which in the years following independence came to represent all non-Indians, refers to an exclusively European identity.

One of the most enigmatic results of the formation of Guatemalan national identity was the reduction of a complicated colonial racial schema—one that included *españoles*, mestizos, *indígenas*, *castas*, and ladinos—into two salient political categories: *indígenas* and ladinos.[9] Of course the collapsing of all non-Indians into the category of ladino occurred mostly at the level of public discourse, and belief that behavioral change could result in racial transformation could only be pushed so far.[10] Guatemalan society continues to comprise multiple racial, ethnic, and class identities, and "whiteness" remains, to a large degree, the social and cultural standard to which other ethnic categories are measured.[11] Ideologies of blood which mark these identities remain powerful, despite the emphasis given to culture.[12] Nevertheless, in the century after independence, the term "race," at least in public nationalist and bureaucratic discourse, became understood in cultural rather than biological terms. All those not engaged in an identifiable indigenous lifestyle were increasingly referred to as ladinos.[13]

Arturo Taracena has argued that the current use of the term "ladino" to refer to all non-Indians was initially a regional phenomenon, emerging in Guatemala's western highlands, Los Altos, during the late colonial and early republican period.[14] In the nineteenth century, a rising class of Creole and mestizo elites first pushed for autonomy from Spain, then independence, and then for their own separate nation. For a brief period from 1838 to 1840, Los Altos broke from Guatemala, and Quetzaltenango—today Guatemala's second most important city—became the capital of the sixth Central American state, the Estado de los Altos.[15] An overwhelming indigenous population, a relatively noncoercive market economy, and a desire to set themselves off from their rivals in the capital led highland elites to promote a national identity that was premised on racial categories but which demanded cultural assimilation. In 1871, when *altense* (highland) coffee planters took over the state, highland terminology governing ethnic relations became generalized throughout the nation.

The emphasis on assimilation makes sense considering the social and political relations that governed the city and its surrounding regions. The economy of the highland region surrounding Quetzaltenango was not based on massive state mobilization of labor such as that which took place in some parts of the Andes and Mexico until later in the nineteenth century, with the planting of coffee. Relatively noncoercive market relations of production allowed for a somewhat blurred line separating the two ethnic groups as there was less interest on the part of the state and local elites to enforce a strict racial divide. Rather than understanding Indians as a caste to be maintained and mobilized for its labor, the highland region's ruling class—Spaniards, Creoles, and eventually ladinos—came to view indigenous culture as an obstacle to their control of land, labor, and revenue. Assimilation would dissolve this obstacle.

Further, many of the highland elites were mestizos who saw in freedom from Spain an opportunity to dismantle the rigid racial hierarchy that had refused them a political voice.[16] "The older the family," wrote Lorenzo Montúfar in 1878, "the clearer is their indigenous provenance."[17] Promoting assimilation and acculturation as forebears of civilization and progress allowed these emerging mestizo elites, both in Quetzaltenango and throughout the new nation, to challenge the racial hierarchy imposed on them by Spaniards and Creoles.

In contrast to Mexican society, there was little pressure in Guatemala from below to push highland elites to develop the equivalent of the Mexican mestizo as an ideal national type. From Morelos to Juárez, to anti-imperialist struggles against the United States and the French, Mexican historians and politicians had to acknowledge and incorporate Indian participation in national history, especially following the Mexican Revolution.[18] This participation forced Mexican nationalists to develop a national archetype that included traits from both "races."

In Guatemala, in sharp contrast, liberals constantly blamed their political failures on indigenous reaction, and nearly uniformly wrote Indians out of their narration of national progress and destiny. The fall of the first liberal state, the failure of the Estado de Los Altos, the endurance of Rafael Carrera's conservative regime, even Guatemala's chronic economic woes, were all blamed on Indians. In Mexico, to become a mestizo nation meant to claim "progressive" elements from an indigenous past; in Guatemala, to become a ladino nation meant to escape a colonial legacy of obstructionism and reaction.

Mixed in Their Very Own Blood

The prose surrounding prevention, illness, and remedy fit this emerging nationalism, and the social relations that produced it, neatly. The notion that indigenous culture was a sickness afflicting Guatemalan society—an affliction usually represented as arising from the social condition that Indians found themselves in rather than something inherent in their blood—forms a recurrent theme in Guatemala's indigenista literature of the 1930s and 1940s.

By the mid-twentieth century Guatemala's long tradition of indigenismo had become radicalized.[19] Much as occurred in Mexico, ladino intellectuals such as David Vela and Miguel Angel Asturias now began to emphasize social and structural reasons, as opposed to a general condemnation of indigenous living habits, for the failure to assimilate Indians into national life.[20] In *El Señor Presidente*, for example, although Asturias still depicted Indians as anonymous victims trapped by their own psychological pathologies, he brings the debate on "the Indian problem" to the level of national politics through an examination of the impact of decades of corruption and dictatorship. Critiques of the treatment of Indians meted out by national and foreign landowners became a prevalent theme in *indigenista* literature.[21] Reformers advocated for increased state intervention (e.g., the foundation, following the 1944 October Revolution, of the Instituto Indigenista Nacional, modeled on the Mexican Instituto Nacional Indigenista) aimed at protecting and assimilating the Indians.[22]

The ascriptive value that Guatemalan ladino nationalists assigned to race—that indigenous culture was degraded (for whatever reason) and needed to be remedied (*indigenistas* also favored the word "regenerated")—was easily represented by the disease metaphor. Flavio Herrera's 1939 novel *El tigre*, for example, offers a classic equation of social exploitation, cultural identity, and physical degeneration. The novel is set on a coastal plantation, and Luis, the *finca*'s foreman, ruminates on the "fate" of indigenous workers suffering from an unidentified ailment:

> They were Indians with yellow, soft swollen faces the color of ripe lemons. With transparent skin and monstrous, bloated bellies. Luis touched them and felt the cysts on their scalps. "What have you given them as a remedy?" "They prefer a witch who robs them of their money." The Indian, death-like, collapsed on a chair . . . shaking with convulsive trembles—his mouth, his nose, his ears, running threads of blood. Luis thought about the melancholy destiny, the fatal augury of this race. Race? . . . suffocated, twisted, beaten down by his environment . . . the Indian . . . spurned by the very mestizo which exploits his flaws . . . forgetting that this Indian is mixed in his very own blood. (46–48)

This passage downplays the importance of blood by acknowledging that "race" (written as an inquiry, not as an affirmation) is defined more by environment and abuse. Indeed, Herrera ends his lament by asserting the essential biological sameness of Indians and mestizos: "mixed in his very own blood." Yet, as in much of the radical *indigenista* writings of the thirties and forties, this common ground cannot be affirmed as long as the Indian remains "beaten down . . . spurned."

At first glance, Herrera (himself a plantation owner) would seem to hold ladino exploitation responsible for the exclusion Indians have suffered. A closer reading reveals that the disease metaphor cuts two ways. For

Herrera, as well as for many of his contemporaries, exploitation and exclusion produced a diseased culture that trapped Indians in their own cultural pathologies. In El tigre, even when help is offered, the sick Indians refuse, preferring a "witch who robs them of their money." Here Herrera echoes a common ladino refrain that Indians are both superstitious and easily tricked. Indeed, according to Herrera, ladinos do not merely exploit Indians, they exploit their (indelible?) "flaws."

This equation of race, exploitation, and social degeneration, repeatedly expressed through the disease metaphor, put an undue burden on Indian society and culture. It bestowed on Maya, in Sontag's apt phrase, an "onerous citizenship" in which they both suffered from and were held responsible for Guatemala's chronic ills. The next section of this essay explores the nineteenth-century roots of this equation.

The 1837 Cholera Epidemic Reconsidered

Following independence from Spain in 1821, liberals attempted to build what they imagined was a modern nation formed by five Central American states.[23] Incessant insurrections by conservative elites, however, gave way in 1837 to a popular rebellion of peasants and Indians.[24] The uprising started in Guatemala's east and was headed by an illiterate mestizo swineherd named José Rafael Carrera. Following the fall of Guatemala City to rebel troops in 1839, Carrera headed to the highlands and forcibly reincorporated the short-lived Estado de los Altos into Guatemala. Carrera went on to rule Guatemala and dominate Central American politics for the next twenty-five years.

Today historians dismiss the notion, first advanced by nineteenth-century liberals, that Indian participation in Carrera's 1837 revolt was an atavistic reaction, spurred on by conservatives and clerics, against state initiatives designed to contain a rampant cholera epidemic. While earlier writers focused on the rumors circulating throughout rural Guatemala that ladinos were poisoning water supplies, scholars now point to loss of land and political autonomy as the prime motives for widespread indigenous opposition to the first liberal state.[25] But in their rush to understand the rebellion as a rational response to increased exploitation, these writers pass over the significance of the coming of cholera both for representing and defining racial and national identities.

A DEFINING DISEASE

The 1837 epidemic was the first major crisis in which Guatemala's new political elites had to deal directly with the population without the mediation of the Crown or the Church, or the distraction of civil war.[26] During this period of intense political uncertainty, as liberals pursued their factional efforts to build an independent, legitimate nation, elite attitudes and responses to the epidemic emerged from the racial and political logic of colonialism.[27]

In Quetzaltenango, municipal officials, as did state agents in other areas of the world, regarded cholera to be a disease of the poor.[28] Quetzaltecos, however, threw ethnicity into the mix, casting cholera as a disease of the indigenous poor. For *altenses*, cholera became a defining disease in three important ways. First, the collapsing of class into ethnicity and equating the result with the disease provided fragmented and politically weak ladinos with an opportunity to culturally consolidate their identity and legitimacy. If economic, political, regional and ethnic differences would not let ladinos define who they were, then Indians and, by equation, cholera helped them to define who they were not. Second, the failure of the national state to respond to their repeated requests for financial aid to fight the epidemic deepened the ladinos' alienation from Guatemala City. As under colonialism, *altenses* continued to resent being caught between the interests of the national government and the highland's indigenous population, and their experience with the epidemic strengthened their resolve to break from Guatemala. Finally, by casting themselves as saviors of "unfortunate indigents," they created for themselves the chance to imagine their vision of the nation as universal. These universalizing assumptions, in turn, provided ladinos with new ideological justification to mobilize city resources and regulate social behavior.

THE DISEASE APPROACHES

Quetzaltecos had ample warning, and plenty of false alarms, of cholera's approach. In 1817 a seemingly new strain of cholera emerged from Lower Bengal to afflict nearly the whole of India.[29] As cholera spread westward, the disease's association with colonialism, race, and poverty, and its sudden and dramatic symptoms, rapid death, and unknown cause worked to generate an exceptional amount of fear, debate, and preparation in western Europe and the Americas.[30] By 1832 cholera was in London, Paris, Quebec, Montreal, New York, and Chicago. In 1835 it reached Mexico and Belize. Bulletins and instructions issued first by the medical school of Guatemala's newly formed Academia de Estudios and then by the emergency health committee kept city officials and regional elites informed of the approach of the disease.[31] In 1834 the municipality stockpiled medical supplies to fight cholera, and in 1835 the national government sent troops to close the border between Los Altos and Mexico due to reports of an outbreak in Chiapas.[32]

Guatemalans likewise kept abreast of the international controversy regarding the cause of the disease. Was cholera transmitted by individuals—that is, was it contagious—or was it caused by the environment—by unsanitary living conditions? The debate was most advanced among Parisian medical professionals, and each side had persuasive evidence to support its position.[33] Contagionists pointed to a long history of successful quarantines, recent advances in vaccination, and a strong correlation between transmission of the disease and troop movements and trade routes.

Notwithstanding these arguments, the anti-contagionist position steadily gained ground. In city after city, cholera brought the hitherto isolated and ignored poverty of the urban underworld to the attention of nineteenth-century reformers. Suddenly, disease was not something that came from without, but something that emerged from within the body politic.[34] Every aspect of the underclass's living habits—the clothes they wore, the liquor they drank, the food they ate and eliminated, the manner in which they disposed of their garbage, the way they buried their dead—was subject to debate, condemnation, and reform. The "strong correlation . . . found among filth, poverty, disease, and death convinced [medical professionals] of the dangers that lie in putrid miasmas, the poisonous air that arose from repulsive matter such as stagnant water, cesspools, rotting garbage, decaying animal carcasses, and rotting corpses."[35] Further, the fact that cholera appeared in disparate areas of a given city and, unlike smallpox, could be repeatedly contracted seemed to undermine the contagionists' argument.[36]

Because both sides made correct assumptions regarding the disease—cholera is transmitted by a water-born bacterium, and sanitary reform does prevent its spread—the debate often became one of confused semantics, serving more to express bourgeois anxieties regarding disease, poverty, and social disorder.[37] Prophylactic initiatives, including quarantines, *cordons sanitaires*, and hygienic reforms, were actually informed by both positions.[38]

As in other Latin American nations, Guatemala's medical establishment was highly influenced by French medical opinion, and doctors closely followed the debate regarding the nature of cholera.[39] One member of the national emergency health committee established during the epidemic, José Luna Arbizú, received his medical training in Paris at the height of the French cholera epidemic.[40] In 1833, the Academia issued an opinion quoting at great length two French doctors who stood on opposing sides.[41] The report related Alexandre Moreau de Jonnes's contagionist argument that cholera was transmitted through trade and troop movements, and took particular notice of Moreau's critique of religious gatherings and pilgrimages. It cited a number of Indian examples, such as a 1825 religious pilgrimage; after cholera attacked "multitudes de indios," thousands died, the corpses infested the water supply and the fleeing survivors spread the disease throughout the region. For the Guatemalan doctors, the local relevance of this correlation between religious rituals, Indians, and disease must have been particularly poignant. The report then gave a number of anti-contagionist arguments. After relating, with a trace of postcolonial insecurity, that even the "powerful nations" do not know the causes of cholera and cannot stop its spread, the report closed with a number of suggestions drawn from both positions: cut off communication with infected areas; establish quarantine houses; prohibit public meetings, both civil and religious, "in order to avoid the bad consequences such meetings can cause during moments of crisis"; ensure that only healthy food is sold in the market; create reserved areas for the sale of fish, meat, fruit; separate prisoners; and supply the poor with healthy food, because that "class eats whatever it finds, even if it is rotten."[42]

On the eve of cholera's outbreak, a degree of bourgeois conceit tempered a growing sense of dread. Indeed, as late as early spring 1837, medical professionals felt that due to its "very pure" air, "steady temperature," "clean streets," and dispersed population, Guatemala would be spared the epidemic.[43] In circulars and reports the Academia stressed that the best way to elude the plague was to avoid all excess: doctors counseled a regular diet of bland food and exercise, but not to the point of exhaustion. Activities which would bring about an extreme mood change—fear, sadness, and anger—as well as "venereal pleasures" were to be avoided.[44] Victorian self-control was thought to be the best prophylactic. One doctor prescribed "innocent distractions, summer walks, gentle conversations" as healthy diversions from the fear of cholera's approach.[45]

Notably, doctors considered foods associated with indigenous culture as harmful. Chiles, spicy foods, and homemade liquor—chicha, pulque (fermented liquors), and aguardiente (distilled cane liquor)—predisposed the body to cholera; wine, however, was "healthy" in moderation.[46] That it had attacked first in Belize, with the majority of its population descended from Africans, likewise contributed to the contradictory opinion that cholera both invaded from without and emerged from within unhealthy lifestyles; indeed, early reports from the coastal department of Izabal insisted that only Africans were dying of the disease.[47]

The first case in Guatemala was reported on March 8, 1837, and a cordon sanitaire was set up in the east to protect the capital.[48] The government ordered eastern towns to clean their streets and establish health committees.[49] By early April, cholera had reached El Salvador, believed by city officials to have been spread by thousands of pilgrims (romeristas) gathered during Easter to worship the Black Christ at Esquipulas.[50] The Federal Congress, based in San Salvador, suspended its sessions; Guatemala's national assembly closed on April 11.[51] As the city's population ignored or resisted efforts to contain the disease's spread, doctors and political leaders grew desperate and besieged.

Many of the early initiatives were drawn from previous experiences in fighting known epidemics such as measles and smallpox, as well as the firsthand experience that Luna Arbizú had had with cholera in Paris.[52] Dr. Luna had interned in the famous Parisian public hospital Hôtel Dieu, the target of popular anger during the French epidemic.[53] The anti-contagionist position, which had come to dominate the French medical profession, undoubtedly influenced his understanding of the disease. The municipality and the *junta de sanidad* ordered houses to be cleaned and trees to be pruned; urged the establishment of local sanitary and charity committees; and prohibited liquor production and sale.[54] The municipality barred fruit from entering the city, believing that it irritated the stomach and thus predisposed the body to the epidemic.[55] Warnings of the disease's imminent approach appeared in the *Boletín de Noticias de la Cólera Morbo*, which began publication on April 4. To combat the indifference of the city's population, the municipality granted special powers to police to inspect houses and enforce sanitary standards.[56] Police were also to search markets and confiscate and destroy any fruit they found.[57]

Cholera struck Guatemala City at the end of April, and within a month, 640 cases and 204 deaths were reported.[58] City officers grew increasingly desperate in the face of the population's intransigence. Not only were people refusing to live up to the new sanitary requirements, the sick were not seeking medical help. Soon, city and health officials no longer acted as if it were an invading disease that needed to be prevented; it was now the population which had to be subdued. The municipality ordered block captains, under penalty of fine and imprisonment, to report sanitary violations and hang white flags on the houses of the infected.[59] Authorities called for a house-by-house search to find those inflicted and administer a cure.[60] The police paid "spies" one peso for each illegal sale of liquor they reported.[61] The municipality increased penalties up to imprisonment for violations of emergency ordinances, and automatically doubled sentences for any crime committed during the epidemic.[62] People caught intoxicated were to be sentenced to public work for five days under police supervision.[63] The ringing of church bells and religious gatherings were prohibited.[64] The municipality, to avoid speculation, confiscated and took charge of distributing wheat.[65] Houses of the sick and individuals entering the city, along with their clothing and goods, were subject to lime, salt, and vinegar fumigation. Even materials that the lower classes used in their daily life were suspect: the municipality prohibited the use of sackcloth and ordered tanneries, whose organic waste was thought to spread the disease, to move their production outside of town.[66]

In April, reports started arriving of disturbances in the countryside.[67] Speculation and shortages were causing unrest, and people were refusing to help form *cordons*.[68] Alcaldes and departmental governors complained that they could not stop the sale of liquor or prohibit religious gatherings, due to "a lack of proper authority."[69] By the beginning of May, rumors circulated that cholera was caused by poisoned water or that the medicine itself was tainted.[70] In San Martín Jilotepeque, dogs and pigs dug up hastily buried corpses; in the city, popular accusations spread that people were being buried alive, forcing authorities to rescind a previous order to inter bodies as fast as possible.[71] It was as if Guatemala, like Paris five years earlier, had lost the ability "to absorb its dead."[72]

Although cholera did not reach the city of Quetzaltenango until June, *altenses* were kept informed of national events through publications such as the *Boletines de Cólera Morbo, El Editor,* and *Boletines Extraordinarios.*[73] These and other like publications of the new post-independence press emerged from the enlightened belief that legitimate government could only be based on an informed public, educated by the proper authorities. Such publications also offered the government a venue through which to demonstrate to the literate that it was effectively managing the crisis, hopefully establishing an appearance of order and authority.

Yet rather than conveying a sense of dispassionate scientific management, the following description of a cholera victim in a nearby town published in the *Boletín de Cólera Morbo* on the eve of cholera's outbreak in Guatemala City must have produced apprehension and dread in those who read it: "The face is pallid and disfigured; the eyes are glassy and sunken; the mouth dry. The face is always covered with an ash-like yellow crust. The respiration is accelerated as if short-winded; the voice is feeble. The pulse . . . is undetectable. [The victim] is very anxious; and he finds himself flat on his back with very little power to move. The skin is cold, particularly at the tip of the nose, the ears, the hands and especially the feet; the whole body is covered with an oily sweat."[74] The *Boletín de Cólera Morbo* went on to report that an autopsy following death revealed empty entrails and a shrunken, bloodless heart.

The ideological shift that converted the disease into an internal political pathogen was captured in the description of another victim in the same issue. After drinking himself into a stupor with *chicha* the day before, the victim contracted cholera. As he vomited, "the *chicha* turned into bloody matter."[75] That *chicha* is a homemade fermented drink closely associated with Indians could not have been lost on the literate public.

A Remedy Worse Than the Disease

It was a short step from the paternal benevolence practiced by the Quetzaltenango municipality during times of famine to the more interventionist posture aimed at administering public health. Citing its "primordial obligation . . . to care for the health" of the population, on 13 April 1837 the municipality contracted, for 1,500 pesos, an English doctor who supposedly had had success treating cholera in Mexico. He was to remain in the city for four months, and if cholera arrived, he was to "visit the houses of the poor . . . providing medicine and treatment" free of charge.[76] From the onset of the cholera days, municipal records inevitably and repeatedly referred to the disease's victims and potential victims as *indigentes*.[77] Considering that, indeed, the vast majority of those afflicted in the highlands were *indígenas*, this choice of cognate was hardly coincidental.[78] On at least one occasion, the city scribe used the word "indigente" when it was clear municipal officials were discussing Indians.[79]

Casting the disease as an affliction endemic to the indigenous poor allowed ladinos the opportunity to consolidate their identity and attempt to project that identity as universal. Equating Indians with cholera emerged from, and helped crystallize, the inchoate nationalist notion of assimilation discussed above. With progress and civilization, Indians would become ladinos, and Guatemala, or at least Los Altos, would become a prosperous ladino nation. Within such a vision, notions of class needed to be understood in cultural or ethnic terms. While "ladino" was to be the universal category which could contain all classes, there was to be no place in the new nation for rich Indians.

Ladinos attempted to establish their political legitimacy by demonstrating that the crisis was under their control. The municipality posted instructions on how best to avoid the disease, set up health and charity committees to distribute medicine and clothes to the afflicted, and dispatched commissions to procure food and other supplies for the needy.[80] Authorities set up a quarantine house and a cordon that prohibited commerce on the routes in from the coast and from Guatemala City.[81] A number of decrees were issued prohibiting the consumption of pork, fruit, and alcohol, and regulating the slaughter of meat.[82] The municipality conscripted prisoners to maintain the cordon and drain fetid ditches and swamps.[83] Perhaps owing to an association of the disease with menstruation, authorities closed the girls' school.[84]

Two obstacles stood in the way of the ladinos' attempt to construct cultural and political hegemony: a lack of funds and popular hostility. On April 3, the municipality requested money from the central government to "provide to the poor, who are the majority of the population, clothes, food, medicine and doctors."[85] The municipality was deeply in debt, having borrowed large sums of money to fund public projects. There were no funds to fight the disease. During an emergency session on April 13, municipal officers debated how best to raise the needed revenue. While they legally could appropriate money from *cofradías* (religious confraternities), as per an 1824 law, it was decided that, considering the anger it would provoke, this "remedy would perhaps be worse than the disease itself."[86]

With no money forthcoming from the national government, authorities became increasingly anxious. Since the beginning of Mariano Gálvez's term as national president in 1831, relations between the highland city and the capital had been tense and strained. Gálvez had suspected Quetzaltenango of being a conservative stronghold and had removed the *jefatura política* (equivalent to governor's office) to San Marcos, antagonizing many Quetzaltecos. The failure of Gálvez to provide financial assistance increased the hostility and alienation felt between *altenses* and *capitalinos*. Except from a few wealthy ladinos such as Manuel Aparicio, requests for voluntary contributions yielded little.[87] On June 8 the municipality, despite its earlier hesitation, ordered that money be taken from *cofradías*.[88] The city priest, however, insisted that the brotherhoods' account books were lost, and K'iche' *cofrades* (members of a *cofradía*) refused to present lists of their assets.[89]

Cholera arrived in the city on June 9, and by the end of July it had killed more than 161 people. As the body count rose, municipal authorities grew increasingly frantic and resentful in the face of public "indifference" and hostility.[90] They could not get enough men to maintain the cordon, staff the health and charity committees (which they complained existed "only in name"), or contribute to the emergency fund.[91] Even though the municipality repeatedly increased the penalties for the sale and use of alcohol, incidents of drunkenness increased, at least according to the authorities. The municipality granted police special powers to go from house to house to inspect for cleanliness and force the infected to seek medical treatment. It also decreed that all fruit trees within the city be destroyed; closed the workshops of tanners and potters, whose ovens were thought to be harmful; and restricted the slaughter and sale of meat to three ladino butchers.[92]

With the arrival of cholera also came notice of unrest throughout the country, including in nearby highland towns. On June 5 the ladino governor of Sololá asked for permission to maintain a standing military force in order to prevent any indigenous uprising that might occur as a result of cholera.[93] On June 25 news came of the Mita revolt in the east.[94] Violence was reported in indigenous pueblos in the department of Sololá, and on August 9 ladinos and Indians in Huehuetenango joined together to protest the new taxes.[95] Confronting widespread rebellion, the national government abandoned efforts to collect the taxes and suspended a number of judicial and land decrees that had previously provoked unrest.[96] On June 26 the municipality received the following instructions from the national government: "In towns where there are a considerable number of ladinos, arm them to avoid whatever trouble the ignorance of the Indians could cause. In completely indigenous towns, if symptoms of discontent are noted and they refuse to receive medicine . . . leave them to their fate . . . arrest the agitators and send them to the capital to be sentenced to public works."[97] The telling use of the word "symptoms" highlights the ladinos' conflation of indigenous behavior with disease.

Conflict in the Time of Cholera

It is harder, obviously, to gauge the Quetzalteco K'iche's' perceptions of cholera. Epidemics were regular occurrences in Los Altos.[98] This generation of community leaders themselves witnessed an outbreak of *calenturas* (fevers) in 1824 and of smallpox in 1826,[99] and many must have been alive during the 1815 epidemic. As cholera broke out and municipal initiatives grew more frantic, the indigenous "indifference" about which ladinos complained turned into active resistance. Infected K'iche's refused to present themselves to the doctor, *cofrades* resisted contributing money, and Indians protested many of the emergency municipal regulations.[100] While this resistance did not evolve into the full-scale insurrection that it did in eastern Guatemala behind Carrera, conflict surrounding ladino attempts to stem cholera does provide an important window onto the city's ethnic relations.

Many of the reforms and decrees cut into the productive and commercial activities of indigenous communities. In Quetzaltenango, the prohibition on liquor and pork sales, the closing of tannery and pottery workshops, the cutting down of fruit trees, and the cordon that cut off trade must have elicited resentment. In mid-July, for example, there is mention that Indians barred from bringing sugar into the city were "angry."[101] And restricting the slaughter and sale of meat to three ladinos must have incensed the city's twenty-five K'iche' butchers.[102]

Not all indigenous resistance, however, can be explained in economic terms. The refusal of many K'iche's to submit to medical treatment needs to be understood in a historical context. In the decades preceding this epidemic, similar municipal initiatives had resulted in violence and death. Likewise, the efficacy, not to mention the salubriousness, of the treatments was by no means assured. One cure advocated by Francisco Quiñones, a doctor working in Quetzaltenango, prescribed four grams of mercury to be taken orally every half hour; it also recommended that menstruating women be stood in a vat of hot water, salt, and mustard, letting the vapors bathe their vulvas.[103] Further, the arrogance and racism of ladino doctors undoubtedly led to brusque and discourteous treatment. In the beginning of August, for example, K'iche's from a rural *cantón* demanded that an abusive doctor be removed.[104]

Mourning rituals were particularly fertile ground for conflict, and throughout Guatemala a number of protests and riots broke out against liberal attempts to regulate burial rites and practices. Since the close of the colonial period, the state had mandated that cemeteries be located outside of towns. The "miasmas" which the decomposing corpses gave off were thought to cause disease, and after centuries of interment there was not much room left in churches. After independence, liberals, in their efforts to define a national identity, made burial reform a priority. During the first decades of independence, however, it remained a mark of status for many to be buried in the church—either under the floor or, for those able to pay the fees, in crypts. In 1840, a U.S. traveler gave a rather graphic account of one such burial. Because the father was "rich," he could afford to bury his son in the earthen floor of the church. After laying the child in his grave and covering him with dirt, the traveler recalled the "brutal and disgusting scene" of how the sexton raised a log and with "all his strength" pounded the dirt "over the head of the child." The father took the mallet and finished pounding: "The child's body must have been crushed to atoms."[105]

As with elite perceptions of cholera's symptoms, such spectacles helped articulate and reduce liberal notions of progress, religious fanaticism, disease, and hygiene to a personal, corporeal realm. The horrific episodes brought to light by cholera and other epidemics—piles of decomposing bodies, corpses disinterred by animals, superstitious rituals which propagated the disease, ungovernable passions fueled by reckless alcohol use and ignorant rumors, unremitting vomiting and diarrhea—represented to ladinos what they were not, and what Guatemala, if it was to become a modern nation, would have to escape.

In 1834, the national government ruled that, henceforth, all burials were to be performed in new cemeteries built outside of towns.[106] Attempts to implement the new policy resulted in what became known as "cemetery revolts" throughout the indigenous zones of Guatemala. Indians from towns such as San Miguel Totonicapán, Momostenango, Quiché, San Martín Jilotepeque, and San Pedro Chipilapa protested the new policy, either violently refusing to abide by it or appealing to local religious or political authorities for suspension of the decree. It is tempting to view these conflicts as a clash between opposing cultural norms and social visions. One historian has suggested that indigenous resistance to the new cemeteries sprang from a desire to maintain spiritual links to their ancestors, and hence spatial proximity to their earthly remains.[107] Many protests logged by Indians over the 1834 decree, however, while suggestive of divine fears, were eminently mundane in nature. In Momostenango, Indians objected that the new cemetery was a mile away. In Quiché and San Pedro Chipilapa, community leaders complained that animals and birds were eating the bodies. And in San Martín, an indigenous authority protested that the ground of the new cemetery was too rocky. Graves could not be dug deep, and the winds blowing into town from that direction carried with them diseases, a belief notably similar to those held by ladino reformers.

In March 1800, Quetzaltenango opened a burial ground just outside the cathedral.[108] Prior to this, most Quetzaltecos, K'iche's, and ladinos had been buried in and around the church building. While the majority of burials following 1800 took place in the new cemetery, interments within the church, mostly in the cathedral but occasionally in one of the four barrio chapels, were still relatively common, particularly for wealthy K'iche's, until the late 1820s.[109]

Following a smallpox epidemic in 1826, the city's health committee had urged the municipality to establish a cemetery outside of town.[110] By the time of the 1837 cholera epidemic, a chapel and adjacent graveyard were functioning about half a kilometer west of the plaza. The new cemetery, however, was not equipped to deal with the large number of bodies produced by cholera. By June 18 corpses were laying exposed on the ground, "particularly those of the *clase indígena*."[111] The epidemic lasted more than four months. The mortality rate was so high, the city priest stopped recording deaths in the church's burial register.[112] Convicts were conscripted to dig collective graves near the church of San Bartolomé, east of the plaza.[113] Burial was to take place as soon as possible, and lime was to be poured on the bodies. Fearing that exposure to the corpses would spread the disease, the municipality banned public mourning and prohibited *cofradías* from singing and accompanying the deceased through the streets.[114]

These measures angered city K'iche's, although the reasons were unspecified. The K'iche' population had already incorporated cemetery burial into their mourning practices, and the protest could have been directed at the crude and disrespectful manner in which bodies were being handled, as well as at municipal restrictions on grieving customs. The opening of the new burial ground was delayed by what the municipality described as a "general restlessness, particularly among Indians," provoked by some "troublemakers of their class that do not recognize the good it will bring."[115] Despite this hostility, the graveyard did go into use for the duration of the epidemic. Fear of further indigenous protest, however, prevented the ladinos from opening a second collective grave.[116]

A Malignant Racism

Julio Cambranes states that when highland liberals of mestizo origin finally gained state power following the 1871 revolution, they held racist views equal to those of any Spaniard.[117] He is right. But now it was a more malignant racism based on culture rather than blood.[118]

Casting Indians as impoverished victims and attributing the spread of cholera to their behavior gave Ladinos the opportunity to project their identity and values as universal and to promote assimilation as the cure. The obsession of Guatemalan ladino reformers with equating squalor and pestilence with indigenous culture bears an uncanny resemblance to a later Latin American social reform movement that historian Nancy Leys Stepan has described as "preventative" or "neo-Lamarckian" eugenics.[119] In the decades before and after the turn of the nineteenth century, Latin American proponents stressed environmental modification as the way to induce permanent racial improvement.[120] This view contrasted with that of advocates of hereditary eugenics, popular in the United States and Europe, who tended to promote regulation of sexual reproduction.

Likewise in Guatemala during the turn of the nineteenth century, neo-Lamarckian assumptions regarding generational improvement were popular among ladino nationalists and reformers. The years 1893 and 1894 were particularly lively for debates regarding the role of Indians in Guatemala's political economy.[121] Intellectuals, politicians, and planters engaged in heated discussion, much of it opportunistic, surrounding the effects of forced labor on indigenous communities. These debates pulled forth the latent tendency on the part of ladinos to collapse class with ethnicity and, congruent with the new role of Indians as semi-proletarianized coffee workers, to associate indigenous culture with hard, demeaning labor.[122] The more charitable of these writers would blame the Spaniards: "¡El Indio! Oh, since the first day of the conquest . . . a slave by birth, a beast of burden."[123] With a liberal sleight of hand in which class is eclipsed in the hopeful glare of progress, Indians were "destined to disappear."[124]

There were, of course, variations on this theme. Throughout the 1890s, the economic boom provided by coffee allowed for a somewhat more generous and imaginative vision of Indians' place in the emerging nation than had been previously expressed. For the more critical and thoughtful thinkers, such as Antonio Batres Jáuregui, the advanced nature of pre-Columbian civilizations was proof that Indians, although now corrupted and decayed, were redeemable and could participate as active members in "public life." Batres was particularly critical of legislation that allowed for increased exploitation of Indians. Yet even Batres, who hoped that some aboriginal "innocent customs" could be retained, believed indigenous culture was ultimately destined to disappear.[125] Exhibiting a decidedly Lamarckian faith in generational improvement through education, technical training, and contact with national society, ladino reformers believed that Indian ethnicity needed to disappear for the nation to progress:

> We need to give Indians the means to leave their communal system; their common and unchanging dress; their barbaric diet of *totopoxte* (large corn tortilla) and chili; their antediluvian languages; their rural, primitive, and rustic homes; In a word, Indians need to be removed from their manner of being—immutable and oriental. It can not be doubted, then, that Indians are very able to develop their civilization and advance progress. It will not be the present generation of *aborígenes* . . . but the new generations, young and flexible, will adjust to the demands of the new century. See . . . how pueblos full of Indians now are confused with the rest of the ladinos. Just a few years ago in Jocotenango, there existed a large number of *aborígenes*, dressed like Indians, speaking their primitive language. Today the children of these *Jocotecos* are nearly all masons and have left their *condición de indios*, becoming ladinos, losing their language and dressing like ordinary people.[126]

Ladino reaction to the cholera epidemic suggests that these neo-Lamarckian assumptions had an important pre-history. An interpretive framework that, as Stepan puts it, "linked a sanitary environment to racial health" allowed ladinos both to escape the blood strictures imposed by Spanish colonialism and to make sense of Guatemala's abiding ethnic divide.[127] At the same time, it allowed ladinos, as promoters of social reform, to inscribe themselves as the agents of national regeneration.

Poverty and disease were no longer considered a fated condition of the lower classes. They were the result of circumstance, behavior, and education. This attitude radically changed the relationship between the government and the governed, and allowed for the proactive social intervention practiced by Guatemalan reformers. With the blood strictures of caste colonialism out of the way, ladinos came to see Indians as capable of improvement through education, behavior modification, and environmental change. Indigenous identity, like poverty and disease, was now something that could be remedied; however, this ideological shift, which set the terms of Guatemalan nationalism, created the conditions for a more profound, vicious racism. Now, despite all the self-serving talk of ladinos regarding the "potential" of Indians to be the political and intellectual equals of Europeans, if Indians did not fulfill that potential, it was their fault. For ladinos, the tendency of cholera to attack Indians was confirmation that it was indigenous culture that needed to change. Cholera thus became an internal pathology caused by a diseased populace.

Epilogue: The Night-Side of Life

The racial assumptions identified in this essay have had horrific consequences in recent Guatemalan history. Beginning in 1981, the Guatemalan army, confronted with a threatening insurgency, targeted Indians in a campaign of torture, rape, execution of children, and massacres. By 1983, the military had committed more than six hundred massacres and had completely destroyed hundreds of indigenous communities. As the Guatemalan Comisión para el Esclarecimiento Histórico (Truth Commission) recently concluded, even if the goal of military strategists was to defeat the insurgency and not to exterminate the Maya, their campaign was genocidal because they killed Maya qua Maya to accomplish their goal.[128]

While the words are different, much of the anticommunist rhetoric that the military used to identify Maya culture as either the real or potential seedbed of insurgency closely parallels the assumptions structuring the disease metaphor: whether cholera or communism, indigenous culture and society bred virulent threats to the nation's well-being.[129] Much like their neo-Lamarckian forebears, military strategists tended to focus on the social characteristics, rather than the biological makeup, that made Indians susceptible to communism, be they poverty, isolationism, or lack of national integration.[130] As one 1972 military intelligence manual put it, "The enemy has the same sociological traits as the inhabitants of our highlands."[131]

The military's counterinsurgency was designed not only to kill Maya, but to "recover" them. We have seen how one thread which runs through ladino racism is the belief that Indians are easily led astray: recall Herrera's Indians who "prefer a witch who robs them of their money." The military's genocidal 1981–83 campaign therefore had two phases. First the army released unrelenting, savage violence designed to separate the indigenous

population from the guerrillas. Then the military took control of humanitarian aid and established model villages, re-education programs, and
civil patrols in order to win back those Indians not "lost" to the insurgency.
In this context emerges the historical logic of President Efraín Ríos Montt's
awful remark made at the height of the slaughter he directed: "Naturally, if
a subversive operation exists in which the Indians are involved with the
guerrillas, the Indians are going to die. However, the army's philosophy is
not to kill the Indians, but to win them back, to help them."[132]

Notes

1   Susan Sontag, *Illness as Metaphor* (New York: Farrar, Straus, and Giroux, 1978). For more
    recent histories of medicine and disease, see David Arnold, *Colonizing the Body: State
    Medicine and Epidemic Disease in Nineteenth-Century India* (Berkeley: University of California
    Press, 1993); Catherine J. Kudlick, *Cholera in Post-Revolutionary Paris: A Cultural History*
    (Berkeley: University of California Press, 1996); Charles Rosenberg, *The Cholera Years: The
    United States in 1832, 1849, and 1866* (Chicago: University of Chicago Press, 1987); Fran-
    cois Delaporte, *Disease and Civilization: The Cholera in Paris, 1832*, trans. Arthur Goldham-
    mer (Cambridge: MIT Press, 1986); and R. J. Evans, "Epidemics and Revolutions: Chol-
    era in Nineteenth-Century Europe," *Past and Present* 120 (Aug. 1988): 123–45.
2   Sontag, *Illness as Metaphor*, 81.
3   See Arnold, *Colonizing the Body.*
4   See Rosenberg, *The Cholera Years.*
5   See Donna J. Guy, *Sex and Danger in Buenos Aires: Prostitution, Family, and Nation* (Lincoln:
    University of Nebraska Press, 1995), especially chapter 3, and Doris Sommer, *Founda-
    tional Fictions: The National Romances of Latin America* (Berkeley: University of California
    Press, 1991).
6   Guy, *Sex and Danger.*
7   See Greg Grandin, *The Blood of Guatemala: A History of Race and Nation* (Durham: Duke
    University Press, 2000), chap. 6.
8   Alan Knight, "Racism, Revolution, and Indigenismo: Mexico, 1910–1940," in *The Idea of
    Race in Latin America, 1870–1940*, ed. Richard Graham (Austin: University of Texas Press,
    1994).
9   For a more detailed description of this process, see Grandin, *Blood*, chaps. 2 and 3.
10 See Diane Nelson, *A Finger in the Wound: Body Politics in Quincentennial Guatemala* (Berkeley:
    University of California Press, 1999), especially the chapter "Bodies that Splatter."
11 Forthcoming work by Ramón Gutiérrez will shed much-needed light on ongoing con-
    structions of Guatemalan "whiteness."
12 Marta Casaus Arzú, *Guatemala: Linaje y Racismo* (Guatemala City: Facultad Latinoameri-
    cana de Ciencias Sociales, 1995), 119–26. See also Carol A. Smith, "Origins of the
    National Question in Guatemala: A Hypothesis," in her edited volume *Guatemalan Indians
    and the State, 1540–1988* (Austin: University of Texas Press, 1990), 86–87.
13 Publicly describing all non-Indians as ladinos started in the colonial period. For exam-
    ple, during colonial times, the highland city of Quetzaltenango was a *pueblo de indios;* the
    church maintained only one set of baptism, marriage, and death books until the mid-
    eighteenth century. At that point it started a separate series of ladino records which

included all non-Indians—marriage books start in 1740, deaths in 1796, and baptisms in the 1780s (the first volume is missing; the second starts in 1789). For example, fourteen-year-old Don Manuel, born in Galicia, Spain (4 September 1804); an anonymous *forestera* (outsider) found dead on the road into town (13 October 1796); a woman with a distinct K'iche' surname, Luiza Antonia Coyoy (9 June 1799); and Don Nicolás Franco (16 December 1807), an important city politician and merchant were all recorded in the first *libro de ladinos difuntos*. See also the city's *padrones*, which in 1813 broke the city's population into four categories—*españoles, mestizos, ladinos o castas, and indios*—yet in 1826 used only the categories *indígenas* and *ladinos*. See Archivo Histórico Arquidiocesano (AHA), legajo 1; expediente 10, 1813, and Archivo Histórico de Quetzaltenango (AHQ), caja (box) 1826.

14 See Taracena's conclusion in *Invención criolla, sueño ladino, pesadilla indígena: Los Altos de Guatemala, de región a estado, 1740–1850* (Antigua: Centro de Investigaciones Regionales de Mesoamérica, 1997).

15 For the most comprehensive history to date of the Estado de los Altos' long rise and quick fall, see Taracena, *Invención criolla*.

16 Casaus Arzú, *Guatemala: Linaje y racismo*, 119–23.

17 Lorenzo Montúfar, *Reseña histórica de Centro América*, 7 vols. (Guatemala: Tipografía de El Progreso, 1878), 1: xi.

18 See Knight, "Racism, Revolution, and Indigenismo."

19 See Knight, "Racism, Revolution and Indigenismo," and Francois Chevalier, "Official 'Indigenism' in Peru in 1920: Origins, Significance, and Socioeconomic Scope," in *Race and Class in Latin America*, ed. Magnus Morner (New York: Columbia University Press, 1970), for similar processes in Mexico and Peru.

20 *El Señor Presidente*, trans. Frances Partridge (New York: Atheneum, 1983). But see Asturias's infamous university thesis, published as *El problema social del indio y otros textos* (Paris: Centre de Recherches de l'Institut d'Etudes Hispaniques, 1971), in which he argues for miscegenation. In his famous "banana trilogy," he moves the discussion of "the Indian problem" into the economic realm; see *Viento fuerte* (Buenos Aires: Editorial Losada, 1950); *El papa verde* (Buenos Aires: Editorial Losada, 1954); and *Los ojos de los enterrados* (Buenos Aires: Editorial Losada, 1960).

21 See Flavio Herrera's *Caos* (Guatemala: Editorial Universitaria, 1949) and *El tigre* (Guatemala: Editorial Universitaria, 1989); and Mario Monteforte Toledo, *Entre la piedra y la cruz* (Guatemala: Editorial "El Libro de Guatemala," 1948) for three novels which explore, somewhat luridly, the impact of migration and plantation labor on Indians.

22 See Dennis Floyd Casey, "Indigenismo: The Guatemalan Experience" (Ph.D. diss., History, University of Kansas, 1979), chap. 6.

23 For two years, from 1821 to 1823, Central America was annexed to independent Mexico.

24 Hazel Ingersoll, "The War of the Mountain: A Study in Reactionary Peasant Insurgency in Guatemala, 1837–1873" (Ph.D. diss., George Washington University, 1972).

25 See Ingersoll, "The War of the Mountain," 45; Michael Forrest Fry, "Agrarian Society in the Guatemalan Montana, 1700–1840" (Ph.D. diss., Tulane, 1988), 226–30; David Mc-Creery, *Rural Guatemala, 1760–1940* (Stanford: Stanford University Press, 1994), 23, 56. For the nineteenth-century liberal polemics, see Montúfar y Rivera Maestre, *Reseña histórica*, 1: x–xi; 2: v–vii.

26 According to the calculation made by one doctor at the end of the nineteenth century, ten thousand Guatemalans died of cholera in 1837 within five months. Francisco Asturias, *Historia de la medicina en Guatemala* (Guatemala: Tipografía Nacional, 1902), 177.

27 See Kudlick, *Cholera*, 31–64, for a similar process in Paris.

28 For France, see Louis Chevalier, *Laboring Classes and Dangerous Classes in Paris during the First Half of the Nineteenth Century*, trans. Frank Jellinek (Princeton: Princeton University Press, 1973); Francios Delaporte, *Disease and Civilization: The Cholera in Paris, 1832*, trans. Arthur Goldhammer (Cambridge: MIT Press, 1986); and Kudlick, *Cholera*. For the United States, see Rosenberg, *The Cholera Years*.

29 Arnold, *Colonizing the Body*, 162.

30 Evans, "Epidemics and Revolutions. See Kudlick, *Cholera*, 53–63, for its association with poverty; see Rosenberg, *The Cholera Years*, 55–64, for the disease's connection with African Americans, Irish, and poverty in U.S. cities; for its association with colonialism and race in India, see Arnold, *Colonizing the Body*, 159–99. See Pedro Molina, *Instrucción, preservativa, y curativa de cólera morbus* (Guatemala: Imprenta Nueva, 1832), for a 1832 guide to cholera written by a Guatemalan physician based on information received from Paris.

31 Archivo de Gobernación de Quetzaltenango (AGQ), 1834, 1835, and 1836. See Grandin, *Blood*, 74–80, for a discussion of shifts in state attitude toward disease that began to take place in the late eighteenth century.

32 See AHQ, Actas, 4 April 1837, for the supplies; see Horacio Figueroa Marroquín, *Biografía del Doctor José Luna Arbizú* (Guatemala: Tipografía Nacional, 1983), 35, for the 1835 scare.

33 Kudlick, *Cholera*, 75–81; for the debate in the United States, see Rosenberg, *The Cholera Years*, 73–81.

34 The Parisian medical community during this time was increasingly influenced by the emerging Lamarckian belief that changes brought about in a species from the environment would be passed down to future generations. While there is debate as to just how influential Lamarck's ideas were when they were first presented at the beginning of the nineteenth century, it is clear that they were part of an intellectual milieu that increasingly focused on environmental regulation as a means to promote generational improvement. See Pietro Corsi, *The Age of Lamarck: Evolutionary Theories in France, 1790–1830*, trans. Jonathan Mendelbaum (Berkeley: University of California Press, 1988), and Nancy Leys Stepan, "The Hour of Eugenics": Race, Gender, and Nation in Latin America (Ithaca: Cornell University Press, 1991), 64–76.

35 Kudlick, *Cholera*, 77.

36 Rosenberg, *The Cholera Years*, 78–79.

37 Kudlick, *Cholera*, 77–78.

38 Rosenberg, *The Cholera Years*, 79–81.

39 In Latin America, French was usually the second language of elites. Medical professionals went to France to receive their training, and many of the scientific works from Europe made their way to Latin American nations in French translation. See Stepan, "The Hour of Eugenics," 72–73.

40 Figueroa Marroquín, *Biografía del Doctor José Luna Arbizú*, 29.

41 The opinion is in Archivo General de Centro América (AGCA), B legajo 1102 expediente 24410; a copy of it is in AGQ, 1834; The French works cited in the opinion are F. J. V. Broussais, *Le choléa-morbus épidémique observé et traité selon la méthode physiologique* (Paris, 1832) and Alexandre Moreau de Jonnès, *Rapport au conseil supérieur de santé sur le choléra-morbus pestilentiel* (Paris, 1832). See also Molina, *Instrucción*; Mariano Padilla, *Método de precaver, conocer, y curar el cólera mórbus* (Guatemala: Academia de Ciencias, 1837); and Pedro Vázquez, *Método curativo del cólera-morbo* (Guatemala: Academia de Ciencias, 1837).

42   AGCA, B 1102 24410.
43   Padilla, *Método de precaver*, 9.
44   Molina, *Instrucción*; Padilla, *Método de precaver*.
45   Padilla, *Método de precaver*, 8.
46   Ibid., 5–6.
47   See AGCA, B 2521 56993, and AGCA, B 2521 56997.
48   AGCA, B 1103 24445 and 24471. For death tolls in the east, see Ingersoll, "The War of the Mountain," 99.
49   See the Acuerdos of 23 September 1836; and 18, 19, 29, and 31 March 1837, in Manuel Pineda de Mont, ed., *Recopilación de las leyes de Guatemala, compuesta y arreglada por don Manuel Pineda de Mont*, 3 vols. (Guatemala: Imprenta de la Paz, 1869–72), 1: 704–10.
50   Ingersoll, "The War of the Mountain," 97.
51   Ibid.
52   See AGCA, B 82.3 1094 24006 for 1826 instructions to prevent the spread of measles, which foreshadowed some of the earlier anticholera initiatives. For José Luna's role in designing the state's response to cholera, see Asturias, *Historia de la medicina*, 523.
53   Figueroa Marroquín, *Biografía del Doctor José Luna Arbizú*, 20; Kudlick, *Cholera*, 187–88.
54   AGCA, B 1102 24446, folio 1. For reproductions of a number of the cholera decrees, see Asturias, *Historia de la medicina*, 159–77.
55   AGCA, B 1103 24471 and AGCA, B 1102 24446, folio 55. See Rosenberg, *The Cholera Years*, 30, for a New York prohibition against raw fruit and vegetables. See AGCA, B 1102 24410, for the French opinion that cherries caused cholera.
56   AGCA, B 1102 24446, folio 55.
57   AGCA, B 1102 24446, folio 55; AGCA, B 3588 82118.
58   AGCA, B 1104 24560.
59   AGCA, B 2521 56993.
60   AGCA, B 1105 24560, folio 51.
61   AGCA, B 1104 24545, folio 49.
62   *Boletín Extraordinario*, 21 April 1837, located in AHQ.
63   AGCA, B 1106 24572, folio 216; and AGCA, B 1105 24560, folio 51.
64   AGCA, B 1104 24538.
65   AGCA, B 1105 24560, folio 32.
66   AGCA, 1105 24560, folio 106.
67   See Ingersoll, "The War of the Mountain," 99–113.
68   AGCA, B 1104 24558 and AGCA, B 3588 82091.
69   AGCA, 1105 24570.
70   AGCA, B 1102 24345, folio 10. These suspicions were not unique to Guatemala's rural population. In 1832, in Paris, rumors spread that cholera was in fact a plot by elements of the bourgeoisie to rid the city of the lower classes. See Kudlick, *Cholera*, 183–92.
71   AGCA, B 3588 82114 and AGCA, B 1104 24545, folio 12.
72   Louis Chevalier, ed. *Le choléa: La premiere épidémie du XIX siecle* (La Roche-sur-Yon: Centrale de L'Ouest, 1958), 13. Quoted in Kudlick, *Cholera*, 3. Illustrating the panic among state agents, the government ordered all public employees to remain at their post, prohibiting them from leaving their towns; *Boletín Extraordinario*, 21 April 1837.
73   The *Boletines de Cólera* were obviously modeled after the *Bulletins du Choléra*, a newsletter distributed in Paris during the 1832 epidemic; they most likely reflect the influence of Dr. José Luna Arbizú, who studied in Paris during its epidemic. See Kudlick, *Cholera*, 123–32.
74   *Boletín de Cólera Morbo*, 21 April.

75 Ibid.
76 AGCA, Actas, 13 April 1837.
77 See, for examples, the numerous documents related to the epidemic in AHQ, caja 1837, and AGQ, 1837. See also AHQ, Actas, 24 April, 30 June, and 5 July 1837.
78 By June 14 cholera was in nearly every indigenous pueblo of the department of Sololá; see AGCA, B 3588 82116. In Chichicastenango by July 31 there were 154 deaths reported; AGCA, B 1106 24576.
79 AHQ, Actas, 5 July 1837.
80 For the broadsheets, see AHQ, Actas, 25 April 1837; for the charity committees, see AHQ, Actas, 13 July 1837; for the commissions, see AHQ, Actas, 24 April and 5 July 1837.
81 For the cordon, see AHQ, Actas, 29 April 1837; for the quarantine, see AHQ, Actas, 16 June 1837.
82 AHQ, Actas, 26 June 1837.
83 AHQ, Actas, 29 April 1837.
84 AHQ, Actas, 19 April 1837.
85 AHQ, Actas, 13 April 1837.
86 AHQ, Actas, 13 April 1837.
87 AHQ, Actas, 12 May, 8 June, and 16 June 1837.
88 AHQ, Actas, 8 June 1837. See also AHQ, Actas, 12 July 1837. The 1826 smallpox attack had led municipal authorities to try to borrow money from *cofradías* as well; see AHQ, Actas, 18 July 1826; likewise, the municipality used *cofradía* money for the water project, a "work of true urgency"; see AGQ, Informes . . . relativos . . . a la . . . obra de la introducción de la agua, 1834.
89 AHQ, Actas, 13 July 1837. Some money was collected, however, as Indians took advantage of an 1848 visit by Guatemala's archbishop to complain that the municipality never paid back the one thousand pesos it appropriated from a *cofradía*. See AHA, tomo 47, Visita de García Peláez.
90 AHQ, Actas, 23 May 1837.
91 AHQ, Actas, 6 and 12 May 1837; AHQ, Actas, 13 July 1837.
92 AHQ, Actas, 26 June 1837, and 13 and 18 July 1837.
93 Taracena Arriola, *Invención criolla*, 308.
94 AHQ, Actas, 25 June 1837.
95 *El Editor*, 31 August 1837.
96 Ingersoll, "The War of the Mountain," 132–33, for the judicial reforms; and McCreery, *Rural Guatemala*, 56, for the suspension of the land laws.
97 AHQ, Actas, 26 June 1837.
98 Murdo MacLeod, *Spanish Central America: A Socioeconomic History, 1520–1720* (Berkeley: University of California Press, 1973), 98–100, lists more than thirty highland epidemics between 1519 and 1746; George Lovell, *Conquest and Survival in Guatemala: A Historical Geography of the Cuchumatán Highlands, 1500–1821* (Montreal: McGill-Queen's University Press, 1992), 149, counts twenty-two for the Cuchumatanes alone. See Sandra L. Orellana, *Indian Medicine in Highland Guatemala: The Pre-Hispanic and Colonial Periods* (Albuquerque: University of New Mexico Press, 1987), 141–58, for a study of how Maya may have reacted to epidemics.
99 AHQ, Actas, 6 April 1824, 28 July 1826.
100 Regarding Indians' refusal to present themselves, one doctor complained that he "had not cured one Indian, because not one has called on my services"; AHQ, caja 1837.
101 AHQ, Actas, 20 July 1837.

102 AHQ, padrón, 1830.
103 AHQ, caja 1837.
104 AGQ, 1837.
105 John L. Stephens, *Incidents of Travel in the Central America, Chiapas, and Yucatan*, 2 vols. (New York: Harper & Brothers, 1841), 2: 371–72.
106 Douglass Creed Sullivan-González, *Piety, Power, and Politics: Religion and Nation Formation in Guatemala, 1821–1871* (Pittsburgh: University of Pittsburgh Press, 1998).
107 Sullivan-González, *Piety, Power, and Politics*, chap. 3.
108 AEQ, Libro de defunción de indígenas, no. 8.
109 On May 19, for example, the widow María Tzó was entombed in the cathedral, in the chapel of the *cofradía* Nuestra Señora del Rosario, and on 5 July 1804, Don Anizeto López was buried in the cathedral; see AEQ, Libro de defunción de indígenas, no. 8. For church burials into the 1820s, see, for examples, AEQ, Libro de defunción de indígenas, no. 10, 22 April 1825, 14 January 1826, 26 January 1826, and 6 February 1826.
110 AHQ, Actas, 28 July 1826.
111 AHQ, caja 1837.
112 See AEQ. For the Libro de indígenas, no. 10, there are no entries between 1 July and 20 October; for the Libro de ladinos, no. 3, there are no entries between 30 June and 9 October; and for the Libro de párvulos, no. 6, there are none between 29 June and 12 November.
113 AHQ, Actas, 30 June 1837.
114 AHQ, Actas, 30 June 1837.
115 AHQ, Actas, 23 June 1837 and 5 July 1837.
116 AHQ, Actas, 18 July 1837.
117 Julio C. Cambranes, *Café y campesinos en Guatemala, 1853–1897* (Guatemala: Editorial Universitaria, 1985), 71. But see Steven Palmer's comparison between Costa Rican and Guatemalan nationalism. Palmer argues against common conceptions of the second liberal state as being influenced by the biological component of Herbert Spencer's social Darwinism. Rather, for prominent liberal thinkers, it was culture and history which made race. See Steven Palmer's "A Liberal Discipline: Inventing Nations in Guatemala and Costa Rica, 1870–1900" (Ph.D., Columbia University, 1990), chap. 7, esp. 174–81. Palmer, however, misses how Guatemalan reformers understood culture, environment, and history within a Lamarckian framework of racial transformation.
118 Alan Knight, in his essay on Mexican *indigenismo*, makes the following point regarding a nationalism based on culture and environment rather than blood: "to equate ethnicity and race, and to suppose that they determine significant ascribed characteristics of such strength and staying power that they are, in practical terms, immutable, is to fall prey to racism, even if those characteristics are not alleged to be biologically determined. In other words, if Mexican Indians are what they are because of environmental pressures—and what they are scarcely admits of change, since it is part of their very being—then the question of whether biological, environmental, or historical factors determined this being is secondary. It is the inescapable ascription that counts." Knight, "Racism, Revolution and Indigenismo," 93.
119 Stepan, "The Hour of Eugenics," 67–76. I thank Diane Nelson for pointing out this connection.
120 Stepan, "The Hour of Eugenics," 84.
121 There is little scholarship on this important period of Guatemalan liberalism. Steven Palmer, "A Liberal Discipline," 189–97, offers the best discussion to date.
122 See, for examples, the debate in *Diario de Centro América*, 10 and 14 April and 5 October

1893, and *La Nueva Era*, 14 and 21 April 1893. For a discussion of the debate, see McCreery, *Rural Guatemala*, 189–94.

123 Antonio Batres Jáuregui, *La América Central ante la historia*, 2 vols. (Guatemala: Marroquín Hermanos "Casa Colorada," 1915), 1: 448.

124 Ibid. Although Batres, it must be said, was less sanguine about the possibilities the future offered. For other examples of the liberal belief in the disappearance of the Indians, see Virgilio Rodríguez Beteta, *Ideologías de la independencia* (Paris: Editorial París-America, 1926), and Villacorta Calderón's *Memorial de Tecpán-Atitlán* and *Prehistoria e historia antigua de Guatemala*, esp. 180.

125 See Batres Jáuregui's *La América Central*, 448, and *Los indios: Su historia y su civilización* (Guatemala: Tipografía La Unión, 1894), pt. 3, chaps. 3 and 4. Batres was the archetype *indigenista* nationalist; he wrote scores of books on *lo Americano*, which, aside from his work on history and indigenous culture, include topics on Creole colloquialism and literature.

126 Batres Jáuregui, *Los indios*, 177–78.

127 Stepan, "The Hour of Eugenics," 85.

128 For the legal reasoning that separates "motive" from "intent" in the Truth Commission's ruling on genocide, see Comisión para el Esclarecimiento Histórico, *Guatemala: Memory de silencio* (Guatemala City: Oficina de Servicios para Proyectos de las Naciones Unidas, 1999), vol. 3, *Las violaciones de los derechos humanos y los hechos de violencia*, 314–423, esp. 316, where the CEH notes that it is "crucial to distinguish between 'the intention to destroy in whole or in part an [ethnic] group' . . . [from] the motives of said intention. In order to be judged genocide, the intention to destroy the group is sufficient, regardless of motives. For example, if the motive which drives an intent to destroy an ethnic group is not based on racism but rather military goals, the crime is still understood as genocidal." See Greg Grandin, "Chronicles of a Guatemalan Genocide Foretold," in *Nepantla* 1, 2 (2000), for a further discussion of the ruling.

129 I want to thank Charles Hale for helping me to think through some of the ideas laid out in the following discussion.

130 See, for example, the speech given by Col. Marco Antonio Sánchez Samayoa on 22 June 1984, reprinted in the Guatemalan military's *Revista Militar* no. 34 (January–April 1985).

131 Centro de Estudios Militares, *Manuel de inteligencia*, G-2, 1972, 217.

132 United States Foreign Broadcast Information Service, Central America, 2 June 1982.

Thomas Miller Klubock

Nationalism, Race, and the Politics of Imperialism:
Workers and North American Capital
in the Chilean Copper Industry

▼

To think of imperialism in terms of race is disastrous. But to neglect the racial
factor as merely incidental is an error only less grave than to make it fundamental.
—C. L. R. James, *The Black Jacobins*

In 1946, workers in Chile's El Teniente copper mine engaged in the longest
strike in the company's history. El Teniente was the world's largest underground copper mine and, with Anaconda's Chuquicamata mine, constituted the engine of Chile's export economy and the jewel of the Kennecott
Copper Company's mining empire. During union assemblies, miners
voiced a fervent antagonism toward their North American employer, rejected efforts by government officials to convince them to end the strike,
and pushed leftist union leaders to take a more militant stance in meetings with company representatives and labor inspectors. In speeches to
the assemblies of more than four thousand miners, workers assailed the
mine's North American managers as "ignorant gringos . . . who for the
sole fact of having blond hair believe themselves to be a superior caste."
They attacked what they referred to as "these criminal, shameless, vagabond gringos" and "soulless gringo thieves."[1]

The strike—which lasted almost a month and then, after an impasse
during arbitration, erupted once again in 1947—was a major factor in
President Gabriel González Videla's decision to bring to a close a decade-
long experiment in coalition government and populist rule in Chile. González Videla sent troops to El Teniente, declared a military state of emergency, and had a number of El Teniente union activists and militants of the
Chilean Communist Party arrested and sent to the Pisagua concentration

camp in northern Chile. He followed this crackdown on organized labor and workers' strikes in the copper mines, as well as strikes in the nitrate fields and coal mines, by expelling Communist ministers from his cabinet and outlawing the Communist Party. González Videla thus satisfied the demands of both the U.S. State Department and the North American copper companies, which had sent various representatives and delegations to alert the Chilean government to their displeasure at the growing power of organized labor and the Communist Party both in the copper industry and nationwide. By 1946–47, Chile had become a test case for U.S. foreign policy in Latin America in the cold war era. Eliminating the Communist Party, which had grown in strength during the 1940s, and reining in Chile's radical and nationalist labor movement, the State Department and Kennecott executives made clear, were the conditions for credits, loans, and expanded investment in the copper industry. Following the repression of the miners' strikes and the Communist Party, Kennecott increased its investment in El Teniente and stepped up production, while the World Bank and the United States Export-Import Bank provided previously withheld loans and credits to the González Videla government.[2]

When I first read the transcripts of the miners' assemblies contained in reports by company spies to the North American company's welfare department, I took these to be fairly routine expressions of workers' antagonism toward their employers, and I interpreted these assemblies as examples of the growing militancy and nationalism of Chilean labor under the populist center-left coalition Popular Front governments that ruled from 1938 to 1952.[3] In retrospect, however, I would argue that phrases like "blond gringos" and "superior caste," as well as the terms "vagabond" and "ignorant," have a significance that goes beyond the formal anti-imperialism and anticapitalism of labor and the Left during this period and reflect the ways in which mine workers experienced class relations in the U.S.-dominated copper industry in terms of racial and ethnic discrimination. Workers' references to caste and blond hair were more than codes for class relations defined by conflicts between Chilean workers and North American managers over labor and production. Social relations in the mining enclave were materially and structurally rooted in the logic of capital accumulation, managerial strategies of labor control, the process of proletarianization, and the organization of production. However, workers' use of signs that invoked race to represent class conflict and describe antagonisms based on nationality constitutes more than a direct or unmediated expression or representation of class relations. That they chose to represent their opposition to the authority of North American managers in the language of race requires that we unpack the operation of racial ideologies and forms of social hierarchy based on racism in the context of North American imperialism, the emergence of nationalist political movements, and the everyday realities of class conflict in the copper mine.

By employing the term "race" in this discussion of the politics of imperialism and the labor movement, I do not mean to suggest that "race" describes the "objective reality" of social groups or social relations in Chile or the copper industry. As many historians and theorists of race have demonstrated, race is not an immutable transhistorical category or essence reducible to biology or culture, but a historical and ideological formation and process based on the ascription of value, meaning, and social power to perceived (or imagined) physical differences that are often defined ideologically as biological or phenotypical. Racial formation takes place through the construction of structures of social power and systems of meaning based on the elaboration of ideological categories and hierarchies that order, regulate, and define racial difference. Thus, racial categories and signs are historical; the ways in which they signify are determined by material social relations and ideologies. They are fixed through the process of social, economic, and ideological hegemony building, and their operation is contested and shifting. In addition, as a way of ascribing meaning and assigning value to perceived difference, race produces social relations as well as being determined by them. This is to say that while "race" does not define any biological or physical reality, ideas about race and the practices of racism establish race as a material element of social relations—as a social reality. The discursive systems that produce racial ideologies and social norms around race both shape other forms of social power, based on class and gender, for example, and manufacture social relations of domination and subordination.[4]

While racial thinking and racism may not have constituted the central logic of class relations in the copper industry, they did inform the ways in which North American capital institutionalized its power through managerial strategies and methods of labor and social discipline, and the ways in which workers built their collective response to the realities of labor and life in the mining camps. Social codes based on racism defined, in part, the conduct of both internal class relations and the operation of North American imperialism. Workers experienced social relations in the copper industry not just in terms of forms of exploitation based on class, but through informal forms of racism directed at Chilean workers by North American bosses and the institutionalization of racial ideas by the North American mining company. Institutional and day-to-day forms of racism gave meaning to, signified, and inscribed the ways in which class relations were structured, acted on, and lived at the level of the everyday.

Mine workers' experience of racism in the copper industry fueled a militant nationalism and labor activism that placed them at the center of the national labor movement, the great strikes of the 1940s, and movements for the expropriation of the U.S.-owned copper mines. Mine workers developed a radical nationalist politics articulated in the formal anti-imperialism of the Left and rooted in the realities of class relations and racial discrimination in the mining camps. In response to the racist disrespect of North American managers for Chilean workers, miners asserted their dignity and respectability as citizens of Chile and members of the Chilean people in opposition to their "disrespectable" and ethnically Other North American bosses. They turned the characterization of workers as backward, ignorant, and roto (broken) on its head by defining North Americans in the same terms and by celebrating the roto, or worker, as the soul of chilenidad, or Chilean national identity. Workers' affirmation of their chilenidad in response to North American racism expressed a nationalism defined in opposition to foreign capital and anti-imperialism. It also articulated workers' assertion of inclusion into the national community as citizens and representatives of the essential attributes of Chilean criollo identity. As a claim to national character, chilenidad implied workers' membership in an ethnic community that was the basis of the nation and nation-state.

The ideology of chilenidad was developed by nationalist elites who critiqued Chile's subordination to foreign capital and European immigration and articulated a xenophobic antagonism to Bolivia and Peru during the first decades of the twentieth century. Elite nationalism drew on nineteenth-century European racial theory to promote an ideology of an ethnically homogeneous Chilean ethnicity or race that would be the foundation of national progress. During the 1930s and 1940s, the Popular Fronts incorporated this nationalism into their populist critique of the landowning "oligarchy" and foreign capital. The Fronts' efforts to promote a reinvigorated chilenidad operated as a vehicle for a militant nationalist working-class politics as well as a cross-class national alliance, which would be the basis for national industrial growth and social reform. Working-class pride in chilenidad echoed the nationalist writings of intellectuals and elites who sought to locate an ethnic, racial, and cultural basis for Chilean identity and national power, as well as the populist and left-wing nationalism of the Popular Fronts' own ideology of chilenidad. In addition, working-class pride in Chilean identity reflected traditions of popular xenophobia and nativism that dated back to nineteenth-century conflicts between Bolivians, Peruvians, and Chileans on the northern frontier in the nitrate mines of the Atacama Desert and the War of the Pacific

(1879–84). Working-class nationalism was woven of different threads, from the radical anti-imperialism of labor and the Left, to the populism of the Popular Fronts, to the ethnic nationalism and xenophobia of elites. Nationalist ideologies of chilenidad could reflect a number of contradictory tendencies, including a radical opposition to the role of foreign capital in the economy and capitalism, an identification with a mythical mestizo national ethnic identity that obscured internal ethnic and class divisions, and a popular nativism and racism.

Ideologies of Race, Nation, and Class in Chile

Working-class nationalism in the copper industry was not elaborated autonomously through workers' encounters with foreign employers. Rather, copper miners' sense of belonging to a Chilean nation and people was established in the context of elites' debates over the racial and cultural foundation of the nation and economic modernization and traditions of working-class nationalism and xenophobia that dated back to the mid-nineteenth century. Ideas about race and internal forms of racism, nationalism, and xenophobia circulating since the nineteenth century provided the background and context for the radical nationalism of the Left and organized labor during the twentieth century. Copper workers' class militancy and anti-imperialism reflected strains of the nationalist discourse produced by intellectuals of a variety of political stripes as well as forms of nationalism and xenophobia present in working-class culture and the Left and labor since the late nineteenth century.

Given the flux of external and internal frontiers during the nineteenth century, the project of constructing a unitary national subject and homogenous national culture was paramount for Chilean intellectuals and reformers. The wars to conquer territories south of the Bío-Bío from Mapuche control and the War of the Pacific with Bolivia and Peru, in which Chile expropriated the northern territories of the Atacama Desert, brought up issues of what would constitute national territory and population. Similarly, the constant migration of landless Chilean peones throughout the economy, as well as to Bolivian and Peruvian nitrate oficinas, created a constantly mobile internal frontier based on the migratory patterns of laborers. National, ethnic, and class differences (the latter increasingly acute with the emergence of a militant labor movement in the north and in Chile's cities and ports after the turn of the century) made it increasingly imperative for elites to build a Chilean national identity. Finally, as foreign capital came to dominate Chile's nitrate and copper export economy, elites concerned with Chile's economic underdevelopment began to draw on racial theory to build nationalist explanations for the country's economic subordination to the United States and Europe.

Nationalist intellectuals combined elements of European positivism, racial theory, and social Darwinism to critique the liberal economic policies that had allowed European and North American capital to dominate the economy. In his famous 1912 work on Chile's lack of economic modernization, *Nuestra inferioridad económica (Our Economic Inferiority)*, Francisco Encina proposed building national industries and establishing industrial education, and attributed foreign control of Chile's major industries, extractive economies, financial sector, and commerce to "the extraordinary economic ineptitude of the national population, owing to the mentality of the race, or in the best of cases, the consequence of a completely inadequate education . . . to fill in the gaps of people who are backwards in their evolution."[5] Similarly, he located the causes of Chilean economic weakness in the fact that "our race, in part because of heredity, in part because of the relatively backward grade of evolution, and partly because of the detestable and inadequate education, vigorous in war and moderately apt in agricultural labor, lacks all the conditions demanded by industrial life."[6] Employing social Darwinist language, Encina noted that the Chilean race was still at "the pastoral stage" of evolution. While the lower classes were only capable of agricultural work, elites were oriented toward occupations like law and medicine rather than commerce and industry. Encina ascribed the problem of this national cultural obstacle to development to the "Spanish ancestry," which left "an unenviable inheritance of Iberian characteristics burdened with Berber and Afro-Semitic blood; the Spaniard has always demonstrated a great incapacity even for the most primitive occupation: the military."[7] For Encina, the bulk of Chile's rural population bore the heavy weight of "stone-age Araucanian culture" in their blood: "There circulates in the veins of our people the blood of the aboriginal Araucanian; and, although this blood is generous it cannot save in three centuries the distance that the European peoples have traveled in close to two thousand years."[8] Thus, he argued that "the Chilean worker isn't capable of sustained and regular work characteristic of well evolved peoples. . . . At base there is intact in him the aboriginal repugnance for manual activity . . . without material necessity to work the Araucanian atavism explodes with violence."[9]

At the same time, however, Encina began to build a case for a strong national identity based in racial theory by arguing for a distinctive Chilean identity "that differentiates the Chilean mestizo both from Europeans and from other Latin Americans: Our race, formed by two ethnic and mixed elements in good biological conditions, has a relative anthropological unity; but in its grade of civilization it not only lacks unity, but is separated in its distinctive spheres by true abysses. . . . Our lower spheres . . . stayed in a state of civilization little superior to that at the end of the barbarian invasions of the Roman empire." Still, searching for some hope for the nation, Encina contended that "among the Hispanic-American races, the Chilean is the strongest and that which has the greater future, even economically speaking" since Chile was favored in its racial "primary material."[10] Encina developed an embryonic nationalist discourse by asserting that the Chilean successes in foreign wars demonstrated that "Chilean primary material is . . . unquestionably superior to the Spanish." The final military defeat of the Mapuche during the 1880s allowed Encina to glorify Chileans' putative mestizo racial stock and its "Araucanian" content in terms of Chile's potential for economic and military progress in competition with its neighbors. Like other nationalist intellectuals, Encina celebrated Chilean mestizaje and the contribution of the militarily heroic "Araucanian" to national identity.

Encina's effort to locate a racial basis for Chilean national identity and a nationalist development policy was echoed in Nicolás Palacios's antiliberal and nationalist treatise La raza chilena.[11] As did Encina, Palacios drew on the social Darwinist ideas inspired by Herbert Spencer to argue for a distinctly Chilean mestizo race based on the blood of "Araucanian Indians" and "Visigothic conquistadors." Palacios contended that the Chilean racial mixture was superior to the Spaniards', and he proposed a unitary Chilean race: "Chile has a particular race, distinct from all the others of the world. . . . Effectively, the Goths and the Araucanians, so different in their physical traits, both possessed with the same clarity and fixedness the characteristic attributes of what are understood as the patriarchal or manly and virile psychology, based on the criterion of the absolute dominance of man over women in the mental spheres."[12] Palacios invoked Spencer's idealization of the patriarchal perfection of the German race and argued that "the legitimate Chilean does not have Latin blood in his veins."[13] In contrast to Encina, Palacios lent his reactionary nationalism a populist tone by glorifying the Chilean roto, the rural and urban worker and miner, as the representative of Chile's manly and potent racial stock. As did other nationalist intellectuals at the turn of the century, Palacios launched virulent attacks against European immigrants, who, he argued, took jobs from Chilean workers. He also attacked foreign companies for contracting foreign technicians and white-collar workers, and paying them higher salaries than their Chilean employees.[14]

The antiliberal nationalism of Palacios and Encina was taken up by other intellectuals who sought to place Chilean economic dependence in the context of North American control of the emergent copper industry and export economy. After the First World War, nationalist reformers interested in promoting Chile's economic development and social progress looked to racial and cultural (the two terms were often conflated) explanations for Chile's "weakness" and "inferiority." They drew on Chileans' lack of a true capitalist culture and labor discipline to explain economic backwardness and North American domination of the national economy. Julio Kaulen, in his study of foreign mining companies, for example, argued that "El Teniente does not have the character of being an adventure that attracts the Chilean entrepreneur. [Low-grade copper mining] is a work of perseverance, which is not a predominant quality in the Chilean."[15] Similarly, Santiago Macchiavello Varas postulated that Chilean entrepreneurs' failure to develop the national copper industry came not from structural constraints such as lack of capital, limited access to North American markets and technologies, or the lack of favorable mining legislation, but from a "short-term" and "short-sighted" perspective on profitability.[16] Chilean capitalists were thought to share many of the cultural defects of Chilean workers: lack of perseverance, short-sightedness, lack of discipline, and lack of enterprising spirit. An ideology of racial and national cultural inferiority structured explanations of Chilean economic backwardness and subordination to North American capital. Nationalists such as Machiavello and Kaulen attacked Chilean elites for their responsibility in handing the economy to foreign capitalists, but with Encina, they also located the origins of dependency in the backwardness and lack of education of Chilean workers.

Nationalism was not only an elite concern and project during this period. As in other parts of Latin America, workers developed their own understandings of the nation and their own nationalist politics.[17] In Chile, working-class nationalism, most militantly articulated in the labor movement of the northern pampas, was often inscribed by racist attitudes toward Peruvians and Bolivians, who were perceived to be more indigenous and, in the case of Peru, more African. Even before the War of the Pacific mobilized workers and miners to fight Bolivians and Peruvians behind nationalist and expansionist flags, Chilean workers had developed a sense of national identity and ethnic difference informed by racist attitudes of superiority. In the northern nitrate fields of Peru's Tarapacá province, the labor force was largely Chilean and Bolivian, with a smaller number of Peruvians.[18] Historian Julio Pinto describes how in 1860, Chilean workers in a Tarapacá nitrate oficina assaulted a company store, calling the Peruvian authorities in the region "negros y cosas peores" (blacks and worse things), as well as "cobardes y flojos zambos" (cowards and lazy mulattos). The workers also shouted nationalist slogans such as "¡Viva Chile!" and "¡Muera Peru!"[19] Similarly, in the 1870s a Chilean consul in Tarapacá reported a "rivalry between Chilean and Bolivian workers: hatreds and antipathies."[20] As Pinto notes, Chilean workers in the northern nitrate industry were known for their disorderly conduct, violence, rowdy behavior, and "exaggerated patriotism."[21]

In the nitrate oficinas, working-class rebelliousness was expressed in both militant nationalist opposition to foreign-owned nitrate companies and nativist antagonism toward Bolivian and Peruvian workers and political authorities. Thus, an 1879 uprising of Chilean workers was sparked by the arrest of a Chilean worker who had stabbed a Bolivian coworker, signifying, for Pinto, a "high grade of nationalist violence associated with profound ethnic, cultural, linguistic differences." By the 1890s, with significant levels of Asian immigration to the Peruvian South and Chilean north, attacks on chino merchants became frequent. In one case, a drunken mob of Chilean workers attacked an Asian-owned business, yelling, "Let's go to the house of the chinos, that is a cursed race and there shouldn't be any in Chile." In another case cited by Pinto, the mixture of working-class militancy with Chilean nationalism expressed itself during a strike in a British-owned nitrate oficina in the symbolism displayed by the strikers: Chilean flags and shouts of "¡Viva Chile!"[22] Chilean nationalism served as a vehicle for expressing class antagonism to foreign capitalists in the north. At the same time, however, Chilean workers articulated this nationalism in an often racist xenophobia directed against fellow workers and small-business owners from Bolivia and Peru, whom they represented as "Indians," "blacks," "chinos," and "zambos" (a mixture of African and Indian).

Working-class nationalism in the ports and nitrate mines of Chile's northern Antofogasta and Tarapacá provinces contributed to the militant socialist and anarchist politics of workers' mancomunales (resistance societies) and unions, the powerful strike movements of the first decade of the twentieth century, Emilio Recabarren's Partido Obrero Socialista (POS) (Socialist Workers' Party), and the Federación Obrera de Chile (FOCH), making the Chilean labor movement one of the most radical in Latin America. But working-class nationalism was also channeled into the middle-class-led ligas patrióticas, which in 1911 mobilized Chilean workers in a campaign to drive Peruvians out of the province of Tarapacá, wrested from Peru in the War of the Pacific. The ligas, with support from mobs composed of Chilean workers, attacked Peruvian social clubs, newspapers, a firehouse, and a mutual aid society to expel Peruvians from Tarapacá. The president of the ligas patrióticas had ties to the worker-supported Balmacedista Liberal Democratic Party, which expressed a virulent nationalism and hostility to the foreign-owned nitrate companies. According to Sergio González, the organization of the *ligas* and the infamous massacre of thousands of workers at the Escuela Santa María de Iquique in 1907 brought an end to the internationalism and solidarity among different ethnic groups and nationalities in the north, effectively crushing the northern labor movement and exacerbating working-class divisions according to nationality, race, and ethnicity. After the massacre, British nitrate companies began to replace Chilean workers with Bolivians, Peruvians, and Asians, who were perceived to be less militant, and to hire Peruvians and Bolivians as company police. Despite the internationalism of the northern unions and *mancomunales*, and denunciations of the *ligas* in Emilio Recabarren's left-wing newspapers, including El *Grito Popular* and El *Despertar de los Trabajadores*, these ethnic and national divisions fueled Chilean workers' support for the *ligas* and antagonism for Bolivian and Peruvian workers, shop owners, and white-collar employees in the north.[23]

National and ethnic divisions among laborers in the northern pampa took concrete form in the tensions between Bolivian and Chilean workers in the Guggenheim-owned Chuquicamata copper mine (the company was later sold to the Anaconda Copper Company), run by a subsidiary, the Chilean Exploration Company (Chilex). Bolivians lived in a segregated community within the copper-mining camps and maintained a separate cultural world with their own social clubs, mutual aid societies, and political clubs. Many Bolivians were indigenous Aymara and were looked down upon by Chilean workers. Tensions between Chileans and Bolivians were exacerbated during the 1920s by the North American company's strategy of hiring Aymara Bolivians, who were believed to be more docile than Chileans, at lower wages, a method that had been employed by British nitrate companies to undermine miners' labor organizations. Chilean workers viewed Bolivians as "passive," lacking in labor militancy, and undercutting the labor market. A 1926 study of Chuquicamata by Ricardo Latcham, who had worked for the company's welfare department, noted that "in the mining regions there is a significant population of Bolivian Indians, feared competitors of the Chileans in the work of extracting copper since they are content with low salaries and make few material demands, and for this they are often preferred by the North American capitalists."[24] Latcham also noted with racist condescension the differences between Chileans and Bolivians, who, he claimed, "confused the limits of rational faith with those of idolatry, superstition and the uncouth fetishism of aborigines."[25] As anthropologist Janet Finn has argued, racial codes that valorized "whiteness" and mestizo identity, and racism toward Bolivian

Aymaras by Chileans defined ethnic relations among workers in Chuquicamata's copper camps.[26]

Chilean workers' antagonism to Bolivians in Chuquicamata drew on decades of national and ethnic hostilities in the Chilean north. However, despite the institutionalization of social and cultural divisions between Chileans and Bolivians in segregated neighborhoods and a segmented labor market, Chuquicamata's unions developed a commitment to class-based internationalism in the name of a shared struggle against capitalism and imperialism. During the 1930s workers, both Bolivian and Chilean, elected a Bolivian, Humberto Mur, to head the mine's union of blue-collar workers (obreros).[27] Mur had entered the political life of the mine's camps through his activities as president of the Centro Boliviano and through his "patriotic acts" in support of the Bolivian army during the Chaco War with Paraguay. In 1938, when Mur was deported by the Alessandri government under the Ley de Residencia (Residency Law) for his union activism, the labor and leftist press rallied to his cause, pointing out that Mur had lived and worked in Chile since 1920 and that six of his eight children had been born in Chile and were thus Chilean. The Antofogasta paper, El Popular, even celebrated Mur as having worked to develop "intense ties between Bolivia and Chile in this region."[28] In the Chuquicamata copper mine, as in the nitrate oficinas and ports, xenophobia and racist attitudes coexisted in tension with forms of solidarity and internationalism that transcended ethnic and national differences and provided a unity between Bolivian and Chilean workers organized in one union of obreros.

It is difficult to draw clear lines of causation between the elite-generated nationalism and racial theory of intellectuals like Encina and Palacios, and the informal racial attitudes, expressions of patriotism, and militant nationalism present in working-class culture.[29] A variety of nationalisms emerged during the late nineteenth and early twentieth centuries in response to the dominance of foreign capital in the Chilean economy. Working-class nationalism lent the right-wing nationalism and racial theory of intellectuals such as Encina and Palacios radical class content and served as a vehicle for the militant politics of the labor movement in strikes, protests, and riots. While antiliberals such as Encina and Palacios grounded their nationalism in the specious racial science of the late nineteenth century and advocated an authoritarian and hierarchical political order rooted in the principles of positivism, workers made nationalism into the basis of an egalitarian anticapitalist and anti-imperialist politics. In addition, radical nationalism coexisted with labor's internationalist commitment to class solidarity among different national and ethnic groups in the struggle against capital. However, as in the case of nationalist intellectuals, working-class nationalism was also at times expressed in nativist hostility to Bolivians and Peruvians, who were defined as more indigenous than Chilean mestizos, and toward Asians. Racism and racial attitudes constituted one element of working-class nationalism and labor militancy in tension with the labor movements' commitment to internationalism. At times, working-class xenophobia, converting nationalism into patriotism, coincided with the racist nationalism of right-wing intellectuals, as during the popular mobilizations led by the *ligas patrióticas* in 1911. In this case, nationalism, rather than being an instrument of class struggle and anti-imperialism, provoked divisions within the labor movement and contributed to the defeat of mass mobilizations from below. In the copper mines, workers inherited both the radical nationalist traditions of the *mancomunales*, FOCh, and POS and the nativist patriotism of the *ligas patrióticas*. In response to their experiences of North American racism in the mining camps, they asserted pride in their Chilean ethnic and national identity, and wove these traditions together in a militant movement for the expropriation of the mining camps.

North American Capital, Chilean Workers,
and Institutional Racism

The Kennecott Copper Company's Chilean subsidiary, the Braden Copper Company, encountered enormous difficulties developing the rich veins of copper ore named El Teniente into an efficient and productive modern copper enterprise. Originally purchased from its Chilean owners in 1904 and controlled by the Guggenheims, El Teniente did not become profitable until production increased after 1914 owing to the introduction of new technologies for extracting and processing low-grade ore, and to expanded international demand for copper during the First World War. Having conquered the difficult terrain of the Andes through innovative engineering and production techniques during the war, the North American company confronted another obstacle to production: Chile's social landscape. The mining company found it difficult to establish a stable, disciplined, and trained source of labor for a mining enterprise that demanded as many as eight thousand workers. El Teniente miners tended to work short stints, accumulate small savings, and then leave for the northern nitrate fields, ports, the capital of Santiago, or surrounding agricultural valleys. Living and working conditions in the mine and its camps were harsh and brutal. Accidents in the mine were frequent, and heavy blizzards, harsh temperatures, and a barren terrain made the mine's camps difficult places to inhabit. Faced with dangerous and grueling labor, most mine workers voted with their feet. During the First World War and throughout the 1920s, as international markets for copper grew rapidly, El Teniente's labor force maintained deeply entrenched patterns of mobility. In 1922, for example, only 9 percent of two thousand workers hired by company agents and labor recruiters stayed on in the mine. High rates of labor turnover and a lack of labor discipline provoked one mine supervisor to complain that "the majority of the lower class labor that we employ at the Mine is absolutely uneducated and ignorant, and are absolutely without responsibility."[30] A 1932 U.S. consulate report on labor conditions in the Chilean copper industry echoed company managers' racially condescending analysis of the sources of labor instability. Noting the ongoing conflict between "the easy temperament of the Chilean working man and the relentless driving policy of Braden," the report argued that "like most Latin American laborers . . . [the Chilean working man] will work long enough to keep the wolf from the door but when the immediate future is provided for they much prefer to loaf."[31]

Mine workers' transience had its origins in the itinerant labor force of landless agricultural laborers (peones) who traveled the Chilean countryside from hacienda to hacienda in search of labor and who migrated to port cities and copper and nitrate mining districts during the off season, following the boom and bust cycles of nitrate production as well as the rhythms of production in the agricultural sector. These traditions of mobility provided workers their most viable form of resistance to the demands of the North American mining company. In his 1923 study of Chile's copper industry, Macchiavello Varas located the cause of mine workers' notorious transience in the harsh conditions of life and labor in the mines, rather than in the cultural defects of the Chilean working class: "the veritable mobility, this life of vagabondage, of the Chilean miner comes not from love of the new, but from the intense suffering that he finds in all the mines."[32]

In response to the difficulties of securing a reliable labor force in El Teniente, the mine's North American managers introduced a social welfare system designed to attract workers to the mine and keep them there. The company's welfare department, established in 1916, provided workers social, cultural, and recreational activities and sponsored a network of vocational and night schools for workers and their families. In addition, the company implemented a new system of bonuses, built improved housing for married workers, and began to increase wages. The goal of this system of corporate welfare, the first to be introduced in Chile, was the reformation of workers' everyday habits and cultural lives through training, education, and "hygienic" social activities. Most important, social welfare aimed to reorder and reform gender relations; it sought to transform a transient and unruly population of men and women (who often migrated independently to the margins of the mine's camps to work in an informal economy of bars and brothels) into a stable population of married male heads of households and female housewives dedicated to the administration of the domestic sphere.[33]

Gendered social welfare policies were designed to produce the cultural uplift of El Teniente's Chilean working-class population and instill the values of domestic responsibility, civic duty, and labor discipline. By forming stable families, participating in sports teams, joining mutual aid societies, and attending vocational schools, workers would leave behind the vice-ridden cultural habits that disrupted production: drinking, frequenting brothels, gambling, and absenteeism. Corporate welfare established a set of apparatuses designed to restructure the ways in which working-class men and women spent both their work and leisure time by disciplining their bodies and behavior through prescriptive recreational, social, and cultural activities. The company's ideology of cultural betterment as a means to social improvement echoed similar corporate welfare policies in the United States that sought to bring cultural and racial uplift to African American migrants and European immigrants through industrial education and social welfare programs that would erase ethnic cultures and produce Americanization.[34]

The company welfare department advertised the benefits of corporate welfare in letters and meetings with Chilean politicians and social reformers: involvement in social works and patriotic activities, better appearance, the elimination of criminality, more robust and stable families based on the foundation of civil marriage, participation in sports clubs, and attendance at vocational schools. Because of "welfare work," the company argued to visiting Chilean politicians, "the worker lives better, his family is well constituted, he earns more, is better educated and more cultured . . . and is a better citizen."[35] In 1936, in a social work thesis at the University of Chile, Stella Joanne Seibert Alphand focused on El Teniente's welfare programs as a model for employer and state practice, arguing that Chileans should learn from "a system based on ideas put in practice in the United States."[36] Like the North American company's managers, she argued that welfare work served "to inculcate education and culture in the worker . . . to give him and his children a little education; place in his muddy mind some principles of respect for hygiene, cleanliness, decency; teach him that there is something more in the world for the worker than vice, drunkenness, and abject poverty." According to Seibert, new ideas about social welfare in Chile "had budded from the seeds sown by the great producers of copper, with their intelligent and generous policies for their workers."[37] In 1931, the publication of the company-controlled miners' union reflected on Braden's social welfare program and pledged to follow the company's prescription for improving workers' lives through cultural improvement rather than collective action. Echoing the company's focus on uplift, the union promised to devote itself to education and "problems of social betterment" since the mass of workers in El Teniente "are the most backward in education and culture." "With education and culture," the union paper editorialized, "the workers' economic state will improve as they leave the traditional vices of our race."[38]

The North American company complemented its social welfare programs with the careful surveillance of daily life in the mine and its camps. Alcohol was banned in a nationally heralded "dry law"; the company required that all romantic or sexual liaisons be formalized in civil marriage; living arrangements were strictly regulated; and a pass system was implemented to control workers' movements in and out of the isolated mining camps. The company's private police force patrolled the camps and workers' barracks in search of bootleg alcohol and illicit sexual activity, detained workers for fighting with foremen and supervisors, and expelled union activists and "rebellious" workers from the mine's camps. The rigorous control of miners' work and nonwork lives was backed by the spatial organization of living arrangements in the camps. The company imported policies of Jim Crow segregation from the United States and established a rigidly divided system of housing and social life for North Americans and Chileans that gave its repressive forms of social control an explicitly racial dimension. As in the copper mines of the U.S. Southwest, where Mexican and Mexican American workers lived in segregated housing apart from Anglo workers and supervisors, in El Teniente North Americans lived in their own community, the *población norteamericana*, in little houses with gardens in stark contrast to Chilean laborers, who lived in austere barracks built of wood and tin.[39] To this day mining community members' most salient memory of their time in El Teniente's camps is of the separate and unequal system of housing. They recall being prohibited from entering the North American district of the camps, describe North American social clubs that banned Chileans, and speak of a bitter sense of racial discrimination. In one oral history, a retired miner remembers sneaking into the North American neighborhood during the 1920s to play on the playground swings (there were no playgrounds in the Chilean districts of the camps). He was caught by the company police and delivered to his father, who beat him out of fear that another such trespass would lead to his dismissal.[40] For the worker, the trauma of the event was a turning point in the development of his political identity; he later became a union leader and militant of the Communist Party.

Other oral history interviews brought forth memories of separate hospital wards, schools, and social clubs. A woman who grew up in the mining camps and remembers her life there and the company's paternalist welfare system with a nostalgic fondness absent in the narratives of the Communist Party militant, still recalls racism: "The *gringos* lived in their own camp with houses, a golf course, and tennis courts . . . while the workers lived in barracks. It was a kind of discrimination."[41] Similarly, a worker recalls that when he arrived in the camps, "what was shocking to me was how many differences there were of all kinds. The American *jefes* lived in a neighborhood that they called American where they lived with the maximum comforts that the common worker didn't have."[42] The memories of these former El Teniente miners and their family members indicate that the discrimination workers felt in the mining camps derived not only from the class exploitation inherent in the organization of production, but also from a system of separation, exclusion, and privilege based on nationality and inflected with racism. Their words demonstrate that subordination in the mining camps was lived as a national and racial, as well as class, experience.

In 1919, José Pezoa Varas traveled to El Teniente to take a position as a teacher in the camps' schools. Appalled by El Teniente's harsh living and working conditions, and outraged by what he perceived to be rampant racial discrimination against Chileans, he left his job after a short period and penned a tract denouncing the North American company, *En el feudo* (*Inside the Fiefdom*).[43] Pezoa Varas noted in his description of El Teniente's racially stratified housing patterns that physical difference and the fear of contact or interaction seemed to be the foundation of the North American domain: "[The North American neighborhood] possessed beauty and comfort, constructed intentionally far from housing destined for Chilean families. The privileged race could thus live without any kind of contact with the humble children of this uncivilized country."[44] Similarly, members of the mining community remember stepping away from North Americans in the camps' passageways because "they applied North American ideas in a Chilean city . . . when a North American passed by, the [Chilean] *obrero*, the *empleado*, the women, or children had to step to one side so as not to touch him, because if they touched him, he complained with the consequence that they fired [the worker] and made him leave the camps."[45]

Pezoa Varas's description of El Teniente's system of Jim Crow was repeated in other observers' studies of Anaconda's northern Chuquicamata copper mine. Ricardo Latcham noted Chuquicamata's North American managers' racist contempt for Chileans, whom they referred to as *nativos malditos*, and argued that what most rankled "of all the evils that exist in Chuquicamata is the Yankee capacity to arrogate to himself the title of superior race and look down on everything that is Chilean. . . . The natives as they call them with scorn are for them an inferior people . . . they impute all the vices, all the backwardness, all the lack of intelligence and all the defects of a barbarous or savage people to the Chileans."[46] Similarly, the northern writer and journalist Eulogio Gutiérrez denounced the Chilex company in *Chuquicamata: Tierras rojas* (1926) ("a certain North American current feels a profound aversion for everything that is Chilean") and the fact that the North Americans used the term "blakman" derogatorily to refer to Chileans.[47] In a section on the wages of "the people of color" Gutiérrez noted that in Chuquicamata, as in El Teniente, the North American "white" was paid more (and in dollars) than the "blakman chileno" (paid in pesos) for the same jobs. He described the ways in which the classification of Chileans as "blacks" or "Indians" "was taken to the extreme of separating the camps and even dividing them in barracks and houses for "white" men and "black" men. "The Europeans and Yankees not only earn higher salaries and wages, paid in dollars, but also enjoy better accommodations and receive better treatment as empleados, while the Chilean obreros, 'blakman,' are badly paid in devalued bills and treated . . . like Indians, like pariahs in their own country . . . even though they do the jobs of empleados." The left-wing Antofagasta paper *El Popular* echoed Latcham and Gutiérrez in 1946 when it argued that North American white-collar employees and supervisors enjoyed privileged salaries and benefits: "the "high-up bosses of [Chuquicamata] . . . view themselves as privileged kings or as belonging to a superior race."[48]

The institutionalization of physical separation based on nationality rendered the system of class relations in the mining camps explicit and meaningful in terms of racism and perceived racial difference. Segregation based on nationality and categorized in racial terms in the mining camps indicated an exercise of domination that went beyond the social boundaries of class. Codes of race informed the day-to-day exercise of class relations by embodying social power and cultural value based on class. The lack of social intercourse, the prohibition on entering North American space, and the taboo against physical contact lent a system of social relations based on class and nationality its material racial dimension. North Americans' disdain for Chileans reflected an explicit racism that shaped forms of discrimination based on nationality and class that Chileans felt deeply. In his short stories about life in the camps, the nationally famous writer Gonzalo Drago, who had worked for the Braden Copper Company, describes a segregated social life in which North Americans expressed only contempt for Chileans, be they white-collar employees (*empleados*) with some education, training, or technical skills, or blue-collar workers (*obreros*). The North Americans' racism took form in frequent expressions of disgust for Chileans. Drago writes about one North American boss, a Mr. Lewis, who expressed his attitude toward "the natives" by saying, " 'Bah, how disgusting!' He would not touch them even with metal gloves for fear of infecting himself. . . . Contact with [Chilean] workers repulsed him, the smell of their badly washed bodies, their corrupt looks, and their indigenous faces."[49]

The physicality of perceived racial difference in El Teniente was made clear in another Drago story of life in the mine centered on the figure of "Mr. Jara," a Chilean employee who identifies with the company. For Drago this identification took on the aspect of a derided racial "passing," as Mr. Jara attempts to appear white by speaking only English and adopting the mannerisms of his North American supervisors. Drago describes how Mr. Jara had arrived at his post in the company through "the everyday use of his flexible spine whenever he was in the presence of a blond boss, authentically Yankee, '*made in the USA.*' " Despite Mr. Jara's employment as an informer for company supervisors, the North Americans "despised him, but made use of his services." Mr. Jara internalizes a sense of racial inferiority and only desires to make himself white: "His physical appearance mortified him. He would have liked to be blond and white with deep blue eyes, but nature had given him markedly indigenous external signs. *Moreno*, with widespread eyes, Roman nose, and thick lips, he was the antithesis of the racial type that he admired; but what most exasperated him was the tenacious rebellion of his hair that covered his head like a grotesque black porcupine."[50] These descriptions display both Chilean workers' sense of racial difference from, and subordination to, North Americans and their rejection of North American pretensions to racial superiority. Drago's story operated as a critique of the North American company not only in terms of class exploitation and a critique of imperialism, but also in terms of the North Americans' racism, and it worked to assert a Chilean ethnic pride and attendant nationalism. In Drago's stories, the opposite of a Mr. Jara is the Chilean who defines true manhood—also *moreno* but described as robust, physically powerful, virile, independent, loyal to his work mates, hardworking, and "straight" or "upright." To this day the phrase "Mr. Jara" is used in the mining camps to denote an "Uncle Tom"—someone who identifies with company power and is disloyal to his class and nationality.

The pride in Chilean national identity articulated in opposition to North

American racism in these texts was based on an assertion of a mestizo ethnic unity. Nationalist writers celebrated both the contribution of indigenous groups to the national ethnic identity and the putative unity of mestizo identity. In rejecting North American racism, they constructed an image of a Chilean national ethnicity free of racial divisions and discrimination. Writers like Drago valorized the contribution of Araucanian Indian groups to Chilean national and ethnic identity, while asserting the racial homogeneity of the Chilean people. Pezoa Varas's first experience with the North American company's racial system came when he was assigned housing and encountered two different barracks, both gray, but called informally the "White Barracks" and "Black Barracks," the former for North Americans and the latter for Chileans. He only fully understood the meaning of the words "white" and "black" when a number of people described to him how an invitation for a dance at the North American social club had circulated the camps with the caution "only for whites." "Who were the whites?" Pezoa asked. "Who were those of the other color? Was it that the outgoing North Americans who had made the invitation had of Chileans the same idea that von Luxburg expressed in an official note about South Americans saying that all of them underneath a light varnish of civilization, are still no more than Indians? Or do they think they are in Yankeeland, the country in which the tenth part of the population is composed of blacks and Chinese?"[51]

Pezoa Varas's text suggests the very real racist discrimination against Chileans by North American supervisors and managers in the camps, and the profound structuring of social life in the camps around invented racial categories. At the same time, however, Pezoa Varas established the dignity of Chilean workers by distinguishing them from "blacks" and "Chinese," and by asserting Chileans' non-Indian status in contrast to North American perceptions of Chilean racial composition. As he rejected North American claims to racial superiority, he also attempted to distinguish Chileans from North American blacks and Chinese as well as from Indians. Similarly, in oral histories, members of the mining community frequently joked that North Americans perceived Chileans to be Indians, emphasizing their mestizo origins while implicitly commenting on perceived North American racism. Their perception that North Americans viewed them as "uncivilized Indians," goes beyond national or class differences to reflect their perception of North American racism. But this rejection of North American racial categories also reflects a claim to mestizaje and ignores the presence of indigenous groups and internal forms of racism.

In a story describing conflicts between North American bosses and Chilean workers, Gonzalo Drago articulated a critique of the internal racial codes and discourses that structured Chilean society based on a disdain for the Indian or indigenous elements of Chilean culture and nationality. One worker, in describing Chilean subordination to North Americans, and the phenomenon of Mr. Jara figures who curry favor with North Americans, argues that the cause of Chilean "weakness" is a sense of racial inferiority that has led Chileans to be dominated socially and economically by North Americans: "I believe that our race, our ethnic formation, is the only cause of our behavior. We must not forget that we carry the Indian underneath our jacket, and disguised with foreign or Spanish last names. We are a hybrid product, incomplete, with little evolution, that feels itself subjugated before any man of a foreign race." He invokes a "racial inferiority complex that poisoned the blood of our ancestors for more than three hundred years."[52] The story criticizes this sense of racial inferiority internalized by its characters and proposes as an alternative pride in Chileans' mestizo racial identity based on the valorization of both the indigenous and Hispanic contribution to Chilean racial stock.

Eulogio Gutiérrez drew on the discredited anthropology and racial theory of Nicolás Palacios to establish the mestizo ethnicity of Chileans as equal to the "Anglo-Saxon" ethnicity of North Americans in his critique of racism and class exploitation in Chuquicamata. Gutiérrez devoted a chapter of his pamphlet to "The Distinct Races of Chuquicamata" and argued that the population of Chuquicamata was "founded on the base of two races—the Anglo-Saxon and the Chilean—since we Chileans not only constitute an ethnic entity, but a race, according to what doctor don Nicolás Palacios has magisterially demonstrated; and both strong races because of their physical and moral make up." As did Pezoa Varas, Gutiérrez distinguished the racism and racial divisions of North American society from a raceless mestizo Chile: "In Chile there is no division of races. Here we are all equal, here there are no blond men of blue blood nor do there exist blacks with a thick lower lip or African pigment . . . the *señores directores* de Chilex are like us, Americans of European origins and must not then classify the Chilean as 'blakman' or 'hombre negro' in contrast to the yankee or white man of the United States."[53] Thus, while critiquing the North Americans' racism and use of the term "blakman" to describe Chileans, Gutiérrez drew on racial theory to define Chileans as a race equal to Anglo-Saxons because of the putative absence of Indians, Africans, and Asians. He celebrated the fact that "in our Chilean race we do not have the Black African with a mofa and livid thick lips." And while denying any racial stratification or division in Chile, he glorified the indigenous contribution to Chile's mestizo racial stock: "We have the honor to still have the vestiges of the ancient Mapuches . . . . the ancient Arauco."[54] Gutiérrez asserted Chilean racial status by insisting on its mestizo nature and the value of the vanquished (and supposedly vanished) Mapuche peoples' contribution to Chilean blood, and by denying the "degenerative" presence of Africans and Asians in the Chilean population. At the same time, he critiqued North American racism and celebrated an alleged absence of racial and ethnic divisions in Chile.

Racism, Sexuality, and Respectability in the Mining Camps

The physical and embodied nature of racial discrimination that defined the dynamics of class relations in El Teniente's camps was made clear in conflicts surrounding sexuality. As the reformation of working-class sociability became a feature of the disciplinary regimes related to enforcing new rhythms of work and producing the proletarianization of the labor force, sexuality became a sphere in which the dynamics of class tensions and ethnic and national relations, defined by racism, were played out. As they succumbed to the demands of proletarianization and the new regime of gender relations in the mining camps, male workers expressed their loss of autonomy in terms of their loss of control of the masculine honor of the itinerant *peón* and *roto*, whose manhood was defined by independence, physical strength and bravery, and sexual freedom. Miners viewed class domination by North American bosses as a form of sexual domination and exploitation inflected by racism. Popular tales of North American bosses raping Chilean women demonstrated the sexual basis of both miners' sense of self and their consciousness of their own exploitation. Male workers lost their dignity and were quit of their manhood because of their inability to guard or control women's sexual virtue. At the same time, these stories contrasted the social respectability of Chilean workers with the degenerate and uncivilized behavior of North American bosses. For nationalist writers and copper miners, the *gringos*, not the Chilean workers, were culturally backward. Workers laid claim to the values of disciplined and proper citizenship and masculinity broadcast by the company welfare department and the state, and defined North Americans as both ethnically Other and disrespectable.

Gonzalo Drago devotes one of his "miners' stories" to the tale of a North American supervisor, Jack Morgan, who is married to "an Englishwoman, skinny and flat like a board . . . she was only good for folding his socks and emptying his pockets."[55] The story holds up the beautiful and "feminine" Chilean woman, the worker Ramiro's wife, Berta, in contrast to the unfeminine and desexualized white/European woman. Morgan desires Berta and eventually rapes her, threatening her not with a weapon or his fists, but with her husband's dismissal and the entire family's eviction from the camps. Upon discovering the rape, Ramiro, who is described as the embodiment of miner manhood ("a strong and rigorous boy who knows his job of mechanic well and never has problems with his *compañeros*" and who "is straight and works hard"), feels "humiliated, mocked, and ashamed," runs out to kill the *gringo canalla* (gringo bastard), and is himself beaten by Morgan and arrested by company police. The collapse of racial, sexual, and class subordination in the story is revealed when the supervisor responds to Ramiro's fury by asking him provocatively, "Who's your woman, you dirty Indian?"[56] This story was not unique in El Teniente and approached the level of the iconographic. In a similar tale, the writer Baltazar Castro, who had worked for the company as an office clerk, describes the attempted rape of a Chilean domestic servant by a North American boss in the camps in his novel of work and life in El Teniente.[57]

Workers' identification of class alienation with sexual and racial exploitation was further articulated in critiques of North American supervisors as morally corrupt. Chilean workers turned North American racist condescension toward Chileans on its head by portraying North Americans as a morally degenerate and backward ethnic group. In terms of Drago's story of Ramiro and Berta, the honorable and respectable masculinity of the Chilean worker and the femininity of his wife are contrasted with the corrupted depravity of the North American boss and his wife's lack of true femininity. Drago upholds the manliness of the Chilean worker Ramiro against the degenerate North American supervisor. The story contrasts the sexual immorality of the boss with the honorable Chilean worker and respectable Chilean housewife. Drawing on the moral prescriptions of the company's gendered social welfare programs, the story mobilizes concepts of respectability, moral rectitude, civilization, and education to critique the exercise of social power by North Americans. Using sexuality, the story turns the company's own condemnation of Chilean workers as uncivilized on its head by portraying North Americans as sexually degenerate, lacking in morality and respectability, and as failing to live up to the prescribed models of appropriate masculine and feminine behavior broadcast by the company's own social welfare department. In fact, both Drago's and Castro's stories of life in the mining camps frequently deploy North Americans' description of Chileans as "uncivilized" in describing North American bosses as vulgar, uncultured, dirty, and drunkards, just as miners in union assemblies denounced North Americans as "vagabonds," "ignorant," and "thieves."[58]

In his polemic against the Braden Copper Company, Pezoa Varas uses similar codes of sexual and social respectability to critique both the class exploitation and North American racism. He described watching "two yankees who formed an interesting pair. Young and beautiful, mounted on horse back she smiled and glanced at the young man who rode at her side with her head uncovered and a bouquet of flowers at her waist. They were not married . . . since she was the wife of one of the principal supervisors."[59] Pezoa Varas implied the sexual immorality of the woman and distinguished her from morally upright Chileans by stating, "I was happy that she was distant from the Chilean district. That way there was no danger that our women adopt the mode of riding bareback . . . neither would they learn the custom of looking for flowers with friends in such distant and solitary places."[60] In this anecdote, Pezoa invoked hegemonic notions of appropriate gendered behavior to critique North Americans by representing North American women as disrespectable sexually and a potentially corrupting influence on Chilean workers, a direct inverse of the company welfare program's stated assumption that the North American company would bring respectable forms of domestic life and gender relations to its Chilean workforce.

Ricardo Latcham also appropriated the racist attitudes of North Americans by describing the "yankee" managers of Chuquicamata as backward, immoral, and degenerate. He described the contradiction between North Americans' claims about the defects of the Chilean race with their own "depraved and dishonest customs . . . their constant drunkenness, their orgies, their shameless licence and dissolution which are an immoral stimulus for the workers." As did Pezoa Varas, he underlined the sexual immorality of North Americans who "swam, men and women, mixed together, in the pool" in the American camp, and who on one occasion at a dance cut the thin silk threads of a Yankee woman's see-through dress, leaving her semi-naked. At the same dance, according to a disapproving Latcham, a "mister" urinated in a spittoon, dirtying the North American social club's carpets.[61]

Other writers used racial theory to condemn the evolutionary backwardness of the North Americans in Chuquicamata, in effect appropriating the language of racial science to build a Chilean national identity and nationalist critique of foreign capital. In Chuquicamata: La tumba del chileno (1928), Marcial Figueroa explicitly defined the control of the Chilean economy by foreign capital in terms of racial and sexual degradation. Figueroa applied the language of eugenics to argue that the North American copper companies "take away our wealth and contribute to the extinction of our race with their miserly salaries." He underlined the links between racial and sexual subordination by asserting that the North American copper industry was leading to racial degradation and a loss of masculine virility among Chilean workers: "The family of our conational is dying, there is emerging a deformed and extremely weak generation, a generation of impotents without spirit, without the vigor of the white and red blood cells, without the rich blood that the past progeny transmitted to us healthy, strong, and valiant."[62] Not only were North American companies extracting Chile's wealth and exploiting its workers, they were also destroying its primary racial material and undermining Chilean manhood.

For Figueroa, the North Americans, not the Chileans, were a backward and degenerate race whose influence was undermining Chile's national strength. He attacked the "directors of this company, the Guggenheim brothers, who, it is said, have the undesirable blood of the Israelite people in their veins" and argued that "taking into consideration the fundamentals of paleography and the findings of some anthropologists about a monogenetic human evolution, that is a common human species . . . that comes from a common root," it was still possible to categorize races by skin color, the shape of the cranium and face, and the proportions of the body.[63] Given these measuring sticks, "the typical characteristics of many of the yankees in Chuqui give us an opportunity to make a small anthropological study of these individuals. . . . We observe in the subjects underneath their grim expression indigent, niggardly, quarrelsome, lying, and scheming [traits]; in addition they have in their face those teratologic signs of degeneration and anomaly. These are a big and protruding mandibula, big incisor teeth, which with their wide cheeks and big ears form a coarse and semi-brutal physique." Figueroa concluded his study of the evolutionary defects of the North American supervisors in Chuquicamata by concluding that "the majority have an atrophied pituitary gland since they lack rational ideas. . . . The idea of evil dominates because they anastomose with the pituitary perpetually maintaining in the brain the genius of evil united with their lack of civilization."[64] For Figueroa, the North American managers' cultural backwardness was directly related to their inferior stage of racial evolutionary development.[65]

Writers such as Latcham, Pezoa Varas, Drago, Gutiérrez, Figueroa, and Castro were not themselves working-class. They worked as white-collar employees of the mining companies, teachers, newspaper reporters, and writers. Yet they sought to describe the realities of working-class experience in the copper industry in the service of a radical and nationalist critique of the dominant role of foreign capital in the Chilean economy. As did Nicolás Palacios, these writers located the foundation of the nation and people in Chilean (male) workers, whose virility, strength, and independence they celebrated. As did Palacios, they employed strands of nineteenth-century racial theory and rhetoric to define North American economic domination and class exploitation in the copper mines in explicit opposition to the systems of institutional racism established in the copper mining camps. This racialized nationalism was cast in a number of molds, from the specious racist and eugenicist celebration of Chilean workers' racial stock in Figueroa, to the racist condescension of Latcham for Bolivian Aymara in the Chuquicamata camps and the assertions by Pezoa Varas and Gutiérrez that Chile was a land of mestizos without ethnic or racial divisions. Typical of *indigenista* and nationalist movements of the time throughout Latin America, they celebrated the Mapuche (or Araucanian, as they put it) contribution to Chilean racial stock and Chile's mestizo national identity without recognizing the realities of ethnic divisions and internal racism in Chile or the contemporary histories of Mapuche communities, which were relegated to some distant heroic and mythologized past.[66] For these intellectuals, the popular subject of Chilean nationalism—the working class, exploited by both foreign capital and imperialism—was mestizo.

These writers' stories and descriptions of life and labor in the copper industry converted working-class experience into formal narratives that reflected a populist nationalism which glorified the masculine and mestizo virility of the Chilean *roto* and identified the *roto* as the pillar of national identity. They published stories and articles in the labor and left-wing press, as well as in the newspapers of middle-class and nationalist political parties. Their texts contributed to the construction of a radical working-class nationalism and mediated between elite ideas about race and nation, working-class experience, and the politics of anti-imperialism. They helped to transmit nationalist ideas and rhetoric, and to convert the racial ideas of elites such as Encina and Palacios into populist and nationalist working-class ideology. As workers built their own ideas about the meaning of the nation and organized a powerful labor movement during the 1930s and 1940s, they appropriated and drew on the ideological precepts and narrative structures of these writers' racially inflected and populist nationalism. Copper miners invoked their status as members of the Chilean people and their status as citizens in conflicts with the North American copper companies and fueled a nationalist movement for the expropriation of the mines.

Anti-Imperialism, Nationalism, and the Politics of Class

With the election of Chile's social-reformist Popular Front coalition in 1938, the El Teniente workers built the mine's first independent unions, headed by militants of the Chilean Communist and Socialist Parties. Although the miners had been organizing strikes and forming unions since 1911, every independent organizing drive and work stoppage had been crushed by the company, and miners' unions had been "company unions" controlled by the dismissal of leftist workers and union leaders who sought to build autonomous labor structures in the mine's camps. Repeated efforts by the Chilean Workers Federation (FOCh) to build an independent union during the 1920s and 1930s had met with repression by the Chilean military and police.[67] In El Teniente, labor legislation passed in 1924 and the 1931 labor code had remained unimplemented. The Popular Front coalition of the Radical, Socialist, and Communist Parties brought significant changes to the North American fiefdom. The Front's program for the modernization of Chile called for state intervention to promote import substitution industrialization, support for the unionization of the urban industrial workforce and white-collar employees, and a series of redistributive social benefits, including price controls on basic necessities, expanded public education initiatives, public works programs, social security benefits, and public health care. In addition, the Popular Front promised to limit the political power of Chile's landed oligarchy and the economic authority of the North American copper companies controlling Chile's major source of foreign revenue.[68]

During the electoral campaign of 1938, however, the Popular Front made a specific effort to assure both landed elites and the United States that its program of social reform and modernization did not threaten their interests. The unionization of industrial workers, social legislation, and state-sponsored industrialization would promote economic development without harming the interests of foreign capital and the large landed estate. Indeed, the very condition of the Front's capacity to govern was its willingness to appease traditional right-wing parties' interests by pledging to ignore agrarian reform and the unionization of rural workers, and its assurances to the United States that it intended to honor debt obligations and respect the position of the copper companies in the national economy. Thus, the Front's presidential candidate, Radical Party leader Pedro Aguirre Cerda, pledged that his coalition represented "responsible parties that want not a revolution, but an ordered social and economic reconstruction."[69] In addition, Aguirre Cerda promised a North American journalist that Chile would continue to service its foreign debt while "attempting . . . to assure that [debt payments] cause the least possible damage to our economic development," and he stated that "Chile is not ready to nationalize or socialize its great copper and nitrate industries. . . . We do not intend to use foreign capital as a football."[70]

At the same time, however, both Aguirre Cerda and the constituent members of the Popular Front, particularly the Communist Party and the new national labor federation, the Confederación de Trabajadores de Chile (CTCh) (Federation of Chilean Workers) which had been organized as the labor arm of the Popular Front, employed a more radical and nationalist rhetoric designed to mobilize unions and the urban working class in the 1938 elections. The CTCh defined its opponents as "the imperialist yoke" and "national oligarchy," while even Aguirre Cerda blasted the social structure "that left 40 percent of all fertile lands uncultivated" and "copper, nitrates, iron, and electrical power in the hands of foreign companies."[71] The Popular Front program used radical nationalist language to attack the "uncontrolled exploitation by imperialistic capital" and vowed to regulate "imperialistic enterprises with the fundamental purpose of defending our national patrimony."[72] The U.S. State Department commented nervously on "the radical and anti-capitalist utterances of Aguirre," but passed them off as campaign rhetoric "designed to stiffen the resolution of his proletarian partisans."[73] To the El Teniente copper miners, many of whom had traveled to the north in search of work during upswings in the nitrate export economy during the 1920s, the nationalist rhetoric of the CTCh and Popular Front politicians held particular resonance and spoke to their everyday experience of class, refracted as it was through the experiences of racism and discrimination in the copper industry.

The active anti-imperialism of union organizers and Popular Front militants helped give form to copper miners' daily experiences of class conflict and racism in the U.S.-owned copper mine. A meeting between the new Popular Front minister of labor, Antonio Paupin, the head of Braden's welfare department, and El Teniente union leaders shortly after the Front assumed power displayed the force of the Chilean Left's nationalism. Paupin and the company representative held a heated debate over mass dismissals in the mine. During the 1938 election campaign the company had dismissed 650 workers, and leftist congressional deputies had denounced the Braden Copper Company's practice of using reductions in production to fire union activists and militants of the Popular Front parties and thus sabotage the Front's political base in the mining camps.[74] According to the head of Braden's welfare department, after one company proposal to allow the dismissal of hundreds of workers, Paupin "jumped up and, smacking his fist on the table, said that the Government could not tolerate a solution of that kind." Paupin informed the representative that "he knew that there were a number of bosses . . . who were little better than slave drivers and nigger [once again referencing North American racial realities] whippers." Paupin burst into anger at another point, shouting, "Here you see is the attitude always taken by these imperialist companies. . . . you may tell your principals . . . that Chile is for Chileans."[75] Paupin's slogan, "Chile for Chileans," was echoed shortly afterward by Popular Front president Pedro Aguirre Cerda, who visited the mine to inspect working and living conditions. In a speech to assembled miners, he stated that he intended to rule for all Chileans and to enforce Chilean laws in the mining enclave, and that the North American mining company had to understand that his government would defend "the national workmen and national interests."[76] The nationalism of the Chilean Popular Front spoke to miners' experience of antagonism toward North American employers in the copper industry. It provided a more formal ideological rendering of miners' sense of racial and national discrimination and subordination. Miners' strikes in 1942 and 1946–47 took on a powerful nationalist and anti-imperialist tone, and the miners' unions, led by militants of the Communist Party, began to demand the expropriation and nationalization of the El Teniente mine.

Despite the radical possibilities present in Popular Front ideology, the coalition's focus on a new imagined national community and the virtues and responsibilities of citizenship obscured internal forms of racism and class hierarchy. The Popular Front promoted an ideal of Chilean national identity based on the myth of a homogeneous, harmonious, and conflict-free mestizaje. Aguirre Cerda embarked on a campaign to inculcate a new patriotism and national culture among peasants, landless laborers, workers, and the urban poor. The chilenidad (Chileanity or Chileanization) campaign sought to redefine a national community in "popular-democratic" terms in contrast to the Chilean oligarchy and foreign capital.[77] The campaign also sought to build a cross-class consensus in favor of the Popular Front's efforts to promote capitalist modernization through a set of import substitution industrialization policies. Essential to the new modern Chilean nation would be a population of trained and disciplined industrial workers and miners who would accept the responsibilities and duties of citizenship. Thus, during his visit to El Teniente, Aguirre Cerda modified his nationalist rhetoric by urging copper miners to exercise self-discipline and restraint, and to cooperate with the company to increase production and thus contribute to the progress of the nation.

Aguirre Cerda adopted as his governing slogan the phrase "to govern is to educate" and initiated the establishment of state social services, schools, and welfare agencies to train and reform the social habits of the emergent urban working class and to cultivate new forms of Chilean national identity and responsible citizenship.[78] As did the North American copper company, the Popular Front government aimed to build progress and modernization through social welfare and cultural uplift. Culturally "backward" rural-urban migrants, peasants, workers, and miners would become members of a newly imagined Chilean national community. In 1939, to implement Aguirre Cerda's slogan "to govern is to educate," the Popular Front government established a new Commission in Defense of the Race and Profitable Use of Free Time under the ministries of the interior and education, defined as "a national organization . . . with the principal mission of elevating the physical, moral, intellectual and social coefficient of all Chileans." The commission sought to combat "the negatives that were deteriorating the Chilean race"—mostly, as historian Patrick Barr notes, infant mortality and poor hygiene.[79] The government's focus on reproduction and hygiene among the urban and rural popular classes echoed the eugenicist ideas of the turn of the century by linking medical, public health, and reproductive policies to the strength of race and nation. Cultural and social reform would promote both national progress and instill the civic values and duties associated with responsible citizenship.

The nationalism of the Left and the Popular Front was contradictory. The Front's ideology of citizenship and economic nationalism provided a political channel for miners to articulate their antagonism toward their North American employer during labor conflicts and legitimized their demands that the government nationalize the copper mine. Yet the Front's nationalist ideology also obfuscated class conflict and internal forms of racism by promoting a homogeneous, ethnically mestizo Chilean national community that would be the subject of Chile's modernization. In addition, the Popular Front's nationalism coincided with the North American copper company's strategies for building a productive labor force by locating progress and development in the racial uplift of the newly configured Chilean "people." The Front's social welfare policies and nationalist campaigns to instill new notions of the virtues and responsibilities of chilenidad served a disciplinary function much like that of the Braden Copper Company's program of corporate welfare.

Workers drew on both the Front's anti-imperialism and its ideology of cultural uplift and progress, developing their own nationalist languages articulated with the intonations of class militancy and racial antagonism. They invoked their status as Chileans and citizens during strikes throughout the 1940s to demand government intervention on their behalf. Following Aguirre Cerda's visit to El Teniente, the miners' union paper appropriated the Front's ideology of the rights of citizenship to argue for the rights of workers in the North American enterprise. The miners' union frequently demanded that the Popular Front government intervene to impose the rule of Chilean law in the North American enclave and endow workers with the rights of Chilean citizens: "We want to show Chilean workers that we live in a country where the Constitution of the State is followed to the letter. . . . the company must understand that we are in Chile and that they should not treat us badly, that they should respect us as free citizens and not treat us as slaves."[80] El Teniente's workers began to draw on nationalist languages of citizenship and rights to articulate their demands to the company, defining themselves as Chileans and identifying themselves with the progress of the nation. Thus, for the miners, what it meant to be a worker and working-class was closely tied to an emergent sense of belonging to a Chilean people. Copper workers transformed their struggles with the mining company into a conflict between all Chilean citizens and foreign capital.

Nationalist attacks on employers in the name of chilenidad were not limited to the copper industry. In the state-subsidized and protected metallurgical and textile industries, workers also phrased their attacks on capital in the language of Chilean patriotism and often invoked race to demand the deportation of Jewish and Middle Eastern factory owners. The Communist Party paper Bandera Roja denounced the presence of foreign capitalists in key sectors of the Chilean economy, titling one article "Out of Chile Gringo Calder!" The paper described Calder as "among the most voracious and bothersome characters who has stepped on Chilean soil . . . representing the most cynical foreign company—the Electric Company." The paper argued that Chile had become "a semi-colonial country beaten by the feudal domination of foreign capitalism" and stated that "the fundamental task of the revolutionary movement consists in struggling against the oppression of the country by foreign capital. . . . the arrival of Mister Guggenheim, Misters Calder, Rothchild, constitutes a threat to Chile."[81] Anti-imperialism took a racist turn in a metal workers union paper's denunciation of the abusive labor practices of an owner of the large Santiago textile factory Hilandería Nacional. In response to fines levied on mostly female workers for broken machinery and damaged cloth, the paper, Músculo, called on textile workers to make their demands on their employer without "any fear of the injustice with which you were treated by the Jew [Elías] Ready. You have a just right since your money is being vilely usurped by the Jew Ready." The union of the MADEMSA metallurgical plant held mass meetings and organized demonstrations in support of the textile workers at which a major chant was "Ready must leave the country!"[82] The union paper argued—in an odd reference, given its own anti-Semitic insinuations—that "Señor Ready you are not in Germany—you've made your factory into a concentration camp" and demanded the factory owner's expulsion from Chile for refusing to respect union rights and "making a mockery of Chilean laws."[83] Later the next year the paper commented that "we have been denouncing the maneuver put in practice by the Jew Elias Ready."[84]

Anti-Arab language was also prominent in the attacks by leftist unions on textile industrialists, many of whom had immigrated from the Middle East. Union and leftist papers frequently phrased their attacks on the exploitative and anti-union practices of textile plant owners in demands that the *turco* industrialists be expelled from Chile for violating Chilean laws and sovereignty. One poem in the union paper *Obrero Textil* denounced the hiring of scabs and violent assaults on strikers by company-hired thugs orchestrated by a *turco* textile plant owner: "The Saracens came / and they beat them [the strikers] up / because God rewards the evil / when they are stronger than the good."[85] The anti-*turco* language employed in attacks on the labor practices of textile industrialists provoked a letter to *Obrero Textil* from one plant owner who claimed to be sympathetic to organized labor's goals, but angered by the anti-Arab tone he had noted. He expressed surprise at a speech to Congress made by the Trotskyist deputy Emilio Zapata (which was reprinted in the union paper), who described the textile industrialists as "slave drivers and called almost all the industrialists turcos in a form as full of contempt as ignorance." The letter argued that "here in Chile there is not one industrialist of 'turco' nationality, we are Arabs, but more than Arabs we are Chileans because we love Chile like our own country." He distinguished between foreign imperialists who extracted Chilean resources and exported the benefits to their own countries from the Arab immigrant who "invests in this land all his labor, all his honestly earned capital in such a way that he can give work to thousands of laborers . . . the Arab does not keep his money abroad."

The writer drew on the nationalist pro-industrial ideology of the Popular Front to distinguish between imperialist foreign companies and those that contributed to the modernization and growth of the Chilean economy. In addition, he identified Arabs' conflicts with British imperialism with Chile's struggles to free itself of North American domination. Arabs had come to Chile "because today we are dominated by brutal English imperialism and we want to die on free soil."[86] As Peter Winn has shown, despite this appeal to Third World internationalism and anti-imperialism, textile workers' movements often drew on anti-*turco* feeling. In fact, as Winn points out, the decision to nationalize the Yarur textile mill under Allende's Popular Unity government in 1971 was influenced by the sense that the factory was an easier target for expropriation than other companies, given the Yarur family's *turco* status.[87]

Workers often appropriated the language of *chilenidad* and the Popular Front's program of cultural uplift to phrase their class-based demands. In

El Teniente, the miners claimed the status of respectable citizens who demanded their rights and legal guarantees as Chileans, while characterizing
the North American managers and supervisors as uncouth imperialists who
violated the law, trampled on the Constitution, and behaved in uncivilized
ways. The union paper *Despertar Minero* frequently denounced the fact that in
El Teniente the company was "violating the Constitution" by attempting to
break the union, and defined "going to union meetings, helping in the
resolution of our problems for the good of our class, elevating our social,
cultural, and economic level . . . as a true support for *chilenidad*."[88] For the
miners, their struggles for an independent union, the implementation of
the labor code in the mining camps, and the nationalization of the copper
mine represented true *chilenidad*. Cultural and social uplift would be accomplished through collective action within the union rather than reliance on
state or corporate welfare programs. Miners worked for the "progress" and
"development" of Chile, while the company sabotaged national modernization by ignoring Chilean laws, provoking strikes with abusive treatment,
and treating Chilean workers like slaves. Thus the miners' union criticized
"the imperialistic company" for impeding "the plan for national reconstruction" by adopting an intransigent posture toward the union's peti-
tions.[89] The North Americans were "soulless" and "ignorant," "thieves"
and "vagabonds," as workers claimed during union assemblies during the
1946–47 strike, while the workers themselves were respectable citizens
who produced the copper that fueled economic growth and fought for the
Constitution and the nation by insisting that the North American company
respect the Chilean Constitution and laws in its "fiefdom." The miners
turned the North American representation of workers as backward to their
own use, invoking their status as respectable and morally upright citizens
and members of the Chilean people, while attacking the company and company managers as "uncivilized" and ethnically Other.

This reversal of terms was reflected, too, in the statements of the metallurgical workers' union paper. *Músculo* commented on the status of the
Chilean worker as *roto*, arguing that for employers and Chilean elites "the
roto belongs to a caste apart, to a blackened race . . . a disgusting and bad
smelling race." For the union paper, however, like many leftist and labor
publications at the time, the *roto* possessed the essential attributes of
Chilean racial stock and constituted the soul of the nation. Drawing on
language that evoked Nicolás Palacios's arguments for the superiority of
the Chilean race, the paper glorified the *roto*'s manly strength, independence, and virility, and turned elites' accusations that workers were "broken ones" and "vagabonds" on their head: "the *roto* is the great lord of
vagabondage and liberty. . . . he has his fate in his hands and in his heart

without horizons. Chilean agility is the *roto* in circulation. The *roto* has drilled the earth and has given to Chile its greatness. . . . he fought the War of the Pacific and constructed *chilenidad*; he has given the country its best men. He is the great force of the future. He is the source of *chilenidad*." The paper commented that *chilenidad* was fashionable, but that no one had mentioned the workers of the countryside, the city, and the desert, "those who through their labor and through fighting wars have made the country's name." Unlike elites who had adopted "foreign manners and customs," the *roto* "lives and dies with the *criollo*." Like the copper miners, the union paper argued that "we workers understand *chilenidad* in terms of our necessities. *Chilenidad* is to put clothing and food in our reach." In a discussion of the minister of education's plans to fortify the race with physical education programs, titled "Our Race and Subsistence," the paper commented sardonically that returning vigor to the race would only be possible by controlling prices and making basic commodities available to the working class. In discussing the Commission for the Defense of the Race, one editorialist for the union paper commented, "Give the people hygienic housing and food and the race will defend itself."[90] Like the copper miners' unions, the metallurgical workers defined (male) workers as the soul of Chilean national identity and the engine of national progress.

Workers drew on a powerful strain of Chilean nationalism that had been developed in the northern mining districts during the late nineteenth century to phrase their antagonism to foreign-born industrial employers and multinational mining companies. As in the mining districts of the north, this nationalism was, at times, inflected with racism. National and ethnic antagonisms shaped industrial workers' and miners' experiences and articulations of class. Often workers drew on dominant discourses of race and nation to define the true national subject and citizen, and the pillar of the Chilean race, as *el roto*, the rural peon, miner, or industrial laborer. They turned racist attributions of backwardness to Chileans and to Chilean workers by foreign employers on the companies themselves in a xenophobic and nationalist pride that fueled class militancy. Thus workers appropriated racial languages and ideologies of nationalism and gave them class content, rephrasing them in terms of class-specific demands and conflicts.

Miners' growing militancy, support for the Left, and demands for nationalization of the copper industry during the 1940s were shaped by their experience of racism as well as by class conflict in the mine. National antagonism, informed by the experience of institutional racism, fueled their opposition to the authority of the North American copper company. Workers drew on new notions of a Chilean people to affirm their own dignity as citizens and workers. They appropriated the terms of North

Americans' racism and the ideology of social welfare and cultural uplift, articulated by both the company and the state, to figure their exploiters as racially Other, degenerate, and backward. At the same time, however, this assertion of a popular *chilenidad* rested on an identification with a putative mestizo Chilean ethnicity and obscured internal ethnic and class hierarchies and divisions. The Braden Copper Company and the Popular Front governments intended welfare programs and cultural improvement to promote social discipline, class cooperation, productivity, and national progress. Miners and workers in the emergent textile and metallurgical industries rendered the Front's nationalism a radical and anticapitalist ideology, and justified their strikes and demands for nationalization of mines and factories by invoking the standards of civilization and progress broadcast by both capital and the state, and by staking their claims to citizenship in the Chilean nation and membership among the Chilean people.

Notes

1 Transcripts of these speeches were recorded in reports to the Braden Copper Company's Welfare Department by company spies. See "Informe sobre la concentración llevada a efecto jueves, 26 de septiembre de 1946"; "Informe sobre reunión extraordinaria general, llevada a efecto . . . lunes, 16 de septiembre de 1946"; and "Informe sobre reunión extraordinaria general, llevada a efecto martes, 17 de septiembre de 1946 en el local del Sindicato Industrial Sewell y Minas" in the archive of the Braden Copper Company located in CODELCO-Chile, División El Teniente, hereafter referred to as ABCC.

2 The best history of this period is Paul Drake, *Socialism and Populism in Chile, 1932–1952* (Urbana: University of Illinois Press, 1978). For histories of labor under the Popular Front, see Alan Angell, *Politics and the Labour Movement in Chile* (London: Oxford University Press, 1972) and Crisóstomo Pizarro, *La huelga obrera en Chile* (Santiago: Ediciones SUR, 1986). For a history of copper miners' strikes during the 1940s, see Thomas Miller Klubock, *Contested Communities: Class, Gender, and Politics in Chile's El Teniente Copper Mine, 1904–1951* (Durham: Duke University Press, 1998).

3 The populist coalition governments that ruled between 1938 and 1948 were headed by the Radical Party and included, at different times and in different configurations, alliances between the Radical, Socialist, Communist, and Democratic Parties.

4 For important theoretical works on race and race formation, see Howard Omi and Howard Winant, *Racial Formation in the United States from the 1960s to the 1980s* (New York: Routledge, 1986); Stuart Hall, "Gramsci's Relevance for the Study of Race and Ethnicity," *Journal of Communications Inquiry* 10 (1986); Paul Gilroy, *There Ain't No Black in the Union Jack* (Chicago: University of Chicago Press, 1988). Among the numerous works on theoretical and methodological approaches to writing about race in Latin America that I have found helpful, the following have been particularly important to this conceptualization of race: Richard Graham, ed., *The Idea of Race in Latin America, 1870–1940* (Austin: University of Texas Press, 1990); Peter Wade, *Blackness and Race Mixture: The Dynamics of Racial Identity in Colombia* (Baltimore: Johns Hopkins University Press, 1993); Jeffrey L. Gould, *To Die in This Way: Nicaraguan Indians and the Myth of Mestizaje, 1880–1965* (Durham: Duke University Press, 1998); Roger Lancaster, *Life Is Hard: Machismo, Danger, and the Intimacy of Power*

in *Nicaragua* (Berkeley: University of California Press, 1992); Pierre-Michel Fontaine, ed., *Race, Class, and Power in Brazil* (Los Angeles: UCLA, Center for Afro-American Studies, 1985); and Michael Hanchard, ed., *Racial Politics in Contemporary Brazil* (Durham: Duke University Press, 1999).

5 Francisco Encina, *Nuestra inferioridad económica* (Santiago: Editorial Universitaria, 1905), 6.

6 Ibid., 29.

7 Ibid., 86.

8 Ibid., 96.

9 Ibid., 112.

10 Ibid., 110–12, 131, and 139.

11 Nicolás Palacios, *La raza chilena* (Valparaíso: Impr. Litografía Alemana, 1904). For an excellent discussion of Palacios and national identity in Chile, see Patrick Barr Melej, "The Four Rs (Reading, Writing, Arithmetic and Raza): Making an Alternative National-ism in Chile," presented at the annual meeting of the Conference on Latin American History, Seattle, January 1998; and Sandra McGee Deutsch, *Las Derechas: The Extreme Right in Argentina, Brazil, and Chile, 1890–1939* (Stanford: Stanford University Press, 1999).

12 Palacios, *La raza chilena*, 5.

13 Ibid., 7.

14 Gabriel Salazar and Julio Pinto, *Historia contemporánea de Chile II* (Santiago: LOM Edi-ciones, 1999), 79.

15 Julio Kaulen, *Las empresas mineras extranjeras en Chile y la economia nacional* (Santiago: 1916).

16 Santiago Macchiavello Varas, "El problema de la industria del cobre y sus proyecciones económicas y sociales" (Santiago: Universidad de Chile, 1923).

17 On subaltern nationalism, see Florencia Mallon, *Peasant and Nation: The Making of Postcolo-nial Mexico and Peru* (Berkeley: University of California Press, 1995).

18 For a path-breaking history of the labor movement in Tarapacá, see Julio Pinto Vallejos, *Trabajos y rebeldías en la pampa salitrera* (Santiago: Editorial Universidad de Santiago, 1998).

19 Ibid., 76.

20 Ibid., 78.

21 Ibid., 79.

22 Ibid., 131 and 139.

23 Sergio A. González Miranda, "De la solidaridad a la xenophobia: Tarapacá 1907–1911," in *A 90 años de los sucesos de la Escuela Santa María de Iquique* (Santiago: LOM Ediciones, 1998), 95; Deutsch, *Las Derechas*, 17–23. For histories of the northern labor movement, see Hernán Ramírez Necochea, *Historia del movimiento obrero, siglo XIX* (Santiago: Edi-ciones LAR, 1956); Elías Lafertte, *Vida de un comunista* (Santiago: Partido Comunista de Chile, 1961). Lafertte, cofounder of the Partido Obrero Socialista (POS) (Socialist Workers' Party) and leader of the Federación Obrera de Chile (FOCH) (Chilean Workers Federation) and Communist Party whose memoirs describe his experiences of labor conflicts and working-class politics in the nitrate *oficinas*, denounces the "chauvinism" of the *ligas patrióticas*, and celebrates the solidarity of the different ethnic and national groups within the northern working class. Lafertte describes the supporters of the *ligas* as "hordes of barbarians" and argues that "in that epoch in which you traveled without a passport and there were no discriminatory barriers and laws that exist today, Argentines, Bolivians, Peruvians were for us exactly like countrymen, with the same rights and duties. What pampino would discriminate against an Argentine or a Peruvian for their nationality?" (63 and 81).

24 Ricardo A. Latcham, *Chuquicamata: Estado yankee* (Santiago: Editorial Nascimento, 1926),

116. See also Janet L. Finn, *Tracing the Veins: Of Copper, Culture, and Community from Butte to Chuquicamata* (Berkeley: University of California Press, 1998), 90–91.

25 Latcham, *Chuquicamata*, 116.

26 Finn, *Tracing the Veins*, 126 and 139.

27 Chilean labor legislation divided unions between blue-collar workers (*obreros*) and white-collar workers (*empleados*).

28 *El Popular*, 4 and 6 October 1938.

29 Alan Knight explores the issue of the relationship between elite racial ideologies and internal forms of racism in Mexico in "Racism, Revolution, and *Indigenismo*: Mexico, 1910–1940," in Graham, ed., *The Idea of Race in Latin America*.

30 H. Mackenzie Walker to L. E. Grant, 2 May 1923, ABCC; Mine superintendent to District Court Judge Julio Maldonado, 22 August 1915, ABCC.

31 U.S. Department of State General Records, RG 59, 825.00/561, U.S. National Archives, hereafter referred to as USNA.

32 Macchiavello Varas, *El problema de la industria de cobre y sus proyecciones económicas y sociales*, 202.

33 See Klubock, *Contested Communities*.

34 See Herbert Gutman, "Work, Society, and Culture in Industrializing America, 1815–1919," in Herbert Gutman, *Work, Culture, and Society in Industrializing America* (New York: Vintage, 1977).

35 Braden Copper Company, "La Ley Seca en los centros industriales: Sus ventajes vistas en la practica en el mineral de El Teniente" (1921); Braden Copper Company, "El Departamento de Bienestar" (1922), both in ABCC.

36 Stella Joanne Seibert Alphand, "Legislación del trabajo y previsión social en El Teniente" (thesis, Universidad de Chile, 1936), 21.

37 Ibid., 29–30.

38 *El Minero*, second fortnight of August 1931.

39 For histories of the copper industry and miners in the United States, see Jonathan Rosenbaum, *Copper Crucible: How the Arizona Miners' Strike of 1983 Recast Labor-Management Relations in America* (Ithaca: ILR Press, 1995); Barbara Kingsolver, *Holding the Line: The Great Arizona Mine Strike of 1983* (Ithaca: ILR Press, 1989).

40 Interview, Orlando Moraga, Rancagua, 1992.

41 Interview, Círculo Social Sewell, Rancagua, 1996.

42 Interview, Luis Vergara, Rancagua, 1992.

43 José Pezoa Varas, *En el feudo: Impressiones sobre la vida obrera del mineral del Teniente* (Rancagua: Imprenta de "La Semana," 1919).

44 Ibid., 88.

45 Interview, Manuel Ahumada, Rancagua, 1991.

46 Latcham, *Chuquicamata*, 46.

47 Eulogio Gutiérrez, *Chuquicamata: Tierras rojas* (Santiago: Editorial Nascimiento, 1926), 133.

48 *El Popular*, 12 April 1946.

49 Gonzalo Drago, *Cobre: Cuentos mineros* (Santiago: Impresa El Esfuerza), 91.

50 Ibid., 109.

51 Pezoa Varas, *En el feudo*, 53.

52 Drago, *Cobre*, 49.

53 Gutiérrez, *Chuquicamata*, 136–37.

54 Ibid., 138.

55 Drago, *Cobre*, 71.

56 Ibid., 74.
57 Baltazar Castro, *Sewell* (Santiago: Editorial Zig-Zag, 1966).
58 See Castro, *Sewell*, and Drago, *Cobre*.
59 Pezoa Varas, *En el feudo*, 89.
60 Ibid., 89–90.
61 Latcham, *Chuquicamata*, 47.
62 Marcial Figueroa, *Chuquicamata: La tumba del chileno* (Antofogasta: Imprenta Castelleana, 1928), 17.
63 Ibid., 21–22.
64 Ibid., 232–33.
65 Nancy Leys Stepan has demonstrated brilliantly the links between the racial ideology of eugenics and the preoccupation with gender and the regulation of sexuality and reproduction in Latin American nationalist ideologies. Nancy Leys Stepan, *"The Hour of Eugenics": Race, Gender, and Nation in Latin America* (Ithaca: Cornell University Press, 1991).
66 For the case of Mexico and the Mexican Revolution, see Knight, "Racism, Revolution, and *Indigenismo*: Mexico, 1910–1940."
67 See Klubock, *Contested Communities*.
68 Drake, *Socialism and Populism in Chile*; Klubock, *Contested Communities*; Karin A. Rosemblatt, "Gendered Compromises: Political Cultures, Socialist Politics, and the State in Chile, 1920–1950" (Ph.D. diss., University of Wisconsin, Madison, 1996).
69 *La Hora*, 18 July 1938.
70 U.S. Department of State General Records, RG 59, 825.00/1085, USNA.
71 Confederación de Trabajadores de Chile, Memoria del Consejo Directivo Nacional, July 1939; *La Hora*, 18 July 1938.
72 *La Nación*, 18 April 1938.
73 U.S. Department of State General Records, RG 59, 825.00/1097, USNA.
74 Chile, Sesión ordinaria de la Cámara de Diputados, 4 de julio de 1938.
75 Memorandum from Mackenzie Walker to assistant general manager F. E. Turton, 7 November 1939, ABCC.
76 *Despertar Minero*, 6 April 1939.
77 For a discussion of the *chilenidad* campaign, see *Despertar Minero*, 1 August 1941.
78 See Rosemblatt, "Gendered Compromises."
79 Quoted in Barr, "The Four Rs (Reading, Writing, Arithmetic, and Raza)," 9.
80 *Despertar Minero*, 11 May 1939.
81 *Bandera Roja*, 2 sem. mayo 1936.
82 *Músculo*, 3 February 1945.
83 Ibid.
84 *Músculo*, June 1945.
85 *Obrero Textil*, June 1937.
86 *Obrero Textil*, 17 October 1936.
87 Peter Winn, *Weavers of Revolution: The Yarur Workers and Chile's Road to Socialism* (London: Oxford University Press, 1986).
88 *Despertar Minero*, 1 August 1941.
89 *Despertar Minero*, 9 April 1939.
90 *Músculo*, 1940.

Heidi Tinsman

Good Wives, Bad Girls, and Unfaithful Men:
Sexual Negotiation and Labor Struggle in
Chile's Agrarian Reform, 1964–73

▼

On February 14, 1972, Hilda Gutiérrez Sánchez, described in judicial records as an "older housewife" living on a state-managed farm in rural Chile, charged a twenty-five-year-old agricultural worker, Juan Pérez Hernández, of attempting to rape her while she was harvesting beans. She told the court that Juan had passed under the barbed wire separating their places of work and sexually propositioned her while four of his male coworkers watched. She said that although she had replied that she was a married woman, Juan threw her to the ground and began ripping her clothes. Hilda claimed she prevented the rape by screaming, at which point all of the men fled, but not before Juan hit her and menaced, "You're lucky I don't have a knife!"[1] All four of Juan's coworkers testified that Hilda was lying. Despite their contradictory accounts (two men reported that Hilda was not even working in the field that day; two others maintained that, while she had been, they had heard no cries of distress), all of the men, together with Juan's father, defended the accused's innocence on the basis of his honor. One testified to Juan's "shy and peaceful character"; another to the fact that Juan was a "responsible and hard worker, a man without vices"; and still another to Juan being a man who "doesn't [sexually] play around and is incapable of this kind of behavior."[2]

Hilda also defended the veracity of her story on the basis of honor. She stressed her married status and attempts to resist even in the face of personal danger (Juan's threat about what he would do with a knife), and she submitted a statement from a local women's organization testifying to her upstanding character. Marked with the thumbprints and signatures of seventeen of her comembers, the document sternly condemned Juan's depravity and called for his severe punishment in order to protect young girls from future attacks. Finally, the women challenged the integrity of the investigation.

> We the undersigned, wish to leave it clear that Sra. Hilda Gutiérrez Sánchez, who we have known for a long time, whose life is without reproach, who is [an elected leader] in this Mothers Center, and who is an exemplar mother, has never been seen with a man other than her husband. . . . We want to clarify that the drunk Juan Pérez Hernández attempted to rape her . . . and ask that justice be done as we consider [this man] a grave danger to all young girls who have to cut beans on this road or pass by it on the way to school. . . . It is clear that [the Pérez Hernández family] has very bad antecedents and we ask that they be expelled from the [county]. . . . We also have reason to believe that the official in charge of the investigation has been swayed by outside influential parties and ask for a new investigation.[3]

Juan responded with an attack on Hilda's sexuality. While finally admitting that he had crossed over the fence to see Hilda, he insisted this had been at her request, that she had asked him if he had a girlfriend and insinuated that she wanted to have sex, and that she had challenged his manliness when he honorably declined: "When I refused, she insulted me for being unmanly and threatened me. I would not do such a thing because I am very Catholic; I'm a friend of her husband's; and she is not desirable."[4]

This case began on Valentine's Day 1972, two years after Salvador Allende Gossens was elected president and began taking Chile down what he hoped would be a peaceful road to socialism. An Agrarian Reform, begun in 1964 by a reformist Christian Democratic government and accelerated by Allende's Popular Unity (Unidad Popular, UP) coalition after 1970, had already expropriated nearly half of Chile's agricultural land and reorganized it into peasant cooperatives and state-managed units like the one where Hilda Gutiérrez and Juan Pérez lived in the Aconcagua Valley, one of Chile's oldest and most productive agricultural regions.[5] The Agrarian Reform had also initiated the massive political mobilization of the rural poor. Almost a quarter million campesino men (most likely including Juan) would join unions by the end of 1972, and tens of thousands of youth and women (including Hilda) were being incorporated into neighborhood organizations.[6] Literacy classes, housewives' committees, expanded housing and health-care services, and Chile's first sex education and family planning programs were all rapidly reshaping the contours of campesino life. Ideas about masculinity and femininity, including ideas about what constituted proper male and female behavior, were in flux as the state and the rural labor movement officially encouraged all campesino men and women to become the politically conscious and organized creators of a new society. Fights about sex had long been important to the way rural men and women negotiated their obligations and entitlements.[7] But during the Agrarian Reform, rural poor people in Aconcagua and elsewhere in rural Chile embraced new sexual expectations and fought about sex in ways that differed from the pre-1964 world of great haciendas and a semi-peon labor system. This signaled how the Agrarian Reform was transforming campesino sexuality, as well as how rural men and women were negotiating the process of political mobilization in sexual ways.

Between 1964 and 1973, married campesina women began to elaborate upon a longstanding female responsibility for the family in order to more closely tie concepts of female respectability to ideals of modern domesticity, and they increasingly objected to what they saw as men's expanded sense of sexual license. Campesino men's concept of masculine worthiness came to straddle two ideals: on one hand, the paternal figure of a responsible head of household, and on the other, the sexually assertive and politically militant comrade whose first loyalty was solidarity with other men. Gendered responses were also generational; the Agrarian Reform had quite different implications for unmarried adolescent girls.[8] After 1964, social reformers and political activists promoted "youth" as a distinct category of cultural experience and social mobilization, encouraging young people to think of themselves as having interests and needs independent from those of their parents and the household. Young women increasingly defied parental control over their sexuality and justified heterosexual encounters on grounds other than the desire to marry.[9] This, in turn, generated alarm among campesino mothers. As the Agrarian Reform accelerated and became more volatile after Allende's election, the multiple gender ideals increasingly clashed. As rumors spread about impending civil war, married campesina women, in particular, increasingly understood the escalating class conflict in terms of a deterioration in sexual responsibility.

New conflicts over sex were apparent in the rape case involving Hilda Gutiérrez and Juan Pérez. In the Aconcagua district of San Felipe where it was filed, the case was highly exceptional.[10] The majority of rape cases that ended up in court in the late 1950s through the early 1970s involved very young women, often prepubescent girls. Determining the veracity of rape charges usually relied on evidence of a girl's prior virginity, sexual ignorance, and/or mental incapacity.[11] Hilda was older, married, a mother, and perfectly sane. Yet she felt strongly enough about the matter to bring Juan to court, and gambled that she might convince the judge to rule in her favor on a different criterion. Significantly, the statement from the mothers center urged the court to recognize and vindicate an older woman's honor in order to spare future dishonor to young girls. In a twist that departed from traditional markers of female virtue in rape cases and revealed a certain generational tension between older and younger women, Hilda's defenders proposed that it was her very status as wife and mother that made her honorable—an implicit contrast to the more sexually suspect predilections of single women and adolescents, whose virtue the mothers center simultaneously claimed would be protected through their action.

The case was also exceptional in that it became a very public affair that appears to have divided the community. It was the only case revealed either in judicial records or in oral histories used for this study that involved an organized response from a women's civic organization, not only invoking women's moral authority to defend a woman's honor, but also questioning the ability of the court to protect it.[12] The reference to "outside influential parties" corrupting the investigation probably pertains to state bureaucrats, labor activists, or political leaders from the Agrarian Reform unit where Juan worked. Hence, the case potentially pitted a housewives' organization against an all-male union, state-managed farm, and/or representatives of the Popular Unity state.

Whatever the missing details, Hilda's case against Juan illustrated the ways in which the Agrarian Reform had reshaped women's and men's self-understandings and differently positioned them within a process of dramatic social transformation. It also critically underscored how gendered expectations and grievances were understood in terms of sexual conflict. In their testimonies, both Hilda and Juan mobilized the official gender ideals that had been promoted by the Agrarian Reform since 1964, and especially after 1970. Hilda presented herself as an upstanding wife and mother, but added evidence of her work in seasonal harvests as a bean-cutter and stressed her political activism and leadership within the mothers center. Juan's defense was built on arguments that he was an honest and hardworking laborer who respected, and was respected by, other men of his state-managed farm or union. Juan attacked Hilda's claim to virtuous female character by maintaining that it was Hilda, not he, who had been sexually irresponsible and aggressive. Invoking double meanings of manliness, he suggested that while he had been manly (righteous) enough to decline Hilda's advances (out of loyalty to the sexual claims of Hilda's husband, his friend), he would have been manly (virile) enough to comply with the proposition were it not for his standards of sexual taste (Hilda was not desirable). Women flatly denounced this masculine posturing. Through the collective voice of the mothers center, they affirmed Hilda's honor and condemned Juan's sexual license (as well as his overindulgence in alcohol) as dangerous enough to merit his expulsion from the community.

Gender Mutualism, Youth Outreach, and Social Mobilization

Between 1964 and 1973 both the Christian Democratic and the Popular Unity governments defined cooperative marriages between hardworking, responsible male breadwinners and domestically able female helpmates as fundamental to building a new rural society.[13] Both also addressed rural adolescents (male and female) as an independent constituency whose education and development were crucial to having strong families and communities in the future. Although similar domestic models had been officially encouraged among the urban and industrial working classes throughout the twentieth century, it was only after 1964 that they were extended by the state on a mass scale to the rural poor.[14] Between 1964 and 1973 the Christian Democrats and the UP redistributed land almost exclusively to married adult men with children based on their status as heads of household.[15] The state ran elaborate technical training programs to prepare men to become stewards of the land, and labor activists swiftly began organizing men into unions. Adult campesina women gained access to land only through husbands and other male family members. With a few exceptions, the Agrarian Reform called upon women to build the new society by becoming modern housewives.[16] Both the Christian Democrats and the UP sponsored organizations like the mothers center to which Hilda belonged, which offered craft and sewing projects and instructed women on how to frugally manage household budgets and serve balanced meals to children.[17] Meanwhile, male and female adolescents were offered educational and social opportunities distinct from those of their parents. Both the Christian Democratic and UP governments, together with political parties and Catholic organizations, established youth clubs and youth training seminars to prepare young people for future productive roles and to mobilize them as a political force distinct from adults.[18]

The policy of giving land to men and promoting domestic partnership built upon existing gender divisions of labor in latifundia society. By 1955 men already comprised 94 percent of all permanent workers on haciendas, and the vast majority of campesina women survived within male-headed families.[19] But the Agrarian Reform substantially transformed the meaning of "agricultural worker" and the possibilities of campesino households. In the 1950s, hacienda workers lived in the abject poverty and extensive servitude of Chile's inquilinaje system, in which more than 80 percent of irrigated land was controlled by less than 10 percent of the population, and semi-peons owed labor on haciendas in return for the use of subsistence plots.[20] Most sectors of Chilean society regarded all campesinos as *inquilinos* and saw them as backward and racially inferior.[21] In contrast, the Agrarian Reform hailed the liberated campesino man as the key to modernizing Chilean agriculture and celebrated new codes of masculine honor based on political militancy, productive independence, and familial responsibility. Both Catholics and Marxists spoke of the Agrarian Reform as a process of turning campesino "children" into "real men" and of making each man his own *patrón*. The rural labor movement gave campesino men a powerful political voice at the national level and urged them to be activist citizens by carrying out strikes and land occupations. Even for men not belonging to Agrarian Reform production units, extensive labor guarantees passed in 1967 and a 600 percent raise in real wages during the decade made male breadwinning a reality in ways it never before had been.[22]

Meanwhile, for adult campesina women, notions of what constituted good and honorable work increasingly emphasized the domestic. Prior to the Agrarian Reform, campesina women cared for children and prepared meals, but they also raised livestock, farmed subsistence plots, sold homemade cheeses, took in outside laundry, and earned wages during harvest seasons and as domestic servants.[23] Although in the large hacienda regions such as the Aconcagua Valley, men's more permanent employment as estate workers was given priority over women's work, both men and women recognized what women did as critical to the household's material survival, and they rarely distinguished between work women did in the house from work done outside it. In contrast, the Agrarian Reform's emphasis on transforming the means of production (defined as the redistribution and cultivation of the large estates) and its focus on men as the primary protagonists in this endeavor forced a definition of what women did as "nonproductive."[24] Between 1964 and 1973 rural women continued to perform almost the exact same types of labor they had in latifundia society, but this work was increasingly referred to as "helping out" or as "home-based," in contrast to men's "breadwinning." Combined with the celebration of women's roles as wives and mothers, "domesticity" and "housewife" emerged as more clear-cut categories for defining women's experience. One mothers center pamphlet described the purpose of assisting campesinas' labor: "The mothers center teaches us how to use available resources in order to create a happy domestic life. . . . we learn to prepare and apply ourselves in the role that corresponds to us as women . . . to help collaborate with [men's] unions, cooperatives, etc."[25]

For adolescent girls, the situation was different. Although they exerted considerable labor on behalf of the household (usually under their mother's supervision), as unmarried daughters most were not directly responsible for fulfilling the new ethos of domestic efficiency.[26] Although they certainly received the message that their future lay in modern homemaking, the Agrarian Reform explicitly encouraged their participation in activities *outside* the campesino household and viewed their paid agricultural work as a positive (if temporary) good. Youth branches of political parties were open to both genders, and although youth training projects were often gender specific (mechanics lessons for boys, handicraft courses for girls), state-sponsored agricultural schools were co-ed, giving small numbers of young women an opportunity to discuss vegetable hybrids and drive tractors alongside young men.[27] In addition, during the Agrarian Reform, young women's paid employment on estates jumped dramatically: whereas in 1964 slightly more than five hundred women earned wages in seasonal agricultural employment in the Aconcagua Valley, by 1975 more than two thousand did.[28] More than 64 percent of such agricultural workers were single, and more than 34 percent under age twenty-five.[29] Although campesina adolescents had worked in multiple capacities in latifundia society, such work usually had been unpaid and on the family's subsistence plot. Access to cash had involved migrating to towns and cities to work as domestics, which accounts for why men significantly outnumbered women in rural Chile throughout the 1940s and 1950s.[30] In contrast, the expanded educational and employment opportunities of the Agrarian Reform encouraged adolescent girls to stay in the countryside and make monetary contributions to their families while living at home.[31]

At the same time that the Agrarian Reform more clearly separated husbands' and wives' responsibilities and distinguished between youths and adults, it emphasized principles of gender harmony and family cooperation. Under both Christian Democratic and Popular Unity leadership, all campesinos were urged to see each other as partners in the joint project of community uplift and class struggle. The rural labor movement promoted the idea that a good wife understood the importance of the Agrarian Reform and supported her husband's struggles.[32] Women were invited to join picket lines and union marches, and praised for providing meals to striking workers.[33] Men were told that a good husband should better esteem these wifely labors. State-run literacy and adult education programs admonished husbands, as a 1968 manual from the state Institute for the Development of Agriculture and Livestock put it, "to respect the vital roles that women play as home managers and educators of children," and to communicate more openly with women "so that wives can appreciate their spouses' daily routines."[34] Meanwhile, male and female adolescents were encouraged (by Christian Democratic and Catholic Church initiatives, in particular) to cheerfully help their parents and to take seriously their educational responsibilities for becoming future citizens.[35]

The celebration of gender and family collaboration built upon long-standing campesino notions of reciprocity within the household, but much more explicitly implied limits to men's unilateral action without female consent and suggested that adolescents did not always have the same interests as their parents. Prior to the Agrarian Reform, married women had exercised authority in decisions regarding children and subsistence gardens, but they did not routinely handle family finances. Men usually had ultimate say about the allocation of family labor (including their wives'), frequently without consulting their spouses.[36] The Agrarian Reform's gender mutualism asked men to confer with women and to obtain their approval, while the idea that women should manage the household budget theoretically gave women control of men's wages. Gender mutualism also provided unprecedented institutional spaces for women. If union membership was reserved for men, the all-female mothers centers provided campesinas with a state-sponsored, nationally recognized structure that represented women's interests as housewives at public and political events.[37] They promoted the idea that a "good" woman was involved in civic life, and in exceptional cases (such as Hilda's charges against Juan), mothers centers provided vehicles for women to collectively defend women's honor and challenge men's behavior.

For rural adolescents, both male and female, the popular mobilization of the 1960s and 1970s created unprecedented social opportunities outside the direct parental gaze. In the 1950s, girls and boys usually had started working by age ten and had labored closely with adult family members, either around the household or on haciendas. Children's interests had been firmly subordinated to parents' decisions about what benefited the household. During the Agrarian Reform, increased education programs and greatly improved living standards enabled young people to stay in school well into their early teens, providing youths space both *away* from parents and *among* their peers.[38] The youth branches of political parties elected separate leaderships and stressed the importance of young people mobilizing around issues specific to their generational needs, including higher education scholarships and rural cultural resources. Under Allende, the tone of youth organizing became explicitly militant. The Left began addressing adolescents more in their capacity as future workers than as future family members, and increasingly espoused the idea that a class-conscious youth could have the most revolutionary potential.[39] The extent to which young campesina women participated in political party youth branches on par with their male counterparts is unclear. Among rural adults, such activities were overwhelmingly male. However, adult men were usually recruited into political parties through their unions (which were 95 percent male), while political activities for young people were centered around school and cultural events that were more gender inclusive.

The ethos of gender mutualism and youth outreach was especially promising for campesina women in matters of sex. In 1964, the Christian Democrats initiated Chile's first national Family Planning Program with heavy financial backing from the Rockefeller Foundation and U.S. Alliance for Progress.[40] Rural clinics were built and hospitals expanded to provide women with gynecological, prenatal, and postpartum care. Family Planning seminars offered basic instruction on human anatomy and contraceptive use, and stressed men's and women's mutual responsibilities as parents. Cartoon pamphlets from the National Health Service and the Chilean affiliate of Planned Parenthood warned campesino men against the foolishness of equating virility with the number of children one fathered, and argued that modern men had manageably sized families that they could adequately support.[41] Campesina women were urged to become more knowledgeable about their bodies and to see female reproductive cycles as natural and healthy. They were also encouraged to collaborate with men in deciding whether smaller families would be achieved by using contraceptives or forgoing sexual intercourse during ovulation.

Under the UP, Family Planning programs went still further. The Ministry of Education began developing a curriculum to teach sex education in the school system so that "Chilean children and adolescents [could] enter into a society in which sex is a natural and happy fact situated in a cultural context free of falsehoods, superstition, fear, and commercial exploitation."[42] Abortion was permitted on a limited scale in state hospitals (although it remained illegal), and the minister of health advocated sex education for adults that would "help [couples] secure the right to separate reproduction from the exercise of their sexual lives."[43] A vocal, but frequently marginalized, feminist camp within the UP linked all of these matters to women's emancipation and revolutionary success. In a pamphlet on women originally published by the UP but not distributed, Communist feminist Virginia Vidál labeled sexual violence, male impotence, and female frigidity as national political problems and boldly argued that women's ability to decouple sexuality, motherhood, and marriage was crucial to building a socialist society: "Not all women want to be mothers, not all women want to join their life with that of a man. Many single mothers are happy, but simply need better [economic] circumstances. . . . They are also entitled to [sexual] happiness."[44]

All of this marked a major change from the past. In oral histories conducted for this study as well as for others, campesina women who grew up in the 1940s and 1950s recalled, almost without exception, that they knew little or nothing about menstruation, sexual intercourse, pregnancy, or childbirth until the very moment that such events occurred in their lives.[45] Women bore "all the children that God sent" (on average, seven), and Chile's rates of maternal death, infant mortality, and abortion were among the highest in the hemisphere.[46] In Aconcagua, 80 percent of rural women eventually married, and another 6 percent lived with permanent partners.[47] Although they saw sex as a "natural" part of marriage and usually viewed children as a blessing and positive sign of feminine fertility, women maintained that they had little control over the terms and frequency of sex with husbands, and that they often associated it with men's violence and inebriation. In Aconcagua, rural women married later than their urban counterparts (on average, at age twenty-four, as opposed to the Santiago average age of twenty-two).[48] Campesinos placed a minimal importance on women's premarital virginity, and pregnancy was frequently a precursor to a couple becoming betrothed. At the same time, adolescent girls and young adult women were expected to marry men with whom they became sexually active because of the high likelihood of a pregnancy. Before such an event, campesino parents attempted to heavily restrict daughters' interactions with men, and once married, wives were expected to be sexually loyal to husbands.

For men, having a wife and many children was a marker of maturity, good fortune, and sexual prowess. But men also defended their right or need for extramarital liaisons, and among men, such activities usually signified manliness. For the almost one-third of male agricultural workers who regularly migrated in search of work, it was not uncommon to have multiple lovers and families throughout the country. Most of these men never married.[49] In the case of permanent hacienda residents, men more jealously guarded their exclusive access to one wife by attempting to restrict women's contact with other men. This was never entirely possible given poor men's labor obligations away from home, the need for women of all ages to work as domestic servants and field hands, and the sexual license (often violent) assumed by a supervisor or patrón. However, the principle of men's right to police women's mobility for sexual reasons was widely accepted, and men often opposed wives' work away from subsistence plots and family residences precisely for this reason.

Family Planning programs were intended to promote less-coercive and -unequal sexual expectations. They defined limiting family size and joint decision making by husbands and wives as "modern" behavior and equated modernity with what was desirable and respectable. Although most Family Planning projects took for granted and reinforced existing principles of female sexual fidelity to husbands, they strongly suggested that men should show *more* fidelity (more respect) to wives, even if this amounted to less than perfect sexual loyalty. They also insisted that adult women should have a say on how and when a couple had sex, and that women, rather than men, should be in charge of enforcing codes of female sexual responsibility.

After the election of Allende, there was significant public discussion about separating issues of sexual fulfillment (especially women's) from procreation. Despite the fact that Virginia Vidál's manifesto on female desire was ultimately quashed as too radical, and that the feminist call to recognize single women's needs never translated into an official endorsement of adolescent girls' access to birth control, these issues were being raised in ways they never before had been. Sex education and expanded gynecological services offered women of all ages and marital statuses more knowledge about their bodies. The de facto permission of abortion encouraged safer and more available pregnancy terminations for single and younger women to whom contraceptives were less available.[50] In addition, the UP moved to abolish distinctions between "illegitimate" children (whose fathers were not married to the mother) and "legitimate" children (whose fathers were married to the mother). Although the government argued that its intent was to "end unfair discrimination against innocent children" (a quarter of all children in the Aconcagua district of San Felipe were born out of wedlock), it simultaneously implied eliminating the legal stigma against the mothers, roughly a third of whom were single adolescents.[51]

Beyond the impact of official efforts to prevent and/or reevaluate adolescent motherhood, young campesinas were increasingly exposed to, and part of, a distinct youth culture that celebrated a generation-specific and independent heterosexuality. Local radio programs and national Catholic broadcasts humorously advised adolescents about dating.[52] Although these shows firmly warned against premarital sex, they looked approvingly on co-ed gatherings as a healthy way for adolescents to emotionally mature and eventually find permanent mates.[53] A favored site for such activity was the youth dance, sponsored by neighborhood clubs and schools, where the traditional campesino rhythms of *cueca* and *ranchero* were displaced by the "international music" of the Beatles and *nueva canción* of Chilean groups like Los Jaivas and Quillapamú.[54] By the late 1960s, televisions were increasingly acquired by Agrarian Reform production units and agricultural schools. They flashed images of young men with long hair and young women in miniskirts, replayed excerpts of popular music concerts in Santiago stadiums, and discussed the activities and political intrigues of university student governments. Such urban accents were made even more immediate by the thousands of university students who descended upon the countryside each summer to volunteer. These youth brigades were co-ed and, although the volunteers usually performed gender-specific work (young men built houses, young women taught literacy), male and female volunteers were regularly seen gathering around campfires to discuss political strategies and share homemade wine. Rumors abounded that they shared the same tents for sleeping quarters.[55]

Although many urban concerns had only indirect relation to campesina life, rural youths were increasingly eager and able to follow the issues and trends of their counterparts in the city and elsewhere. A 1971 survey conducted by the Catholic Rural Education Institute among 1,200 rural young people in the Central Valley found that 70 percent of adolescents listened to urban radio programs or viewed television on a regular basis, and they had a "great interest in accessing culture and information," especially on national political news and international music.[56] The ability of campesino adolescents to participate in new forms of sociability was further facilitated by increased employment opportunities and higher wages, which put more spending money into the pockets of young men, and perhaps a minimal amount into those of young women. All together, the Agrarian Reform's promotion of "youth" as a category, and the cultural image of independence attached to it, had real appeal to rural young people. It fostered a generational sense that their needs and interests were distinct from those of their parents and connected to a wider world. It also suggested that young people could and should create social spaces autonomous from adult control.

The Agrarian Reform's promotion of gender mutualism among married adults was similarly popular among campesina women. Married women welcomed the public validation of their child-rearing and household labors, while the directive for husbands to collaborate with and respect their wives gave new teeth to older notions of reciprocity. Men's dramatically increased wages, combined with the promise of access to land, improved the entire family's standard of living and eased women's responsibility for making ends meet. Importantly, there was no widespread opposition by campesina women to the Agrarian Reform's redistribution of land to male "heads of household." Most campesina women already lived in male-dominated families in which subsistence plots were entrusted to men, even if women's agricultural labor was critical to the household's survival. What was new and welcome was not the primacy of men's economic activities, but the expectation (and increased reality) that men would support their dependents in ways that diminished women's burdens and allowed them to dedicate themselves to the now more ennobled office of wife and mother.

Gender and Generational Struggles

But husbands and wives, parents and adolescents, often disagreed sharply over what constituted good behavior. Adult rural men were enthusiastic about being taken seriously as economic producers, but whereas wives interpreted the ethos of gender mutualism to mean that husbands should give them more respect and autonomy, men often interpreted it to mean that women should support and obey their husbands.[57] This rift was aggravated by the Agrarian Reform's celebration of a brand of campesino manhood that emphasized male agency, militancy, and being one's own boss. Men's political maturity was measured both by an ability to collectively stand up to employers and to take charge of one's own household. As an organizer-training manual explained, campesino men needed to act on the consciousness that they could give their own orders rather than meekly follow those of others: "We are subjects conscious of our worth, dedicated to fighting to build a more humane world, rationally and through critical consciousness. Otherwise we are domesticated, permitting others to decide things for us, always at the orders of others."[58]

Although the word "domesticate" (domesticar) implied a broad range of relationships of containment and subordination, it was most closely associated with women and, in particular, with female domestic servants. Women and servants naturally took orders from others. The manual juxtaposed political consciousness and masculine autonomy with femininity and female spaces. In contrast to women and the domestic realm, unions allowed men to decide things for themselves, placing them in the world of action. Indeed, to be truly manly, a man exercised his authority as household head by giving commands at home. In some ways, this encouraged men to continue exercising tight (or even tighter) controls over women as displays of a restored masculinity. Men were particularly wary of the state's and the labor movement's education and organizing efforts for women. In oral histories, both men and women recalled that husbands often objected to their wives' participation in mothers centers because it distracted from their responsibilities at home. They also claimed that men frequently forbade wives to attend literacy programs or union marches because they saw politics as inappropriate for women and because such activities would presumably allow women contact with men outside their family.[59] Some women bitterly recalled their lives as becoming more isolated after the Agrarian

Reform because men's much higher wages curbed the need for married women to take seasonal agricultural jobs or domestic service positions.[60]

For adolescent girls, things were different. As young women stayed in school longer and had increased opportunities to join youth organizations, they had the opportunity to spend *more* time away from home and parental supervision. In oral histories, women who had been adolescents and those who had been parents during the Agrarian Reform recalled fights between mothers and daughters, and less frequently between fathers and daughters, over the extent of young women's extra-household activities. Adolescent girls were regularly obliged by parents to quit school early, although they still attended three to four years more than they had in the 1950s. And although parents welcomed youth education programs, they were far more likely to send a son than a daughter to the new agricultural schools, arguing that a daughter's labor was needed around the household and that technical training was more important to a boy's future than to a girl's. Attending youth dances or political clubs was sometimes forbidden outright, and where it was allowed, girls were often accompanied by brothers.

Campesino women and men also disagreed over the meaning of campesino economic obligations within the family. Married men did not readily hand wages over to wives despite the fact that women were being told that they should manage household budgets. Men saw their much-improved incomes as a reward for their labor and political work, and understood control over money to be part of being a household head. However, as wages replaced payments in-kind, women were increasingly dependent on cash to provide meals and clothing. Men's decisions over *how much* money women needed and *who* would make cash purchases clashed with women's growing sense of entitlement to men's earning power. As Anita Hernández, a campesina from the village of Santa María, explained in an oral history: "I thought, 'Well, he's making more money now so he should give me more for the children.' Of course, he always said that *he* would buy what we needed, but he never did and he would leave me with only a few bits of change to buy bread . . . it was difficult to confront him, you see, he was hard . . . it made me so mad!"[61] In some cases, women abandoned all hope of partnership with their spouses. Sonia Araya, a campesina from Los Andes, became so frustrated that she asked her husband's *patrón* to give her a portion of his wages each month, "seeing that my own husband couldn't be counted on."[62]

Adult women also fought about money with their daughters. Campesina mothers presumed the right to direct and benefit from the labor of daughters. As the Agrarian Reform began providing young women with better-paid and more-numerous agricultural jobs, daughters had new access to cash while living in the parental household. Almost all daughters turned their wages over to their parents, usually to their mother, but there was always the chance that a daughter might reserve a small sum for herself. This was enabled by new labor legislation that phased out payments in-kind and mandated that each worker receive his or her own cash wage personally.[63] In oral histories, fights between mothers and daughters over a daughter's wages were far less common than those over adult men's wages, but when they occurred, they usually revolved around not whether the daughter's keeping a few pesos for herself would destitute the family, but rather the girl's *entitlement* to take such action.[64] Daughters spending money on themselves even for small things like a hair comb symbolized their ability to act independently of maternal authority as well as outside the principle of female sacrifice for the family.[65]

Encompassing and permeating all of these conflicts over what constituted "good" male and female behavior were fights about sex. Chile's Family Planning programs had mixed results, and women had difficulty getting men to cooperate sexually. Between 1965 and 1975, reported rates of infant mortality in Aconcagua plunged 39 percent, and those on mater-nal death declined 35 percent; yet by 1973 only 6 percent of rural women reportedly used clinic-dispensed contraceptives.[66] In oral histories, most rural women said they had no idea that sex education programs were available; those who did complained that they rarely had the time or means to attend.[67] Most important, both campesina women and health-care of-ficials reported widespread male opposition to Family Planning.[68] Men feared that women's greater access to sexual knowledge and birth control would allow wives to be sexually promiscuous and/or make women sterile. Even when men shared women's desire for smaller families, they saw Family Planning as unacceptably threatening connections between manli-ness, procreation, and a husband's sexual authority over his wife. As one campesino man succinctly explained in an oral history, "Women [were] supposed to have] the children that God sent and to take care of them. If not, why have a wife?"[69] Partly in response to this attitude, Family Planning programs required married women to have the written consent of hus-bands to use contraceptives, and with the exception of some minimal attention to single women under the UP, Family Planning almost exclu-sively targeted married couples.[70] This marked a meaningful break with the pre-Agrarian-Reform world, wherein women of all marital statuses man-ufactured homemade (and largely ineffective) contraceptive remedies. Al-though the Family Planning programs enormously advanced the ability to impede pregnancies, they gave men control over a practice previously dom-inated by women, and defined legitimate contraception as that used within marriage.

But women challenged men's notions about sexual obligation and entitlement within marriage. Rural fertility rates statistically declined by a remarkable 35 percent between 1964 and 1975—a change which, given that medical contraceptives were not widely used, suggests that women were able to enlist men's cooperation in avoiding pregnancy.[71] Women invoked principles of gender mutualism to place limits on conjugal sex and to demand respectful reciprocity from men. Somewhat paradoxically, the extent of this challenge is evident in the many domestic quarrels that ended in a man using violence against his wife. Between 1964 and 1973, women in the Aconcagua department of San Felipe filed an annual average of twenty charges of physical bodily harm (lesiones) against husbands and permanent partners, and almost three-quarters involved poor and campesina women.[72] In oral histories, both men and women recalled wife beating as a regular dynamic in rural marriages during the 1960s. As I have argued elsewhere, wife-beating cases during the 1960s and early 1970s overwhelmingly involved men's insistence that wives, by definition, owed them exclusive sexual and domestic services on demand.[73] Men physically disciplined wives for supposed flirtations with other men, for withholding or being unable to have sex, and for failing to complete specific household duties. Women, on the other hand, often claimed they had the right to deny men certain wifely obligations because men had failed to fulfill their roles as breadwinners and respectful husbands.

Typical of these cases was Eugenia Puebla who, in October 1969, filed charges against her husband, Onofre Poza, an agricultural worker, for splitting her lip open because his lunch was not ready when he came home at noon and because she refused to have sex with him.[74] Eugenia testified that she purposely had not prepared her husband's lunch because that morning "he [had] left [her] at home with all the work [and] had come home drunk."[75] She maintained that Onofre became enraged about the lunch and "grabbed [her] by the shoulders so that [she would] sleep with him." Eugenia told the judge that when she resisted, her husband started "beating and kicking her."[76] Onofre's testimony was quite different. While admitting that he hit his wife, he said nothing (either in defense or in denial) about trying to sexually force himself on Eugenia. Instead, he maintained that his wife also had been physically violent to him, that she was responsible for her own injuries, and that he had actually received his lunch after all: "My wife served me lunch and it was cold. . . . I complained and she screamed [at me]. This made me mad so I gave her a little slap on the face. She then took a jar and threw it at my head. Then she ran into the street and fell down, which is why her face is like it is."[77]

Prior to the Agrarian Reform, men had also beaten their wives for failing to serve meals and refusing to have sex. What is interesting about cases of wife beating from the late 1960s and early 1970s is that women more explicitly referenced "wifely obligations" (whether it be sex or dinner) as something that they owed on the condition that their husbands fulfilled their roles as good spouses. Eugenia intentionally denied her husband his lunch (or served him a cold one) because, in her opinion, Onofre had failed to properly work that morning and because he had arrived drunk. She insisted that there were limits to her sexual obligation to her husband, and that she had the right to refuse angry and drunken advances. It is not that, prior to the Agrarian Reform, campesina women didn't expect things from husbands or set limits. Notions of unequal but reciprocal rights and obligations—what Steve Stern has called patriarchal pacts—were central to rural marriages in latifundia society.[78] But the official promotion of gender mutualism and the much trumpeted ideal of campesino men becoming able and responsible heads of household more sharply defined marriage arrangements and gave women reason to demand more-cooperative behavior from men. Significantly, Onofre did not defend his actions, as was common in the 1950s, as an open-ended marital right to physically discipline his wife.[79] Rather, he implied that he had acted *responsibly* as a husband (he had given her a little slap when she screamed at him) and blamed his wife's own failure to exercise similar restraint (her recourse to jar throwing and hysterics) for the resulting bloody lip.

Some women went so far as to interpret gender mutualism to mean that they were entitled to break off relationships and pursue new ones when a partner failed to uphold his end of the bargain. In 1970, Sonia Bruna told the court that her common-law husband, José Muñoz, an agricultural worker, had beaten her in the face after she "decided [that she] wanted nothing more to do with him and was seeking other company."[80] José admitted to his actions but defended them on grounds of his marital right to castigate his partner for infidelity. As he stated in his testimony, "We were making a married life together and I surprised her talking with another man. I asked her for an explanation, and since I had already pardoned her for a similar situation, I hit her in the face."[81]

Sonia's boldness reflected the particular assertiveness of the small proportion of campesina women (only 6 percent) who cohabitated with their partners as opposed to legally marrying them. Common-law wives were far more likely than official wives to bring judicial charges against men, both because judges had little power to remove a legally married man from his house and because common-law wives insisted that they were not permanently bound to the men with whom they lived.[82] Sonia deemed José to be an incompetent husband (for reasons not apparent in her testimony) and attempted to leave her spouse rather than continue enduring his unacceptable behavior. Whether or not Sonia was actually seeking the sexual company of the man with whom José caught her talking, she clearly felt she had a right to do so. She did not see herself as being obliged to honor wifely duties (including sexual loyalty) under any and all circumstances, and she saw it as her prerogative, not José's, to determine when affection and loyalty would be transferred to another man.

Interestingly, some of the rawest tensions between campesino men and women occurred not over women's sexual fidelity, but over men's. If men demanded sexual faithfulness from wives, they jealously guarded their own sexual license outside marriage. Women's objections to men's liaisons were one of the most common causes for fights that ended in wife beating. Prior to the Agrarian Reform, women's opposition to husbands' extramarital relationships had provoked conjugal fights, but during the 1960s and early 1970s, women's suspicion of such activity and their anxiety about it grew substantially. In the available judicial cases of wife beating filed in San Felipe between 1968 and 1973, almost a third involved women's accusations of spousal infidelity.[83] Similarly, in oral histories conducted for this study and several others, memories of male abandonment and sexual betrayal figure centrally in women's narratives; even many men remembered the Agrarian Reform as a time of considerable strain on campesino marriages.

Women had reason to worry. The rural labor movement approved of men's sexual prowess as an integral part of worker militancy and provided men with more opportunities to interact with women other than their wives. In oral histories, men recalled the all-male drinking sessions that followed union meetings as much as a time for sharing jokes and fantasies about women as for discussing labor politics.[84] Such competitive banter served to confirm men's common membership in a fraternity that excluded women and to emphasize the link between men's heterosexual accomplishments and masculine agency. When labor confederations sponsored weekend training sessions for campesinos in Santiago, they often provided entertainment featuring all-female dance troupes. When union activities involved acts of solidarity with other unions, men traveled to other countries where they lodged in another señora's home and enjoyed the host region's modest festivities of drinking and dancing.[85]

Interactions with women ranged from jocular flirting to full affairs and the creation of second families. The rural labor press devoted special comic pages to cartoons of men seducing voluptuous, often half-naked women, or of men who were henpecked or denied sex by their wives.[86] Such jokes revealed a certain misogynist anxiety about female sexuality and men's ability to control it, while encouraging the idea that male sexual access to, and control of, women was inherent to union manhood. In one oral history, a former union president recalled that many men discovered that they not only had increased opportunities to pursue female company, but that their status as "union men" actually heightened their sexual cachet in some women's eyes: "[During the Agrarian Reform], a lot of men took advantage of being out of the house to meet women and to be with them. . . . There were so many women! And they liked you a lot for being a leader, for having pride. Men found this very exciting. It made them feel that they could go around getting lots of women."[87]

Paradoxically, if extramarital sex was an acceptable, and sometimes celebrated, component of Agrarian Reform union manhood, it violated ideals of gender mutualism that the Agrarian Reform (including the rural labor movement) was simultaneously promoting to women—namely, the principle of husbands respecting wives and providing for families.[88] This ideal was increasingly important to women's survival. As the Agrarian Reform reinforced women's material dependence on men by excluding them from land redistribution, it made women's ability to benefit from the Reform contingent on an alliance with a participating male. Added to this was women's need for cash and men's reticence to part with "their" money. The expansion of paid agricultural employment for women afforded only minor relief. Such jobs were seasonal, lasting only a few months, and although well compensated, they rarely paid enough to allow women to live independently from men.

If married women and men clashed over the meaning of sexual obligations and entitlements within marriage, they jointly came into conflict with adolescent children, particularly daughters, over the ways that the emerging ethos of youth independence and heterosexual socializing undercut parental authority. The expanded social opportunities for youth clashed with adult expectations about hierarchy in the family. In oral histories, men and women who were adult parents during the Agrarian Reform complained that their adolescent sons and daughters attended functions without parental permission and violated curfews. Incredulous parents were told that school had ended late, that the bus had broken down, or that their children had passed by to visit relatives. Although, in principle, most parents welcomed new youth education projects as a way for children to acquire skills and technical knowledge, they appeared more willing to send male children than female. More often than not, this discrepancy was enforced by campesina mothers who insisted that their daughters' labor was needed at home and who frowned on the heterosexual character of youth activities as morally dangerous. Echoing husbands' rationale for forbidding wives' participation in mothers centers and unions, such mothers argued that their daughters' place was "in the house" and that "politics was for men."[89] Given the importance of adolescent girls' labor to the household, daughters' prolonged absences from home would have been a strain for adult women. But perhaps even more important, girls' extra-household activities challenged mothers' sense of authority over daughters (always greater than that over adolescent sons) and, in particular, infringed on their ability to monitor a daughter's sexuality.

Not coincidentally, one of the most literal ways in which daughters challenged parental (and, in particular, maternal) authority was by running away from home. Between 1960 and 1973, rural parents in the Aconcagua district of San Felipe filed an average of eighteen cases each year against daughters or their male partners for "abandoning the home."[90] Although these cases represent only a tiny fraction of parental and adolescent inter-actions, they are exceptional more for the fact that they ended up in court than for the generational tensions they reveal—tensions that were widely experienced, even if on less polarized or publicly acknowledged levels. Home abandonment cases overwhelmingly involved situations in which adolescent girls ran away from home to live with male partners. Campe-sino parents filed charges either against their daughter for "abandoning home" or against her male partner for "inducing abandonment." In the vast majority of cases (some 70 percent) it was adult women, usually moth-ers, who initiated the proceedings.[91] Mothers usually requested that the judge punish the male partner and force their daughter to return home; occasionally they demanded that the court compel the couple to marry.

Between 1960 and the early 1970s, changes in circumstances under which young women fled their homes and in the justification they gave in court reveal shifts in how adolescent women negotiated parental authority. In the late 1950s through the mid-1960s, most home abandonment cases resulted from young women's efforts to override parental opposition to a marriage: adolescent girls ran away from home with men to whom their mothers, in particular, objected. In court, the girls went to elaborate lengths to stress that these men were their fiancés (*novios*), that their rela-tionship had already become sexual, and that they intended to marry. Prov-ing that a relationship had become sexual—and, therefore, that there was a likelihood that the young woman would become pregnant—usually per-suaded the judge and the young woman's mother that the optimal situation was for the couple to get married.[92] In most cases, young women also testified to the considerable physical and emotional abuse that they had suffered in the parental household above and beyond being forbidden to see or marry their partners. Crucially, however, no matter how extensive the level of parental abuse, *only* in cases where a daughter could establish the sexual nature of her relationship (and the most convincing way was by being pregnant) *and* her intent to marry did the girl succeed in preventing the court from sending her back to her parents.[93]

In contrast, by the late 1960s and early 1970s, a number of home abandonment cases involved girls who *temporarily* ran away from home for reasons of escape or leisure. Strikingly, in court these young women testified that they had no intention of marrying the men with whom they fled or of making such flight permanent. Typical of these instances was seventeen-year-old Luisa Fernández, who ran away from home in September 1972 with her girlfriend, Susana Guerra, also seventeen, and their boyfriends (*pololos*) to Valparaíso.[94] Luisa's mother accused the boyfriends of abducting the girls in order to have sex with them and otherwise "have a good time." Both Luisa and Susana insisted that they had run away from home because their parents beat them and forbade them to go out with friends. They testified that while they had smoked marijuana on two occasions, they had never had sex with their boyfriends and had not planned to remain in Valparaíso past the end of the month. Similarly, in June 1973, the mother of seventeen-year-old Olivia Contreras filed charges against her daughter for running away to live with her boyfriend, Nicanór Urgueta, on an Agrarian Reform production unit.[95] The mother requested that the judge either force the couple to marry or demand Olivia's return. Five days later, Olivia returned home, stating that she had gone with Nicanór just for a party and that although she had had sex with her friend, she did not have a relationship with him. Olivia's mother agreed to drop her legal request that the couple get married when it was determined that Olivia was not pregnant.

In both cases, and others like them, adolescent girls asserted a right to escape their parental homes for short-term periods of leisure and casual sexual-romantic liaisons with men. Their mothers objected that such action placed their daughters in "moral danger" (*peligro moral*) and insisted on their right as parents to prohibit sexual activity not directed toward the object of marriage. The young women's actions marked a significant challenge to contemporary mother/daughter relationships as well as to popular perceptions of the link between female sexuality and male authority. In most home abandonment cases of the early and mid-1960s, daughters escaped parental households by establishing that they had traded the stewardship of their sexuality by parents for that by a husband. In contrast, by the early 1970s some young women were arguing that freedom from their parents was not contingent on forming permanent unions with men, and that not all heterosexual and romantic activity necessarily had to end in marriage. This indicated less an explicit notion about adolescent entitlement to sexual freedom than it did a general erosion of parental (especially maternal) authority. Young women defended their associations with men in terms of their right to activities independent of their mothers' desires rather than as a general license to be sexually active. While daughters insisted that heterosexual interactions be decoupled from marriage, they saw freedom *from* mothers rather than freedom *with* men as the central issue. Whereas these two relationships had been causally linked as a trade-off half a generation earlier, some young women now maintained that they were separate.

Increased anxiety about daughters' sexuality is also evident in court records involving rape. Between 1960 and 1973, there was an annual average of seven rape cases in the San Felipe courts, an estimated two-thirds of which involved young girls between eight and twelve years old whom parents alleged had been raped by neighbors or strangers.[96] In slightly more than half of the available cases, rape charges were initiated by the girl's mother or female guardian, and in most other cases by the father.[97] Parents substantiated their allegations by stressing their child's innocence: they pointed to the girl's age, produced medical "evidence" of the girl's "deflowering," and often argued that their child was mentally "retarded."[98] However, between 1969 and 1973, several rape cases involved adolescent girls whose willingness or ability to use traditional markers of female sexual innocence was far more difficult. In at least three cases, young women denied charges filed by their parents that they had been raped.[99] In 1971, fourteen-year-old Silvia Tapia flatly repudiated her mother's testimony that she had been "kidnapped and raped, but too ashamed to tell." Instead she told the judge that she had been "going with" the accused for six months "against the wishes of (her mother)" and that the couple had engaged in "voluntary sexual relations" on three occasions.[100]

Daughters' negations of rape charges filed on their behalf by mothers suggests deep disagreements between mothers and daughters over the appropriate sexual behavior of unmarried female adolescents. It also highlights the different meanings that mothers and daughters could attribute to sexual intercourse. Most important, however, such cases indicate the extent of frustration that some mothers felt with their inability to control a daughter's sexual conduct. Surely most mothers were already aware if a daughter insisted that a particular sexual encounter had been consensual, and yet they filed formal rape charges anyway. There may have been instances in which mothers acted over and above the will of their daughters out of a belief that their children were incapable of denouncing sexual violence. Yet the firm testimony of daughters like Silvia suggests that there were also cases in which mothers appealed to a judge to condemn a daughter's willfully consensual sexual activity. In such instances, parents turned to the courts for an authority that they felt they no longer possessed.

Rape cases in which the alleged victim denied the existence of rape were rare. A far more common scenario depicted in court records from the late 1960s and early 1970s involved adolescent girls who were allegedly raped by boyfriends or acquaintances with whom they willingly socialized. In such cases, it became almost impossible to establish a young woman's victim status according to the traditional indicators of female sexual innocence. Instead, any evidence suggesting that a young woman had willingly sought the company of the accused man in other social (and possibly sexual) circumstances immediately compromised the young woman's qualification as a true victim, and therefore also her definition as a proper daughter.

For example, in June 1973, the mother of fourteen-year-old Elisa Saavedra filed charges of kidnapping and rape on her daughter's behalf against a bus driver and an agricultural worker.[101] In her original testimony, Elisa's mother claimed that her daughter had been "forced to board a bus by two unknown men" and was taken to the "outskirts of town, held down, and raped." She further testified that her daughter "had never dated," "was not coquettish with men," and had been "so traumatized" by the incident that she did not admit the rape to her mother "until after her soiled underpants were discovered." Over the next two months of court hearings, however, this traditional picture of female victimization became more complicated. Elisa herself told the judge that she had "voluntarily boarded the bus," and other passengers testified that the bus had not departed for the "outskirts of town" but, rather, had continued on its route to town "full of people." Elisa continued to maintain that she had been raped but altered her mother's story to say that, once in town, the men had "locked her in the bus," a story that was undermined when two of Elisa's school friends alleged that Elisa was "crazy for young men" and "everybody knew it." Finally, the rape charges were dropped altogether when Elisa confessed that the men were "not strangers," that she had formerly "gone with" the agricultural worker, and that she had accompanied the men to town "in order to have a drink."

Elisa's connection to the accused disqualified her from possibly obtaining judicial redress for rape. She could not claim sexual violence at the hands of company she had solicited. Her plight resembled that of many other adolescent girls and older women, the vast majority of whom probably never appealed to the Juzgado de Crimen in cases of sexual violence precisely because they could not fit the court's and society's narrow definition of female sexual vulnerability. Yet one of the most interesting things about cases like Elisa's is its illustration of the relatively wider social opportunities enjoyed by rural adolescent girls in the early 1970s, and the problems and anxieties that such opportunities produced. The expanded education options and improved transportation systems enabled by the Agrarian Reform allowed at least some young campesinas the chance to take unchaperoned trips to town and to pursue heterosexual friendship and romance. Going to town to have a drink with male friends would have been an almost impossible event for an unmarried campesina adolescent a generation earlier. As Elisa's case exemplifies, however, such new forms of socializing were problematic for girls and their families. Cultural assumptions that unescorted single women were sexually vulnerable and sexually available to men persisted alongside newer ideas about youth independence. Adolescent girls' casual or romantic contact with men could involve danger and violence as well as pleasure. Yet as judicial records indicate, the courts and many parents refused to recognize that women could be victimized within consensual relationships. This not only placed blame for unwanted advances and sexual violence on young women themselves, but also confirmed maternal fears that the new opportunities for young people were allowing daughters to pursue risky behavior.

Mothers' fears about daughters' expanded social opportunities were closely wedded to alarm that sexual interactions were increasingly being separated from men's obligation to marry their sexual partners. Longstanding concerns that sexually active daughters would be abused and/or become material burdens on their families were now coupled with adult women's feeling that campesino men were more sexually irresponsible and parents less in control generally. Daughters not only seemed to move more freely outside of their homes, but also seemed increasingly uninterested in using sexuality exclusively for the purpose of securing a marriage. Such anxiety was reinforced by a significant rise in adolescent pregnancy and single motherhood. In 1964, 18 percent of all births registered in the department of San Felipe corresponded to unmarried women whose children were either "illegitimate" or "natural"; in 1972, this figure was 23 percent.[102] Likewise, whereas in 1965, adolescent girls under age twenty had accounted for 23 percent of illegitimate births, by 1972 they accounted for 28 percent.[103] Although the percentage of adolescent girls who married had risen slightly by 1970 (from 10 percent in 1960 to 12 percent in 1970), and women were marrying at younger ages than they had in the 1960s (on average at age twenty-three, as opposed to age twenty-four), there were greater numbers of single adolescent mothers.[104] Given the connection between conjugal unions and a woman's ability to benefit from the Agrarian Reform, daughters appeared at a higher risk of becoming unmarried mothers at precisely the moment marriage was ever more important to a woman's survival.

Beginning in the late 1960s and intensifying during the Popular Unity government after 1970, married campesina women's concerns about their daughters' sexuality combined with worries about campesino men's infidelity to create a sense of "crisis." These fears flowed both from the ways that Agrarian Reform had reshaped the campesino family and, more specifically, from a painful gap between the official vision of family mutualism and what women actually experienced within their households as hardship and uncertainty. Family structures of authority and obligation seemed to be breaking down at the very time the family was being publicly touted as a means for achieving working-class solidarity and uplift.

Certainly the late Agrarian Reform years were a time of exceptionally divisive conflict. In the last years of Christian Democratic government, there were thousands of illegal strikes and land occupations by impatient campesinos demanding immediate inclusion in the Agrarian Reform—an urgency that only escalated with the subsequent election of Allende. The UP's promise to build a socialist society was met with a ferocious and internationally backed opposition, deepening already profound class and partisan conflicts, and setting off a wave of organized and often violent sabotage. Between Allende's November 1970 inauguration and mid-1973, there were more than 8,200 strikes and 6,000 property occupations nationwide, nearly a third of which took place in the countryside.[105] Most of these actions were aimed at pushing the government to expropriate land more quickly, but there were also numerous acts of opposition to the UP agenda.

The rural labor movement splintered into warring partisan factions, ending the loose collaboration and solidarity that had characterized rural unions in the 1960s and bringing campesinos to blows with each other over the judiciousness of specific policies. (There was particular campesino opposition to the expropriation of medium-size estates and the creation of permanent collective production units.) Landowners formed vigilante "white guards" to menace campesinos; in response, university students instructed the rural poor in the rudimentary construction of Molotov cocktails. By late 1971, a U.S. boycott and merchant hoarding combined with campesinos' unprecedented earning power to spur three-digit inflation and consumer shortages. The following year a national strike led by truckers against the UP paralyzed much of the economy and set off a wave of violent demonstrations. Among the most visible anti-UP protestors were large groups of women who marched through the streets of Santiago banging empty pots and pans and decrying the "Marxist attack on families." Although such activities disproportionally involved middle-class and elite women, significant numbers of working-class housewives also participated.[106]

In the Aconcagua Valley and most other sectors of rural Chile, there was no equivalent organized anti-UP protest by campesina women. Poor rural women overwhelmingly supported the goal of accelerating the Agrarian Reform, with almost one-third of women in rural Aconcagua voting for Allende in 1970 and another 36 percent voting for an explicitly Left-leaning Christian Democratic candidate, Radomiro Tomic, whose Agrarian Reform platform was arguably more radical than that of the UP.[107] Moreover, in subsequent municipal and congressional elections in 1971 and 1973, rural women's support for UP candidates rose significantly, surpassing 36 percent.[108] However, campesina women's enthusiasm for Popular Unity was apparently cooler than that of campesino men, more than 40 percent of whom voted for Allende in 1970, and more than 50 percent of whom supported UP candidates in 1971 and 1973.[109] Although electoral patterns are in themselves problematic since campesina women in Aconcagua voted in significantly lower numbers than men, oral histories of both men and women referenced a female ambivalence and sometimes hostility to specific Popular Unity policies.[110]

Importantly, this greater female dissatisfaction was a *matter of degree* whose causes were deeply gendered, rather than a *gender division* that set rural women's political sensibilities apart from, and in opposition to, those of most rural men's. It flowed not, as many contemporary actors and later scholarly commentators implied, from women's religiousness, innate conservatism, or the failure of the Agrarian Reform to take women into account.[111] Rather, it sprang from the ways that the Agrarian Reform had already addressed women: it had refigured married women's sexual and social vulnerability to men, and unequally positioned women and men to participate in the political struggles that reached crisis proportion after Allende's election. Married campesina women experienced the impact of political polarization in isolated and family-centered ways in contrast to the vastly more collective and institutional spaces afforded men. Although mothers centers and female support activities for unions offered women unprecedented civic roles, only a minority of women were ever directly involved (between 10 and 25 percent), and such activities heavily emphasized domestic responsibilities.[112] In contrast, almost 90 percent of campesino men in Chile's primary agricultural districts belonged to unions, which were themselves entrusted with the national mission of reorganizing the means of production.[113] Whether or not a man supported Allende's plans to build a socialist economy, and regardless of how vicious fights with his peers became, a man was generally more apprised than was a woman of the structural reasons for conflict. A man was also much more likely to be directly involved as a protagonist in the strikes, land occupations, and demonstrations that constituted that conflict. While both men and women felt the strain of escalating class struggle, wives were less well positioned than their male family members to see such conflict as connected to specific political projects that they could directly influence. As tensions mounted, women interpreted the negative costs of class struggle as *family* crisis: a belief that their authority as wives and mothers was eroding, and that men were no longer fulfilling the role of responsible and respectful provider and husband.

The situation of adolescent girls was different. Daughters did not bear the same household responsibilities as their mothers (even if their household labor was significant), and since most were still unmarried, the issue of men (not) fulfilling their obligations was more indirectly experienced. Moreover, girls welcomed the Agrarian Reform's youth outreach programs, expanded seasonal employment opportunities, and the flourishing of a more independent youth culture. Although, as their mothers were, adolescent girls were excluded from unions, and their participation in youth activities trailed that of campesino boys, many associated the rapid change of the early 1970s with relative freedom and excitement.

For married women, however, the UP was more often associated with heightened worry. Political cleavages permeated all facets of community life, rupturing old friendships and networks of reciprocity through which adult women had borrowed food and watched each other's children. Basic consumption issues became politicized as access to housing, food rations, and scholarships became more tied to a family's partisan sympathies. Men were often absent from home for long periods of time in order to participate in land occupations, strikes, and training seminars. Husbands shirked financial obligations to families, often going weeks without giving wives money. Rumors abounded about vigilante violence and mass firings. Since many husbands told wives little or nothing about their activities, and women felt unwelcome at union meetings, campesinas were often not in a position to verify such claims or to evaluate the strategy behind them. As the contentious fullness of men's political lives grew ever more at odds with married women's familial concerns, wives interpreted the cost of political mobilization in terms of male fidelity. In particular, husbands' prolonged absences led women to fear that men were using "union business" as a camouflage for sexual affairs. Women saw men's sexual promiscuity as directly linked to (and caused by) men's failure to be responsible providers and cooperative partners. All of this, combined with their concern as mothers about waning control over daughters, came to symbolize what was going wrong. Political crisis was increasingly understood as sexual crisis.

Certainly gender relations both within and outside the campesino household seem to have become more volatile and violent. Even a cursory glance at judicial records suggests that married women were either complaining more and/or had more to complain about. In the department of San Felipe, the annual average of wife-beating cases during the UP more than tripled from the level during the Christian Democratic years, jumping from twelve cases per year during the 1964–70 period to thirty-eight cases per year during the 1971–73 period.[114] Similarly, the average number of home abandonment cases leapt from fifteen per year during 1964–70 to thirty-five per year during 1971–73.[115] The number of rape and attempted rape cases rose from an average of five per year during the Christian Democratic years to an average of fifteen per year during the UP years.[116] These increases mirrored the general rise in violence throughout society as campesinos clashed with employers and with each other. By 1972, more than 50 percent of all judicial cases in San Felipe involved physical violence, up from 35 percent in the late 1960s and almost triple the level prior to Agrarian Reform.[117] Yet the rise in wife-beating, home abandonment, and rape cases was not a mere corollary to class conflict, but the result of very specific inequalities in sexual power that the Agrarian Reform made more obvious and, in some cases, exacerbated. On one hand, the rise in reported cases may well reflect adult campesinas' emboldened faith that during the Agrarian Reform (and the UP period in particular), the courts would more aggressively protect and vindicate poor women. Likewise, as already noted, the Agrarian Reform's promotion of gender mutualism encouraged women to set limits on men's behavior.[118] On the other hand, none of this precludes the possibility (so consistently claimed in oral histories) that the Popular Unity years were also a time of *increased* violent conflict between men and women as well as of *more* defiant behavior by daughters.

In oral histories, the differences between men's and women's recollections of the Agrarian Reform—and the UP years, in particular—are striking. Even men who were very bitter about and opposed to the Popular Unity agenda (more than 40 percent of men in Aconcagua and nationwide belonged to opposition unions) referred to the entire Agrarian Reform as a tremendously exciting time in which they traveled outside their home counties for the first time in their lives, met other men (and women) from elsewhere in the country, and felt taken seriously by political parties, state bureaucrats, and even landowners. They recalled heady moments of winning strikes, forcing (or preventing) land expropriations, and becoming, in a sense, "one's own boss." In contrast, women who were wives during the period often remembered late Agrarian Reform years, in particular, as times of violent marital fights, long periods of being alone, and men's repeated betrayals, as well as times of declining respect from, and control over, children. Interestingly, men sometimes acknowledged the discrepancy between male and female experiences. Armando Gómez, the former president of a pro-UP union in the county of Putaendo, went so far as to suggest that men's greater social (and sexual) opportunities had cost women's support: "Lots of men had troubles with their women. They'd arrive home and there would be a big fight because the wife thought he had been out going around town [with other women]. A lot of women didn't give their support to the Agrarian Reform for this reason."[119]

The former president of the oppositional Christian Democratic union, Jorge Tejedo, had similar recollections, but was more partisan in apportioning blame: "The conflict during the UP was really hard on women. Men would leave the house at four in the afternoon and not come back until three in the morning. . . . Or sometimes, these family men would leave for three or four days when occupying an estate, etc. And you can imagine what women thought of men spending nights out of the house! I saw many marriages broken into pieces over this."[120]

Poignantly, although both Armando and Jorge professed to have enjoyed their wives' full support—implying that while other men abused their absences from home, they had not—their wives remembered things quite differently. Jorge's wife, Ana, reported that her husband beat her viciously when she complained about his nighttime absences and accused him of sexual affairs with female clerical staff at union headquarters. At one point she threatened to send their children to a sister outside Valparaíso because "he cared about politics and other women, and nothing about his family."[121] Armando's wife, Elena, had memories similar to Ana's. She maintained that Armando had numerous affairs on his trips as union president and that in 1971 he left her to live with a lover he had taken in the town of San Felipe. He ceased to take an interest in their three children and only erratically passed by their home on the Agrarian Reform production unit to leave her money. She was finally forced to approach the Christian Democratic president of the production unit, a political enemy of her husband, to plead that he allow her to purchase goods on credit that would later be charged to Armando. She recalled, "Those were terrible years for me really. . . . It was so difficult . . . [Armando] ran around in all that politics—oh, it was chaos, so much fighting. . . . And it made me ashamed to go to [Armando's political rival], but he gave me no choice. I had the children and he made me do all the sacrificing."[122]

Both Elena and Ana supported the Agrarian Reform. Although Ana shared her husband's antipathy for the UP, Elena professed loyalty to Allende, and both women praised the Agrarian Reform's general goal to empower the rural poor and ennoble campesino families. Yet both women saw their husbands' affairs, which had so jeopardized their security, as related to "politics" (men's involvement in unions and labor struggles) and to the "chaos" of the UP years (a period of strained and openly conflictive relations within the rural community). This connection reflects neither campesina women's simple hostility to politics nor their rejection of the Agrarian Reform's goals. Rather, it points to women's sexually inscribed vulnerability within the Agrarian Reform's specific process of political struggle. Women expected and needed husbands' loyalty, and bitterly resented and fought other claims on male fidelity. This arrangement was sustained by the Agrarian Reform's promotion of domesticity and its decision to make women's ability to benefit from the Agrarian Reform contingent on a sexual alliance with a participating male. A husband's affair entailed the danger that he might divert his income or land opportunities to another woman, leaving a wife to fend for herself.

Married campesina women did not stop supporting the Agrarian Reform, and more than a third remained openly positive about Allende. Campesina women continued to applaud the Agrarian Reform's redistributive goals and lay claim to its message of gender cooperation and family unity. On the whole, they did not reject either their exclusion from unions or from direct land redistribution. Most supported accelerated expropriations. What women objected to was not the UP's Agrarian Reform, but the way class conflict threatened to erase certain gender ideals and material realities that Agrarian Reform, including the UP version, had created. In both its Christian Democratic and Popular Unity forms, Agrarian Reform had urged married women to expect husbands to be able providers and responsible (loyal) heads of family, and to expect children to be cooperative and respectful. Women welcomed these ideals as an improvement on the already existing dynamic of female dependence on men and parental authority over children. They struggled not over women's access to land and union membership, but over the meanings of husbands' and daughters' "respect" and "responsibility" to them.

For campesino men the ideal of the responsible husband existed in tension with the requirements of other masculine signifiers, including worker militancy, male combativeness, loyalty to fellow men, and a general sexual prowess with women. During the Popular Unity years, these multiple ideals came under extraordinary stress. As men's energies were ever more absorbed in political conflicts away from their households, their commitment to other men seemed to take precedence over family commitments, frustrating women's needs at home and fueling a sense of abandonment.[123] Men also felt this rupture but were primarily consumed by the breakdown in male solidarity. Militancy now privileged combativeness against fellow workers as much as against the *patrón;* loyalty to one's fellow campesinos was now only partial. But whereas men assessed the cost of social struggle in terms of the courage to withstand and win fights against political factions of other campesino men, married women saw the price in terms of male abandonment, family dysfunction, and their own ability to survive. The central paradox was that while the Agrarian Reform had reinforced married women's dependence on men as reliable partners, it had instructed men that their ability to be good household heads depended first on their ability to militantly defend class interests. In addition, while it had touted family unity as the basis of social uplift, its opportunities for young people undermined adult women's sense of authority over daughters. Given campesina women's marginalization from the primary vehicles of political struggle, when class conflict escalated, the contradictions between these ideals hit women hardest.

Notes

1 Case File S370;28128, San Felipe Juzgado de Crimen, San Felipe (hereafter, Juzgado de Crimen).
2 Ibid.
3 Ibid.
4 Ibid.
5 The Agrarian Reform was begun in earnest in 1964 by the Christian Democratic government preceding Allende. Between 1964 and 1973, the Chilean state expropriated 9,861,516 hectares of land. The Aconcagua Valley lies 100 kilometers north of Santiago and, at the time of the Agrarian Reform, was part of the province of Aconcagua. Aconcagua Valley consisted of nine *comunas* (counties) organized into two administrative departments, San Felipe and Los Andes. Aconcagua province (as opposed to the valley) consisted of these two departments, plus the additional department of Petorca, which is not part of this study.
6 In 1962, the number of unionized rural workers in Chile numbered less than 2,000. Between 1967 and 1968, the number of rural union members registered at the Ministry of Labor jumped to 76,000, and by early 1973, that number soared to over 225,000 (Luis Salinas, *Trayectoria de la organización campesina* [Santiago: AGRA, 1985]). Mothers Centers, associations of women formed first in mass by the Christian Democrats and later by the UP and trade unions, included 1,000,000 members by 1973 (including urban and rural women) (Teresa Valdés and Marisa Weinstein, Isabel Toledo, Lilian Letelier, "Centros de madres, 1973–1989: Solo disciplinamiento?" Documento de Trabajo, no. 416, FLACSO, 1989, 22).
7 Historian Gabriel Salazár has written at length about gender conflicts between rural men and women in the nineteenth century. See Salazár, *Labradores, peones, y proletarios: Formación y crisis de la sociedad popular chilena del siglo XIX* (Santiago: Sur Profesionales, 1986).

8   Karin Rosemblatt and Steve Stern have each given specific attention to how gendered experience and culture are differentiated by generation as well as by marital and employment status. See Karin A. Rosemblatt, "Gendered Compromises: Political Cultures, Socialist Politics, and the State in Chile, 1920–1950" (Ph.D. diss., Univ. of Wisconsin Madison, 1996); Steve Stern, *The Secret History of Gender: Women, Men, and Power in Late Colonial Mexico* (Chapel Hill: University of North Carolina Press, 1995).

9   There were also important generational implications for unmarried adolescent boys. However, given the Agrarian Reform's policy focus on men, adolescent boys were addressed as potential full members and protagonists in land reform and unionization efforts, not just as "youths" in youth-outreach projects. Although their situation differed substantially from fathers and other married men with children, the *degree* of generational difference was less than in the case of mothers and daughters. For reasons of space and focus, this article will only address the consequences of generational differences between women and girls.

10 Out of 114 rape cases filed at the San Felipe Juzgado de Crimen between 1958 and 1973, 70 were available for examination in this study. Thirty-six involved persons were listed as "agricultural workers" or "campesinos," while another 12 involved very poor people who probably made part of their livelihood from agriculture. Only 4 cases involved married women or women under age 25. "Registro de Crimen," Juzgado de Crimen, years 1955–73.

11 "Registro de Crimen," Juzgado de Crimen.

12 Between 1991 and 1993, I conducted ninety-five interviews and oral histories with a wide range of campesinos and labor leaders (fifty women, forty-five men). I interviewed single and married men and women, people who had been working adults during the 1960s and 1970s, former members of Agrarian Reform production units, and members of all political factions. In 1997 I conducted an additional ten interviews. Many of my interviewees were campesinos in the Aconcagua town of Santa María, where I was working for a nonprofit organization associated with a union of temporary fruit workers in 1992–93. From here I branched out to the Santa María workers' acquaintances and former comrades.

13 This is the central thesis of my dissertation. See Heidi Tinsman, "Unequal Uplift: The Sexual Politics of Gender, Work, and Community in the Chilean Agrarian Reform, 1950–1973" (Ph.D. diss., Yale University, 1996).

14 Elizabeth Hutchison argues that at the turn of the century in Santiago and Valparaíso, social reformers and trade unionists advocated a domestic partnership in which working-class men provided for domesticated housewives ("Working Women of Santiago: Gender and Social Transformation in Urban Chile" [Ph.D. diss., University of California, Berkeley, 1995]). Thomas Klubock argues that working-class domesticity was promoted in the 1930s and 1940s by corporations like the Braden Copper Company in the El Teniente copper mine, and that it centrally shaped mid-twentieth-century labor law and politics (*Contested Communities: Class, Gender, and Politics in Chile's El Teniente Copper Mine, 1904–1951* [Durham: Duke University Press, 1998]). Karin Rosemblatt ("Gendered Compromises") argues that working-class domesticity was promoted by the Chilean state and provided the model for welfare-state politics beginning with the Popular Front governments of the 1930s and 1940s.

15 Several excellent studies detail women's structural exclusion from land redistribution. See Patricia Garrett, "Growing Apart: The Experiences of Rural Men and Women in Central Chile" (Ph.D. diss., University of Wisconsin, Madison, 1978); Carmen Diana

Deere and Magdalena León, eds., *Rural Women and State Policy: Feminist Perspectives on Latin America* (Boulder: Westview Press, 1987); Xímena Valdés, *Mujer, trabajo, y medio ambiente: Los nudos de la modernización agraria* (Santiago: CEM, 1992).

16 Under the UP, collective Agrarian Reform units called Centros de Reforma Agraria (CERAs) were established and were open to women, youth, and single male agricultural workers. However, the vast majority of Agrarian Reform units were based on the *asentamiento* established under the Christian Democrats, offering membership only to "heads of household." According to most researchers, CERAs did not succeed in recruiting female members because of widespread male opposition and lack of adequate training. Patricia Garrett estimated that less than 5 percent of CERA members were women ("Growing Apart").

17 For a description of the mothers centers' changing goals and activities, see Edda Gaviola, Lorella Lopresti, and Claudia Rojas, "Los Centros de madres: Una forma de organización para la mujer rural," unpublished manuscript, ISIS, Santiago, 1988; Teresa Valdés et al., "Centros de madres, 1973–1989"; Patricia Garrett, "Growing Apart." Also see various reports on mothers centers in the periodical literature, including *Campo Nuevo* (May, June, Nov., Dec. 1968; *La Nación*, 3 Jan. 1966, p. 3; 2 July 1966, p. 4; *El Trabajo*, 1 July 1969, p. 7; 23 May 1970, p. 6.

18 Newspapers provided ample coverage of new programs for rural young people. For examples, see *La Nación*, 16 Feb. 1970; 1 Feb. 1972; 7 Jan. 1973; 13 Apr. 1973. *El Siglo*, 19 Aug. 1968; 4 Jun. 1972; 14 May 1973. *El Trabajo*, 10 May 1970; 14 Jun. 1971; 25 Jun. 1971; 20 Aug. 1973. Also see Heidi Tinsman, chapter 10, "Unequal Uplift."

19 Patricia Garrett, "Growing Apart"; Xímena Valdés, *La posición de la mujer en la hacienda* (Santiago: CEM, 1988).

20 Author's calculations from cuadros 1 and 4, *Censo agropecuario: Aconcagua*, 1954–1955.

21 Inquilinos were campesinos who exchanged their labor on an estate in return for a combination of benefits, including access to small plots of land, pasture rights, cash remuneration, and in-kind payments of food, housing, fuel, and agricultural products. Traditionally, inquilinos resided within the estate on plots of land and in houses allotted to them by the landowner. They were permitted to use the land *regalía* for subsistence and petty commercial purposes in exchange for an obligation to work throughout the agricultural year for the landowner on the rest of the estate. Inquilinos were also required to provide the estate with an additional laborer called an *obligado* ("an obliged one") during seasonal peaks and to pay this laborer from his/her own earnings. By the eve of the Agrarian Reform in 1964, inquilinos comprised only a quarter of the wage-labor force in Aconcagua, with the majority of estate workers being permanent and seasonal laborers. Nonetheless, the inquilino labor relation, including with the extreme dependence on payment in kind and lack of organizing rights, centrally shaped all rural labor contracts.

On the eve of Agrarian Reform, 82 percent of all land in Aconcagua belonged to 9 percent of the population, and more than half of all agricultural workers made less than the *sueldo vitál*—the minimum cost of survival, not the minimum wage. Another 31 percent made only the *sueldo vitál*. *Censo Agropecuario*, 1964–65.

22 The 1967 Law of Campesino Unionization (Law 16.250) overturned legislation dating from the 1940s that, in practice, had made rural unions illegal. It loosened the criteria for joining and leading unions, allowed countywide collective bargaining, and created a mechanism for the joint government-employer-worker financing of unions. Legislation passed in 1962 and 1965 gradually phased out the practice of paying rural workers in-kind and mandated that all rural workers be paid in cash wages equal to or above the

minimum wage. National wage laws, collective bargaining, and employer eagerness to persuade workers not to unionize combined to rapidly raise real wages. See Brian Loveman, *Struggle in the Countryside* (Bloomington: University of Indiana Press, 1976; *Estadísticas Laborales*, INE, 1992).

23 Various oral histories by author. These details are also recorded in other studies and collections of oral histories. See Xímena Valdés, *La Posición de la mujer en la hacienda*; and Sonia Montecino, Kirai de León, and Xímena Valdés, eds., *Historias testimoniales de mujeres del campo* (Santiago: CEDEM, 1983).

24 The tendency for women's labor to be defined in more domestic terms following the mechanization and "modernization" of agricultural work has characterized numerous agrarian reforms and has been documented in several previous studies. In particular, see the various essays in Carmen Diana Deere and Magdalena León, eds., *Rural Women and State Policy*; Magdalena León, Cheywa Spindel, Carmen Diana Deere, *La mujer y la política agraria en América Latina* (Mexico City: Siglo XXI, 1986).

25 *Boletín Centro de Madres*, Movimiento Campesino Independiente, cited in Almino Affonso and Sergio Gómez, Emilio Kline, Pablo Ramírez, *Movimiento campesino chileno*, vol. 1 (Santiago: ICIRA, 1970), 228.

26 In 1960, only 10 percent of campesina adolescents (women between twelve and twenty years of age) in the departments of Los Andes and San Felipe were reportedly married or cohabitating with men (cuadro 5, *Censo de población: Aconcagua*, 1960).

27 Between 1966 and 1973, local and national newspapers were full of articles describing new educational and recreational programs sponsored by the state and different political parties for rural young people. For examples, see *La Nación*, 18 July 1965, p. 21; 23 Jan. 1972, p. 2; 7 Jan. 1973, p. 16; 14 Mar. 1973, p. 14; 13 April 1973, p. 6. *El Trabajo*, suplemento, 6 July 1968; *El Siglo*, 19 Aug. 1969, p. 15.

28 Cuadro 6.3, *Censo agropecuario, Aconcagua*, 1964–1965; cuadro 11.A, *Censo agropecuario, Aconcagua*, 1975–1976. Despite the fact that the 1975–76 census was conducted two years after Allende's overthrow, the military regime did not fully begin dismantling the Agrarian Reform until 1976; therefore, I consider that the 1975–76 census reflects changes that occurred prior to the coup.

29 Unfortunately, the 1975–76 agricultural census did not categorize women workers by specific ages. However, in the 1970 *Censo de población*, conducted the year Allende assumed office, 64 percent of women listed as working in agriculture in Chile were categorized as never married (50 percent) or widowed (14 percent). Thirty-four percent were listed as under age twenty-five. Since this data includes *all* agricultural workers, wage-earning and non-wage-earning, the actual percentage of single and young wage-earning women was probably significantly higher than these figures (Cuadro 30, *Censo de población: Chile*, 1970).

30 In the 1960 census, the rural population in Chile was 52 percent male and 48 percent female (*Censo de Población: Chile*, 1960).

31 David Hojoman has argued that land reform under the Popular Unity government provided an improved standard of living that encouraged women to stay in rural areas and curtailed female migration to cities to look for work as domestics. See Hojoman, "Land Reform, Female Migration, and the Market for Domestic Service in Chile," *Journal of Latin American Studies* 21: 105–32.

32 For an example, see *Campo Nuevo*, Mar. 1964; *Tierra y Libertád*, May 1962; and *El Siglo*, 30 May 1967 and 16 Aug. 1969.

33 The rural labor press frequently commented on women's support activities as evidence

that the Agrarian Reform was a project in "family uplift." For examples, see *Nuevo Campo*, Sept. 1967, p. 2; Oct. 1967, p. 1; Apr. 1968; and *Tierra y Libertád*, Jan. 1964, p. 2; Apr. 1963; Nov. 1963.

34 "Marco Nacional de Programación," INDAP, Santiago, 1968, 9–10; "Primer reunión, nacional de institutos públicos y privados sobre el desarrollo de la comunidad," Consejo Nacional de Promoción Popular, photocopied memo, 1968, 22, Archivo del Ministerio de Vivienda, Santiago.

35 This perspective was particularly championed by the Catholic lay education association, Instituto de Educación Rural; see Memoria del IER, 1970–1971," Santiago, 1971, Archivo Instituto Pastor Rural, Santiago.

36 For a detailed analysis of this dynamic, based on oral histories and judicial records of domestic conflicts, see chapter 2 of Tinsman, "Unequal Uplift."

37 Delegations from mothers centers were present at strikes, land occupations, and ceremonies marking the expropriation of estates. For examples, see *Nuevo Campo*, Nov. and Dec. 1968; *La Nación*, 3 Jan. 1966; 2 July 1968, p. 3; *El Trabajo*, 1 July 1969, p. 7.

38 In the province of Aconcagua, less than 30 percent of rural men and women in their early twenties had attended school for four years or more in 1960; by 1970, fully 62 percent of men and women in their twenties had attended more than four years of school (cuadro 14c, *Censo de población, Aconcagua, 1960*; cuadro 40, *Censo de población, Aconcagua, 1970*).

39 For example, in 1971, the UP's director of the corporation of Agrarian Reform, David Baytelman, called campesino youths the "authentic" and most important engine of mass mobilization (*La Nación*, 1 Oct. 1971, p. 4).

40 "Síntesis historica de la planificación familiar en Chile," APROFA, Santiago, 1974.

41 According to agency records, APROFA published and distributed more than eighty thousand pamphlets, bulletins, and cartoon books between 1966 and 1972 ("APROFA: Diez años de labor," *Boletín APROFA* (Aug. 1972): 6–7).

42 Conference speaker at 1971 Ministry of Education seminar, quoted in the bulletin of the affiliate of International Planned Parenthood, APRORA. *Boletín APROFA* (Nov. 1971): 2.

43 Historian Xímena Jiles has reported that the UP allowed abortions to be conducted for medical reasons and scientific research at Barros Luco Hospital in Santiago. See Jiles, *De la miel a los implantes: Historia de las políticas de regulación de la fecundidad en Chile* (Santiago: CISEC-CESOC, 1992). Minister of health quoted from the 1971 Ministry of Education seminar, cited in *Boletín APROFA* (Nov. 1971).

44 Virginia Vidál, *La Emancipación de la mujer chilena* (Santiago: Editorial Quimantú, 1972), 49–52.

45 In the interviews of women I conducted for this study, only two women professed to have had any substantial knowledge about sexuality prior to puberty and the commencement of sexual relations with men. Other researchers have also found this to be true. See Xímena Jiles, *De la miel a los implantes*; Patricia Garrett, "Growing Apart"; Armand Mattelart and Michele Mattelart, *La mujer chilena en una nueva sociedad* (Santiago: Pacífico, 1968).

46 In 1960, Chile's infant mortality rate was 120.3 deaths per 1,000 births; in 1964, the maternal death rate was 28.3 deaths per 1,000 mothers (*Estadísticas APROFA*, 1960–1992, APROFA, Santiago, 1993). In 1965, APROFA reported that there was an annual number of 140,000 abortions, or one abortion for every 2 live births (*Boletín del Comité Chileno de Protección de la Familia* (July 1965).

47 These figures are for women between the ages of thirty-five and fifty in 1960 (cuadro 5, *Censo de población: Aconcagua, 1960*).

48 Demografía, Aconcagua, 1960, INE, 1960.

49 Cuadro 5, Censo de población, Aconcagua, 1960.

50 While the estimated rate of abortion in Chile remained stable in relation to pregnancy between 1970 and 1973, maternal death from abortion diminished by more than 25 percent. "Births, Abortions, and the Progress of Chile," *Field Staff Reports* (American University) 19, 2 (1972); and *Estadísticas APROFA*, Santiago, 1992. Lack of documentation makes it impossible to ascertain to what extent the decline in abortion-related death was due to an increase in the number of abortions being performed in clinical facilities. The decisions of medical professionals and local SNS branches to administer abortions were arbitrary and highly personal. In many areas, traditional healers and midwives probably continued to perform the majority of abortions. Yet the very fact that abortions were being performed in even a limited capacity by the state health care system surely weakened the anxiety of medical professionals that abortion would be criminally prosecuted, probably encouraging women to seek safer conditions. One study claimed that whereas in the early 1960s abortion had been three times more frequent among poor women as among middle-class women, in the early 1970s it was five times greater (see Dr. Onofre Avedano, "El Aborto: Problema médico, social, y jurídico," unpublished paper, APROFA, December 1972, 3).

51 Legislation abolishing the distinction between illegitimate and legitimate children was introduced, but not passed, by the time of Allende's overthrow. Nonetheless, its very proposal was already having an impact on how births were officially recorded. In the department of San Felipe, the Registro Civil stopped distinguishing between illegitimate, natural, and legitimate children in the beginning of 1971. In 1972, 23 percent of all births in the department of San Felipe were by women who were not married to the father of their child, and fully 27.5 percent of all these births were by mothers under the age of twenty. Author's study of *Registro de nacimiento: San Felipe, 1964–73.*

52 The Catholic Church published a youth magazine and ran a weekly radio show, both called "Sucro y Semilla," and both discussing a range of topics pertinent to youths, including fashion and dating advice. Various issues of *Sucro y Semilla*, Archivo INPRU.

53 "Memoria del IER, 1970–1971," Archivo INPRU; monthly advertisements in El Trabajo.

54 Local newspapers frequently advertised youth club activities, including both educational and recreational events. For examples, see El Trabajo, 16 Apr. 1971, 15 Jun. 1971, 14 July 1971, and 14 Jun. 1972; and La Aurora, 11 Mar. 1971, 15 May 1971, and 6 Jun. 1973.

55 Various oral histories, including Carlos Ordenas, Calle Medio, 7 Sept. 1997; Miguel Acevedo, San Esteben, 7 Sept. 1997; and Lucilia Flores, San Esteben, 14 Sept. 1997.

56 The survey was conducted by the Catholic Instituto Educación Rural (IER) and involved interviews with 606 male adolescents and 550 female adolescents throughout the Central Valley, including the departments of San Felipe and Los Andes. Unfortunately, however, the conclusions reported in IER's annual report do not distinguish between male and female responses, nor do they classify responses by department. The survey reported that almost 30 percent of those interviewed cited "national political news" as their main investment in mass communication, while another 30 percent expressed a primary interest in contemporary music. IER, *Memoria del IER, 1970–1971*, 24, Archivo INPRU.

57 Various oral histories, including Leandro Reyes, Catemu, 25 May 1993; and Emilio Torres, Santa María, 25 May 1993.

58 Triunfo Campesino, "Capcitación," manual for union education, circa 1969. Author's photocopy from original manual belonging to former Triunfo union president Jorge Tejedo, San Felipe.

59 Various oral histories, including Elena Vergara, Putaendo, 4 June 1993; and María Trujillo, Santa María, 26 Oct. 1992.

60 Ibid.

61 Oral history of Anita Hernández, Santa María, 12 Apr. 1993. To protect the privacy of all interviewees, the names of all people quoted from oral histories have been altered.

62 Oral history of Sonia Araya, Los Andes, 2 June 1993.

63 The practice of paying rural laborers largely in-kind instead of in cash wages was fundamental to the inquilino labor system predating the Agrarian Reform, and was abolished in stages throughout the late 1950s and 1960s. It was also not uncommon for wages of working dependents (including children and wives) to be given to the (male) household head or put toward the worker's debt at employer-owned stores.

64 Various oral histories, including María Trujillo, Santa María, 26 Oct. 1992; and María García, Santa María, 4 Nov. 1992.

65 In her study on political culture and gender during the Chilean Popular Front, Karin Rosemblatt has argued that women's gendered position and "problems" shifted meaningfully throughout a woman's life cycle. Single (usually younger) working women were inserted into a distinct web of power dynamics, which changed substantially once they were married and devoting their labor to the family. See Rosemblatt, "Gendered Compromises." Steve Stern has argued that single, older women (especially widows) occupied yet another set of gendered situations and that such women could simultaneously be relatively more independent and more vilified. See Stern, The Secret History of Gender.

66 Estadísticas APROFA, 1960–1992, Santiago, 1993. Also see Ana María Silva Dreyer, "Tendencias generales de la fecundidad," Instituto de la Mujer: Informativo no. 3, 1990, 9–10.

67 This sentiment was expressed by at least three-quarters of the women I interviewed as well as by women interviewed by other researchers on the Agrarian Reform. See Garrett, "Growing Apart"; Valdés, et al., Historias testimoniales; Mattelart and Mattelart, La mujer chilena; and José Cancino, Germán Gonzalez, Juan Méndez, Claudio Zúniga, "Hábitos, creéncias, y costumbres populares del puerperio y recién nacido," unpublished paper in author's possession, Universidad de Chile, Valparaíso, 1982, 19–22.

68 Interview with Dr. Luis Ortega, San Felipe SNS, 16 Mar. 1998; various oral histories.

69 Oral history of Emilio Ibáñez, 10 Nov. 1992.

70 Interview with Dr. Luis Ortega, SNS San Felipe, San Felipe, 16 Mar. 1993; Xímena Jiles, De la miel a los implantes.

71 Ana María Silva Dreyer, "Tendencias generales de la fecundidad," 9–10.

72 Author's calculations from the "Registro de Crimen," Juzgado de Crimen, San Felipe. Of the 240 cases of physical harm against filed between 1964 and 1973, only 70 were available for study; of these, almost three-quarters involved rural poor people, at least one of which was listed as earning a livelihood in agriculture.

73 Heidi Tinsman, "Esposas golpeadas: Violencia domestica y control sexual en Chile rural, 1958–1988," in Disaplina y desacato: Estudios de genero en la historia de Chile, siglos XIX y XX, ed. Lorena Gody, Elizabeth Hutchison, Karin Rosemblatt, and Soledad Zárate (Santiago: SUR/CEDEM, 1995); "Household Patrones: Wife-Beating and Sexual Control in Rural Chile," in The Gendered Worlds of Latin American Women Workers, ed. Daniel James and John French (Durham: Duke University Press, 1997).

74 Case file S350;26768, Juzgado de Crimen.

75 Ibid.

76 Ibid.

77 Ibid.

78 Steve Stern, The Secret History of Gender.

79 Ibid.
80 Case file B27;27615, Juzgado de Crimen.
81 Ibid.
82 Elsewhere I have discussed common-law wives' very different legal position within marriage. See Heidi Tinsman, "Household Patrones."
83 Eighteen cases of wife beating examined for this study involved female objections to men's extramarital sexual activities.
84 Various oral histories, including Raúl Fuentes, Santa María, 15 Nov. 1992; Emilio Ibáñez, Santa María, 10 Nov. 1992.
85 Oral histories of Pedro Muñoz, San Esteben, 11 Mar. 1993, and Jorge Tejedo, San Felipe, 20 Oct. 1992. For a fuller discussion of the masculine, and even misogynist, nature of the rural labor movement, see chapter 3 in Heidi Tinsman, "Unequal Uplift."
86 Various issues of El Siglo, 1960–73; Nuevo Campo, 1967–68; and Reforma Agraria, 1960–62.
87 Oral history of Armando Gómez, Putaendo, 14 June 1993.
88 Thomas Klubock and Karin Rosemblatt have argued that, as institutions, Chilean labor unions and Popular Front governments in the 1930s and 1940s frowned on sexual promiscuity and attempted to create an upstanding and "moral" working class composed of men who responsibly headed families. Klubock, in particular, contrasts the moralizing mission of unions with the enduring sexual (and sexist) promiscuity defiantly pursued by rank-and-file men. See Klubock, Contested Communities; Karin Alejandra Rosemblatt, "Domesticating Men: State-Building and Class Compromise in Popular-Front Chile," in The Hidden Histories of Gender and the State in Latin America, ed. Elizabeth Dore and Maxine Molyneux (Durham: Duke University Press, 2000). I argue that, in the rural context of the 1960s and 1970s, this distinction was more blurred: labor activists both championed male responsibility to the campesino family and condoned a sexually assertive working-class male persona.
89 Oral history of María Ordenas, Calle Medio, 7 Sept. 1997.
90 Author's calculations from the "Registro de Crimen."
91 Of 274 cases of home abandonment filed at the Juzgado de Crimen between 1958 and 1973, only half were available for examination, and 89 involved campesina or very poor town-dwelling families. Of these, women (usually mothers, but occasionally a guardian aunt or grandmother) initiated the charges 70 percent of the time. Fathers initiated charges in 16 percent of the cases; in the remaining cases, the record was unclear.
92 For a fuller analysis of home abandonment cases between 1955 and 1964, as well as during the Agrarian Reform period, see chapter 2 in Tinsman, "Unequal Uplift."
93 The dynamics of home abandonment cases are highly reminiscent of court trials involving "honor" throughout the colonial era and into the nineteenth century. As several scholars have argued, premarital sex commonly followed a promise of marriage but took place before the formal marriage ceremony as a way of solidifying a union. In cases where men backed down from marriage promises or denied them, families of the affected woman took the suitor to court to seek redress in the form of a marriage, money, or criminal sentence. Parents also went to court to prevent children from marrying undesirable parties. See the various essays in Asunción Lavrin, ed., Sexuality and Marriage in Colonial Latin America (Lincoln: University of Nebraska Press, 1989); Ramón Gutiérrez, When Jesus Came, the Corn Mothers Went Away: Sexuality and Marriage in Colonial New Mexico (Stanford: Stanford University Press, 1991); Patricia Seed, To Love, Honor, and Obey in Colonial Mexico: Conflicts Over Marriage Choice, 1574–1821 (Stanford: Stanford University Press, 1988).
94 Case file no. S373;28295, Juzgado de Crimen.

95 Case file no. 378;28837, Juzgado de Crimen.
96 There were 114 charges of rape and attempted rape filed at the San Felipe Juzgado de Crimen between 1958 and 1973 ("Registro de Crimen"). Of these cases, only 70 were available for examination. Thirty-six involved people who were specified as "agricultural workers," and in another twelve, the parties were poor, but it was unclear if they were campesinos. Of the cases available for examination, only four involved women under age twenty-five.
97 Mothers or female guardians of alleged victims initiated rape charges in 54 percent of the available cases; fathers, and male guardians initiated charges in 36 percent of these cases.
98 Of the forty-three rape or attempted rape charges filed in San Felipe between 1971 and 1973, twenty-seven were available for examination. Of these, seventeen involved the rape of young girls, one involved the attempted rape of an older married woman, and nine the rape of adolescent girls.
99 See case files S374;27906, S370;27835, and S345;27924, Juzgado de Crimen.
100 Case file no. S374;27906, Juzgado de Crimen.
101 Case file no. S378;28846, Juzgado de Crimen.
102 Author's study of "Registro de Nacimiento," department of San Felipe, 1964–86.
103 Ibid.
104 For data on marriage rates for women by age, see *Censo de población: Aconcagua*, 1960 and 1970. Women between the ages of 20 and 29 also married in higher percentages in 1970 than they had in 1960. In 1960, 57 percent of all women between 20 and 29 years of age were married. In 1970 this figure rose to 60 percent. For data on average marriage ages, see *Demografía: Aconcagua*, 1960, 1968, and 1970. In 1970 the average marriage age for rural women in Aconcagua was 22.8 years; in 1968 it was 23.6; in 1960 it was 24.
105 The numbers of strikes industry-wide in Chile per year were as follows: 1,867 in 1970; 2,576 in 1971; 3,278 in 1972; and 2,048 in 1973. The numbers of strikes in rural areas were as follows: 523 in 1970; 1,580 in 1971; 1,758 in 1972; and 317 in the first three months of 1973. (For 1970 and 1973, *Estadísticas laborales*, INE, 1976, 96–100; for 1971 and 1972, Solon Barraclough and J. A. Fernández, *Diagnóstico de la reforma agraria en Chile* [Mexico City: Siglo XXI, 1974], 134). The numbers of *tomas de tierra* in agriculture nationwide were as follows: 456 in 1970; 1,128 in 1971; 1,273 in 1972; 309 in January–April 1972 (José Bengoa, *Historia del movimiento campesino* [Santiago: GIA, 1983]).
106 For an excellent discussion of women's mobilization against the UP, see Lisa Baldez, "In the Name of the Public and the Private: Conservative and Progressive Women's Movements in Chile, 1970–1996" (Ph.D. diss., University of San Diego, 1997); Margaret Power, "Right Wing Women and Chilean Politics: 1964–1973" (Ph.D. diss., University of Illinois, Chicago, 1997). Also see Elsa Chaney, "The Mobilization of Women in Allende's Chile," in *Women in Politics*, ed. Jane Jaquette (New York: John Wiley and Sons, 1974); Edda Gaviola Artigas, Lorella Lopresti Martínez, and Claudia Rojas, "La participación política de la mujer chilena entre los años 1964–1973" (ISIS, Santiago, 1987); María de los Angeles Crummett, "El poder feminino: The Mobilization of Women against Socialism in Chile," *Latin American Perspectives* 4, no. 4 (fall 1977): 103–13; Michele Mattelart, "Chile: The Feminine Side of the Coup or When Bourgeois Women Take to the Streets," *NACLA: Latin America and Empire Report* 9, no. 6 (1975): 14–25.
107 In the Aconcagua Valley counties with majority rural populations (excluding the comunas of San Felipe and Los Andes), 27.5 percent voted for Allende in 1970, and 36.6

percent voted for Tomic, the Christian Democratic candidate whose Agrarian Reform platform was almost identical to the UP's in its call for eliminating all latifundia and reorganizing land into collectively farmed terrain (Dirección del Registro Electoral, Santiago).

108 In the municipal elections of April 1971, 36.7 percent of women in the Aconcagua Valley cast votes for candidates pertaining to Popular Unity parties. In rural *comunas* where the Left was particularly strong, such as Catemu and Rinconada, up to 50 percent of women who voted did so for UP candidates ("Elección ordinaria de regidores, 4 de abril, 1971," Dirección del Registro Electoral, Santiago). Likewise, in the March 1973 elections for congressional delegates, 36.2 percent of all female voters cast ballots for UP candidates; in rural *comunas* such as Curimón, Catemu, Panquehue, Calle Larga, and Rinconada, well over 40 percent of the female vote went to UP candidates ("Elección Ordinaria Parlamentaria (Diputados), 4 de marzo, 1973," Dirección del Registro Electoral, Santiago).

109 In the rural *comunas* of the Aconcagua Valley (excluding San Felipe and Los Andes), 40.6 percent of men voted for Allende in 1970 and 31.3 percent for Tomic (Dirección del Registro Electoral). In the 1971 municipal elections, 47 percent of men in the Aconcagua Valley as a whole cast ballots for UP candidates; in *comunas* such as Rinconada and Catemu, male votes for the UP exceeded 57 percent ("Elección Ordinaria de Regidores, 4 de abril, 1971," Dirección del Registro Electoral, Santiago). Likewise, in the 1973 congressional elections, 49 percent of men throughout the Aconcagua Valley cast votes for UP candidates, and in all predominately rural *comunas* (excluding San Felipe and Los Andes), the male vote for UP candidates exceeded 50 percent ("Elección Ordinaria Parlamentaria (Diputados), 4 de marzo, 1973," Dirección del Registro Electoral, Santiago).

110 In the rural comunas of the Aconcagua Valley (not including the cities of San Felipe and Los Andes), 25–30 percent fewer women voted than men. Even accounting for the fact that men outnumbered women in rural areas, the difference was considerable. Strikingly, women's voter participation was lowest in the rural counties where the UP did best (San Esteben, Catemu, Putaendo), suggesting that the Left failed to mobilize women (or convince men to let women vote) in its own strongholds.

111 Edda Gaviola Artigas et al., "La Participación de la mujer chilena entre los años 1964–1973"; Elsa Chaney, "The Mobilization of Women in Allende's Chile," in Jaquette, *Women in Politics;* "Women in Latin American Politics: The Case of Peru and Chile," in *Male and Female in Latin America,* ed. Ann Pescatello (Austin: University of Texas Press, 1973), 131; *Supermadre: Women in Politics in Latin America* (Austin: University of Texas Press, 1979); Michael Francis and Patricia A. Kyle, "Chile: The Power of Women at the Polls," in *Integrating the Neglected Majority: Government Responses to Demands for New Sex Roles,* ed. Patricia Kyle (New Brunswick, N.J.: Rutgers University Press, 1976); Michael Francis and Patricia Kyle, "Women at the Polls: The Case of Chile, 1970–1971," *Comparative Political Studies* 11, no. 3 (October 1978); Steven M. Nouse, "Voting in Chile: The Feminine Response," in *Citizen and State: Political Participation in Latin America,* ed. John Booth and Mitchell Seligson (New York: Holmes Meier, 1978); Norma Stoltz Chinchilla, "Mobilizing Women: Revolution in the Revolution," in Jaquette, *Women in Politics;* Nathaniel Davis, *The Last Two Years of Salvador Allende* (Ithaca: Cornell University Press, 1984); María de los Angeles Crummett, "El Poder feminino"; Michele Mattelart, "Chile: The Feminine Side of the Coup"; Lisa Baldez, "In the Name of the Public and the Private"; Margaret Power, "Right Wing Women."

112 Garrett, "Growing Apart."
113 Ibid.
114 In 1971 there were thirty-four cases of *lesiones* involving male violence against women filed at the San Felipe Juzgado de Crimen. In 1972 there were thirty such cases; in 1973 there were fifty cases. In contrast, between 1964 and 1970, there was a total of eighty-four cases, or an annual average of twelve cases (author's calculations from the "Registro de Crimen," Juzgado de Crimen).
115 Author's calculations from the "Registro de Crimen."
116 Ibid.
117 Records of judicial criminal cases in San Felipe made distinctions between crimes committed with violence and those that were not. Between 1960 and 1972, there was a continuous increase in the number of crimes listed as involving violence. In 1960 the percent of crimes involving violence was 21 percent; in 1964, 26 percent; in 1968, 35 percent; in 1972, 51 percent; and in 1973, 34 percent (author's calculations from the "Registro de Crimen").
118 As Thomas Klubock has argued in his study on copper miners and the Chilean Popular Front, increased complaints to authorities by women about sexual violence accompanied the political opening afforded by working-class mobilization and benefited from the creation of social welfare institutions. See Thomas Klubock, *Contested Communities*.
119 Oral history of Armando Gómez, Putaendo, 22 May 1993.
120 Oral history of Jorge Tejedo, San Felipe, 14 June 1993.
121 Oral history of Ana Saavedra, San Felipe, 15 Apr. 1993.
122 Oral history of Elena Vergara, Putaendo, 14 June 1993. This story is also recounted in the interview of "Inés" in *Hombres y mujeres de Putaendo: Sus discursos y sus visiones* (Santiago: CEM, 1988), 119–20.
123 The impact of escalating class struggle on Campesino masculinity is more fully explored in chapters 9 and 10 of Tinsman, "Unequal Uplift."

IV
Historians and the Making of History
▼

Florencia E. Mallon

Bearing Witness in Hard Times: Ethnography and
Testimonio in a Postrevolutionary Age

▼

"He is not an 'average' anything," wrote Sidney Mintz in the last paragraph
of his introduction to *Worker in the Cane* (1960), "neither an average man,
nor an average Puerto Rican, nor an average Puerto Rican lower-class sugar
cane worker." He was, of course, referring to Don Taso Zayas, the man
whose life history (and, Mintz admitted, whose conversion to Pentecostal
Protestantism after a lifetime of leftist and union politics) formed the
central drama of the book. Mintz continued, "He has lived just one life and
not all of that. He doesn't think of himself as representative of anything,
and he is right. His solutions to life's problems may not be the best ones,
either, but he seems satisfied with his choices. I have tried to put down his
story in the context of what I could understand about the circumstances
under which he lived and lives."[1]

Worker in the Cane is an early example of *testimonio* or life history, written at
a time when in Latin America the genre was still dominated by the polished, seamless narratives constructed by Oscar Lewis out of his own and
his research assistants' interviews.[2] In contrast to many later *testimonios*,
which began from a personal relationship politically constituted, *Worker in*
the Cane emerged from Mintz's participation in Julian H. Steward's broad,
multiperson project of ethnographic fieldwork titled "The People of Puerto
Rico." Along with John V. Murra, Steward supervised a team of graduate
student researchers, among whom was Sidney Mintz. After completing his
earlier project, Mintz went back to follow up with Don Taso Zayas and
produce the life history.

Worker in the Cane openly struggled with many of the issues that would
later be "discovered" in the debates of the 1980s and 1990s: how far to

Isolde Reuque (center) and Rigoberta Menchú (second from right) pose for a photograph along with other participants in the 1992 Indigenous Tour of Europe. From the personal archives of Isolde Reuque.

"doctor" or organize the narrative; how clear to make the relationship between subject/narrator and editor; whether or not to include alternative perspectives provided by other family members. Not only did Mintz include interviews with Doña Elí Villarronga, Don Taso's wife, but he also left in his questions and included a lengthy explanation in the introduction about how they had met, and how, after the interview process, Mintz organized the material. With many of these innovative techniques, Mintz prefigured the debates around concepts like ethnographic authority and ethnographic narrative. He also produced a *testimonio* featuring a man who did not claim any special or representative status for an oppressed group, but simply thought he had lived the best life he could.[3]

Why did a dialogic life history about a Latin American worker, published in 1960, get left out of the recent boom in discussion and criticism of *testimonio* and life history? One reason, I believe, is that the critiques of ethnography and *testimonio* have tended to occupy the attention of different groups of scholars. Increasingly considered a literary genre, *testimonio* has generally been dissected by literary critics and other practitioners of cultural studies. Ethnography, on the other hand, has tended to be debated within anthropology and to focus on the "scientific" versus "literary" elements of the discipline: narrative choice versus narrative distance; the reading of texts versus falsifiable hypotheses. Because *Worker in the Cane* is both *testimonio* and ethnography, and emerges from a relationship that spans more than a decade, it does not fit the categories and periodizations established for the two separate genres, and either simply falls through the cracks of intellectual taxonomy or gets discarded because it constitutes an anomaly. But precisely because it constitutes an anomaly, foreshadowing many of the issues and problems we now face in addressing ethnography and life history, I believe we need to take seriously the issues it raises about the practice of ethnography and *testimonio*, many of which are startlingly relevant in our postrevolutionary times.

To begin with, *Worker in the Cane* provides an early and understated example of what critics of ethnographic authority were vociferously calling for in the mid-1980s, a dialogic approach. By including statements written by Don Taso himself in response to Mintz's initial request that he tell the story of his life, by interspersing more-formal interviews (with questions left in) with more monographically presented information, and by juxtaposing Don Taso's and Doña Elí's version of events, Mintz creates almost a postmodern ethnography. According to Stephen Tyler, a postmodern ethnography "foregrounds dialogue as opposed to monologue, and emphasizes the cooperative and collaborative nature of the ethnographic situation in contrast to the ideology of the transcendental observer. In fact, it rejects the ideology of 'observer-observed,' there being nothing observed and no one who is observer. There is instead the mutual, dialogic production of a discourse, a story of sorts."[4]

Particularly in Mintz's struggle to understand Don Taso's conversion to Pentecostalism, however, the earlier "cooperative and collaborative nature" and the lack of observer and observed seem to fall away. Mintz was so convinced of Don Taso's rational intellectual gifts that he simply could not fathom the man's attraction to a charismatic religion—a fact that spoke more to Mintz's worldview than to Don Taso's. At the end of the book, in fact, Mintz spends two chapters attempting an objective, structural explanation of the factors that brought about this change in his friend's behavior. At this point the book begins to resemble a text described by James Clifford, Marjorie Shostak's *Nisa*, which seems to struggle with some of the same issues. "Difference invades the text," Clifford comments. "It can no longer be represented; it must be enacted."[5]

But does this tension, Mintz's ultimate inability simply to accept Don Taso's conversion (and Don Taso's knowledge that Mintz would not accept it, and his discomfort with explaining how he received the spirit and spoke in tongues) doom the ethnography or the *testimonio*? I think not. Instead, it opens up the tensions, the arguments, the mutual process of influence, even of confrontation, that form part of a deep dialogic relationship. Indeed, through the various phases of the friendship, its deepening mutual acceptance and affection, difference is enacted rather than represented. And in so doing, Mintz and Zayas provide us with a deeper and more respectful answer to the "naive questions"—"How do you write polyphonic ethnographies? How do I make my dissertation reflexive?"—than the tendency among postmodern anthropologists to simply ignore them or, rather than answer, critique the questions.[6] The answer provided by Mintz, Don Taso and Doña Elí is that reflexive, polyphonic narrative is crafted only imperfectly, and is successful if it is possible to maintain an openness to mutual difference and a willingness to acknowledge the weaknesses or contradictions in our own assumptions.

By focusing on an individual and his family, therefore, and on their relationship with a foreign anthropologist, *Worker in the Cane* provides an early example of how dialogic ethnography might begin to look, and suggests some techniques for rendering the dialogue in the text. It is even more unusual or anomalous, however, as a text within the genre *testimonio*. It is not the testimony of a woman or of a political activist (male or female, member of a guerrilla group or of a social movement), and it does not claim to represent a social group or a set of experiences generated in a community through a collective historical process. Though contemporaneous with the life histories of Oscar Lewis, it does not bury the marks of conversation nor assume the voice of an omniscient narrator. And finally, before the publication of Miguel Barnet's *Autobiography of a Runaway Slave*, before the stamp of approval given to the genre by the Casa de las Américas with the creation of its *testimonio* prize (1970), and quite removed from the dramatic revolutionary processes initiated in Cuba in 1959, *Worker in the Cane* challenges the later division John Beverley suggests between *testimonio* and life history. Not only is "the intentionality of the *recorder*—usually a social scientist" not dominant, but neither is the resulting narration "data." Instead, as Beverley then proposes for *testimonio*, Don Taso Zayas's narration clearly "involves . . . a problem of repression, poverty, subalternity, . . . struggle for survival, and so on."[7]

One aspect of recent debates about *testimonio* that *Worker in the Cane* does not prefigure is the concern with whether or not the subaltern can speak, and whether or not an attempt to represent or mediate the voices of the marginalized is a pertinent or viable endeavor. George Yúdice wrote, "Testimonial writing shares several features with what is currently called postmodernity, the rejection of master discourses or prevailing frameworks of interpreting the world and the increasing importance of the marginal." But "the task of the deconstructionists has not been to vindicate or emancipate the marginalized elements," he added, "but rather to detect the traces

Isolde Reuque reaches the climactic point of her well-received speech in Assisi, Italy, during the 1992 Indigenous Tour of Europe. From the personal archives of Isolde Reuque.

left behind as they are consumed in the projection of 'natural,' 'rational,' and 'logical' states of affairs." In such a context, Yúdice concluded, the Other or marginalized "has no existence except as the absence that difference establishes."[8]

Initially some scholars influenced by postmodernism, including John Beverley and Yúdice himself, welcomed *testimonio* as a literary genre precisely because it provided a venue through which the presence of the Other could be reestablished and legitimized, potentially destabilizing the canon and calling into question the "natural" or "logical" state of affairs. What made this possible, according to these scholars, was the embeddedness of *testimonio* in resistance movements, guerrilla struggles, peoples' struggles in the Third World. In such a situation, the mediation of the intellectual who recorded and organized the narrative became an act of solidarity rather than an act of cannibalism. As Beverley initially conceptualized it, *testimonio* was a form of literary production giving voice to a "collective popular-democratic subject, the *pueblo* or 'people,' " in which the "deep and inescapable contradictions" between the narrator/subject and the editor could potentially be resolved through solidarity, through "a sense of sisterhood and mutuality in the struggle against a common system of oppression."[9]

But what happens in today's postrevolutionary world, when struggles for liberation have been defeated or, at best, marginalized? The same scholars who earlier celebrated *testimonio*'s power to transgress are now having second thoughts. As before, it is John Beverley who summarizes it best when he suggests that the historical moment that gave *testimonio* its urgency has now passed. Begun as a genre during the revolutionary upswing of the 1960s, he suggests, it came into its own as a form of *denuncia* during the authoritarianism and repression of the 1970s and 1980s. "It was the Real, the voice of the body in pain, of the disappeared, of the losers in the rush to marketize." It also provided a corrective within literature by demonstrating that Latin American boom writers were not the only valid voice for Latin American peoples. And finally, *testimonio* provided a counter, through the foregrounding of people's social and solidarity movements, to the enduring assumptions about politics led and organized by vanguards and parties.

At the end of the twentieth century, however, Beverley concluded that the genre became "detached from these contexts," losing "its special aesthetic and ideological power." Precisely as *testimonio* has been increasingly incorporated as a genre into academic literary discourse, it has lost—according to most of the contributors to the volume *The Real Thing*—its "authenticity," its original legitimacy and power to transgress. Added to this, according to Javier Sanjinés, are the forces of globalization and marketization that have destroyed the material and political conditions that earlier made possible the social movements and dreamed utopias from which *testimonio* sprung. "What is left today," asked Beverley, "of the desire called testimonio?" And he answers, "Chiapas."[10]

While bearing witness in Chiapas through the same general form of *testimonio* as solidarity and *denuncia* is a worthy and crucial endeavor, I would like to suggest here an additional path that reemerges with the sea change, both intellectual and political, brought about by the defeat of really existing socialism. Though following "states of emergency" from one part of the Third World to another has been, and will continue to be, decisive, especially in the project of saving lives and denouncing human rights abuses, the multiplication and extension of these situations has desensitized or overloaded our consciences and consciousness. In addition, once an "emergency" passes and the human press of solidarity and *denuncia* moves on, can we and should we focus on the remaining, perhaps less immediately dramatic, issues of poverty, subordination, oppression, hunger, malnutrition, and political exclusion? If so, through what methods and with what goals? It is here that I think, once again, *Worker in the Cane* provides some helpful suggestions.

Researched and written at a moment of cold-war conservative backlash in the United States, by a member of a leftist generation deeply impacted by McCarthyism, *Worker in the Cane* bears witness in hard times. Don Taso Zayas is a disappointed union and leftist activist, a man who has suffered the blows of political party *caudillismo* and petty corruption, who ultimately finds partial solace and a sense of meaning in Pentecostalism. Within the limits of his own assumptions and beliefs, Sidney Mintz bears witness to this process and develops a lifelong friendship with the man, ultimately both celebrating and grieving the complexity and limitations of one man's life. "Taso's story has no moral," writes Mintz in the epilogue describing his last visit in 1956. "Perhaps it is enough that his life should seem so much better to him now. Or perhaps the reader will see the waste I think I see: the waste of a mind that stands above the others as the violet sprays of the *flor de caña* tower above the cane. But the story should evoke no pity, for that is a sentiment which degrades the meaning of Taso's life to himself and to those who know and love him."[11]

Beginning from these reflections on Mintz in the context of recent trends in anthropology and literary criticism, I would like to suggest that an alternative path for the crisis of *testimonio* and ethnographic authority may lie in the conflictual and creative articulation of ethnography and testimonial, life history and fieldwork, prefigured by *Worker in the Cane*. I believe it is not only possible but necessary, and even urgent, to look beyond the crisis of legitimacy generated in a particular kind of *testimonio*—the politically grounded, "state of emergency"–created solidarity text—to the refashioning of texts that claim their legitimacy elsewhere. That legitimacy, I believe, lies not in the reconstruction of old forms of ethnographic authority, but in the rethinking of the deep relationships of dialogue and connection made possible by ethnographic fieldwork.

This essay is a first and partial exploration of these possibilities, through a discussion of some of the problems and challenges I encountered while doing archival research and fieldwork in Chile in 1996–97. After a dramatic, nearly decade-long struggle against the Pinochet dictatorship ended in 1990 with the election of Patricio Aylwin, most of the foreign human rights activists, political observers and hangers-on, and general international solidarity representatives and cheerleaders went home. In a situation where international observers and peace-oriented foundations and funding agencies declared Chile transformed and democratically healthy, local activists in a variety of social movements were left to sort through the pieces of the antidictatorship movement in a new climate of modernization, economic growth, and military impunity. Slowly a post-transition pall settled over a broad range of participants in the powerful 1980s mobilizations: the much vaunted, much longed for, and much celebrated *democracia* did not turn out to be all that it was cracked up to be. Deep reflection and attempted political reconstruction—as well as ever more bittersweet yearnings for a democracy that seemingly could not be again (and even, occasionally and ironically, for the forms of unity and solidarity possible under authoritarianism)—fell on ever deafer international ears.

This was the situation when I arrived, long after the press of *denuncia*, solidarity, and *testimonio* had moved on—mainly, as Beverley observes, to Chiapas. It was in this context that I began to form relationships, in the southern region of Temuco, with individual Mapuche activists and Mapuche indigenous communities. Because these are not only theoretical or textual relationships, although they do involve theory and texts, I have chosen to organize my reflections around the two deepest networks of connection I was able to establish with communities, families, and individuals in the course of my work in southern Chile. Of the two, one concerns the genre of *testimonio* and my friendship with a Mapuche feminist intellectual. The other involves my ongoing relationship with a community, and the extended Ailío family which composes a good part of it. By focusing my discussion around these concrete cases, and the challenges they presented for me and the people I got to know, I wish to begin a conversation about the many ways in which anthropologists, historians, and others can continue to bear witness in hard times.

The Crafting of Testimonio: Isolde Reuque,
the Reuque Paillalef Family, and Me

I met Isolde Reuque Paillalef for the first time on November 29, 1996. We had talked on the phone a couple of times in preparation for our meeting, and I had heard a summary of her role as a feminist Mapuche leader from my Santiago colleague María Elena Valenzuela, who had gotten to know Isolde on the Chilean delegation to Beijing earlier that same year. We met for coffee at the Café Raíces, a short-lived experiment in pan-indigenous Latin American culture, music, jewelry, and cuisine that existed in downtown Temuco for about eight months. Though we did not know it at the time, the café was pretty much on its last legs when we began to get to know each other at one of its tables.

What was clear to me then were my reasons for being interested in an intellectual relationship with Isolde Reuque. Having taught a course on oral history and testimonial literature less than a year before, having read the most current experiments with the testimonial genre as well as revisiting some of the classics, and having begun to read the early critiques coming from feminist and postmodern literary criticism, I was determined to explore the possibilities for collaborating with a Mapuche woman on a feminist testimonial. I was seeking a horizontal relationship, insofar as that was possible. I was not interested in telling the story of a "typical peasant," however one might define such a person. Instead, I wanted to collaborate on a testimonial whose author/subject would reflect and dialogue with me on the cultural and political complexities of her people.

From what I already knew at the time of our first conversation, Isolde Reuque could very well be exactly the person I was looking for. I had already interviewed another woman who was a Mapuche intellectual and leader, a woman who held a position of some importance in the indigenous state agency, the Corporación Nacional de Desarrollo Indígena (CONADI) (National Indigenous Development Corporation), and had gotten along very well with her. But for a series of reasons, the most important of which was that she was always too busy at her job, we had not been able to find time for a second conversation. The other Mapuche leader I had interviewed was an eminently urban woman. While I was not looking for the "exotic" by focusing on the countryside, and although I was only four months into an incredibly complex research project, still at a loss as to the overall conceptualization, I had already read enough in secondary and primary sources to understand that the relationship between urban and rural, between community and town, was conflictual and complex in Mapuche culture. From early in the twentieth century, organizations of urban Mapuche intellectuals had attempted to erase their cultural differences and integrate into mainstream Chilean culture. Indeed, by the 1930s, only a few Mapuche intellectuals continued to revindicate the religious and family traditions that many acculturated Mapuche urbanites themselves labeled as "barbarian."[12] Even though my earlier interviewee was of a different generation, in which respect for rural Mapuche traditions was now de rigeur among urbanites as well, I began to suspect that her lack of personal rural experience would limit how far our conversation could progress. Indeed, in my conversation with María Elena in Santiago, I had asked whether Isolde had a connection to a rural community. María Elena had emphasized that she did.

Isolde and I got along famously. She was humorous, sharp, honest, and self-possessed. When I read the transcription of our first interview before my next trip to Temuco, about a month later, I could see a number of places where I had tried very hard to show her I "knew stuff," that I was not just another dumb outsider, in my case both *wigka* (non-Mapuche) and half-gringa. But she was very patient with me and didn't hold my ignorance and posturing against me, even when I interrupted an important discussion to try to show what I knew. We got along so well, in fact, that somewhere along the way, during that first conversation, I laid my intellectual cards out on the table. I remember telling her (though this did not end up on tape) that I would like to explore the possibility of collaborating with her on a life history or testimony. I proposed some conditions: first, that she would be the primary author, appearing first on the title page, and that my name would appear lower down, as "with Florencia Mallon"; second, that she would receive transcripts of all conversations and would have the last word as to the version that got published; third, that I would be in charge of transcriptions and of organizing the text into some kind of narrative form, though she would then have final editing rights; fourth, that she and I would both have the opportunity to write our own introductions and conclusions to the text; and finally, that this would involve a fair amount of work for both of us over the next few months. She seemed immediately interested, and we agreed to meet again the next week, before I left Temuco.

At the time, I modeled my offer on the example of testimonio that had most recently inspired me: the collaborative work edited by Lynn Stephen concerning María Teresa Tula's life and the Committee of Mothers and Relatives of the Political Prisoners, Disappeared and Assassinated of El Salvador (COMADRES). Among all the books of testimonio I had read, this one had most inspired me to think about potentially more horizontal ways of collaborating on a testimonial.[13] It would be much later, however, before

I began to understand why, from Isolde's own personal point of view, the offer to help write her life story seemed so attractive. She did mention at the time that it was something she had been thinking of doing, but never could find enough time to sit at the computer and actually write. And she invited me to her house, a two-story structure she and her husband had built piecemeal since their marriage, in the Pedro de Valdivia neighborhood of Temuco.

I arrived at her house, near the northwestern edge of the city, around teatime on December 3, 1996. I struggled uphill along three blocks of dirt road from the bus stop with a backpack full of notes and copies from my day's research as well as my laptop computer. I came armed with a bag of high-quality *mate* I had bought in the downtown market. (I had gotten many strange stares, as a *wigka* outsider buying *mate*, because in southern Chile drinking *mate* is usually a marker of Mapuche ethnic identity.) Bringing *mate* was a signal that I was willing to stay for a while, to share a *mate* brew with those present and let the conversation go where it may. I had listened to our first interview a couple of times and came equipped with a series of questions about the Mapuche movement and Isolde's role in it that probably signaled to her that I was serious. We talked for more than three hours, and at various points her husband and one of her younger sisters joined in. For the first time she talked openly and in detail about her frustrations in the Mapuche movement, and I began to get a clearer picture of the political complexities of her role, and that of other Mapuche leaders.

My next visit to Temuco was in January 1997, and I spent the entire month doing research and fieldwork in the region. Because of my own rushed schedule (I had my teenage son with me, who was on summer vacation) as well as Isolde's own numerous commitments, the whole time we were unable to meet for more than half an hour. I even had to deliver her copy of our first interviews' transcriptions to a neighbor. I began to understand what she had meant, the first time we talked, about never finding enough time to sit down and write. In fact, I began to fear that the testimonial might not materialize. On the bright side, however, a solid month of research in Temuco archives, combined with intense fieldwork in the community of Ailío, brought me over the top of my first conceptual mountain range on the project as a whole, and gave me a much clearer view of where I was headed.

February was summer vacation month in Chile, so when I returned to Temuco in mid-March, I came determined to go into full gear on the interviews with Isolde. From the time of our first interview, when Isolde had told me a bit about her community, I had been wanting to visit Chanco with her and get to know her family and neighbors, and perhaps do some research about the community as well. Every time I subsequently proposed this to her, she seemed interested but would talk vaguely about when we might go. So on March 14, having just arrived from Santiago, I called her and pushed the issue of her community once again. This time we agreed on a visit that very weekend. Since on Saturday I was going with the Ailío community to visit the new lands they had recently purchased with government money, we agreed to travel to Chanco on Sunday.

With Isolde's help I put together several bags of groceries at the local supermarket, which we presented to her mother upon arrival. During an afternoon of eating, talking, and sharing a *mate* brew with Isolde's parents, sister, and daughter, I managed a short interview with her father, Don Ernesto Reuque, the *logko*, or head, of the community, about his life and work experiences. Isolde's younger sister Elvira also introduced me to some of the members of the community's youth group she had helped organize, and showed me the library she was accumulating to help them with their schoolwork.

The first visit to Isolde's community and family seemed to go well, and I think it helped set the tone for our interview in Temuco, at her house, the following Wednesday. Along with her sister Elvira, Isolde was in a more intimate and reflective mood. The three of us talked about what it was like to be a woman in Mapuche culture, the difficulties with establishing a companionate romantic relationship, and why Isolde felt so comfortable, intellectually and politically, with her parents-in-law. There was something about that conversation—which also included a description of the hardships Isolde had faced giving birth to her daughter, out of wedlock, many years before—that convinced me an important hurdle had been cleared. The three of us also worked on a tentative outline for the book and began discussing possible titles.

I called again in April, upon returning to the south, and learned a small crisis had developed. One of the elders in the community with whom we had talked on our previous visit, suggesting that we get together on my next trip for an interview and a photograph, had decided that he would not talk for free. When he discussed the situation with his daughters, they had apparently told him that Isolde must be making a lot of money doing a book with a gringa and that he should get some, too. A photograph for a calendar paid a lot of money, they calculated, so a photo for a book must pay a lot more. Isolde had told him that it was all right, that there were other people in the community and that we did not have to talk to him. Isolde's mother had found out first and had been upset. Isolde sounded pretty upset on the phone, too, but we agreed that we would go to Chanco anyway.

Only later did two subtexts emerge for me in this situation. The first was that Isolde's family was being protective of me and of the relationship they had developed with me. In a challenge to them from within their community, they already felt, for whatever combination of reasons, that they needed to take my side. Second, the assumptions being made by the old man and his daughters probably reinforced Isolde's sense of being an outsider, even in her own culture and community, something her outside political activism had also increased.

We traveled to Chanco on Saturday, April 19, planning to come back the following day. In addition to spending the night with her family, we would have plenty of space to continue our interviews as well as to meet other members of her community. Said and done, except when we arrived at her family's house, after the introductions, initial conversation, and sharing of a *mate* brew, Isolde informed us that she would have to return to Temuco for a political meeting, but that I could stay the night, and she and I could talk on Sunday when she returned! When I pointed out, somewhat frustrated, that this was not what I had envisioned, and why didn't she tell me about this change of plans while we were still in Temuco, Isolde laughed and said something to the effect of "Why not take this as a golden opportunity? You get to talk to my family, even gossip about me, without my being present!"

We did not gossip about her, but her mother Doña Martina Paillalef, her younger sister Elvira, her daughter Liliana, her older brother Lionel, and I spent nearly two hours talking over wine and *mate* in the family kitchen. On two cassette tapes we recorded our discussion of topics as diverse as the origins myth of the Paillalef lineage (which Lionel had read in a book), Doña Martina's childhood, what it was like to go to school as a Mapuche child, the ups and downs of the Ley Indígena and the transition to democratic rule, and the complexities of cultural preservation in a minority setting. We ended up laughing and joking, and Lionel threatened to steal a Swiss army knife of mine to which he had taken a liking (before leaving Chile, I gave it to him as a gift). When Isolde returned the next morning, she received positive reports from all concerned, and in the afternoon we found a relatively secluded spot where we could continue our conversation. That day we filled four cassette tapes with a series of discussions about the most important events and moments in the development of the Mapuche movement, using my accumulated research in the newspapers of the time as a starting point. Isolde also made suggestions about which newspapers and additional dates I should consult when I returned to Santiago. At some point we also decided to include in the book the conversation I had had with her family.

These April interviews marked a watershed in our project. Though it was always difficult for us to know how far we had gone (until one night in May, when sitting at the kitchen table in her house in Temuco, the fact that we had finished suddenly hit us in the face), in April we were both sure we had advanced more than halfway. On my laptop computer we composed a final draft of the book outline that would become our map through the final interviews. But our watershed was about more than the volume of interviews already recorded; it was also about trust. Returning on the bus to Temuco that night, Isolde confided in me that she had never before brought an outside researcher to work in her own community. Though she had collaborated with a number of other scholars and had introduced people to her family in a personal or social sense, earlier research collaborations had usually featured her in-laws rather than her own kin. Opening her family and her community to me had been a sign of trust, as well as a test; luckily I had passed muster and been accepted. In June, at a seminar held in Temuco with representatives from several of the Mapuche communities where I had done research, people were asked what they had gotten from their collaboration with me. Isolde said, with gentle and playful humor, that she had learned things about her community she had never known, not only by going with me to interview some of the elders, but also (she could not resist a chuckle) from the conversations they held after I had left.

During the four years since I left Chile, I have reflected many times on the friendship Isolde and I are still building. On one side, I have thought a great deal about the differences between us—of life experience and cultural background; social position, education, professional connections; economic privilege and country of residence, with all the differential access this entails. I have also considered how the balance of power between us has changed over time. If we started from an initial position in which I depended a great deal more on her—trusting that she would teach me about the Mapuche people and their experiences, that she would take me to her community and help me understand—we have now gotten to a place where, even if she has authorship, right of ownership and of final revision over her text, I have the contacts for publication and have supervised and negotiated an advanced contract for the English translation.[14] In this sense her desire—her need to share her point of view about the conflicts and successes, pain and happiness that she has seen and experienced in the Mapuche movement over the past quarter century—must necessarily find ultimate realization through my professional and academic connections. All of this makes our friendship a complex relationship that operates at multiple levels; I cannot presume a false and easy equality between us. In fact, all the debates, all the criticisms that have emerged from within anthropology in the last twenty years prevent me from pretending an equality of circumstances between the two of us.[15]

At the same time, I do not want to misinterpret or exaggerate the differences that separate us. On one side they are important and are based on such structural, overdetermined factors as social class, imperialism, even the Spanish Conquest and more than five hundred years of racism. But on the other side, the two of us have managed to build a friendship that involves two specific people who, for a series of distinct reasons, have been able to communicate with and appreciate each other despite the barriers and differences that separate us. Thus I would also like to reflect a bit on which factors I have come to see as important in the construction of our friendship.

I have come to believe that Isolde Reuque and I became friends because we both felt like outsiders in our own environments. During one of our conversations, when she was explaining to me why she had stayed with her husband despite their many problems, she said it was because they were both "like black sheep." This expression, especially its sense of connection in marginality, also has a great deal of relevance for me. In Isolde's case, it denotes her experience as a Mapuche leader who, despite being one of the founding members of the first Mapuche ethnic organization in 1978, had to learn *mapunzugun* as an adult because it had not been spoken in her house. Even though she spent years traveling throughout the south of Chile helping other communities revive Mapuche culture and ritual, in her own community people had stopped celebrating the *gillatun*, the most important Mapuche religious and communal ceremony, twenty years before. As she remembers, although a new cycle of rituals was begun in Chanco in 1980, it was aways harder to be a "prophet in one's own land."

In addition, in a Mapuche social movement where many activists were on the political left, Isolde was always a political moderate and espoused a deep and sincere Catholic faith, which caused her more than a few problems. Yet at the same time she is a profoundly radical person in how she lives her life, because she criticizes honestly, both friend and foe, and always begins with herself. She does not beat around the bush, even when it makes her less than popular with her political allies or the elites of her political party. Her courage and honesty, even when we had different political beliefs, made possible a friendship based on trust, and also inspired in me a profound admiration.

For my part, I learned when I returned to Chile in 1996, after more than twenty years, that I really did not belong anywhere. Despite my long absence my Chilean family, originally from the traditional landowning elite, accepted me back with deep and unconditional love, and welcomed my husband and children warmly and affectionately. Nonetheless, I felt out of place in the post-Pinochet prosperity of Santiago's upper-class neighborhoods and sought desperately to find an alternative way of connecting to the land where I was born, preferably along the margins of dominant society. At the same time I did not entirely reject the privilege provided by my family connections, using it strategically in order to schedule an interview with a southern landowning family and gaining their confidence by telling them that a great-uncle of mine had been president of the republic. When I expressed my distaste to Isolde about having done this, she laughed at me, but I think the mocking was tinged with affection, and with a form of recognition based on her own familiarity with the pain of living on the boundaries of a social and cultural world.

In short, I think we both needed the testimonio we began crafting, and the friendship that arose alongside it. Ever more isolated within an ethnic movement to which she had given the previous quarter century of her life, forced to witness its ebbing strength at the precise moment when the dynamic unity of its first ten years would have been crucial for self-defense, Isolde needed the platform provided by the book we were aiming to write.[16] She is a person who does her best writing in an oral format. (She insisted to me, repeatedly, that this is a general Mapuche trait. Few Mapuches, she said, have taken well to the written medium; they are much better at long and florid speeches.) Thus she needed me, and the research assistants I contracted for in Santiago, to transform her spoken thoughts into a written narrative. For my part, I needed the vindication, recognition, and simple acceptance I received from Isolde, her daughter, her sister, and the rest of her family. I needed an interlocutor from within Mapuche society who could help me understand and evaluate the many complexities—cultural, political, social—I had encountered; in Isolde, her sister Elvira, and her husband Juan, I found exactly that. And finally, given the closed and insular nature of the "Mapuche studies" community into which, as an outsider, I found it hard to enter, I also hungered for the approval she gave me as an analyst of her society and culture who cared deeply and looked beyond the surface.

While our sharing of outsider status has brought us closer, it has also posed unique challenges in the presentation and acceptance of the text we are producing. When Isolde's sister Elvira said to me, mockingly and affectionately. "Tía, eres una bisagra cultural" ("Auntie, you're a cultural hinge"), she hit on a characteristic that not only describes me, but also Isolde herself. This makes the testimonio's more-recognizable or traditional relationship between subject and scribe a little harder to reproduce. When an early draft of the testimonio was criticized, in an anonymous review process in Chile, because I had not gained access to the "real" Mapuche cultural world, Isolde reacted by suggesting that this was not up to me, since she was really the mediator between two worlds whose efforts I was helping record. In addition, Isolde's reflections about politics and strategy are not a well-established genre for a Mapuche woman. In 1983, when Rolf Foerster recorded the life history of Martín Painemal Huenchual, a Communist leader with fifty years of militance in the Chilean labor movement, he helped break new ground in our understanding of Mapuche political activism. Most recently, with the publication of Sonia Montecino's innovative biography of *machi* Carmela Romero Antivil (1999), a female leader/intellectual has also become the center of ethnographic attention. Yet a gender division of labor has been maintained in these life stories: the man occupies the public, political world and dialogues with dominant society, while the woman preserves traditional knowledge, heals, and dreams. Isolde's life, and her telling of it, breaks through these categories in ways that are both multiple and difficult to grasp.[17]

The result of this process is a book in progress. In the first year after I left Chile, I managed to complete the organization of an initial draft of the book-length *testimonio* that had emerged from our conversations. In August 1998 I traveled again to Temuco, and with Isolde and her husband Juan, we went over the text, correcting some errors in *mapunzugun* and taking out some personal references or other comments that, when making the transition from a personal conversation to a written text, no longer seemed appropriate. I also took Isolde a first draft of the editor's introduction, on which she made comments, after which we recorded an introduction and conclusion based on a reading of everything written to that point. In August 1999, we recorded an epilogue that brought up to date the political and personal changes she and her people had experienced over the previous year, and we are hoping that the expeditious publication of the book will finally keep its expansion from continuing! Our text is thus a reflection of conversations that have not ended, of friendships still deepening and in progress; upon publication it is inevitable that it will freeze in time a whole set of experiences, a life, a network of friendships and social relations that continue to evolve and grow.

In February 1998, when I sent her the first two complete chapters, I also included with the package a copy of Rigoberta Menchú's first memoir. I knew that Isolde and Menchú had been part of the same indigenous tour of Europe in 1992, but I also explained to her on the telephone what was my other motivation for sending her the book. "When your book is translated into English," I said, "in the United States people will inevitably compare you to Rigoberta Menchú. It's important to begin thinking about what that comparison might mean."

We had that conversation before David Stoll's critique of Menchú became public, but I had already heard rumors that a U.S. anthropologist had been questioning the "truth" of her autobiography. I also knew that Menchú's second memoir was about to appear, and that she had retained principal authorship over that one. Thus a reflection about the similarities and differences between Menchú's first autobiography and Isolde's work, especially the different contexts in which they were written and the distinct political motivations that inspired them, seemed crucial to me. I also thought that such a reflection might help us think comparatively and historically about what constitutes a life history, something that has not been done systematically despite the immense international attention and acclaim Menchú's first testimony received.[18]

Isolde and I have since discussed, most notably in our most recent conversations in August 1999, the similarities and differences between her *testimonio* and Menchú's, especially the contexts in which they were written and the distinct political agendas that underlie each. When Menchú recorded her testimony, she had been recently exiled and was visiting Paris, still coping with the multiple traumas she had undergone in Guatemala and wanting fervently to communicate to an international public the situation of her people. Isolde, on the other hand, recorded her testimony in her home region, facing an indigenous movement on the wane, willing and able to reflect deeply on the gains and losses of the previous two decades. Isolde's ability, at a different historical moment, to be more critical and open about internal divisions and problems, as well as about the difficulties of feminist organizing in an indigenous movement, makes her *testimonio* reflexive where Menchú's was urgent. At the same time, sharing as they did a stage in the 1992 indigenous walking tour of Europe, they share as well the desire and commitment to speak about and for indigenous cultures that have survived centuries despite overwhelming odds.

What often does not get discussed in relation to Menchú's first *testimonio*, however, is its specific and "atypical" nature within the testimonial genre. An inclusive list of texts would be too long and complex to reproduce here, but it is interesting to note that, before the texts of revolutionary solidarity so celebrated in the 1980s and 1990s—which would include, in addition to Menchú's book, Margaret Randall's texts on Nicaragua, the testimony of María Teresa Tula mentioned earlier, and the story of Bolivian tin mine activist Domitila Barrios de Chungara—a distinct life history and testimonial tradition had already emerged from anthropology. This would include, among other works, the books by Oscar Lewis, the "testimonial novel" and oral histories produced by Elena Poniatowska (who worked as one of Lewis's research assistants in Mexico City) and Miguel Barnet, and the classic works by Sidney Mintz on Taso Zayas, and June Nash on Bolivian mine workers.[19]

Within this great variety of texts, what stands out about Menchú's work is that it is the only one that is not based on some kind of encounter with the community and/or culture of the narrator/subject. With all the differences among them, and even in the other cases in which texts were produced with a clear political purpose—such as the testimonies of Tula or Barrios de Chungara, or the books edited by Margaret Randall—we find that the works emerge from some kind of encounter between the editor and the narrator/subject's world. In Menchú's case, in contrast, the testimonio emerges from a series of interviews done in Burgos Debray's house in Paris, and the original purpose was apparently not to produce a testimonial book, but a magazine article. According to what Burgos Debray said to Stoll in a subsequent interview, it was only after Menchú had left that the editor discovered she had enough material for a book.[20]

Of course, at no point do I wish to suggest that an encounter with the culture or community of a narrator/subject somehow assures a form of "objectivity" that would otherwise be absent. It is precisely the ethnographer's false objectivity that began to be criticized within anthropology in the 1980s, and I have no desire to attempt its resuscitation. At the same time, however, I believe that a dialogue with the narrator/subject's community or culture makes for a richer and more complex text. For the reasons already described, such a dialogue and the resulting complexity were not a part of Menchú's first testimony. What does it say about our own intellectual world that it is precisely this book, among all possible texts in the genre, that becomes the most read, the most cited, and the most celebrated of all testimonial narratives?

In part, the attractiveness of Rigoberta Menchú's autobiography lies precisely in the clarity and simplicity of the message. A young indigenous woman who has experienced unimaginable suffering bears witness to that suffering and calls for international solidarity. A more complex, perhaps even contradictory, message, or a reflection at multiple levels that might evoke human imperfections and the lack of unblemished heroisms—such a testimony would not have had the same impact on the international community. Throughout Latin America, moreover, military dictatorships were abusing the human rights of the populations under their control and then trying to cover up their actions. Wide and well-organized disinformation campaigns were being challenged only by the individual testimonies of repression's victims, whose truth strove to be heard at the international level. The eloquence of individual testimony, of the victim's truth, was a formidable weapon used by movements against repression in the Latin American countries, by international human rights organizations, and also by the truth or restitution commissions set up in several Latin American countries after the fall of military regimes. At a moment of national and international emergency throughout Latin America, therefore, Menchú's personal testimony was acutely moving and powerful. Perhaps it is not superfluous to mention, in this context, the staggering nature of the genocidal violence experienced in Guatemala during more than three decades of civil war, which according to the recently released report of the Guatemalan Truth Commission resulted in the deaths of around 200,000 Guatemalans, more than 90 percent of whom were killed by the army.[21]

In such a context, it is easy to lose sight of the difference that can exist between truth as a weapon of *denuncia* or condemnation, and truth as a subject of academic debate. In Menchú's first testimony, truth exists as *denuncia* in the face of repression, pain, and military abuse. When seen at this level, even Stoll agrees that Rigoberta Menchú's truth belongs to all poor Guatemalans. But when Menchú's *testimonio* was transformed into an emblematic academic text, *denuncia* became ethnography. This transformation impoverished debates on culture and experience because any difference of opinion became seen as an attack on the legitimacy of the *denuncia* itself. It also impoverished the role of *denuncia* as a weapon in the struggle for human rights by conflating the testimony of abuse and pain given by repression's victims with a social or cultural text. Ultimately, this transformation also demonstrated that, at a certain level, we are still searching for the simple and transparent voice of the Other: We still have difficulty accepting multiplicity and contradiction.[22]

Perhaps it is only now, when we have passed into a different political stage, that it becomes possible to reflect more deeply about the complexities and contradictions of subaltern voices and actions. Can we find new ways to narrate and analyze the problems that remain when the war or dictatorship is over—problems that may appear less dramatic yet are no less painful or intractable, such as poverty, subordination, political exclusion, malnutrition, and cultural discrimination? Isolde Reuque's testimony—thought, spoken, and written in a post-crisis process of deep reflection—challenges us to begin. It calls on us to take up once again, though now in a new context, earlier forms of testimony or life history that formed part of long-term ethnographic work, and the deep yet consciously complex relationships fostered by anthropological research. A creative yet always conflictual relationship between testimony and ethnography, between life history and fieldwork, suggests an alternative path that may take us beyond the crisis of testimonial narrative as a form of *denuncia*. Without rebuilding our old illusions of scientific objectivity, but accepting the challenge and responsibility associated with a dialogic and postmodern ethnographic conversation, we can begin to open new and deeper narrative forms in our continuing search for ways to tell the stories of ordinary human beings. And while my collaboration with Isolde Reuque has emphasized the individual personal story in the context of an ethnographic relationship with her family and community, my work with the community of Nicolás Ailío has attempted to weave multiple individual stories into the fabric of a multilayered collective narrative.

When a Historian Is Approved in Community Assembly: Fashioning a Collective Ethnography in Nicolás Ailío

The same day I met Isolde Reuque, I had earlier visited the Centro de Estudios Simón Bolívar (CESB), a frayed and ramshackle grassroots organization run by Enrique Pérez, a chainsmoking radical leftist who had returned from exile in 1989. Enrique and the CESB had been recommended to me by a local anthropologist when I had explained my interest in locating a Mapuche community that, during the socialist experiment of Salvador Allende's Popular Unity government, had collaborated with the Movimiento de Izquierda Revolucionaria (MIR) (Movement of the Revolutionary Left) through its peasant front known as the Movimiento Campesino Revolucionario (MCR). Since Enrique had been a member of the MIR and had worked with a number of Mapuche communities in the region, this anthropologist had thought him a good potential contact, and I had not been disappointed.

During my earlier visit in October, I had managed to meet with Enrique briefly. We had agreed that I would begin research in the local Asuntos Indígenas archive, which housed the records of the original land grants, or *títulos de merced*, given to the region's Mapuche communities after their final military defeat in the 1880s. He had given me a list of the communities with which he was presently collaborating that might make good case studies, and I had promised to research at least some of them before our next meeting. By the time I called him in November, I had found some extremely interesting documents concerning the community of Nicolás Ailío, and coincidentally the leaders from that community were meeting with him that very week. Enrique invited me to drop by the CESB while they were there and talk with them.

After I was introduced to the president and secretary of the community, Don Heriberto Ailío and Don José Garrido, I shared with them copies of the documents I had found. Immediately Don Heriberto began commenting on them, incident by incident, adding information to what was available on the page. Our discussion of the Popular Unity years was especially intense. Don Heriberto talked about their occupation of a local hacienda, Rucalán, early one morning, and how they threw the landowner out. Subsequently Rucalán would become an agrarian reform center. He also mentioned that in 1972 they had carried out a second land occupation in order to seek restitution of forty-five hectares that had been taken from the community only two years after they received their original land grant in 1906—an abuse amply documented in the archival materials we were discussing.[23]

Even though Enrique had worked with the community during the Popular Unity government and thought he knew its history quite well, he reacted with surprise when Don Heriberto remembered this second land occupation. As a result of the documents I had found, therefore, it became clear to all involved that a dialogue between human memory and the archival record might be beneficial for the community and help clear up points of forgetfulness. I was invited to join Enrique on his next visit to Ailío, which was to happen the next day. Needless to say, I was thrilled, since hearing the voices and perspectives of some of the actors in Ailío's drama was especially inspiring for me and made the documents come alive. "What a story of struggle and survival," I wrote in Spanish in my field notebook that night. "I want to accompany them, become a sort of secretary of memory, sharing my notes, my discoveries, offering them the material I am finding in order to facilitate their process of re-membering. They, too, can be my teachers. I hope our common process of re-membering works out."

I waited around a lot on the following day, first for the perennially late Enrique to appear at my pensión, then for the community of Ailío to finish its meeting. When I was almost sure that they would never call me in, I was invited into the community assembly, and Don Heriberto Ailío introduced me to the twenty or so members who were gathered there. He said I was a historian and that I had already found interesting documents about the community in the Temuco archives and had given copies to them. He asked me to explain to the community what I would be doing, and to explain what kind of help I needed. Not entirely prepared for the situation, I fumbled a bit as I tried to explain the process of collecting oral history: how I wanted to get different people's stories and visions of community life, and then put them together into a larger story that would teach all of us something new, simply by combining different perspectives. People seemed interested in this idea, though concerned about how much time they might need to spend with me. Then one of the men in the room brought up a doubt. "It seems that foreigners have come into Mapuche communities a lot," he said, "and after we talk with them, take time off from our work for them, they take the results home and we never hear from them again. I think you should leave a report of your findings with us before you leave. That way we get something back right away." The assembly agreed, and I said I thought it was an excellent idea. We set a date for my next visit, at the beginning of January. Don Heriberto designated René Ailío, a younger leader in the community, as my host for that visit, and I promised to arrive at René's house on January 4.

The collective ethnography I envisioned at the beginning of my relationship with the community of Ailío, about which I wrote with such starry-eyed idealism in my field notebook, turned out a little differently from what I had expected. When I finally arrived, a week late, at René Ailío's house, I slowly began to understand that I had ventured into a very complicated, and intensely emotional, moment in the history of the community. René's family was a part of the group in the community that was not moving to the new land that was being bought with a government subsidy acquired through CONADI's Land Fund, a special program meant to provide limited restitution to Mapuche communities and families who had lost their land in the century after the so-called Pacification. Don Heriberto, on the other hand, was leading the group that had put together the application to CONADI and expected to move to Huellanto Alto—a region past Gorbea, a town south of Temuco, then east toward the Andes Mountains—as soon as the paperwork on the purchase of approximately 180 hectares could be completed. The prospect of moving, of dividing a community into halves, of some people getting access to new land while others did not—all these changes threatened to tear the community apart. The assembly I had attended in November 1996 had combined people from both groups, those who were leaving and those who were staying; at that moment the accepted common discourse was that the community would still be one, that people would continue to cooperate and to work together. The mood was similar the following Thursday, December 5, when I accompanied Don Heriberto, Enrique, Don "Chami" and others to Huellanto Alto to look over the land they were buying. But as time passed over the next couple of months, the fissure between the two groups began to deepen.

In retrospect, I think Don Heriberto and many of the other people present at the original assembly saw me as a potential healer of the rift, in the sense that I could help people remember their common history of struggle and privation—the history that made them a community and, at least in terms of the original land grant, an extended family or lineage. As a consummate politician and experienced organizer, Don Heriberto wanted my presence to keep alive for people their deeper motivations in the struggle for land so that the process of moving, and of negotiating with those who were staying, could be easier. For me, certainly, the fact that Ailío was about to receive from the Chilean government a subsidized land grant in recognition of the previous century of exploitation made for a particularly compelling finale to the story I wanted to tell. The fact that the community had collaborated with the MCR and occupied an hacienda during the Allende years, and that as a result several people had been imprisoned and tortured by the military, also made it an ideal case to explore in depth. For different reasons, then, we all participated enthusiastically in the common project of reconstituting community memory. As the months passed, however, and as I became an interlocutor both for those who left and for those who stayed at the original site, my role seemed to become less a healer of the rift, and more a force that could potentially deepen it.

The common historical memory that existed in the community was a bare-bones affair composed of the following basic facts and events. In 1908, only two years after the community was given a land-title grant (título de merced) to 120 hectares, a local landowner by the name of Duhalde usurped forty-five of them. Despite a series of legal attempts at restitution, the community was drastically reduced in size, and this led quickly to poverty and land hunger. To make matters worse, the Duhalde family sold the estate created in part from Ailío's lands to the state, which then divided it up into smaller parcels and auctioned these off to small proprietors. By the 1960s desperation had set in, but when state policy turned toward agrarian reform, some people insisted that only the restitution of the original lands was legitimate, while others were willing to try something different as long as they got access to additional land to farm. Part of the underlying disagreement here concerned the importance and legitimacy of Mapuche traditions, and the need to revindicate the specific land on which the community's identity had been constructed. This political and cultural disagreement deepened during the years of Salvador Allende's Popular Unity government and cracked wide open after the military coup.

Each of the factions that had emerged in the late 1960s articulated these events and facts into quite a distinct narrative that ended in a broader moral lesson. For René Ailío's family, especially his father, Don Antonio Ailío, the centerpiece of the story was the original usurpation of the forty-five hectares and the ability to endure and survive afterward, despite the failure of all attempts at restitution. "That happened many years ago," Don Antonio explained to me during that initial visit, embarking on a narrative of violent dispossession whose rhythms and imagery suggested it had been repeated many times over the years. It began with the actions of a man named Duhalde who fenced off a whole section of the community with the wood from native trees he had first cut down. It continued with the forced eviction of Don Antonio's young and recently married parents, and the burning of their humble home. And it ended with Duhalde being murdered by a business associate to whom he owed money, because, as Don Antonio explained, Duhalde was an arrogant man who did "bad works." René's brother Antonio, who had clearly heard this story many times before, had his own particular spin on its moral. "He [Duhalde] thought he was king of these lands," he said, "but he didn't know that there's another King upstairs, another King Who's on top of him, Who got to order him around."[24] Now this story did not end with the restitution of land, for it was a story of suffering and endurance rather than of victory. But it did end with a kind of moral restitution, for the murder of Duhalde was a classic morality tale that cut to the very heart of local relations with an easy, quick, and satisfying thrust: the exploitative landowner, rotten and corrupt to his very core, will sooner or later be hoisted on his own petard.

For Don Heriberto Ailío, on the other hand, and in general for those who had participated in the agrarian reform, the December 1970 takeover of Rucalán was the centerpiece of a story about overcoming exploitation through direct action. This version of the community's history was the same through 1965, when agrarian reform provided a new opening toward campesino issues and encouraged the community once again to begin restitution proceedings. Unfortunately, because the process of subdivision and sale had been so complicated, the trial dragged on, and people began to lose hope—something which, in the face of extreme and grinding poverty, was a truly devastating prospect. So what to do? In 1969 a local committee composed of members of Ailío and surrounding communities was organized to discuss the issue. Among the alternatives considered was the occupation of a nearby landed estate, and as discussions proceeded, the people most active on the local committee, which increasingly had a presence of MIR activists through the MCR, began to focus on the *fundo* Rucalán. They felt that court-based strategies of Mapuche restitution had proven unsuccessful, and that justice would only be achieved through direct action, technically illegal, of both Mapuche and non-Mapuche peasants. That was the rationale that underlay the invasion of Rucalán, and it created a rupture within the community that was only deepened three years later by the military coup.[25]

If the lesson in Don Antonio's story was one of endurance and moral superiority, the agrarian reform narrative emphasized the need for political militance and innovation in the face of a failed traditional strategy of legal restitution. Those who participated in the agrarian reform presented two pieces of evidence as proof of the correctness of their position: first, that a short-lived restitution of a portion of the original forty-five hectares came about only after another de facto occupation, despite a legal finding in the community's favor; and second, that the two and a half years spent on the agrarian reform center created on Rucalán were the only years of prosperity their generation had ever known. The rejoinder from Don Antonio, as representative of the anti-land-invasion position, was that the 1973 coup and subsequent repression had made clear that illegal occupations were wrong. Indeed, the culmination of Don Antonio's morality tale of endurance was precisely that 1973 had proven the importance of doing things "the right way" (por las buenas).[26]

I'm convinced that an open discussion of these different narratives and interpretations of community history, especially in the context of the tensions generated by the move, ultimately helped to justify and deepen divisions. This was intensified as well by my dialogic and participatory research methods, and by the community's own demand that I share the research results with them before I left. Over the next six months or so I used transcriptions of previous interviews, results of my conversations with other members of the community, and photocopies of newspaper articles and other documents to elicit responses and interpretations from my interviewees. I also presented two research reports to both sectors of the community, in Huellanto Alto and at the original site in Tranapuente. Especially in Huellanto Alto, Don Heriberto Ailío and his sister Eduardina actively engaged my analysis and disputed the interpretations of people with whom they disagreed. On March 20, 1997, an assembly of people in Huellanto Alto took time away from their discussions of survival strategies in an extremely challenging new setting to discuss my first report on the community's history.[27]

In the long run, then, by tying together the remembered but dispersed threads of the community's history, my work actually helped make clear to people why the division in the community was necessary. Lest I grant myself too much agency in the process, it is also important to point out that the very implementation of the Ley Indígena—which had created CONADI and the Land Fund in the first place—opened fissures among different sectors of the Mapuche movement and in other communities as well. The lack of funding to help get people on their feet once they moved to Huellanto Alto further created a sense of desperation that contributed to division and a lack of solidarity. Rather than being the causal factor in the rift, I became its narrator and witness, and shared the results of my witnessing with community leaders. I continue to work with them from a distance, talking with the new agricultural experts who are trying to help them, attempting to aid in the search for financing, and continuing to witness the present as it unfolds.

Beyond witnessing, however, I am also engaged in fashioning a collective history or ethnography of the community in the genre commonly termed a "community study." In the year or so that I have spent producing nearly a full draft, unforeseen problems of voice, perspective, and narrative line have emerged directly from the community's history of divisions, as well as from my methodology of dialogic ethnography and deep immersion. One of these is simply the fact that the very success of my efforts at immersion has provided me with so many versions of events that it often becomes impossible to include them all. Ironically, once moved beyond the problem of accessing "the popular," I found that narrating all the conflicting "populars" can be even more challenging! And how do I decide which of the many stories I have been given, and trusted to respect and honor, should be left out? A further quandary facing me as I struggle to be a worthy guardian of people's stories is the question of how far to intervene in people's silences. How much do I say about women's marginalization, for example, or on gender in the construction of people's social and cultural identities, when neither women nor men highlighted this directly in their testimonies? If I allow the story itself to suggest these issues, as the testimonies did for me, will that be enough? I have not resolved these questions yet and will face them again as I revise the first draft of the book and as I share it with people in the community.

I have already learned, however, that nonintervention in people's narratives does not, in and of itself, result in greater respect for the spirit of the stories they have entrusted to me. This has become clear in the numerous scuffles over interpretation in which I have already been engaged. From the first community meeting I attended, I emphasized that my purpose was to hear different stories and combine them into one larger history, thus declaring up front my interpretative autonomy. Nevertheless, the deep differences of opinion among community members inevitably result in a desire for each side to see their position highlighted in my text. Because we have engaged in conversations about historical interpretation for nearly three years now, the sense I get is that the leaders, especially in Huellanto Alto, where I have received the most consistent welcome and feedback, expect the book to reflect their point of view. This is particularly the case because the process itself has resulted in a sense of ownership and participation by all in the formulation of the narrative. "So," Don Heriberto Ailío asked me when I visited in August 1998, "how's that book we're writing coming along?"

A particularly good example of the interpretative tussles we have had over the book occurred in our discussions of the military operation of Nehuentúe. On August 29, 1973, personnel from the Third Helicopters Group of the Chilean Air Force (FACH) joined with the army regiment Tucapel, headquartered in the provincial capital of Temuco, to carry out a major sweep of the area between Carahue and Puerto Saavedra, an area that included Ailío and the ex-*fundo* Rucalán, which had become an agrarian reform center. This military operation, which was carried out autonomously from the authority of the civilian government, was justified as part of the overall campaign to control arms possession among the civilian population because, according to the commander of the Tucapel regiment, the MIR had established an arms factory and guerrilla school there.[28]

When I first discussed the Nehuentúe operation with Don Heriberto Ailío, he gave me the same version of events that he had likely repeated, over and over, during the torture sessions that followed his arrest in September 1973. There were no weapons, he said. They had been doing nothing wrong. The military had made up the whole story and had planted the weapons later exhibited at the Tucapel regiment. The peasants arrested in connection with the Nehuentúe operation had never been successfully charged with any crime, even though most of them were jailed for at least two years. What more proof could anyone want, especially at a time like the mid-1970s, when the rules of evidence that governed military tribunals were lax at best? Clearly, in Don Heriberto's memory and estimation, the prisoners of Nehuentúe were innocent victims, almost lambs taken to the slaughter.[29]

Initially, therefore, my forays into other documentation on the incident, particularly in the local and national press, were motivated by my desire to help expose the military's lies and thus provide support for Don Heriberto's version. As I dug, two conflicting images of Nehuentúe and the local population offered competing claims to truth. One was provided by the opposition to the UP government, as represented in Temuco's newspaper El Diario Austral and the national opposition press, most notably El Mercurio. In these the local peasants were portrayed as either conspiratorial revolutionaries ready to attack all peace-loving citizens in their homes, or as innocent dupes in a violent extreme-left conspiracy, during which the MIR had turned the Nehuentúe region into its first fortress or bunker. In this context, the Nehuentúe military operation was rendered as a liberation from MIR domination, and any protests against human rights abuses labeled slanderous prevarications.[30]

The other version of events was given by publications that either supported or stood to the left of the UP government. In addition to the MIR publication Punto Final, which on the very same day of the coup published an in-depth interview with a Mapuche woman who witnessed the operation, pro-government publications such as Puro Chile, Clarín, and La Nación published a series of articles blaming the right for fabricating the conspiracy, and characterizing as ridiculous any charges that Mapuche peasants, who barely had enough money to buy their daily necessities, could have been involved in stockpiling weapons or participating in military training. In this context, the charges of torture presented by local inhabitants against the military emerged as violations against the bodies of hardworking, upstanding, innocent citizens.[31] These two opposing versions would define the discursive options, both within the military and among its prisoners, for years to come.

The longer I investigated the Nehuentúe case, the more I became convinced that the two opposing versions of events had become articulated in a mutual dance whose choreography actually made it harder to understand what had happened. Not surprisingly, it turned out to be easier to prove the falsehood of the military version. To begin with, the charges published in *El Mercurio* and *Las Ultimas Noticias*—about the fifty guerrillas who had been arrested, or the existence of a bunker, mortars, and machine guns on the *ex-fundo* Nehuentúe, or the authoritarian domination of the region by longhaired commandos with mandarin-like moustaches—are nothing short of laughable today.[32] But even the more sober version of the military's position, which emphasized stockpiles of weapons and a guerrilla school, are not supported by available evidence, not even that provided by Iturriaga himself in the press conference he gave on September 5, 1973. There he exhibited the confiscated arms and ammunition, photographs of which were published in the local press. In these photographs we see little more than a few shotguns, sticks, revolvers, and some Molotov cocktails. Even the most famous weapons, the "anti-tank" bombs also known as *vietnamitas* which, according to Iturriaga, were capable of blowing up something the size of a city block, turned out to be homemade, in pots and pans; in the picture there are about twenty. This does not a weapons factory make. In addition, I have found no evidence, direct or indirect, to support the existence of a guerrilla school in the area. In fact, as one of the MIR organizers who had worked in the area pointed out, it would have been foolhardy to train there, since the *ex-fundo* Nehuentúe was in full view of the local police post![33]

The relative ease with which the military's version can today be disproved should not blind us, however, to the fact that at the time of the coup, and throughout the subsequent years of the dictatorship, it emerged as dominant. This dominance was assured, of course, by press censorship and the feeding of untrue stories to the surviving newspapers. It was also assured through repression and violence. Through a combination of arrests, torture, and disinformation, the military managed to hide the dimensions of human rights abuses in the Nehuentúe operation, as well as the fact that it was a dress rehearsal for the coup, one of several carried out across Chile during August 1973. By the end of September 1973, there was

no longer any public awareness that in Nehuentúe the military had practiced all the tactics it would later use in the post-coup repression: invasion
and destruction of private residences; intimidation of the civilian population; beatings and torture, including the methods that later became well
known (hanging people by their feet, applying electricity to their testicles,
submerging heads in septic water, forcing people to drink water until they
were bloated and then jumping on their stomachs, hanging people from
helicopters and then submerging them in the river). An awareness of these
facts, which is present in the leftist press before September 11, was quickly
erased by a campaign of disinformation concerning the motives and methods of the action.[34]

"I lied because they paid me," screamed a headline in Temuco's *Diario
Austral* on September 28, 1973, less than three weeks after the coup. In the
article, a Mapuche woman whose name was given as Gertrudis Quidel
Quidel confessed she had been paid by members of the deposed leftist
government to lie about the events in Nehuentúe. The article went on to
explain that Quidel was the real name of the woman who, in the days
immediately before the coup, had gone on national television under the
alias "Margarita" to "denounce tortures and beatings supposedly carried
out by the armed forces" in Nehuentúe. We are informed here, by contrast,
that Quidel had seen nothing in Nehuentúe because, when the "airplanes"
arrived, she had suffered an attack of nerves and went immediately to the
hospital in Puerto Saavedra. When she returned to the site, a mysterious
journalist later identified as Fireley Elgueta had written up, on a typewriter,
what she was supposed to say. She was then taken to Temuco, where the
intendant, or local representative of the national government, had given
her money to go to Santiago and tell this story. In the capital city she had
met with Allende, who also gave her money. Finally, Quidel claimed, when
she returned to the region, the same journalist told her that the army was
going to kill her for the story she had told, but if she changed it, militants
from the MIR would kill her. The MIR militants who had worked in
Nehuentúe, according to Quidel, "had been the bosses, and who could she
turn to if they were the ones who gave the orders?" The article concluded by
stating that, sometimes, Quidel had been forced to use up to three hundred
pounds of flour preparing their meals.[35]

This news story appeared the day after the ex-intendant of Cautín and the
journalist named by Quidel had been arrested in connection with the case.
Ex-intendant Sergio Fonseca was kept under house arrest, while Fireley
Elgueta, a female journalist who had worked for the Ministry of Agriculture
in the Temuco region, was arrested in Santiago, tortured, and sent to
Temuco to face a military tribunal. Under existing martial law, the charge
was extremely serious: insulting the armed forces.[36]

Gertrudis Quidel was the same woman who in Santiago, in the days immediately before the coup, had given testimony under the name of Margarita Paillao about the human rights abuses in Nehuentúe. Fireley Elgueta was named to accompany her at a meeting of government officials from the Ministry of Agriculture in Temuco, where it had been unanimously decided that the information from Nehuentúe was serious enough to take personally to the capital city. The delegation to Santiago, which included Doña Gertrudis and Elgueta, had gone to speak to the Minister of Agriculture first, but given the seriousness of the case, they had subsequently been invited to speak directly to President Salvador Allende. Present at the meeting with Allende where the delegation repeated its testimony was FACH commander General Gustavo Leigh, shortly thereafter one of the members of the military junta. When Leigh heard testimony about the participation of the Temuco branch of the FACH, he went pale and began taking furious notes. It was on the day subsequent to his arrival in Temuco, in the second half of September, that arrest orders went out for ex-intendant Fonseca and Elgueta.

Doña Gertrudis was tortured at army headquarters in Temuco, and the soldiers also threatened the lives of her children to force her to change her story. When Fireley Elgueta was brought to the jail in Temuco, the two women were brought face to face. At that very moment Doña Gertrudis was coming back to the jail from military headquarters, where people were always taken to be interrogated. Her escorts brought her down a line of women prisoners, among whom stood Elgueta. At first Doña Gertrudis pretended not to recognize the journalist in an effort to protect her. But the inconsistencies between the two women's stories made it clear that Doña Gertrudis was lying. Shortly after she admitted her lie she was released, a broken woman.[37]

People from Ailío remember that, later, Doña Gertrudis began dating a policeman. They also say that, one day, with the visitors the Nehuentúe prisoners received in jail, came the news that she went out one night with her boyfriend and left Luciano Ernesto, the son she had with jailed peasant leader Orlando Beltrán, alone in the house. While she was out, the house caught fire, and the child died in the flames. When Beltrán received the news, he became gravely ill. After he was released from jail in 1978, he simply disappeared; it seems that he went to Santiago to live with his first wife and later died there. Doña Gertrudis stayed on in Nehuentúe, working for a family named Garrido who sharecropped for Astorga on part of the forty-five hectares Ailío had lost so many years before. She began a relationship with the son, Ramón Garrido, and they had a daughter. But tragedy pursued her, it seems. First the mother of the Garrido family died, and then the little girl; finally, Ramón's father died as well. Doña Gertrudis then developed cancer, and despite Ramón Garrido's best efforts, she died in 1979. People said she had been bewitched, since the illness consumed her bones and shrunk her down to a fraction of her original size.[38]

Under such conditions, when people's bodies and lives were routinely destroyed in order to ensure the dominance of the military's version of events, it is hardly surprising that survivors like Don Heriberto Ailío would hold on tenaciously to the counter-version, the version of their own innocence which, in the broader scheme of things, contained a great deal more truth in any case. The rendition of those arrested as innocent victims received further support from the human rights movement during the dictatorship, as well as from the most widely and publicly circulated versions of the post-1990 discourse developed by the Commission on Truth and Reconciliation, which emphasized the body counts of the "victims" of repression.[39] But in the long run, one dimension common to all these stories of innocence and abuse became increasingly troubling to me: by rendering people as the "victims" of military repression, the stories tended to remove their individual agency, political legitimacy, and human complexity. I became convinced that representing people as Christ-like sacrificial lambs, while comprehensible and perhaps inevitable under the conditions existing in Chile after September 1973, sold short the fact that many of them had been involved in morally defensible, if sometimes shortsighted, efforts to achieve social justice. Was there a way to emphasize and preserve their innocence while at the same time respecting their political vision and activism?

This was my main concern when I interviewed Don Heriberto Ailío again in April 1997. By that point I had found enough evidence in other sources to confirm the existence of some weapons, and at least the informal manufacture of some grenades, in Nehuentúe.[40] When I showed him the newspaper photographs and asked him what he thought, Don Heriberto answered:

> Well, the truth is that there were some, but they weren't very many, because that depends on money, and we were poor. There's other weapons that they put into the pile at the end, so they could declare we had a guerrilla school, and that we were making weapons and ammunition, but that wasn't true, it wasn't as much as they put in the newspaper. So these are pure lies. Yes, we were preparing ourselves, just like they were preparing themselves, we couldn't just be there with our arms crossed, we had to prepare. We knew they were preparing themselves for a coup, and to repress the poor, to repress the people.[41]

As this particular interview progressed, it became possible for Don Heriberto to free himself from the discursive confines of excessive innocence and thus to reflect more openly on the nature and consequences of political activism in his home region. No longer fettered by the need to render himself and his colleagues as neophytes, spurred on by my sharing other documents I had found concerning the Centro de Reforma Agraria Arnoldo Ríos (the ex-*fundo* Rucalán), Don Heriberto wove a complex and coherent narrative about why it became necessary to take direct action during the years of the UP. He also expressed deep pride at what they were able to accomplish on Rucalán—how much they were able to improve the property and make it produce. This success and prosperity would, of course, be interrupted by the Nehuentúe military operation and the deepening repression that followed the September 11 coup. Although Don Heriberto was able to escape the first roundup, around September 18 he turned himself in because the military was putting pressure on his family. The questions about his role on the *asentamiento* Arnoldo Ríos began immdiately, as did his denials. But even as Don Heriberto denied everything and protected his friends and *compañeros*, he also showed pride at what they had accomplished. It was a pride intimately related to a sense of justification and legitimation that it had been correct to take direct action at Rucalán because the occupants had subsequently proved, through their hard work, that they were worthy of the support the Allende government had provided.

The lesson I learned from this first scuffle over interpretation was that it made sense to investigate deeper and not simply to bear witness to the original version of events presented by the participants. When I put conflicting evidence on the table in my next interview with Don Heriberto, the results were not pleasant; he was angry, and our conversation was a great deal more tense than previously. Yet at the same time, the conflict elicited more-complex and powerful memories about the politics of the period that ultimately made for a better, even more fully sympathetic, narrative of the events. And this was something that, in the long run, would prove satisfying to Don Heriberto and other agrarian reform veterans.

The situation was a bit different with the second point of conflict emerging from my investigation of Nehuentúe. Starting from Doña Gertrudis, who still today is remembered by the ex-prisoners of Nehuentúe and their families as a traitor, I began to consider the question of local complicity in the operation and subsequent repression. Don Heriberto first alerted me to a second local case of betrayal when he expressed anger at those who had not managed to keep quiet, as he had. A young man from Ailío, not even eighteen, ended up breaking under torture during the Nehuentúe operation: "He had been in the community, and became enthusiastic, he got involved in the movement and wanted to help. But as a young boy he was weak, and he turned the rest of the people in. He was weak. Now if we decide we can't turn people in, if we're really going to be a part of the movement, we can't do that. But he did, he turned in people who really were involved in serious things, people who were involved on the military side of things, and we didn't like that."[42]

When I pressed him further, Don Heriberto admitted that it was tough to blame someone for talking under torture, especially someone so young. Hugo Ailío was sixteen when he was arrested in August 1973. As Hugo explained to me in August 1999, a patrol came to his house at 3 A.M. and treated him very gently in front of his parents, even calling him "son." When his mother began to cry, the sergeant in charge told her, "Don't worry, ma'am, the boy is going to make a statement, and tomorrow we'll bring him right back." But as soon as they were out of the house, the soldiers began to mistreat him, hitting him with their rifle butts, and once they got to the landowner's house at the ex-*fundo* Nehuentúe, a soldier hit him with a chain that had a lead medallion attached to the end, opening a gash in his head. Then they took him into the house, making him wait in the hall before entering, as they explained, "the torture chamber." Indeed, as Hugo remembers it, the psychological torture involved in waiting was in many ways the most effective way to break someone down. While in the hall, and later shut up in a closet while he heard the moans and screams of another prisoner being tortured, Hugo imagined what was in store for him. He remembered what he had read about Nazi tortures "and the tears rolled down my cheeks." When it was finally his turn, he was so afraid that, at first, he admitted a few things. Then he tried to stop, denying that he knew people, but at that point they began to pressure him harder, hitting him, applying electricity to his head, the soles of his feet, his mouth, lips, and nose. The moment came when he simply could not stand it any longer. Though the combination of everything finally got to him, the worst was the electricity. "I just started quacking like a duck."[43]

I have yet to share with Don Heriberto the results of my interview with Hugo Ailío. I know I will at some point before "that book we're writing" goes to press, since the Spanish version of the manuscript will be delivered to them before it is submitted to publishing houses. And while I cannot say I know how he will react, I'm confident that the additional human complexity Hugo provides at various points in the book will, in the long run, endow the story with a depth that can only be seen as positive. This is what I learned from researching Nehuentúe, from not allowing my discomfort at eliciting anger or grief to stop me from telling the best and most honest story I could.

Indeed, by the time I finished my systematic and dogged reconstruction of the Nehuentúe operation, interviewing ten people, reading accounts in seven different publications, piecing together documents from the partially gutted archive of the Intendencia in Temuco, and convincing several reticent individuals to tell me as full a story as they could, I had come to doubt the wisdom, as well as the viability, of a quest that focused excessively on the "real" story or "the truth." When faced with the military's denials that abuse had happened in Nehuentúe, a quest for truth was clearly the appropriate response; the same was the case when faced with repeated denials about the presence of weapons on the *centros de reforma agraria*. But in the end, an important part of the story lay also in the layers of prevarication and partial truth that, over the years, had enveloped the Nehuentúe events. In these layers, like the rings of an old tree's bark, lay embedded a crucial story about what had gone before, about why and how people remembered what they remembered. The layers were crisscrossed with pain and betrayal, with personal and political justifications and legitimations, and with the ongoing need to grieve a splintered dream of social justice.

Perhaps for this reason, as well as the military's brutal invention of a blood-soaked ballet of guilt and justification, people participated in a common choreography that danced around the demonization or beatification of the Mapuche peasants. Debating issues at that level kept the opposing sides clear and clean, lining up all Leftists and ex-UP people against the military and its allies. As I learned en route, with my various interviews of those involved, it was much more painful to dig deeper. For when I did, the emerging kernels of another truth were particularly difficult to bear: a utopian class alliance smashed and betrayed; some activists informing on others or changing sides under pressure; people still too afraid of the consequences to be willing to give their real names; a few still nursing a tattered longing for equality, and insisting that the efforts and sacrifices of the time were not entirely wasted. When all is said and done, a lot more emerged in the quest for the weapons at Nehuentúe than whether or not all the rifles in the picture really did belong to the local MIR committee. More than the ownership of the weapons, what ends up mattering—and is also more difficult to ascertain—is whether anyone can still claim to own the common dream, the vision of a more just future, that Chilean soldiers and FACH helicopters aimed to shatter that winter morning in August 1973.

Conclusions: Bearing Witness in Hard Times

As an ethnographer, historian, and testimonial scribe working in Chile after the crush of *denuncia* had moved on, I became, in about equal parts, an archaeologist of stories and discourses buried by time and suffering; a weaver of narratives dispersed by military disinformation and political division; a mourner of broken dreams and lost solidarities; and an inter-locutor for reflections about past losses and future possibilities. As Sidney Mintz wrote about Don Taso Zayas almost forty years ago, I, too, wish "to evoke no pity, for that is a sentiment which degrades the meaning" of the struggles and reflections I have witnessed and recorded. That meaning is clearly multifaceted and, in my experience, goes far beyond what Georg Gugelberger suggests when he concludes that "in the end there is only 'mourning,' 'travail du deuil' as Jacques Derrida has called it."[44]

Isolde Reuque and I recorded her testimonio in her own country and region, facing an indigenous movement in retreat. I was witness and scribe as she sorted through twenty-five years of political activism, first in the human rights movement, then as a founding member of the Mapuche indigenous movement of the 1970s and 1980s. She was able, at a different historical moment, to take honest and critical stock of the internal divi-sions and problems of the movements in which she had participated, and of the difficulties of organizing a feminist movement within the Mapuche movement and with the Mapuche people. By revealing and analyzing the profound and painful contradictions that exist within popular movements, Isolde presents herself and us with a deep challenge: Is it possible to renew and reconstruct a commitment to social justice without also reconstructing an excessively simplistic and heroic vision of popular politics? Without the illusion of an easy answer, Isolde shares with us her reflections and experi-ence.

At one point in our conversations, Isolde spoke of a deep depression she entered in the mid-1980s, when the Mapuche organization she helped found was taken over by Mapuche militants from the Chilean Communist Party. The resulting split expelled a significant number of the least radical Mapuche communities, and she, along with several other leaders, was forced out. It was only after a trip to New Mexico, where she met a Hopi grandmother who had been an activist all her life, that Isolde began to emerge from her slump. "I think this was an emotional moment, full of feeling, strength and also pain," she told me. This encounter with another indigenous leader and female elder, symbolized by the gift of a turquoise ring Isolde still wears, represented for her the need to look beyond present defeats to the past and the future, and to become part of a chain of struggle that did not begin and would not end with her. The setbacks suffered by the Mapuche movement served, then, as a catalyst, both in her efforts to see beyond the immediate process and in her construction of her own political identity as stubbornly optimistic. To this day Isolde sees in her initial experience of organizing the Mapuche movement her greatest lessons, and in the communities and traditions of her people the greatest wisdom, not because of some romantic and ancestral purity, but precisely because of survival despite overwhelming odds. "The greatest beauty I have within me," she told me one day,

comes from my travels through Mapuche communities, through the communities in Chiloé, the communities close to the rivers, the lakes, where I find Ngenechen [God], where I can communicate directly with that superior being, when I find, I don't know what, but I can cry, laugh, sing; my poetry springs forth, my verses, and I can dream and surround myself in reality, all at once. I think there's much in the wind that blows in each one of those places. Where I've most easily been able to find that superior being is in the places where someone says there's nothing else to be done. There I find something that speaks to me. When a flower is reborn amidst all that filth, it tells you there's still a moment of hope, and that our love for the earth, for nature, for human beings, must open each day toward the world, toward people, toward all of us.[45]

A stubborn optimism, with eyes wide open, a romanticism that does not idealize reality—this more than anything else characterizes Isolde Reuque. Her romanticism and optimism mix in a complex way with an eminently practical view of the world. Throughout her life history she repeats, again and again, the phrase "We have to do what we can, not what we wish to do." Creatively negotiating the contradiction between the possible and the desirable, between the ideal and the possible, Isolde Reuque narrates a life in which she has reconstructed her optimism again and again, finding in it the strength to keep going. That is why we agreed to title her book "When a Flower Is Reborn," which symbolizes not only her stubborn spirit, but also our shared hope that in the twenty-first century the rebirth of the Mapuche movement and of aspirations for social justice will help heal the wounds inflicted on Chilean society by a recent and excessive love of modernity and the market.

The title I gave to my final report to the community of Nicolás Ailío, which the people in Huellanto Alto approved, was "The Copihue Flower's Blood." This title, too, had many layers of meaning. It was first suggested to me by the fact that, in the middle of the new land that the government had helped them purchase, the families from Ailío found a patch of native forest with red copihues in bloom. But after I thought more about it, I also liked the fact that the copihue is the Chilean national flower, and that the reference to a bleeding red copihue starkly represented the historic suffering of the Mapuche people in their relationship with the Chilean nation-state. Specifically for the community of Ailío, the metaphor also incorporated the experience of repression suffered under military dictatorship. Indeed, in the letter I received in 1997 from Don Heriberto Ailío and Don Chami Garrido in representation of the Huellanto Alto community, they spoke of their desire to welcome me back to their midst, to the "copihue flower's blood."

In the case of Ailío, I continue to be witness and scribe, maybe even facilitator, of a mourning process. Utopias have failed, and neighbor has turned against neighbor. The wounds have been deep and enduring, and I don't think they will ever completely heal. Yet, as is the case for Isolde Reuque, the leaders of Ailío continue to seek ways to learn from the past. In this context, healing comes with the settling and cultivation of new land, even as new problems send some of the settlers back to the old Ailío in Tranapuente. As the historian approved in community assembly, I know my role must continue to be one of empathetic challenge. I can't pull any punches when demanding a deeper and more honest consideration of the painful questions such healing allows to bubble forth, but at the same time, the more intimately I understand people's lives, the clearer it becomes that some things must remain, appropriately, off the page.

As I continue to participate in the present and future lives of the Reuque Paillalef family and the community of Ailío, we will all continue to write, talk, struggle, and act. On one hand, Isolde's political activism and stature as a leader privilege her personal story and her ability to tell it. Her identity as a public intellectual makes the relationship we have established more of a horizontal one, even as it is clearly marked by inequalities of power between region and center, academy and social movements in Chile itself, between the academies of Chile and the United States. It is not too difficult to envision our common participation in national and international conferences, perhaps even a book tour once the volume comes out. The dialogue we have established will continue to prosper if we are able to work out the challenges of these potential new stages in our relationship.

On the other hand, my connection with the community of Ailío will continue to be more fully that of intellectual mediator and narrator. Don Heriberto and Doña Eduardina Ailío, both deeply reflective and complex local intellectuals and leaders, lack the formal education and regional political status to gain easy access to the forums in which Isolde feels comfortable. Here I envision ongoing discussions of the community's history, my personal help with connections that might facilitate funding for community projects, potential regional seminars and projects on development and human rights, and when I finish and publish the community history of Ailío, perhaps a book presentation in Santiago and Temuco to which are invited the leaders of both parts of the original community.[46]

The many subtle and complex voices and stories I have been able to listen to and record in the Temuco region are but a small sampling of what is available to us as we bear witness in hard times. As postmodern ethnographers and scribes, we can hear and help braid these stories into new plaits of meaning that have impact on all our lives in a postrevolutionary age. Part of the work associated with these new narratives is, of course, the work of grieving, and unless we recognize the losses suffered and the pain incurred, it is impossible to move effectively to the next stage. At the same time, as both Isolde Reuque and the community of Ailío make clear, the defeat of revolutionary options has not broken the chain between past and future that today's social struggles represent and reproduce. As Isolde learned in her encounter with her fellow activist the Hopi grandmother, a key element in that chain is the ability to communicate across generations. On one side, then, our struggle to hear and record these experiences, and to participate in debating what they mean, suggests that the work of grieving is essential in any effort to envision the future. On the other side, however, the same process makes clear that continuing to search and struggle for social justice must move us beyond a self-indulgent entanglement in the mourning itself.

Notes

The research that forms the basis of this essay was carried out in Chile in 1996–97, on a sabbatical grant from the University of Wisconsin, Madison, with additional support from the John Simon Guggenheim Foundation and a Landes Fellowship from the Research Institute for the Study of Man. Follow-up visits (August 1998 and August 1999) were financed through a Wisconsin Alumni Research Foundation Mid-Career Award and a travel grant from the International Institute, University of Wisconsin, Madison. Space does not permit me to individually thank all the people who made this work possible, but I could not let the essay go to press without mentioning at least the following individuals and institutions. With regards to Isolde Reuque's *testimonio*, I would like to thank María Elena Valenzuela, who first put me in touch with Isolde; Isolde Reuque herself, of course, and her husband Juan Sánchez Curihuentro; Isolde's parents, Don Ernesto Reuque and Doña Martina Paillalef; Isolde's daughter Liliana Reuque; and Isolde's brother and sister, Lionel and Elvira. In relation to the community of Nicolás Ailío, I would like to thank Aldo Vidal, Enrique Pérez, Gustavo and Luis Peralta, Angélica Celis, and Gonzalo Leiva; and in the community, Eduardina, Heriberto, Robustiano, Antonio Sr. and Antonio Jr., René, and Hugo Ailío; José Garrido; Juana Pincheira; Felicia Concha de Ailío; Marta Antinao de Ailío; Luis Ernesto Quijón; and many others who shared food and stories with me. Magaly Ortiz has transcribed most of the tapes of the interviews with Isolde and with the community; she stands as my greatest hero. In Temuco, the Instituto de Estudios Indígenas at the Universidad de la Frontera and the Centro de Estudios Socioculturales at the Universidad Católica de Temuco both provided needed support and logistical help at various points. Colleagues at both institutions—most notably José Aylwin, Teresa Durán, Jaime Flores, and Jorge Pinto—have given me consistent support over the years. The friendships and assistance of Roberta Bacic, Víctor Maturana, and Elisabeth Brevis are also gratefully acknowledged. To those I've neglected to mention, I can only offer my sincere apologies.

1   Sidney Mintz, Worker in the Cane: A Puerto Rican Life History, 2d ed. (New York: W. W. Norton and Co., 1974), 11.

2   See, for example, Oscar Lewis, Five Families: Mexican Case Studies in the Culture of Poverty (New York: Basic Books, 1959); The Children of Sánchez: Autobiography of a Mexican Family (New York: Random House, 1961); and Pedro Martínez: A Mexican Peasant and His Family (New York: Random House, 1964).

3   For a recent analysis of, and reflection on, Worker in the Cane, see Francisco A. Scarano, "Las huellas esquivas de la memoria: Antropología e historia en Taso, trabajador de la caña," in Sidney W. Mintz, Taso, trabajador de la caña, 1st Spanish edition (Río Piedras, Puerto Rico: Ediciones Huracán, 1988), 9–50.

4   Stephen A. Tyler, "Post-Modern Ethnography: From Document of the Occult to Occult Document," in James Clifford and George E. Marcus, Writing Culture: The Poetics and Politics of Ethnography (Berkeley: University of California Press, 1986), 122–40, quotation on 126.

5   James Clifford, "On Ethnographic Allegory," in Clifford and Marcus, Writing Culture, 98–121, quotation on 104.

6   George E. Marcus, "A Broad(er)side to the Canon: Being a Partial Account of a Year of Travel among Textual Communities in the Realm of Humanities Centers, and Including a Collection of Artificial Curiosities," in George E. Marcus, Rereading Cultural Anthropology (Durham: Duke University Press, 1992), 103–23, especially 113.

7   John Beverley, "The Margin at the Center: On Testimonio (Testimonial Narrative)," 1989, reprinted in Georg M. Gugelberger, ed., The Real Thing: Testimonial Discourse and Latin America (Durham: Duke University Press, 1996), 23–41, quotation on 26.

8   George Yúdice, "Testimonio and Postmodernism," 1991, reprinted in Gugelberger, The Real Thing, 42–57, quotations on 49 and 50, respectively.

9   Beverley, "The Margin at the Center," 31 and 33.

10 John Beverley, "The Real Thing," in Gugelberger, The Real Thing, 266–86, quotations on 281–82; Javier Sanjinés C., "Beyond Testimonial Discourse: New Popular Trends in Bolivia," in Gugelberger, 254–65; and other authors in the same volume, especially Gugelberger's introduction, 1–19.

11 Mintz, Worker in the Cane, 277.

12 On the early-twentieth-century Mapuche organizations, see Rolf Foerster and Sonia Montecino, Organizaciones, líderes, y contiendas mapuches, 1900–1910 (Santiago: Centro de Estudios de la Mujer, 1988).

13 Lynn Stephen, ed., Hear My Testimony: María Teresa Tula, Human Rights Activist of El Salvador (Boston: South End Press, 1994).

14 Isolde Reuque Paillalef, When a Flower Is Reborn: The Life and Times of a Mapuche Feminist, ed. and trans. Florencia E. Mallon (Durham: Duke University Press, forthcoming).

15 Perhaps an extreme example of pretended horizontality or equality occurs in Ruth Behar, Translated Woman: Crossing the Border with Esperanza's Story (Boston: Beacon Press, 1993), a life history of a Mexican peasant woman. Behar compares her conflictual experiences as the middle-class daughter of a strict, authoritarian Cuban father who, in front of her, tore up the letters she had sent him and later as a North American academic who did not receive the recognition she felt she deserved, with the life of a peasant woman who knew

bitter poverty and dangerous and repeated physical abuse from her father, her husband, and her mother-in-law.

16 By the time we had recorded the introduction and conclusion to her book in August 1998, a revitalized Mapuche movement had begun to confront the Chilean state and the large lumber companies over the ownership and exploitation of forest resources in Lumaco and other parts of the IX Region. Since then similar conflicts have erupted farther north, in the region of Arauco, and in August 1999 Isolde and I recorded her further reflections on this process. Though the Mapuche movement is no longer in retreat in the same way, the urgency of incorporating lessons learned in the earlier cycle of mobilization has not diminished. If anything, it may have increased, especially since one of Isolde's perceptions is that the present mobilization and militance may have many parallels with the first cycle of ethnic mobilization between 1978 and 1982.

17 Martín Painemal Huenchual, with Rolf Foerster, *Vida de un dirigente mapuche* (Santiago: Grupo de Investigaciones Agrarias, Academia de Humanismo Cristiano, 1983); and Sonia Montecino, *Sueño con menguante: Biografía de una machi* (Santiago: Editorial Sudamericana, 1999).

18 The original Spanish edition of Menchú's first testimony was published in Spain: Elisabeth Burgos, *Me llamo Rigoberta Menchú y así me nació la conciencia* (Barcelona: Editorial Argos Vergara, 1983). By 1997, the Spanish text had gone through fourteen editions and had been translated into many languages, including, of course, into English.

19 Margaret Randall, *Christians in the Nicaraguan Revolution* (Vancouver: New Star Books, 1983); *Todas estamos despiertas: Testimonios de la mujer nicaragüense de hoy* (Mexico City: Siglo XXI Editores, 1980); *Sandino's Daughters Revisited: Feminism in Nicaragua* (New Brunswick, N.J.: Rutgers University Press, 1994); Domitila Barrios de Chungara, with Moema Viezzer, "Si me permiten hablar—": *Testimonio de Domitila, una mujer de las minas de Bolivia* (Mexico City: Siglo XXI Editores, 1977); Oscar Lewis, *The Children of Sánchez: Autobiography of a Mexican Family* (New York: Random House, 1961), *A Death in the Sánchez Family* (New York: Random House, 1969), *Five Families: Mexican Case Studies in the Culture of Poverty* (New York: Basic Books, 1959), *Living the Revolution: An Oral History of Contemporary Cuba* (Urbana: University of Illinois Press, 1977), *Four Women: Living the Revolution* (Urbana: University of Illinois Press, 1977), *Pedro Martínez: A Mexican Peasant and His Family* (New York: Random House, 1964), and *La Vida: A Puerto Rican Family in the Culture of Poverty* (New York: Random House, 1966); Elena Poniatowska, *Fuerte es el silencio* (Mexico City: Ediciones Era, 1982), *Hasta no verte, Jesús mío* (Mexico City: Ediciones Era, 1969), *Nada, nadie: Las voces del temblor* (Mexico City: Ediciones Era, 1988), and *La noche de Tlatelolco: Testimonios de historia oral* (Mexico City: Ediciones Era, 1971); and Miguel Barnet, *Canción de Rachel* (Buenos Aires: Editorial Galerna, 1969) and *Biografía de un cimarrón* (Buenos Aires: Editorial Galerna, 1968). Elena Poniatowska's role as research assistant to Oscar Lewis is mentioned in Susan M. Rigdon, *The Culture Facade: Art, Science, and Politics in the Work of Oscar Lewis* (Urbana: University of Illinois Press, 1988). See also June Nash, *We Eat the Mines and the Mines Eat Us: Dependency and Exploitation in Bolivian Tin Mines* (New York: Columbia University Press, 1979), and *I Spent My Life in the Mines* (New York: Columbia University Press, 1992).

Testimonial and life history texts in Chilean literature, especially those relating to Mapuche culture, include: Pascual Coña, *Testimonio de un cacique mapuche*, dictated to Father Ernesto Wilhelm de Mosebach, 3d ed. (Santiago: Pehuén, 1984); Sonia Montecino Aguirre, *Grupo de mujeres de la ciudad: Una experiencia múltiple* (Santiago: Programa de Estudios y Capacitación de la Mujer Campesina e Indígena, Círculo de Estudios de la

Mujer, Academia de Humanismo Cristiano, 1983), *Mujeres de la tierra* (Santiago: CEM-PEMCI, 1984), and *Los sueños de Lucinda Nahuelhual* (Santiago: Programa de Estudios y Capacitación de la Mujer Campesina e Indígena, PEMCI, Círculo de Estudios de la Mujer, Academia de Humanismo Cristiano, 1984); Painemal Huenchual, with Rolf Foerster, *Vida de un dirigente mapuche*; and Montecino, *Sueño con menguante*.

20 David Stoll, *Rigoberta Menchú and the Story of All Poor Guatemalans* (Boulder, CO: Westview Press, 1999), 185. At the same time we should not lose sight of the fact that by the time Stoll interviewed Burgos Debray, their interests were converging, according to Menchú's long-time mentor and Guatemalan historian Arturo Taracena, because Burgos Debray was in the process of distancing herself from the Latin American Left. Taracena's version of how Menchú's first testimony was produced appears in Peter Canby's review of Stoll and Menchú, *New York Review of Books* 46, 6 (8 April 1999): 28–33. In addition to a detailed narrative about his role in the production of the first testimonial, a role Burgos Debray seems to have buried for quite a while, Aracena apparently confirms (32) that Burgos Debray's original intention was to write a magazine article.

21 Indeed, one of the unfortunate tendencies in the Stoll book is to lose sight of the amazing disparity between the firepower and cruelty of the army and of the guerrillas, a disparity clearly reflected in the commission's figures. For the Truth Commission report, see *The New York Times*, 27 Feb. 1999, p. A4, and 1 Mar. 1999, p. A10. See also the summary available on the Web at http://worldpolicy.org/americas/guatindex.html.

22 An important contrast can be seen, in this context, between the treatment received by Menchú's text and other memoirs of repression or *denuncia* which, because they are not by indigenous authors, are not transformed into ethnography. For the Guatemalan case we have the testimony of guerrilla fighter Mario Payeras, published originally in Spanish as *Días de la selva* (Havana: Casa de las Américas, 1980). Interestingly, in an essay comparing the two *testimonios* Marc Zimmerman refers to Payeras by his last name and to Menchú as "Rigoberta," even in the title to the piece ("Testimonio in Guatemala: Payeras, Rigoberta, and Beyond," in Gugelberger, *The Real Thing*, 101–29). Among all the authors Zimmerman discusses, Menchú is the only woman, the only indigenous person, and the only one to whom he refers by first name. Why is it that ethnographic intimacy only applies in the case of a *denuncia* text produced by an indigenous woman?

   Among the many texts of *denuncia* produced for the Chilean case, see Luz Arce, *El infierno* (Santiago: Planeta, 1993); Sergio Bitar, *Isla 10* (Santiago: Pehuén, 1987); CODEPU, *Chile: Recuerdos de la guerra: Valdivia-Neltume-Chihuio-Liquiñe* (Santiago: CODEPU-Emisión, n.d.); Hernán Valdés, *Tejas Verdes (Diario de un campo de concentración en Chile* (Barcelona: Editorial Laia, 1978). Interestingly, in the Chilean case the Mapuche experience of repression has not received much attention in its own right, with the exception of Roberta Bacic et al., *Memorias recientes de mi pueblo, 1973–1990, Araucanía: Muerte y desaparición forzada en la Araucanía: Una aproximación étnica* (Temuco: Centro de Estudios Socio Culturales, Universidad Católica de Temuco, 1997).

23 The documents about the community I had been able to consult were housed at CONADI, Archivo de Asuntos Indígenas, Título de Merced N° 1112–Comunidad de Nicolás Ailío, 29 de diciembre de 1906; T.M. 1112-Carpeta Administrativa, Juzgado de Indios de Imperial, Expediente N° 20-Restitución y Usurpación de Terrenos, Reducción Nicolás Ailío (representada por Andrés Torres), con Duhalde, José, en Tranapuente, Nehuentúe, iniciado el 25 de abril de 1930.

24 Interview with Don Antonio Ailío, Community of Ailío-Tranapuente, 10 January 1997.

25 Interviews with Don Antonio Ailío, Community of Ailío-Tranapuente, 10 Jan. 1997; and

Don Heriberto Ailío, Comunidad de Ailío-Tranapuente, 18 Jan. 1997; and Temuco, 18 Apr. 1997.

26   Ibid.

27   Field notes for meeting in Ailío-Gorbea, 20 Mar. 1997.

28   *El Diario Austral*, Temuco, Monday, 3 Sept. 1973, p. 1; and subsequent press conference given by Iturriaga on Wednesday, 5 Sept., *El Diario Austral*, Wed. 5 Sept. 1973, pp. 1, 2.

29   Interview with Don Heriberto Ailío, 18 Jan. 1997.

30   In addition to the articles already cited from *El Diario Austral*, see also *El Mercurio*, 4 Sept. 1973, pp. 1, 10; 5 Sept. 1973, p. 1; 11 Sept. 1973, p. 21; *Las Ultimas Noticias*, 1 Sept. 1973, p. 1; 3 Sept. 1973, p. 1; 4 Sept. 1973, p. 2.

31   *Clarín*, 5 Sept. 1973, p. 4; 6 Sept. 1973, p. 10; *La Nación*, 6 Sept. 1973, p. 32; *Puro Chile*, 5 Sept. 1973, p. 2; 5 Sept. 1973, p. 4; 6 Sept. 1973, p. 9.

32   *Las Ultimas Noticias*, 3 Sept. 1973, p. 1; 4 Sept. 1973, p. 2; *El Mercurio*, 4 Sept. 1973, pp. 1, 10; 5 Sept. 1973, p. 1; 11 Sept. 1973, p. 21.

33   For the press conference and photographs, see *El Diario Austral*, Wednesday, 5 Sept. 1973, pp. 1 and 2. The photograph appears on p. 1. I have also taken into account the versions of a number of people who lived and worked in the area during that time: Don Heriberto Ailío, interviews on 18 Jan. and 18 Apr. 1997; Enrique Pérez, 14 Apr. 1997; and Mario Castro, 15 Apr. 1997. The comment about the location of the *fundo* in relation to the police post is from an interview with Francisco Sepúlveda (name changed), Santiago, 9 May 1998.

34   See "El sur bajo régimen militar," *Punto Final*, for a summary of the methods of torture used in Nehuentúe. See also Intendencia de Cautín, Correspondencia Recibida, 1973: "Informe de Nepomuceno Paillalef Lefinao, Director Zonal de Agricultura Subrogante, al Intendente de Cautín don Sergio Fonseca," Temuco, 31 Aug. 1973; and "Declaración pública de los obreros y campesinos de Puerto Saavedra y Carahue," Provincia de Cautín, 2 Sept. 1973.

35   "La mapuche de 'Vamos Mujer' en TV-7: 'Mentí porque me pagaron,'" *El Diario Austral*, Friday, 28 Sept. 1973, pp. 1 and 8.

36   Interview with Sergio Fonseca, Temuco, 19 May 1997; interview with a person close to the *intendencia* who wished to remain anonymous: Gloria Muñoz (name changed), Santiago, 16 May 1997.

37   Interview with Gonzalo Leiva, Temuco, 23 June 1997; Gloria Muñoz, Santiago, 16 May 1997; e-mail confirmation of meeting in the Moneda by Ariel Dorfman, Chapel Hill, North Carolina, 25 Feb. 1998. In the interviews I carried out in the IX Region in August 1999, it became clear that Gertrudis was the Mapuche woman's real name. However, it was not until I returned to Madison and began perusing the various community census materials I'd collected that I was also able to confirm that her last name was indeed Quidel. Interviews with Don Heriberto Ailío, Huellanto Alto, 10 Aug. 1999; Don Robustiano and Doña Eduardina Ailío, Tranapuente, 14 Aug. 1999; Doña Patricia Valenzuela, Nehuentúe, 20 Aug. 1999. Census materials were found in CONADI, Archivo de Asuntos Indígenas, T.M. 1381—Andrés Curiman, Carpeta Administrativa: Ministerio de Tierras y Colonización, Dirección de Asuntos Indígenas, Zonal Temuco, "Censo de la Comunidad de Andrés Curimán," 30 May–4 June 1963, ficha no. 24 (31 May).

38   Interviews with Enrique Pérez, Temuco, 14 Apr. 1997; Gloria Muñoz, Santiago, 15 May 1997; Don Heriberto Ailío, Temuco, 18 Apr. 1997, Huellanto Alto, 10 Aug. 1999; Don Robustiano and Doña Eduardina Ailío, Tranapuente, 14 Aug. 1999; and Doña Patricia Valenzuela, Nehuentúe, 20 Aug. 1999. While Don Robustiano, Doña Eduardina, Don

Heriberto Ailío, and Enrique Pérez all remember the incident with the burning of Luciano Ernesto, Doña Patricia Valenzuela, who lives in Nehuentúe, did not remember it.

39 The published three-volume report by the Comisión de Verdad y Reconciliación takes great care to discuss the political activities of the individual "victims," not as justification for what was done to them, but for the purposes of accuracy. This was not, however, the way in which the findings were publicized most extensively. I am grateful to Steve J. Stern, personal communication, for help in making this distinction.

40 By 18 Apr. 1997, when our interview took place, I already had copies of the 5 Sept. 1973 press conference report in El Diario Austral, as well as an interview with Mario Castro (15 Apr. 1997) in which he confirmed having seen grenades on Nehuentúe and having even participated in making them.

41 Interview with Don Heriberto Ailío, Temuco, 18 Apr. 1997.

42 Ibid.

43 Interview with Don Hugo Ailío, Concepción, 12 Aug. 1999.

44 Georg M. Gugelberger, introduction to The Real Thing, 1–19, quotation on 18.

45 Reuque, When a Flower Is Reborn, chapter 4.

46 Perhaps it goes without saying that any royalties coming from such a community study would go to benefit the community.

Daniel James

Afterword: A Final Reflection
on the Political

▼

"What is it that must first precede the conveying of history? Must there not be the conveying of a double passion, an eros for the past and an ardor for the others in whose name there is a felt urgency to speak? To convey that-which-was in the light of this passion is to become a historian. Because the past is irrecoverable and the others in whose stead the historian speaks are dead, unknowable, she cannot hope that her passion will be reciprocated. To be a historian then is to accept the destiny of the spurned lover—to write, to photograph, film, televise, archive and simulate the past not merely as its memory bank but as binding oneself by a promise to the dead to tell the truth about the past. Nietzsche may have been right in proclaiming that remembering the past is a sick passion; yet without the necrophilia of the historian who gives herself over to overcoming the past's passing into oblivion there would only be the finality of death."—Edith Wyschogrod, "An Ethics of Remembering"

Although the essays in this book were presented at a conference in honor of Emilia Viotti da Costa held at Yale University in 1998, the editor has specifically eschewed the canonical form of a traditional festschrift. That is all to the good—the genre has a tendency to produce well-meaning if rather lifeless commentaries on the life work of distinguished scholars by appropriately deferential younger colleagues and former students. Here, instead, the reader is offered a wide-ranging collection of essays on Latin American and Caribbean history drawn together under the theme of "Reclaiming the Political" in Latin American history. Viotti da Costa is referred to explicitly in some of the texts, footnoted in others, and provides an essay herself. The tone is cool, analytical, and dedicated to the extensive array of historical issues at hand. This is, as I say, largely a good thing consistent with her own dislike of sentimentalism.

And yet, I would like, in these last few pages, to change the key somewhat. The absence of sentimental reminiscence should not be mistaken for the absence of affect, or lack of emotion. While this collection is not conceived as a festschrift, I think that it is still worth reclaiming the most literal linguistic meaning of the term with its clear implication of a festival, a celebration of a life's work. There are many facets of Emilia's (let me register the change of key by referring to her by her first name) work that we could celebrate. Her role as a teacher and mentor would, of course, be one. Indeed, this collection is above all a testimony to her profound influence on the academic lives of her many graduate students. Her stature as a graduate teacher can be measured in many ways. The quality of the essays in this book is one measure, as is the breadth of their subject matter. The positions that her former students now occupy within the academy would be another. To this I could also add my own personal observation as a colleague for nine years: she was quite simply the best graduate teacher I have ever seen. Over the years, in a vain effort to replicate some of that success, I have tried to analyze wherein lay the essence of this achievement.

In part, I think that it was her ability to communicate sympathy to her students. This was an intellectual sympathy and should not be confused with empathy. She was not nurturing in some general, empathetic way. She did not believe in an "in loco parentis" approach to her students. She cared about them, certainly, but this did not mean that she necessarily sought to be their friends. Above all, she was interested in their intellectual development as historians. She wanted to help provide them the tools and, ultimately, the self-confidence to realize their potential as scholars. This did not mean cloning either her specific research interests or her preferred conceptual tools. She knew what any parent discovers: children eventually end up rebelling against, rejecting, changing, or developing the original parental guidelines. Emilia welcomed this. She had the self-confidence and generosity to not be threatened by the independence and intellectual development of her students.

I think that generosity is another key to her impact on her students. This could be expressed in terms of the amount of time she dedicated to them. She read everything they wrote with a detailed, critical eye. She was also generous in another sense: she was generous with her enthusiasms, her own intellectual discoveries. Above all, she was generous in conveying that double passion about the past of which Edith Wyschogrod speaks in the epigraph to this afterword. It was this passion and the intellectual ethics that it implied that stayed with her students, that got into their heads. As

Jeff Gould expressed it in the introduction to his book on Nicaragua, *To Lead as Equals*, "In Chinandega, I often found myself wondering, 'How would Emilia read this document or respond to this informant's testimony?'"[1]

The other, fundamental thing that Emilia shared generously with her students and colleagues was the example of her own practice as a historian. She was such a persistent presence for Jeff Gould in the Nicaraguan countryside (or for myself in an Argentine meatpacking community, for Tom Klubock in a Chilean mining community, for Mary Ann Mahony in the cacao zone of Bahia, for Florencia Mallon in the highlands of Peru—the list could go on) not only because of the forcefulness of her personality, or the passion of her commitment to history, but because of the inspiration she provided through her own practice of the craft of writing history. In the end this inspiration is what is most worth celebrating in this afterword to a non-festschrift. Models (I hesitate to say intellectual heroines) are important for aspiring historians as they act as exemplars of history's range of possibilities and measures of excellence and difference between generational sensibilities. An appreciation of Emilia's own writings also points us toward how she conceived of the relationship between history and politics, the organizing nexus of this diverse collection of essays by her former students.

Underlying the conceptual organization of this collection around the theme of Latin Americanist history and politics is a notion that I would define as "the dream of the organic intellectual." This dream of Gramscian inspiration reflects the desire of a cohort of historians, among whom I include myself, to engage the practice of history with broader movements for social and political change. The story that we tell to express this desire (at least in the chapters that explicitly engage this theme) is one of loss. We tell the story of slippage from a moment of optimism in the 1970s through the early 1980s when a politicized historical scholarship could seek foundation in concrete hopes for social and political change in Latin America to the current situation of neoliberal victory and radical disenchantment that has undermined the earlier optimism. While I do not doubt that this narrative effectively embodies a genuine sense of intellectual and political trajectory that many of us feel, I suspect that it is one that Emilia would say is based on an illusion.

For Emilia a historical narrative is always deeply political, it is always already politically situated. We should not fool ourselves, she might say, that historians in the academy can achieve some sort of more intimate, "organic" connection. The historian can acquire the status of a public intellectual in some circumstances but this should not be confused with the goal of historical practice and historical writing. Thus, for her there is, I think, no nostalgia for a lost moment when history and politics were more intimately mixed; there is no need to "reclaim the political" since, in her understanding of the term, it has never been absent (as Gil Joseph indeed points out in his introduction).

Emilia's understanding of the relationship of history and politics is writ large in her own writings and nowhere more powerfully than in her extraordinary book on the Demerara slave rebellion of 1823, *Crown of Glory, Tears of Blood*.[2] We should first note that the book demonstrates what a lifetime of writing and teaching have also indicated—that Emilia has a profound belief in history and its potential intelligibility. Indeed, it is this intelligibility that preserves for her the possibility of human emancipation. The influence of her studies in France in the 1950s—and particularly the influence of Sartre—is evident. Her historiographical vocabulary is one that still speaks of praxis, and the notion of history as aggregated human praxes, freedom and necessity, and totalization—the Sartrean notion of the constantly developing process of making history that is intrinsically part of the human condition. Yet, as all her writings make clear—and as she tirelessly reiterated in discussions—she does not subscribe to a voluntarist celebration of human agency (any more than did Sartre). She has always been consistent about this and was careful to reemphasize in the introduction to *Crown of Glory, Tears of Blood* that "History is not the result of some transcendental 'human agency,' but neither are men and women the puppets of historical 'forces.' Their actions constitute the point at which the constant tension between freedom and necessity is momentarily resolved" (xviii).

This belief in the intelligibility of history carries with it a commitment to what I think she would not be averse to calling "grand narrative." What might this mean? In part it is embodied in the scope of the text. The range of the historical actors is astonishing: John Smith and the missionaries, the slaves themselves, the slaveowners, the British political elite, and the British working class. This is also a truly Atlantic history as she traces the mutually reinforcing influences between Demerara and the United Kingdom, and in particular the role of slave rebellion and the abolition movement in the construction of an imperial ideology and consensus by the mid-nineteenth century. While the book is centered on the Demerara rebellion of 1823, its narrative goes back to late eighteenth-century Europe and forward to the era of the late nineteenth-century imperial consolidation. Thus, certainly narrative scope and ambition are involved.

Beyond the issue of narrative range there is also a fundamental belief in narrative form and its political potential. For Emilia, in constructing her narratives the historian performs the task of taking the past and bringing it into the present to speak to us and to be interrogated by us, to help illuminate present dilemmas and future dreams. As she says at the end of her introduction: "As historians we understand that history never repeats itself. But we transform historical events into metaphors and see universality in uniqueness. Otherwise history would be a museum of curiosities, and historians nothing but antiquarians. The slave rebellion of 1823 and the Reverend Smith's predicament have universal value" (xix). It is this universal value that is the fundamental political grounding of historical narratives, and it gives John Smith's story and that of the Demerara slaves a function other than that of arid, empirical replication of the past.

Such a narrative goal inevitably involves the author in a wide range of representations of the past, and she is well aware of the difference between representation and replication. She would share, I am sure, Greg Dening's contention that "even the most accurate replication is not representation. The energy expended in replication squeezes out everything else. Ultimately such replication is the stultifying nostalgia of re-enactments and living museums."[3] Crowns of Glory contains a very conscious deliberation on her own strategies of representation. In this sense the book could be regarded as a contribution to the construction of what Jacques Ranciere has called a "poetics of knowledge" as a basis for a revived historical enterprise adequate to the political needs of the contemporary democratic era.[4] For Ranciere such a poetics involves a triple contract that is certainly scientific in that it seeks to understand the laws governing large-scale social, political, and economic changes. But it is also both narrative and political in that it involves reinscribing the anonymous victims of history through a narrative vehicle that is based on character, episode, and event.

What is perhaps most notable about this text is the way in which it engages with many of the elements of postmodern and postcolonial skepticism and pessimism concerning strategies of historical representation, about the difficulty (if not impossibility) of hearing the subaltern voice, about the coercive power of grand narratives. Yet she remains faithful to the narrative element in Ranciere's poetics of knowledge. Other than the introduction there is little of the explicit theorizing we have come to expect in contemporary history texts. Crowns of Glory is a most paradoxical book in that it is a profoundly theoretically informed text that apparently contains little explicit theoretical apparatus. She fashions a text that both lives up to its status as (social) scientific discourse but not at the expense of its narrative (and hence political) capacity.

This book is, she tells us, somewhat akin to a "polyphonic novel," aiming to hear and represent multiple voices and stories. This certainly enables her to undermine the monologic force of the traditional grand narrative. She is interested in the different stories that the historical actors construct and that are subsumed, and repressed, by the "story of the rebellion." But she will not let her narrative (which both authorizes and encompasses theirs) degenerate into a babelic cacophony. She tells us explicitly that she has refused to give up the narrator's privileges and responsibilities. She will be the arbitrating presence, the authorial voice that ultimately shapes the historical narrative and its representations.

Yet what is the nature of this authorial voice? It is certainly different from that of some of her peers in professional stature and political inclination. The difference, for example, between the voice of E. P. Thompson and that of the author of *Crowns of Glory* is notable. Emilia's is a more distanced, cooler, less emotional narrative register. The difference may in part be due to a difference in formative cultural influences. Thompson adopted as his own the English Romantic tradition. Emilia's heritage was linked (in part through the influence of the Annales school) to a much more sociological tradition. It also has to do, I think, with an explicit narrative choice that she makes concerning how to best convey and represent the range of emotion present in her actors and evinced in her retelling of their story. She might be said to be aware of "Diderot's Paradox." Greg Dening describes, in the essay referred to above, the essence of this paradox that Diderot enunciated after observing the actor David Garrick: "The more great actors seemed to be overwhelmed by the emotion of their role, the cooler they were, and the more in control." Extending the paradox beyond the field of acting to other forms of representation Dening notes: "Passion and discipline, natural and artificial, immediate meanings mediated by cultivated signs—Diderot discovered his paradox in the necessity of combining these oppositions to make the complete representation. It is the same paradox that pursues historians when they represent the past."[5] I think that Emilia intuitively understood the need to hold the two parts of this paradox in tension. The cooler tone we find in *Crowns of Glory* is, therefore, a deliberate narrative choice, a demonstration of emotional control rather than lack of passion as she seeks to convey to an audience all too willing to empathize the essence of the historical experience of actors caught up in an inhumane system.

Renato Rosaldo once pointed out that the narrative of *The Making of the English Working Class* is structured by a fundamentally melodramatic aesthetic that involves the identification of Thompson, the author, with the side of the victims, and heroes, of his narrative. Thompson was able to place himself directly within his own narrative in part because he saw himself as the direct heir of the historical tradition he was recovering. His historical writing was directed, in part, toward the recovery, and constitution, of a social memory for the English working class. Fred Inglis refers, in an essay on Thompson, to his books as "large historical novels written for the present," aimed at giving the English working class a new past to live from and thus a new understanding of the present and its possibilities.[6] This resulted in Thompson's unique narrative emotional range whereby he challenged his readers to identify with (as he himself did) the moral dilemmas and decisions of his historical agents—dilemmas about values, community, and solidarity that were as pertinent to English workers of the mid-twentieth century as they were to the artisans of the early nineteenth century. As Rosaldo notes, this left little room for the omniscient narrator since the conflicts that anchor the plot have still to be resolved.

Emilia would, I think, agree with the notion that one of history's basic goals is to tell stories for the present. The last lines of her introduction are quite explicit on this. The story of the rebellion and the Reverend Smith are important because "they remind us of the many missionaries and lay people who, imbued with a sense of mission, a deep commitment to human brotherhood, and a strong passion for justice, became scapegoats in other times and other places. They remind us, also, that the slaves' struggle for freedom and dignity continued to be re-enacted under new guises and new scripts long after 'emancipation.' That is what makes the story of John Smith and the Demerara slave rebellion worth telling" (xix). For her, as for Thompson, the social memory embodied in historical narrative is directed, in a Benjaminian sense, toward the present. It does not partake of a nostalgic flight toward the past and it is this present-directedness that constitutes the essence of history as a political practice.

It is clear, however, that Emilia's situation also differs from that of Thompson. Both the vocabulary and the range of sensibilities available to her are different. The site of enunciation of a historical discourse matters. She was for a large part of her mature scholarly life an exile, writing in a foreign language, cut off from the wellsprings of social and political practice that had inspired her youth. The Brazilian military regime that effectively ended her scholarly career in her homeland in 1969 also forestalled the development of any deeper, more "organic," link with broader social, historical forces. What the regime and its puppets in the University of São Paulo could not do, of course, was to prevent her from pursuing her calling as a politically committed historian. *Crowns of Glory* is no less an example of the power of such committed scholarship as is *The Making of the English Working Class*.

Nevertheless, the conditions under which this commitment to social justice and human freedom were exercised had changed. The tone and guiding aesthetic of *Crowns of Glory* differs from that of Thompson's classic. Its sympathies are extraordinarily large and generous though they are expressed in a minor key. Indeed, in some ways we could say that her range of sympathy is greater than Thompson's. Her powerful evocation of the figure of John Smith, the evangelical missionary, and her moving depiction of his human and religious dilemmas, can be contrasted with Thompson's famously unsympathetic account of English Methodism. Emilia's narrative is at its most restrained, most understated, at precisely its most emotionally wrenching moments. I think that her narrating of the death of Quamina, one of the leaders of the rebellion, is a fine example of the effectiveness of this technique:

> [Primo] said that Quamina had told them they were entitled to their freedom; that if they wished they could leave him in the bush and return to the plantations as some others had, but they would be fools to do so. He intended to remain in the bush. No white man would take him alive. And if they took him by surprise he would kill himself. Primo also said that Quamina and his party had been in the bush for days. . . . Suspecting that Quamina would not be far off McTurk ordered his group to continue the search. They finally spotted him in an area of heavy bushes where he could not be easily seized. The Indian who saw him first ordered him to stop, but Quamina neither stopped nor ran. Instead he went on walking without looking back, as if he had not heard the order. He seemed to be determined to be killed rather than arrested. As he was about to go out of sight the Indian shot him through the arm and temple. Quamina had kept his promise: no white man would take him alive. He carried no arms, only a knife and a bible were found in his pockets. His body was carried back to Success by slaves who had been caught during the raids. On September 17, a gibbet was erected on the road in front of Success. Surrounded by the assembled slaves of the plantation, a party of militia under arms, and Indians, Quamina's body was hung up in chains. (229)

This haunting passage draws its power from its restraint, from the sparseness of its literary devices. The narrator maintains her distance, refusing to explicitly evoke outrage, pity, or sympathy. The sparsity of this narrative also means that the narrator does not offer us a figure—either hero or victim—with whom we can empathetically identify. Prior to this passage there are sections of the book where in her role as guardian of history's status as a (social) scientific discourse Emilia has brilliantly addressed the problems involved in seeking to understand the meaning of slave lives and resistance from the colonial archives. In this endeavor she argues eloquently for the need to derive clues from a greater knowledge of African cultures. And yet, in this scene, she follows her narrator's novelistic instinct, which in the end perhaps best preserves her subject's humanity. Quamina walks away, without turning his head, thus rejecting his tormentors and choosing death over continued slavery. But we could also read this as symbolically walking away from future historians who would seek to appropriate him and know him. He will not fully enter the colonial archive.

Generations change and new generations of historians seek different solutions to old and new questions. Sometimes they end up reinventing old answers to old questions disguised in a new rhetoric. Truly influential teachers and mentors such as Emilia Viotti da Costa offer their students (and younger colleagues) the inestimable gift of their teaching and writings as living examples of the practice of a critical intelligence. The power of this gift seems to me to be demonstrated in the essays in this volume. There are many differences in emphasis—one might even use the word tensions—between some of the concepts and categories deployed by the contributors and Emilia's own work. Certainly, gender as a category is more explicitly present in several of these essays, the use of oral testimony and notions of memory and commemoration might also provoke something of a raised eyebrow and quizzically skeptical look on her part, as would the use of the term "fragment." Emilia will celebrate these differences and joyfully explore the tensions, both critiquing and learning from the dialogue. And when this is done and we reach some consensus, or agree to disagree, on these issues, we will still be faced with some dark night of the soul when we question why we do what we do and what it might mean to write politically committed history whether at the beginning of the twenty-first century or in 1969. As we seek for some road map that would help us to get beyond the triumphalism of this moment in global capitalism and the fatalistic acquiescence of academic scholarship that it engenders, then we can think ourselves lucky to be able to reach out to her teaching and writing for guidance and inspiration.

Notes

1 Jeffrey L. Gould, To Lead as Equals. Rural Protest and Political Consciousness in Chinandega, Nicaragua, 1912–1979. Chapel Hill: University of North Carolina Press, 1990, x.
2 Emilia Viotti da Costa, Crowns of Glory, Tears of Blood. The Demerara Slave Rebellion of 1823. Oxford: Oxford University Press, 1994.
3 Greg Dening, "The Theatricality of History Making and the Paradoxes of Acting," in Dening, Performances. Chicago: University of Chicago Press, 1995, 127.
4 Jacques Ranciere, The Names of History. On the Poetics of Knowledge. Minneapolis: University of Minnesota Press, 1994.
5 Dening, Performances, 122.
6 Fred Inglis, Radical Earnestness. English Social Theory 1880–1980. Oxford: Martin Robertson, 1982, 199.

Contributors

▼

EMILIA VIOTTI DA COSTA is Professor Emeritus of History at Yale University. After graduate studies at the École Pratique des Hautes Études, VIème Section, Sorbonne, and at the University of São Paulo, she taught at the University of São Paulo for fifteen years before moving to the United States in 1970. After visiting appointments at Tulane University, the University of Illinois at Urbana-Champaign, and Smith College, she joined the faculty at Yale, where she taught from 1973 to 1999. She is the author of numerous books, including *Da senzala à colônia* (4th ed., Livraria Editora Ciencias Humanas, 1998 [1966]); *Da monarquía à república* (6th ed., Editorial Grijalbo, 1994 [1977]); *The Brazilian Empire: Myths and Histories* (rev. ed., University of North Carolina Press, 2000 [1985]); and *Crowns of Glory, Tears of Blood: The Demerara Slave Rebellion of 1823* (Oxford University Press, 1994).

JEFFREY L. GOULD is Professor of History and Director of the Center for Latin American and Caribbean Studies at Indiana University. He is the author of *To Die in This Way: Nicaraguan Indians and the Myth of Mestizaje* (Duke University Press, 1998) and *To Lead as Equals: Rural Protest and Political Consciousness in Chinandega, Nicaragua, 1912–1979* (University of North Carolina Press, 1990).

GREG GRANDIN worked with the Guatemalan Truth Commission and currently teaches Latin American History at New York University. He is the author of *The Blood of Guatemala: A History of Race and Nation* (Duke University Press, 2000). He is currently working on a new book, "The Cold War from Below: Mayan Marxists and the Defeat of Social Democracy."

DANIEL JAMES is Mendel Professor of History at Indiana University. He is the author of *Doña María's Story: Life History, Memory, and Political Identity* (Duke University Press, 2000) and *Resistance and Integration: Peronism and the Argentine Working Class, 1946–1976* (Cambridge University Press, 1988), and the editor (with John D. French) of *The Gendered Worlds of Latin American Women Workers: From Household and Factory to the Union Hall and Ballot Box* (Duke University Press, 1997).

GILBERT M. JOSEPH is Farnam Professor of History and Director of Latin American and Iberian Studies at Yale University and Editor of the *Hispanic American Historical Review*. His most recent books are *Summer of Discontent, Seasons of Upheaval: Elite Politics and Rural Insur-*

gency in Yucatán, 1876–1915 (Stanford University Press, 1996), coauthored with Allen Wells; *Close Encounters of Empire: Writing the Cultural History of U.S.–Latin American Relations* (Duke University Press, 1998), coedited with Catherine LeGrand and Ricardo Salvatore; and *Fragments of a Golden Age: The Politics of Culture in Mexico Since 1940* (Duke University Press, 2001), coedited with Anne Rubenstein and Eric Zolov.

THOMAS MILLER KLUBOCK is Associate Professor of History at the State University of New York, Stony Brook. He is the author of *Contested Communities: Class, Gender, and Politics in Chile's El Teniente Copper Mine, 1904–1951* (Duke University Press, 1998). He is currently working on a labor and environmental history of Chile's southern forests.

MARY ANN MAHONY is Assistant Professor of History at the University of Notre Dame and Fellow of the Helen Kellogg Institute for International Studies. The author of several articles on colonial and modern Brazilian history, she is currently finishing a book titled "Revisiting the Violent Land: Bahia's Cacao Area, 1850–1937."

FLORENCIA E. MALLON teaches modern Latin American history at the University of Wisconsin-Madison. She is the author of *The Defense of Community in Peru's Central Highlands: Peasant Struggle and Capitalist Transition, 1860–1940* (Princeton University Press, 1983) and *Peasant and Nation: The Making of Postcolonial Mexico and Peru* (University of California Press, 1995). She is currently translating the testimony of Rosa Isolde Reuque Paillef, *When a Flower Is Reborn: The Life and Times of a Mapuche Feminist* (forthcoming, Duke University Press), and writing a book called "Broken Promises, Cobbled Dreams: The Mapuche Indigenous Community of Nicolás Ailío and the Chilean State, 1906–1999."

DIANA PATON teaches history at the University of Newcastle, England. A specialist in Caribbean history, her research interests are gender, slave emancipation, and state formation. Her edition of *A Narrative of Events . . . by James Williams*, one of a few autobiographical narratives by former Caribbean slaves, was published by Duke University Press in 2001. She is currently working on a book on punishment and the penal system in Jamaica in the era of slave emancipation (1780–1870), and is coediting a volume of essays, *Gender and Slave Emancipation in the Atlantic World*, with Pamela Scully.

STEVEN J. STERN is Professor of History at the University of Wisconsin-Madison. His research interests and publications span the colonial and national periods and several regions within Latin America. His most recent book is the edited collection *Shining and Other Paths: War and Society in Peru, 1980–1995* (Duke University Press, 1998), and he is completing a volume on struggles over collective memory in Chile after the crisis of 1973.

HEIDI TINSMAN is Assistant Professor of History at the University of California at Irvine. Her book *Unequal Uplift: The Sexual Politics of Gender and Labor in the Chilean Agrarian Reform, 1950–1973* is forthcoming from Duke University Press. She is also the author of several articles on neoliberalism, gender, and rural labor during Chile's military dictatorship between 1973 and 1990, and is currently conducting research for a book on temporary workers in Chile's fruit-export sector.

BARBARA S. WEINSTEIN is Professor of History at the University of Maryland-College Park. In addition to numerous articles on modern Brazil, she is the author of *The Amazon Rubber Boom, 1850–1920* (Stanford University Press, 1983) and *For Social Peace in Brazil: Industrialists and the Remaking of the Working Class in São Paulo, 1920–1964* (University of North Carolina Press, 1998). Her current project, to be published by Duke University Press, is a study of regional and national identities in twentieth-century Brazil.

Index

▼

Abandonment, 285, 287–289, 294–296, 298

Abolition: in Britain, 83, 88, 91, 93, 95; in Brazil, 81–95, 104, 108, 110, 113, 120, 122; in Cuba, 39, 81–84; in Jamaica, 175–196

Abolitionists, 175–176

Abortion, 276, 278

Absenteeism, 244

Academia de Estudios, 211–213

Aconcagua Valley, 269–270, 273–274, 277–278, 282, 283, 287, 293, 295

Adamista Group, 107, 109–110, 112, 114, 125

Adolescents, 272–282, 286–291, 294, 297–298

Adoption, 185

Africa, 28, 93, 189–190, 213, 238–239, 250–251, 362

African Americans, 244

Afro-Brazilians, 85, 94, 103, 106, 111, 131

Afro-Caribbeans, 186, 189

Afro-Jamaicans, 175–196

Afro-Semites, 236

Agency, 21, 35–36, 38–43, 49, 51–52, 84, 86, 147–149, 358

Aguilar, Ramón, 155

Aguirre Cerda, Pedro, 256–259

Ahuachapán, 141, 144–146

Ailío, Antonio, 334–336

Ailío, Edwardina (Eduardina), 336, 348

Ailío, Heriberto, 331–333, 335–338, 342–344, 348

Ailío, Hugo, 344

Ailío, Nicolás, 331, 347

Ailío, René, 334–335

Ailío community, 321–324, 332–335, 338, 341, 347–349

Ailío family, 318

Akan, 190

Alcohol, 212, 214–217, 219, 244–245, 285

Alessandri, Arturo, 241

Alger, Horatio, 121

Aliança Renovadora Nacional (ARENA), 163

Allende Gossens, Salvador, 53–54, 261, 269–270, 275, 278, 292–293, 297, 331, 334, 340–341, 343

Almada cemetery, 130

Alvarado, Salvador, 45–46

Alves, Fermino, 106

Alves Dias, Miguel José, 106

Alves family, 130

Amado, Jorge, 120–123, 125–26, 128, 130–131

American Historical Review, 21

Americanization, 244

Americas, 190, 211

Anaconda Copper Company, 231, 240

Anarchism, 239

Andean region, 40, 42–43, 46, 48, 207, 242, 333

Anderson, Benedict, 95

Andrews, George Reid, 81

Anglo-Americans, 190, 245, 250

Cofradías, 217–218

Coimbra, 105, 117

Cold War, 27–28, 49, 232

Collor, Fernando, 128

Colonialism, 25, 27, 40, 43, 105–106, 113, 115, 117, 126, 130, 161, 175, 177–178, 180, 189, 191–192, 208, 211, 221–223, 325

Colonists, 103, 106, 117, 155, 176, 237

Columbia University, 123

Columbus, Christopher, 154

Comisión para el Esclarecimiento Histórico, 223

Commemoration, 363

Commisão Executiva do Plano da Lavoura Cacauerira, 124–125, 127, 128

Commission in Defense of the Race and Profitable Use of Free Time, 259, 263

Commission on Truth and Reconciliation, 342

Committee of Mothers and Relatives of the Political Prisoners, Disappeared and Assassinated of El Salvador, 320

Communism, 121, 138, 144, 147–149, 151, 153, 160, 223, 232, 276

Communist Party: in Bahia, 120–122; in Brazil, 123, 125; in Chile, 231–232, 246, 256–258, 260, 327; in El Salvador, 145–146

Comparative research, 87, 92, 95

Confederación de Trabajadores de Chile, 257

Consciousness, 23, 25, 37, 42–46, 49–50, 52, 81–82, 103, 162, 280, 317

Conselheiro, Antônio, 112

Conservatism, 53, 120, 208, 210

Constitution of Chile, 262

Consumerism, 17, 29, 56

Contreras, Manuel, 54

Contreras, Olivia, 288–289

Cooke, Andrew, 195

Cooperativism, 119

Copper mining, 231–264

Cordons sanitaires, 212–216, 218

Corporación Nacional de Desarrollo Indígena, 319, 333, 336

Corporate welfare, 243–246, 252, 257

Costa, Affonso, 114

Credit, 104, 116, 118–120, 125, 232

Creoles, 207–208, 263

Cuba, 39, 49, 81–83, 86, 92, 314

Cuisnahuat, 148, 155–156

Cultural determinism, 177

Cultural movements, 143. See also Youth culture

Cunha Matos, Raymundo José da, 87–88

Cusamuluco, 155

Dance, 138, 278, 285, 339

Davis, David Brion, 86

Dean, Warren, 81, 83–84

Debray, Burgos, 329

Demerara, 358–363

Democratization, 51, 53–56, 95, 163, 318

Demography, 82, 104, 159, 206

Demonstrations, 292–294

Dening, Greg, 359–360

Dependency theory, 20, 37, 39, 238

Derrida, Jacques, 23–25, 346

Desbravadores, 124–126

Despertar Minero, 262

Development, 118, 123, 235, 238, 262

Dialectics, 19–20, 22, 38–40, 47

Dictatorship, 49, 51, 54, 209, 318, 329–330, 339, 342

Diderot's paradox, 360

Dinont, Christina, 182

Dinont, John, 182

Dirty wars, 53

Disappeared persons, 53

Discourse analysis, 23

Disease. See Illness

Douglas, Sarah, 185

Drago, Gonzalo, 247–252, 254

Dress, 138, 140–141, 144–145, 153–154, 156–157, 159, 160, 163–164, 278

Duhalde family, 334–335

Eagleton, Terry, 23

Education, 106, 108, 115–116, 120, 155, 157, 193, 223–224, 236, 243–246, 248, 256, 258–259, 269, 272, 274–276, 279–282, 286, 291, 294, 348. See also Literacy

El Canelo, 156, 160

El Carrizal, 160

El Despertar de los Trabajadores, 240

El Diario Austral, 338, 340

Gould, Jeff, 357
Gramsci, Antonio, 36, 47, 49, 357
Guatemala, 27, 157, 205–224, 327–330
Guatemala City, 210–211, 214–216
Guerin, Daniel, 24
Guerra, Susana, 288–289
Guerreiro de Freitas, Antônio Fernando, 127
Guerrilla movements, 316, 339
Guevara, Ernesto "Ché", 53
Gugelberger, Georg, 346
Gutiérrez, Eulogio, 247, 250, 254–255
Gutiérrez Sánchez, Hilda, 268–271, 275
Guy, Donna, 206

Haber, Stephen, 47–48
Hacendados, 158
Haitian Revolution, 95
Hale, Charles R., 162
Hammond, James, 89
Hanover Estate, 181
Hanover parish, 180
Hanson, Eleanor, 185
Hanson, Lucy, 185
Hanson, Marcus, 185
Hanson, Penells, 185
Hanson, Rachel, 185
Hawlbachs, Maurice, 131
Hegemony, 25, 35–40, 45, 49, 51–52, 189, 233
Hernández, Anita, 281
Herrera, Flavio, 209–210, 223
Heywood, Grace, 185
Hilandería Nacional, 260
Hispanic American Historical Review, 7
Historical Society, 3
Historiography: of Brazilian slavery, 81–95; of Caribbean slavery, 175–177, 183–185, 188, 194; current trends in, 21–22, 34, 41, 50, 53, 357; and linguistics, 19, 21–25, 42, 49, 90; and revisionism, 18, 25–26; and structuralism, 19, 24, 35, 38–41, 50, 82–83, 86, 95; and theoretical roots in 1950s, 19–20; and trends in the 1960s, 18–19, 21–25, 28–29, 35–37, 50, 81–82
History: and culture, 8, 22, 29, 41–50; differences between North and Latin American, 5, 8–11, 34, 56–57, 83, 113, 122–123,

127, 348; as micro-history, 22, 86; and politics, 4–5, 7, 29, 32–57; and state of scholarship, 3–4, 10–13; and teaching, 32–33; state-sponsored, 112–113, 115, 117, 208
Hite, Katherine, 57
Homosexuals, 206
Honduras, 140
Honor, 268–269, 271, 273
Hopi, 346, 249
Hôtel Dieu, 214
Huehuetenango, 218
Huellanto Alto, 333, 336–337, 347–348
Human rights, 317, 339, 342
Hunt, Lynn, 23
Hybridity, 206, 250

Ianni, Octávio, 82
Identity, 19, 48–49, 82–84, 92–93, 102, 105–108, 110, 115, 139–143, 153–154, 157, 159, 162–163, 206–224, 234–235, 246, 248–249, 258–259, 262–264
Ideology, 177, 188–192, 194, 206, 215, 232–235, 241, 244, 253, 255, 258–259, 264, 313, 316, 358
Ildefonso, Ramiro, 106–107
Ilhéus, 103–132
Ilhéus Commercial Association, 114
Illness, 205–224
Imperialism, 231–264, 325
India, 211
Indians. See Indigenous peoples
Indígenas. See Indigenous peoples
Indigenismo, 208–209
Indigenous activism, 138–139, 152–154, 157, 159, 163, 255, 319–349
Indigenous peoples, 103–106, 113, 115, 121, 126, 138–164, 205–224, 239, 249–250, 318–349
Indigenous rights, 49, 143
Indigenous Tour of Europe, 315, 328
Industrialization, 206, 256, 258, 261. *See also* Modernization
Inglis, Fred, 360–361
Inquilinaje, 272–273
Institute for the Development of Agriculture and Livestock, 274
Instituto Indigenista Nacional, 209

Instituto Nacional Indigenista, 209
Insurrection, 43, 121, 141, 210
Intellectuals: in Brazil, 91–93, 111, 113, 117,
124, 127; in Central America, 139, 141–
142; in Chile, 235–238, 241–242, 318–
320, 327, 348; in El Salvador, 148; gener-
ally, 205–206, 221, 316; in Guatemala,
208; in U.S. South, 92
Intendencia, 345
Intergenerational relations, 161–162, 191,
195, 270–272, 274–275, 281, 286–298
Internationalism, 240–241, 261
International organizations, 318
Interviews, 21, 157, 311, 321–349. *See also*
Oral history
Isaacman, Allen, 7
Isabel, Princess, 82
Itabuna, 109
Iturriaga, 339
Izalco, 138, 145–146, 148–151, 155–156

James, C. L. R., 231
James, Daniel, 56
Jara, Victor, 51
Jayaque, Cumbre de, 146
Jesuits, 103, 105–106, 113, 115
Jews, 206, 260–261
Joseph, Gilbert M., 44–48, 358
Juárez, 208
Juayúa, 146–148, 150, 155
Judicial process, 84
Junta de sanidad, 214
Juzgado de Crimen, 290

Kaulen, Julio, 238
Kennecott Copper Company, 231, 242
K'iche', 217–220
Kinship, 177, 184–185, 188
Kirk, Neville, 23
Klubock, Tom, 357
Kruschevsky, Leopolodo, 107
Kubitschek, Juscelino, 124
Kuhn, Thomas, 47

Labor: and employment patterns, 178, 180;
history of, 25–26; organization, 102, 125,
131, 143–144, 232, 235, 245–246, 255–
256, 276; mobility, 178, 183; movements,

25–26, 148, 150, 234, 242, 280, 292, 327;
and nationalism, 232, 238; relations, 182;
and rural regulation, 207; systems of, 82–
83, 89–91. *See also Desbravadores;* Free la-
bor; Migrant labor; Slavery; Sharecrop-
ping; Strikes; Wage labor
Ladinos, 140, 147–156, 160–163, 206–224
La Libertad, 141, 145
La Matanza, 138–164
La Nación, 338
Land: grants, 332–333, 335; occupations,
273, 292, 294, 332, 334, 336; and reform,
102
Land Fund, 333, 336
Language, 140–141, 145, 153–156, 160–161,
163–164, 327. *See also* Historiography, and
linguistics
Larson, Brooke, 42
Las Hojas, 160
Las Ultimas Noticias, 339
Latcham, Ricardo, 240, 246–247, 253–255
Latin America, 190, 205, 211, 221
Lavigne, Eusínio Gaston, 116–119, 121, 123–
124
Leigh, Gustavo, 341
Le Monde, 17
Lemos Peixoto, Amando de, 119
Leninism, 153
Leolino de Souza, Teotônio, 125
Lewis, Maggy (Ann Palmer), 179
Lewis, Oscar, 311, 314, 328
Ley de Residencia, 241
Ley Indígena, 336
Liberalism, 88, 92, 139, 143, 208, 210, 219, 221
Ligas Patrióticas, 239–240, 242
Literacy, 105, 107, 274
Literary criticism, 319
Livestock, 175, 273
Lomnitz, Claudio, 38
London, 178, 211
Los Altos, 207, 211, 216, 218
Los Andes, 281
Los Gramales, 160
Lower Bengal, 211
Lucea, 195
Lué, Rosario, 156
Luna Arbizú, José, 212, 214
Lyon, Edmund, 179, 181

Macchiavello Varas, Santiago, 238, 243
Machado, Maria Helena, 84
MADEMSA metallurgical plant, 260
Mahoe plantation, 181
Mahony, Mary Ann, 357
Mallon, Florencia, 44–49, 56, 320–349, 357
Manchioneal, 193
Mancomunales, 239–240
Mangabeira, João, 112
Manumission, 90
Mapuches, 237, 250, 255, 318–349
Markets, 82, 88, 116, 120, 126, 188–189, 191, 207, 214
Maroons, 82, 175
Marriage, 106–107, 110, 115–116, 121, 125, 152, 159, 177, 180, 185–186, 189, 192–193, 244–245, 268–298
Marshall, Woodville, 183–185
Martínez, Maximilian Hernández, 145, 149
Marxism, 11, 19, 27, 37, 49, 81–82, 273, 292
Masculinity, 158, 195, 237, 251–252, 254–255, 268–272, 274, 277, 280, 285–286, 297
Mata, Gabino, 150–151, 156, 159
Matagalpa, 162
Mate, 321–322
Material analysis, 8, 37
Materialism, 81, 83, 87, 95, 177
Mattos de Castro, Hebe, 84
Maya, 45–46, 206, 210, 223
Measles, 214
Memory, 21, 53, 56, 103, 131–132, 139, 148–151, 153, 159–163, 245–246, 295–296, 332, 334, 355, 361, 363
Menchú, Rigoberta, 327–330
Merchants, 104, 106, 125
Merleau-Ponty, Maurice, 19
Mestizaje, 139–143, 161–163, 249, 258
Mestizos (mestiços), 111, 207–208, 210, 221, 235–237, 242, 249–250, 255, 259
Metallurgy, 260, 263–264
Methodism, 362
Mexican Americans, 245
Mexican Revolution, 45–47, 208
Mexico, 40, 45–47, 51–52, 56, 141, 143, 206–208, 211, 216
Mexico City, 328
Middle East, 260–261

Migrant labor, 90, 94, 103, 110, 115, 117, 180, 243–244
Military regimes, 51, 329; in Brazil, 125–127, 361; in Chile, 329, 334, 338, 342–345; in Guatemala, 223–224; in El Salvador, 140, 147, 149, 151, 160
Millenarianism, 43, 152
Minas Gerais, 105
Miners, 231–235, 238–264; assemblies, 232
Ministry of Agriculture (Chile), 340–341
Ministry of Education (Chile), 276
Ministry of Fazenda, 124
Mintz, Sidney, 177, 185, 311–314, 317, 328, 346
Misogyny, 285–286
Missionaries, 175–176, 189, 195
Mississippi, 86–87
Mita revolt, 218
Modernity, 85, 91–92, 95, 110, 122–123, 219, 277
Modernization, 20, 37, 91–92, 94–95, 108–109, 112–113, 123, 157, 235–236, 256, 258, 261, 273, 318
Mojica, Fabián, 153
Momostenango, 220
Momsen, Janet, 188
Monarchy. See Brazilian monarchy
Moniz Barreto, Octavio, 119
Montecino, Sonia, 327
Montreal, 211
Moral economy, 37, 42–43, 48, 82–83, 87–90, 252
Morant Bay, 187, 195
Moreau de Jonnes, Alexander, 212–213
Morelos, 208
Moreno Fraginals, Manuel, 39, 81–83, 95
Morgan, Jack, 251–252
Motherhood, 179–180, 269, 271, 277–278, 280–282, 286–291, 294, 297–298
Movimiento Campesino Revolucionario, 331, 334–335
Movimiento de Izquierda Revolucionaria, 331, 335, 338, 340, 345
Mozambique, 27
Multiculturalism, 163
Municipal politics: in Guatemala, 217; in El Salvador, 145; in Ilhéus, 109, 112, 114–115, 118

Muñoz, José, 284–285
Mur, Humberto, 241
Murilo de Carvalho, José, 81, 83
Murra, John V., 311
Músculo, 260, 262
Music, 278–279, 319
Mutual aid societies, 239–240
Mutualism, 275–276, 279–280, 283–284, 286, 292
Myth, 102–103, 132, 139–140, 235

Nabuco de Araújo, José Tomaz, 92–93
Nahuatl, 138–140, 144, 148, 154–156, 160–161, 163–164
Nahuizalco, 138, 147, 149–152, 155–156, 163–164
Narratives, 53, 81, 84–86, 95, 102–103, 117, 122, 127–131, 138, 147, 149, 152, 161–162, 208, 246, 255, 330, 336–337, 343, 357–362
Nash, June, 328
National Congress (Guatemala), 214
National Guard (El Salvador), 146, 152
National Health Service (Chile), 276
Nationalism: in Brazil, 88–89, 92, 95, 118; in Chile, 231–264; in Guatemala, 206–224; in Peru, 43–44; and revolution in El Salvador, 139, 142, 160–162; in scholarship, 175; in the U.S. South, 92
Nation-building, 139, 141, 210, 222
Nationhood, 88–89, 92
National Geographic, 156
Nativism, 234–235. See also Xenophobia
Nehuentúe, 337–345
Neo-Lamarkianism, 221–223
Neoliberalism, 3, 12–13, 49, 52–53, 56, 163
"New" Cultural History, 47–48
New Mexico, 346
New York, 89, 211
Ngenechen, 347
Nicaragua, 140–141, 143, 159, 161–162, 328
Nitrate, 232, 234–235, 238–240, 243, 256–257
Nora, Pierre, 21

Obrero Textil, 261
October Revolution, 209
Oldrey, William, 179

Oliveira, Basílio de, 114
Oliveira, Cypriano, 106–107; daughter of, 107
Oral history, 21, 154, 246, 276, 280–282, 285, 295, 319, 332. See also Interviews; Testimony
Orange Valley, 179
Ortner, Sherry, 176
Oughton, Samuel, 195

Paget, Hugh, 183
Paillao, Margarita. See Quidel, Gertrudis
Painemal Huenchual, Martín, 327
Palacios, Nicolás, 237, 241, 250, 254–255, 262
Palmer, Brian, 22
Pan American Union, 123
Paraguay, 241
Paraiba Valley, 130
Parenthood, 272–282, 286–291, 297–298
Paris, 17, 115, 125, 211–212, 214–215, 328–329
Partido Obrero Socialista, 239, 242
Partido Revolucionario Institucional, 52
Paternalism, 237, 246
Patriarchy, 157–159, 186, 237, 270, 273, 284, 288
Patriotism, 241–242, 244, 258, 260. See also Nationalism
Paulistas, 82–84, 86–87, 93–94, 111
Paupin, Antonio, 257–258
Peasant leagues, 125
Pedro II, Emperor Dom, 105
Peixoto de Brito, 90
Pentecostalism, 311, 313, 317
Pereira de Vasconcelos, Bernardo, 88
Pereira Filho, Carlos, 124, 128
Pereira Gallo, Fortunato, 105
Pérez, Enrique, 331–333
Pérez Brignoli, Héctor, 160
Pérez Hernández, Juan, 268–272, 275
Perrot, Michelle, 27
Peru, 43–45, 56–57, 206, 234–235, 238–240, 242
Pessoa Costa e Silva, Antônio da, 108–116, 126
Pessoistas, 113–114, 125
Pezoa Varas, José, 246, 249–250, 252–255

Library of Congress Cataloging-in-Publication Data
Reclaiming the political in Latin American history; essays from the North /
edited by Gilbert M. Joseph; with a foreword by Elena Poniatowska
p. cm.—(American encounters/global interactions)
Includes index
ISBN 0-8223-2779-1 (cloth: alk. paper)—ISBN 0-8223-2789-9 (pbk.: alk. paper)
1. Latin America—Historiography. 2. Historiography—Political aspects—Latin America.
I. Joseph, G. M. (Gilbert Michael), 1947– II. Series.
F1409.7.R43 2001 980'.007'2—dc21 2001040504